The Myth and Reality of Slavery in Eastern Connecticut

The Myth and Reality of Slavery in Eastern Connecticut

The Brownes of Salem and Absentee Land Ownership

by
Bruce P. Stark

The Connecticut Press
Cheshire, CT
2023

First printing, 2023

Library of Congress Cataloging in Publication Data
Stark, Bruce P., author
    The Myth and Reality of Slavery in Eastern Connecticut:
    The Brownes of Salem and Absentee Land Ownership
    Includes illustrations, tables, maps, annotations, bibliography
    and index, 298 pps.
    ISBN soft cover edition: 979-8-218-00089-9
    Library of Congress Control Number: 2022910173

1. History - America - Colonial Connecticut - Black Americans | Slavery
2 The Brownes of Salem, CT | 3 Absentee Land Ownership in Colonial
Connecticut | 4. Lyme, Connecticut | 5.American Revolution

Dedicated to
Patricia Bodak and Warren Bodak Stark
wife and son
the most important people in my life

vi

TABLE OF CONTENTS

ILLUSTRATIONS, MAPS & TABLES

Illustrations

Tables

Maps

x

APPENDICES

ACKNOWLEDGMENTS

A number of people have been of great assistance in helping me prepare this work and it is difficult to know where to begin. The staff in History & Genealogy of the Connecticut State Library deserve to be first thanked. I worked in the Archives Unit of the Library for a dozen years and can attest to their friendship and professionalism. The people who deserve special mention for their assistance on this project are Kristi Finnan, Kevin Johnson, Carolyn Picciano, Jeannie Sherman, and Mel Smith. These are the people who sit at the front lines, have great knowledge of the collections, and are always ready to provide assistance.

Archivists from several institutions have been extremely helpful. Andrew Bayley and especially Karla Ingermann from the Bermuda Archives Centre have been unfailingly generous in providing me with copies both of original documents concerning Governor William Browne and transcripts thereof. In addition, town and city clerks Gayle Forman and Joanie Campbell of Colchester, Jonathan Ayala of New London, and especially Linda Winzer of Lyme have been of great assistance.

I have also been in contact with with archivists in a number of other repositories, including David Haugaard, Kaitlyn Pettengill, and Alexander Till at the Historical Society of Pennsylvania and Paul Johnson at The National Archives of the United Kingdom and thank them for their assistance. Appreciation also to the Connecticut State Library and Wahoo Art for permission to reproduce illustrations. In addition, thanks to John Van Epps of the Connecticut Conference of the United Church of Christ and the staff at the Connecticut Historical Society, in particular for granting permission to use images from *Chronicles of a Connecticut Farm*. In addition, kudos to Peter J. Malia of The Connecticut Press who has guided this manuscript to completion, for I never knew how much work is required to get a book ready for publication until going through this process.

Another person deserving special notice is Doug Conroy who in his research at the National Archives of Great Britain found and copied the records of the confiscation of the estate of Governor William Browne for me. Without his assistance, this manuscript would have been incomplete. He also kindly read and critiqued the manuscript. Peter P. Hinks has a wealth of knowledge on the history of slavery in Connecticut and has been unfailingly generous in sharing his expertise. He read and critiqued the entire manuscript. In addition, Paul Grant-Costa and Crawford Westbrook have shared their knowledge of Connecticut primary sources with me for which I am greatly appreciative.

A special thank you to my parents Reginald Warren and Hazel Purinton Stark who afforded me the opportunity to grow up in Lyme and thus have the background to be able to tell this story. My father was a Lyme native and his side of the family has had associations with the town dating back to the seventeenth century. My mother was a newcomer from Hartford. Although she had visited Hamburg Cove as a youth, she came to town in 1927 to teach in a one-room school. My parents married in 1928 and they provided a wonderful home for me and my two brothers and two sisters.

Lastly, and most importantly, I thank my wife Patty for enduring my constant trips to archives repositories and all the time spent in front of the computer inputting and correcting a text that has gotten longer and longer, not to mention the clutter of my research files in the family room. She has graciously soldiered through the years spent on research and writing. Indeed, my debt to Patty goes deeper. We first met when I was doing research on a different subject at Manuscripts & Archives, Yale University Library where she worked. Had I never known her, I never would have embarked on an archives career. More than twenty-five years later, as an archivist at the Connecticut State Library, I began to work on the sources, court, General Assembly, and municipal records that made this work possible.

Bruce P. Stark
Lyme, CT
May 2022

ABBREVIATIONS

AmLC	American Loyalist Claims
ANB	*American National Biography*
AO	Audit Office
AOP	Audit Office Papers
CA	Connecticut Archives
CH	*Connecticut History*
CHS	The Connecticut Historical Society, Hartford, CT
CLR	Colchester Land Records
CPR	Colchester Probate District Court Records
ColchesterBMD	Colchester Births, Marriages, Deaths
CollMHS	*Collections of the Massachusetts Historical Society Colony Records*
Colony Records	*The Public Records of the Colony of Connecticut*
CSC	Connecticut Superior Court
CSL	Connecticut State Library, Hartford, CT
CTH	Colchester Town Hall
DAB	*Dictionary of American Biography*
EIHC	*Essex Institute Historical Collections*
EHLR	East Haddam Land Records
EssexQCR	*Records and Files of the Quarterly Courts of Essex County*
HCC	Hartford County Court Records, CSL
HSC	Hartford County Superior Court Records, CSL
LLR	Lyme Land Records
LTH	Lyme Town Hall
LTR	Lyme Town Records
MSA	Massachusetts State Archives
NAUK	National Archives of United Kingdom
NEHGR	*New England Historical and Genealogical Register*
NLCC	New London County Court Records, CSL
NLLR	New London Land Records
NLPR	New London Probate District Court Records, CSL
NLSC	New London County Superior Court Records, CSL
NPR	Norwich Probate, CSL
PbyS	Papers by Subject, Connecticut Court Records, CSL
RG	Record Group, CSL
SalemTR	*Town Records of Salem, Massachusetts*
State Records	*The Public Records of the State of Connecticut*
WCC	Windham County Court Records, CSL
WMQ	*William and Mary Quarterly*

Chapter 1

Setting the Stage

Research often leads one in unusual directions and takes unexpected turns. A newspaper story written on June 10, 2001 upended my research focus. *The Day* of New London published a front-page lead by Maria Hileman on a "slave plantation" in Salem, Connecticut titled "Rewriting Slavery's History." The subheading proclaimed, "In Salem, archeologists dig into an old plantation." The article began with the following:

> The image most Americans have of slavery on the cotton plantations of the South is about to be shattered. Or, at the very least, the historic panorama of that period of American history will soon be expanded to include thousands of acres in southeastern Connecticut and Rhode Island. Archeology intended to prove that generations of American historians have been off on the wrong track is taking place this month and July in rural Salem on what was once a 13,000-acre slave plantation in the heart of what later became the "free" North.

The chief researcher on site, Gerald Sawyer, stated that "we're rewriting history." Slavery "was once huge here, and this plantation was bigger than many in the South. When this comes out, it will shake up a lot of people."[1] The "plantation" was owned by three generations of Browne family absentee landlords from Salem, Massachusetts. Concerning slavery in Salem, the article proclaimed that the first overseer "brought in 60 families of Africans - as many as 120 people - to clear his first 4,000 acre purchase" and "in 1759 a later overseer, John Mumford, Jr., brought in another group of blacks to work the land." Near the end of the article, Sawyer told students assisting with the archeological dig that "what you're involved in is rewriting the history of this country."[2] To borrow a modern phrase, the story quickly became viral.[3]

---

[1] The second archeologist was Professor Warren R. Perry of Central Connecticut State University.

[2] Maria Hileman, "Rewriting Slavery's History," *The Day* (New London), June 10, 2001, A1, A6. The article was one of four on the front page of the Sunday edition of the newspaper. It also filled all of page A6 and contained four illustrations. They consisted of Gerald Sawyer with archeology students on page 1; plus Warren Perry with volunteers; Central Connecticut student Janet Woodruff, Warren Perry and William Bingham on whose land the dig occurred; and a drawing of a Cuban sugar plantation, all on page 6.

[3] See, "Dig Into History Yields Another View Of 'Free' North," *Hartford Courant*, June 11, 2001; Jon B. Case, "Northern slavery is well-documented, *The Day*, August 3, 2001; Sydney Schwartz, "Yankee Slavery," *Archeology*, 54, no. 5 (September/October 2001); Lucretia Bingham, "Hallowed Ground," *Smithsonian*, 32, no. 8 (November 2001), 30, 32; David Pencek, "A hidden history revealed," *Norwich Bulletin*, January 13, 2002; Karin Crompton, "Archeologists explore Salem site," *The Day*, September 1, 2002; Tom Gidwitz, "Freeing Captive History," *Archeology*, 58, no. 2 (March/April 2005); Steve Slosberg, "Auctioning our slaves our legacy, too," *The Day*. February 20, 2005; Cindy Lee Corriveau, *Images of America: Salem* (Charleston, SC:

Additional publicity came in September 2002 when the *Hartford Courant*, the newspaper with the largest circulation in the state, published *Complicity: How Connecticut Chained Itself to Slavery*, a special issue of its weekly and now defunct *Northeast* magazine. The eighty-page study gave the issue even greater historical legs.[4] The first chapter, written by Joel Lang, is called "The Plantation Next Door" and began with this sentence: "The most disturbing evidence of Connecticut's long and profitable complicity with slavery lies hidden in plain sight in the town of Salem, in the fields and woods around an ice cream dairy bar [Salem Valley Farms] near Routes 11 and 82" where archaeologists were "painstakingly uncovering the remnants of a plantation." Archeologists Gerald Sawyer and Warren Perry are again featured and the same assertions made: "a 13,000-acre plantation" and "60 slave families." Lang added that "the Salem plantation, previously no more than a footnote in history books, is stunning in scale."[5]

The two articles, however, contained several errors that the average reader would never pick up, but which should have raised red flags about the main hypothesis.[6] These assertions remained unchecked and became further embedded in the scholarly community five years later when *Connecticut History* published an article on the archeological evidence of slavery in early Connecticut in which many of the same statements

---

Arcadia Publishing, 2006), 127; Matthew Warshauer, *Connecticut in the American Civil War: Slavery, Sacrifice, and Survival* (Middletown, CT: Wesleyan University Press, 2011), 9, 226. Archeologists Gerald Sawyer and Warren Perry got much of their information from Alfred Bingham (1905-1998) who lived on a portion of the estate. Alfred M. Bingham, "Squatter Settlements of Freed Slaves in New England," *Connecticut Historical Society Bulletin*, 41 (July 1976), 76.

[4] Christopher Collier, then Connecticut State Historian, called *Complicity*, little better than "the hyperbolic ranting of deluded writers" and wrote that the *Hartford Courant* devoted all the resources to this publication because it likely "feel[s] complicit in the slavery that existed in Connecticut in the 18th and 19 centuries." Christopher Collier, "The hyperbolic ranting of deluded writers," *Hartford Courant*, December 1, 2002. The author thanks late Professor Collier for alerting him to and providing a copy of his letter.

[5] Joel Lang et al, *Complicity: How Connecticut Chained Itself to Slavery*, special issue *Northeast* magazine, September 29, 2002, 6. *Complicity* was the joint product of seven authors, each of whom was responsible for one or more chapters. In addition to Joel Lang, the authors consisted of Anne Farrow, Rick Green, Liz Petry, Steve Grant, Tina A. Brown, and Matthew Kauffman.
   In the same breathless chapter, one that includes a picture of Sawyer and Perry, Lang stated that what the archeologists had found after three summers of work would never "become a Sturbridge Village of Colonial slavery," but "they've identified foundations of sawmills that slaves may have operated, huge roots cellars they may have dug, rude stone shelters they may have lived in after being cast off, and stone cairns marking where they probably were buried." Ibid, 6-7. Note the mays and the probably in the sentence.

[6] Maria Hileman's article, often quoting Sawyer, contained a number of mistakes, beginning with a figure of 13,000 acres for the "plantation." The real total was around 9,650 acres. "Rewriting Slavery's History" also overestimated the number of Africans imported to North America in the seventeenth and eighteenth centuries. It states that some 1,341,000 kidnapped blacks were shipped to British possessions in the Caribbean and North America in the seventeenth century, while the actual number was around 141,000 and overestimated the total eighteenth century Atlantic slave trade by about one million. In addition, the statement was made that in 1715 there were 1,500 slaves in Connecticut, while the real total was less than half that number and reported that in 1774 some 2,000 Africans were living in New London County, when the census total was 1,194 Negroes and 842 Indians. Lastly, "Rewriting" provided incorrect figures for the number of slaves in Colchester and Lyme. *Complicity* repeated some of these statements and also wrongly concluded that carpenter Daniel Galusha, one of the early settlers in the area, was a black man. "Rewriting Slavery's History"; Lang et al, *Complicity*, 13; Bruce P. Stark, "The Myth and Reality of Slavery in Salem, Connecticut." *Connecticut History*, 50, no. 2 (Fall 2011), 171-72.

were repeated.[7] A second article published in 2013 two years after the author's 2011 essay and one in which the author was cited repeated the story that "Massachusetts native Samuel Browne founded Connecticut's plantation."[8]

I am from Lyme, a town neighboring Salem, live within five road miles of the border to the former Browne estate, remember people of color living in the area when I was a child, and had done a good deal of research on African Americans in Connecticut, yet until the 2001 story in *The Day* had never heard of a "slave plantation" in the next town.[9] After retiring in 2009, I undertook the task of trying to determine whether or not the archeologists were correct in their belief that three generations of absentee landlords from Salem, Massachusetts established and ran a slave plantation in rural eastern Connecticut managed by agents and overseers. Research in early Connecticut General Assembly records, newspapers, diaries, court records, land records, probate records, eighteenth-century secondary sources, and the Loyalist claim to the British government presented by Governor William Browne of Bermuda who last owned the estate, demonstrated that, although slaves lived on the property from around 1759 until the time the state confiscated the lands in 1779, it was not a slave plantation. The author also examined secondary sources to determine the sources for the slave plantation formulation and published the results of this investigation in *Connecticut History* in 2011.[10]

While doing this research, I became convinced that the tale of the so-called "slave plantation" represented only a relatively small part of a much larger story on slavery in southeastern Connecticut, the settlement of what is now Salem, absentee landownership, and tenancy in the region. A wider net, therefore, had to be cast in order to put the story into its proper historical context.

A number of scholars in the last few decades have been studying the history of slavery and African Americans in the state, much of it presented at annual meetings of the Association for the Study of Connecticut History, most of which is unpublished.[11] The bulk of the published literature consists of popular accounts like the apology of the *Hartford Courant* for printing runaway slave advertisements,[12] "Rewriting Slavery's

---

7 Janet Woodruff, Gerald F. Sawyer, and Warren R. Perry, "How Archeology Exposes the Nature of African Captivity and Freedom in Eighteenth Century Connecticut," *CH*, 46, no. 2 (2007), 157. In the section on "New Salem Plantation," the authors claimed that most of the modern town of Salem "was built on the site of an eighteenth-century provisioning plantation encompassing about 13,000 acres and worked by over a hundred captive African laborers."

8 Robert P. Forbes, "Grating the Nutmeg: Slavery and Racism in Connecticut from the Colonial Era to the Civil War," *CH,* 52, no. 2 (Fall 2013), 174.

9 The people of color consisted of Joe Caples, Buster Giguere, Rebecca Maria Hyde, and Tom Hyde. They are long since deceased and the last remnant of longtime people of color in the town died with them.

10 Bruce P. Stark, "The Myth and Reality of Slavery in Salem, Connecticut," *CH*, 50, no. 2 (Fall 2011), 158-81.

11 The growth of the interest in the history of minorities in Connecticut came after the national trend had fully flowered. The foundational work, Kenneth M. Stampp, *The Peculiar Institution: Slavery in the Ante-Bellum South* (New York: Vintage Books, 1956), quickly led to a wave of research that has continued until the present. For an excellent overview of the first rash of these studies, see Peter H. Wood, "'I Did the Best I Could for My Day: The Study of Early Black History during the Second Reconstruction, 1960 to 1976," *William and Mary Quarterly,* Third Series, XXXV (April 1978), 185-225.

12 The *Courant* published its apology on July 4, 2000 some four months after Aetna, Inc., the Hartford based

History," and *Complicity*, stories that are not grounded in a thorough study of primary sources. They provide a clear demonstration of the vast distance that exists between well-founded scholarly understandings of slavery and popular consciousness of the institution.[13] The major exception to this rule is found in plethora of scholarship on the life and times of slave Venture Smith who obtained his freedom and prospered in white society.[14] Venture is the one African American from Connecticut who has become well known, but primarily to specialists. In 2018, however, his story became much more widely heralded with the publication of Russell Shorto's *Revolution Song*, a popular history of the American Revolution.[15]

One cannot examine historical journals for the last sixty years without seeing numerous articles and book reviews on African American and Native American history, a response to generations of neglect. One searches largely in vain, however, for studies that track the influence of wealthy white families like the Brownes of Salem, Massachusetts, unless they can be tied into stories about underclasses of people of color.[16] Unfortunately, a thorough analysis of the Brownes and their impact on Massachusetts and southeastern Connecticut history is difficult to reconstruct due to the disappearance of family papers from the seventeenth century to the American Revolution.[17]

---

insurance company, issued its atonement for insuring the lives of slaves during the 1850s. The article, "Courant Complicity In An Old Wrong," with the subheading, "Newspaper's Founder Published Ads In Support Of The Sale and Capture Of Slaves," was the featured story on pages A1 and A5. It generated considerable reader reaction, including one from the author. The paper published twelve response letters, three cheers, six jeers, and three that pointed out errors in the original story. *Courant*, July 4, 2000, A1, A5; Ibid, July 9, 2000, C1, C4.

13 It is likewise overly simplistic to concentrate solely on chattel slavery to the neglect of the institutions of apprenticeship and indentureship. See, for example, John Donoghue, "'Out of the Land of Bondage': The English Revolution and the Atlantic Origins of Abolition, *American Historical Review*, 115 (October 2010), 943-74.

14 Smith was an illiterate slave from Africa who purchased his freedom in 1765 and became a farmer in Haddam Neck. The *New London Bee* published his story in 1798. This unique and oft cited autobiography is a work of seminal importance in African American history. The two most accessible versions are *Five Black Lives*, Introduction by Arno Bontemps (Middletown: Wesleyan University Press, 1971), 1-34 and Venture Smith, *A Narrative of the Life and Adventures of Venture, a Native of Africa* (New-London), docsouth.unc.edu/neh/venture/smith.html

For secondary works of substance on Venture, see, Robert E. Desrocher, Jr., "'Not Fade Away': The Narrative of Venture Smith, an African American in the Early Republic," *The Journal of American History*, 84 (June 1997), 40-66; Peter P. Hinks, Book Review Essay on Chandler B. Saint and George A. Krimsky, *Making Freedom: The Extraordinary Life of Venture Smith*, in *CH*, 49, no. 1 (Spring 2010), 134-43; Peter P. Hinks, "'Nought from nought leaves nought': Figuring Venture Smith," a review essay of James Brewer Stewart, ed., *Venture Smith and the Business of Slavery and Freedom*, in *WMQ*, 65 (July 2011), 490-99; James Brewer Stewart, ed., *Venture Smith and the Business of Slavery and Freedom* (Amherst, MA: University of Massachusetts Press, 2010); John Wood Sweet, "Venture Smith, from Slavery to Freedom, connecticuthistory.org/venture-smith-from-slavery-to-freedom/. For another discussion of Venture and his life, see Anne Farrow, Joel Lang, and Jennifer Frank, *Complicity: How the North Promoted, Prolonged, and Profited from Slavery* (New York: Ballantine Books, 2005), 61-75.

15 Russell Shorto, *Revolution Song: A Story of American Freedom* (New York: W. W. Norton & Company, 2018). Venture is one of six main characters in the book.

16 See, for example, C. S. Manegold, *Ten Hills Farm: The Forgotten History of Slavery in the North* (Princeton, NJ; Princeton University Press, 2010).

17 The possibility exists that the papers were discarded after death. It is also remotely possible that the records

No correspondence has been found between Colonel Samuel Browne (1669-1731), Samuel Browne, Jr. (1708-1742), and William Browne (1737-1802) with their Connecticut agents and representatives, men like Samuel Gilbert, James Harris, and John Mumford. An extensive collection of family papers did exist at one time and is mentioned in two letters of William Browne (1709-1763), uncle of the Loyalist, to an English correspondent.[18] The only known holding of Browne correspondence is located in Bermuda at the National Archives and Records Centre, where he served as governor from 1781 to 1788. The letters began in 1778, when he was living in exile in England, and continued until 1796.[19] Governor Browne retained possession, however, of considerable documentation on his grandfather's purchases and his most recent leases, as the Loyalist claim for Property No. 1 (Appendix F) contains phrases like "Produces Deed from James Harris to Colonel Browne" and "produces Leases to prove as above."[20]

The author has found just five letters that relate to his Connecticut estate. The standard bibliography on American Loyalists contains several citations to William Browne materials, but nothing that casts further light on the subject.[21] Thus, the story of the Brownes and their vast landholdings must be reconstructed almost exclusively from Connecticut sources, primarily land, court, and General Assembly records, and we know more about the confiscation of the estate in 1779 and what happened to the lands thereafter than we do for the sixty years that it endured. We also know a good deal about the Massachusetts political career of Loyalist William Browne, through newspaper articles, published primary sources, information in Massachusetts scholarly journals, and the edited papers of Governor Francis Bernard, Governor Thomas Hutchinson, and the Saltonstall family, not to mention his life in exile as governor of Bermuda. It should be possible, therefore, to write a biography of the last Browne absentee.

---

are still extant and located in some unknown attic or repository in Great Britain. With the plethora of documentation on the history of Essex County and Salem, however, scholars can reconstruct a detailed history of the Brownes up to the American Revolution. Nevertheless, historical trends make it highly unlikely that anyone will undertake the task of studying this prominent white family.

18 "Browne Family Letters," *New England Historical and Genealogical Register*, 25 (October 1871), 353-54. The short article reproduced four letters concerning Francis Browne, a cousin of William Browne, the first settler, that were sent to the journal by Colonel Joseph Lemuel Chester of London. One states that Francis "kept up a Correspondence with his Cussens [sic], my grandfather and my great-uncle." The second mentions "Mr. Francis Browne's Letters to my grandfather." The likelihood exists that the bulk of the Browne family papers were lost during the turbulent time between August 1774 and March 1776 when Colonel William Browne fled from Salem to safety in British occupied Boston, departed with the British troops in 1776, and sailed to Great Britain.

19 The Letters of William Browne, Esq. of Salem, Mass., Bermuda National Trust Collection, Bermuda Archives and Government Records Centre. Archivist Karla Ingerman kindly provided the author with transcripts of selected letters.

20 Browne had to produce convincing evidence to document his losses. One such piece was as follows: "Produces Deed from James Harris for Colonel Samuel Browne for 4000 Acres in Lyme Township in Consideration of £1600 Currency of New England - - £666 Sterling dated 1718. Produces Survey of said 4000 Acres." The Claim also refers to deeds and copies of documents, but the originals have not been found. In addition, Browne stated that he had "saved his Plate and Linen" and produced a deed to ownership of half of a pew in the Salem meeting house. Memorial of William Browne, American Loyalist Claims, Audit Office Papers, AO 12/10, 223-26, 235-36, National Archives of the United Kingdom.

21 Gregory Palmer, *A Bibliography of Loyalist Source Material in the United States, Canada, and Great Britain* (Westport, CT and London: Meckler Publishing, 1982).

The best and, indeed, the only reliable source on the history of the Browne estate in Salem, Connecticut is an obscure privately printed work of just fifty copies written by Mary E. Perkins called *Chronicles of a Connecticut Farm, 1769-1905.*[22] The book is divided into four sections: historical introduction, genealogical introduction, chronicles, and concludes with a seventy page appendix that contains copies of relevant grants, surveys, deeds, and wills. The historical introduction contains information on boundaries, the founding of Salem, early settlers, the absentees and their lands, and the confiscation of the Browne estate. The genealogical section has chapters on the Mumford, Christophers, Woodbridge, and Shaw families. The last three had children who married Mumfords. The chronicles section focuses on the houses built upon the estate. For those interested in tracking land ownership, the appendix is indispensable. Perkins was a careful and thorough researcher and her work is a reliable and invaluable source.[23]

The life of the second major actor in the story, James Harris (1673-1758) of New London and Colchester, the man who sold Colonel Samuel Browne the bulk of his Salem property, is well documented through a variety of Connecticut primary sources. They include several series of the Connecticut Archives, e.g. early records of the General Assembly at the Connecticut State Library, land records, and, most significantly, court records. An interesting and important person, he receives a good deal of well deserved attention and I am pleased to have rescued him from obscurity. The last agents for the Browne family, John Mumford and John Mumford, Jr., the men who managed the estate when slavery was introduced until it was seized by the state, are also chronicled. In addition, the author has made an effort to recover what can be learned about the Browne slaves and last tenants. The lives of former slaves Pomp Henry and Caesar Beckwith and renters John Henry and William Carr have proven to be particularly interesting.

This story also reveals the extent to which mostly unimproved and vacant lands were bought and sold for investment and/or speculative purposes. Wealthy men from throughout New England speculated in land, although few had the resources of a potentate like Colonel Samuel Browne to be able to buy and control huge tracts of land in several colonies. Harris bought and then sold most of the land he acquired to wealthy investors from Massachusetts and Rhode Island. Browne and Harris followed different patterns. The Salem, Massachusetts man purchased for long term investment purposes, while Harris usually bought in order to rapidly sell at a profit. In addition, what I hope this study also reveals is how important court records are in chronicling eighteenth-century lives.[24] It also concerns an under documented group, tenants. In

---

[22] Mary E. Perkins, *Chronicles of a Connecticut Farm, 1769-1805* (Boston: Privately Printed, 1905). The work was commissioned by Mr. and Mrs. Alfred Mitchell. Alfred Mitchell was descended from the Mumford overseers of the estate and he owned part of the Browne property, consisting of the Mumford and Woodbridge homesteads. The original work is almost impossible to find in hard copy, although it is available online. The author examined the book at the Connecticut State Library during the 1970s, but it had vanished by the time he returned to the subject more than thirty years later. Paul Grant-Costa borrowed a copy from the Yale University Library and the author made a photocopy of significant portions of the work.

[23] She did not supply footnotes and, therefore, the sources for much of her information cannot be determined. The appendix, however, gives citations to all the deeds and surveys.

[24] While the author served as Assistant State Archivist at the Connecticut State Library, the Library with financial support from the National Historical Publications and Records Commission undertook a project

the absence of contracts between landowner and renter, the best source for information on these often elusive farmers is court records. These materials contain documentation when things went wrong - the tenant failed to pay rent or otherwise failed to honor his contract and instances in which the absentee did not properly fulfill his duties.

As will be seen, the book brings several stories together that all coalesce in the small and unimportant town of Salem. The Browne story concerns one the wealthiest and most powerful families in colonial Massachusetts, one that is little known today. This is likewise a tale of land speculation and absentee land ownership. Third, it is a story of parish and town formation. It is also a narrative of tenant farmers, a story of slavery and its disappearance in southeastern Connecticut, and also an account of a false narrative that has become accepted as truth in popular culture. Finally, research on this work led to a short study of Loyalism and to biographical information on a number of men whose lives are in some way connected to either New Salem Society or the family most responsible for its formation.

The book consists of eleven chapters. Chapter 2 discusses the early history of Lyme and Colchester, the two towns from which New Salem Society was formed, as parish and town formation are an important part of early Connecticut history. The success of these two towns and the new parishes formed within them and the sometimes complex stories associated with the incorporation of new societies form a marked contrast to the trials of New Salem and is, therefore, discussed at some length.[25] Chapter 3 concerns James Harris, the New London speculator who sold Colonel Samuel Browne of Salem, Massachusetts the bulk of his land in southeastern Connecticut and fills in the contours of his life. The history of the Browne family and the acquisition of vast Connecticut lands by the wealthy Salem merchant are the focuses of Chapter 4. The next one concerns the establishment of New Salem Society, its struggles, and what is known about the Browne properties until around 1760. The growth, development, and decline of slavery in New London County is the subject of Chapter 6, while the political career of William Browne, the coming of the Mumfords to New Salem, the advent of slavery on his lands there, and his efforts to increase profits from his Connecticut lands are found in Chapter 7. The following chapter discusses the confiscation of the estate, the disposition of the lands, and Browne's effort to gain compensation for what had been lost, while Chapters 9 and 10 relate the stories of what happened to the Browne slaves and the last tenants. An epilogue chapter concerns twenty-first century memories of events in eighteenth-century New Salem with emphasis on the story of the growth of the inaccurate slave plantation narrative.

The Brownes of Salem concludes with six appendices, the first outlining the many court cases involving James Harris of Colchester and New London, the second on those of the Browne family, the third on Browne and related families relationships, the fourth listing Browne tenants, a fifth on tenant contracts, and a last one containing transcriptions of key documents on the confiscation of the estate of William Browne.

The text contains a good deal of discussion on debt and, therefore, some defi-

---

to process, arrange, conserve, and describe records of the New London County Court, New London County Superior Court, and Litchfield County Court.

25 The importance of the topics discussed in chapters 2 and 5 almost prompted me to add the words "Parish Formation" to the title.

nitions may be of use.[26] Its three major forms are debt by book, debt by note, and debt by bond. **Debts by book** are incurred by those owing money to shopkeepers that were recorded in a book. Farmers often lacked the funds to pay for their goods at times of purchase. Debtors built accounts over time and often creditors were not paid until they sued for collection. **Debts by note** were promissory notes recorded on slips of paper or notes by which borrowers agreed to pay back to the persons who loaned the sums, both principal and interest, at an agreed upon date. Each note contained the signature of the borrower and almost always those of witnesses to the contract. **Debts by bond** were formal contracts and used for those borrowing substantial sums of money or for services to be performed like clearing of land or building walls.[27] Bonds contained the written names of witnesses and the signatures and seals of the parties involved.

This work has retained the structure and format as originally conceived with chapters on the subjects described above. As, however, more and more research was undertaken, I decided to enhance the account with additional information. First, although I had always planned to devote a chapter to James Harris, the decision to focus so much on his legal difficulties came much later. Appendix A provides extensive detail on the results of this research. Second, the chapter on "Slavery in Eastern Connecticut" has been augmented by the attempt to determine if the absentee Browne estate and those of others in the region matched the parameters of the slave estates in the Narragansett region of Rhode Island. Third, I intended to devote a chapter to what happened to the twelve Browne slaves after the State of Connecticut confiscated the estate, but the desire to give equal attention to the last tenants was decided upon much later. Lastly, the idea for appendices evolved during the course of research and writing. I hope that readers will find these additions both important and interesting.

The author does not claim that he has remade the historical landscape by offering a striking new interpretation of Connecticut's past, but he has mined sources like account books, has absorbed and integrated court records into the narrative, and has provided illumination on several little known aspects of the region's history, including the significance of tenancy in communities in which non-residents owned large quantities of land.[28] All in an effort to tell an interesting and largely unknown story.

A number of quotations and some transcriptions of documents are included. Original spelling and capitalization have been retained, but have sometimes punctuation has been added and superscripts have not been used, hence ye and not y^e. Citations are given to a number of court cases and land transactions. Original spelling is generally used, except that "and" replaces "&," "Jr." replaces "Junr", and titles like colonel are omitted. The reader may notice, therefore, some differences in the spelling of names in the text and in quotations and footnotes, as the author decided to use the original form for first names and surnames in these two instances.

Please note that until 1752 the British world used the Julian calendar which

---

[26] See also the Glossary on page 247.

[27] As with other important legal documents, bonds began with the following words: "Know all men by these preents."

[28] The text and appendices contain citations to well over 200 lawsuits and other filings before four county courts and the Connecticut Superior Court. This total does not include the figures gathered on court cases chronicled in Appendices A and B.

was eleven days off from the more accurate Gregorian calendar and the new year officially began on March 25. Hence, dates between January 1 and March 24 are recorded
as, for example, February 1743/4.

I started the research on this work in 2012 and, as most historians understand,
the project has taken far longer than originally anticipated. The long gestation of this
work was due to several circumstances in addition to the factors discussed above. First,
research is an avocation of retirement and done in fits and spirts. Second, I suffered
a severe illness in February-March 2018 and this has caused at least a year's delay in
completing this project. Third, the longer the research process the more relevant sources
were discovered. For example, had I not decided to focus so extensively on the information found in court records, the project would have been finished much earlier. And,
the more one relies on these treasures the more sections of them need to be examined,
like the no docket files in New London County Court Records and several series of
Papers by Subject. Lastly, the COVID-19 outbreak in the spring of 2020 caused further
delays due to the closure of the Connecticut State Library, but it also provided me the
opportunity to check additional sources such as several Loyalist studies and the seventeenth-century records of the Quarterly Court of Essex County. The result is more detail
in the text, although these additions have not altered the contours of the story.

Chapter 2

Lyme and Colchester

This story centers on the huge Browne estate in what became the town of Salem in 1819, a community formed from the northeastern or Paugwonk section of Lyme and the southeastern part of Colchester, although a small slice of Montville was also included. The history of Salem, therefore, begins with that of Lyme and Colchester.[1]

Lyme was founded in 1665.[2] The town, originally part of Saybrook that was established in 1635, was located on the east side of the Connecticut River and its first settler, Matthew Griswold, received land there in 1645.[3] On March 10, 1663/4, the Connecticut General Court granted a petition from Saybrook "to set up a plantation on the east side of the great [Connecticut] Riuer."[4] Less than two years later, on February 13, 1665, articles of agreement between Saybrook and the handful of settlers on the east side of the river, known as "The Loving Parting," formally set off the new plantation as a distinct entity. The legislature ordered that the new "Plantation on ye East side ye River over ag[ains]t Saybrooke for ye future be named Lyme" in May 1667.[5]

The new town encompassed an area of around 120 square miles once the Connecticut General Court determined the boundaries and subsequent surveys were

---

1 Paugwonk was the name given to a large seventeenth-century purchase from Native Americans on the upper reaches of the Eight Mile River that later made up a significant portion of the town of Salem. Arthur H. Hughes and Morse S. Allen, *Connecticut Place Names* (Hartford: The Connecticut Historical Society, 1976), 494.

2 The common belief is that the name Lyme came from Lyme Regis, but the authorities on Connecticut place names state that it is just as likely that the name came from Lymn, the ancestral home of the Lees, one of the town's founding families, or is of Celtic origin. The Thomas Lee House, dating to around 1666, is located on Route 156 in the Niantic portion of East Lyme. Ibid, 228.

For more detailed information on the early history of Lyme, the following four works are very helpful. Christopher Collier, "Saybrook and Lyme: Secular Settlements in a Puritan Commonwealth," in George J. Willauer, Jr., ed., *A Lyme Miscellany, 1776-1976* (Middletown: Wesleyan University Press, 1977), 9-28; May Hall James, *The Educational History of Old Lyme, Connecticut 1635-1935* (New Haven: Yale University Press, 1939), 3-27; Perkins, *Connecticut Farm*, 8-19; Bruce P. Stark, *Lyme, Connecticut: From Founding to Independence* (Lyme: [Lyme Bicentennial Commission], 1976), 1-15.

3 Descendants of Matthew Griswold still live on a portion of the property in Old Lyme acquired by the first member of this prominent family.

4 J. Hammond Trumbull, ed., *The Public Records of the Colony of Connecticut* (Hartford: Brown & Parsons, 1850), I, 419.

5 James, *Educational History*, 17-20; Perkins, *Connecticut Farm*, 17-20; Stark, *Lyme*, 1; *Colony Records*, II, 60.

made.[6] The Connecticut River and Long Island Sound formed the western and southern boundaries of the new community. In October 1668, the Court imprecisely fixed the northern boundary of Lyme at the southern bounds of "Thirty Mile Island plantation," called "Haddum."[7] The eastern boundary was inexactly established in May 1672. The colony government appointed three commissioners to measure five miles east from Connecticut River and four miles west of "Pequot River."[8] That area remained in dispute between these two markers until an October 1673 act of the legislature divided it equally between Lyme and New London.[9]

The southern part of the new town, present day Old Lyme and Niantic portion of East Lyme, was originally part of Saybrook, while title to the area of the modern town of Lyme and the southern half of Salem came from Indian deeds. Captain Sannup or Sanhop, a sachem of the Niantic tribe, deeded a tract of land eight miles square to Matthew Griswold and five others on the Connecticut River some twelve or thirteen miles from its mouth on June 6, 1664. This land later formed sections of East Haddam, Colchester, and Salem.[10] Five years later William Lord of Saybrook purchased a large tract from Chapeto, a relative of Uncas, the Mohegan Sachem, that encompassed the entire Eight Mile River valley, except for the cove near Eight Mile Island.[11]

Lord later sold the land to the town. In May 1672, the General Court confirmed Lyme's title to it with the stipulation that Joshua, Sachem of the Niantics, "shall have layd out to him a sufficiency of upland to plant for himselfe and men . . . [on] the north side of Eight Mile River," property that reverted to Lyme after his death in 1676.[12] Most of this section of town, later called Joshuatown, was acquired by Richard Ely. The Lord and Ely tracts composed most of the north part of town, later the North or Third Parish, and now Lyme.[13]

Almost all of the Lyme portion of Salem became the property of Matthew Griswold, Jr. as part of his fourth division, e.g. "land at Pagunk," when in January 1691/2, the town granted him all remaining lands in the northeast corner of Lyme except for those previously conveyed to his father at Paugwonk. The town set the price at £14 "in provision pay."[14] Griswold's heirs later sold this tract to James Harris of New London.

Settlement gradually spread over the course of two generations from the Lieu-

---

6 *Connecticut Register and Manual 2003* (Hartford: Secretary of the State, 2003), 426. 471, 520, 541.

7 *Colony Records*, II, 97, 108. Formal boundary surveys were undertaken by Richard Lord and Joseph Peck in 1700 and by county surveyor John Plumbe in 1718. Perkins, *Connecticut Farm*, 183-85.

8 The Thames River. At the mouth of this body of water, stood New London, Connecticut's largest and most important port during the eighteenth century.

9 *Colony Records*, II, 174, 213.

10 Ibid, III, 200.

11 Hamburg Cove.

12 Eight Mile Island and Eight Mile River so named because they were around eight miles from the mouth of Connecticut River at Saybrook. Hughes and Allen, *Connecticut Place Names*, 279.

13 Stark, *Lyme*, 3-4; *Colony Records*, II, 174.

14 Perkins, *Connecticut Farm*, 183; Jean Chandler Burr, ed., *Lyme Records, 1667-1730: A Literal Transcription of the Minutes of the Town Meetings with Marginal Notations, to which hath been Appended Land Grants and Ear Marks* (Stonington: The Pequot Press, Inc., 1968), 74.

tenant River and Duck River areas in what is now Old Lyme near the mouth of Connecticut River east along the coast of Long Island Sound to Mile Creek, Four Mile River, Bride Brook, and Niantic Bay and north to the Hamburg Cove, Joshuatown, and Selden Cove areas on the Connecticut River shore.

The town built its first meeting house on a hill between the Duck and Black Hall Rivers around 1670.[15] As population increased, those living in outlying sections of town began agitating for separate parishes both for personal and religious reasons because they lived several miles from the church and had to travel over poor roads to attend worship services. The process often began with the organization of a new militia company.

Population expanded most rapidly to the east. The inhabitants "at Nahantick" in Lyme petitioned the General Assembly, first, to organize a separate militia company or trainband and, second, for parish privileges. The Niantic petitioners stated in October 1708 that they wished to become "a distinct military company."[16] The General Assembly agreed and appointed Thomas Bradford as lieutenant and George Waye ensign in May 1709. In an April 29, 1718 memorial, twenty-six inhabitants of the East Quarter asked for parish privileges, the "Liberty to Call and Settle a minister amongst our selves." They stated that they numbered around thirty families, had estates valued at £1,982 and lived so far from the meetinghouse that it was almost impossible for them to regularly attend worship services. Despite opposition from a majority in the town, the General Court established "Niantick Quarter" as a separate society in October 1719 and set the boundaries of Lyme's Second Society two years later.[17]

The Third or North Society came next, but its organization was complicated by events in the northern areas of the town, both the northwest region bordering on what became East Haddam and northeast section bounding on Colchester, subsequently New Salem. The effort to establish a separate society began in January 1720/1 with a petition signed by nineteen men in which they requested to be granted the "Liberty to be a society by our selves and Call a minister amongst us that so ye gospell may be preached in those Remot[e] parts of ye Town." They affirmed their willingness to pay their share of the salary of the elderly Reverend Moses Noyes (1643-1729) and that of an assistant pastor until Noyes' death.[18] The town voted to approve this proposed memorial on January 23, 1720/1, but the northerners took no further immediate action, perhaps due to delays associated with finding a new associate minister who was not hired until January 1721/2.[19]

---

15 Located on or near Meetinghouse Lane in Old Lyme.

16 *Colony Records*, V, 68, 95.

17 The petition was signed by twenty-six heads of households. Connecticut Archives, Ecclesiastical Affairs, Series 1, III, 25, Connecticut State Library; *Colony Records*, VI, 160, 274; Stark, *Lyme*, 9-10.

The new parish hired its first minister, George Griswold (1692-1761), a son of Matthew Griswold, Jr., in 1720 and formally ordained him in 1724. A graduate of Yale College, Class of 1717, he remained as pastor of the church in the Second Society until death. Stark, *Lyme*, 10; Franklin Bowditch Dexter, ed., *Biographical Sketches of the Graduates of Yale College*, Vol. 1, 1701-1745 (New York: Henry Holt and Company, 1885), 168-70.

18 The town first voted to hire an assistant minister in February 1717/8. He stayed just two years, the second remained only four months, and the third drowned in December 1722. Stark, *Lyme*, 8-9.

19 Burr, ed., *Lyme Records*, 61,156-57; Stark, *Lyme*, 8-9. The town released the North Society from helping to pay the minister's salary in 1728.

Another petition for parish privileges soon followed from residents of the southern part of Haddam who lived on the east side of Connecticut River and the northwest section for Lyme. Sixteen landowners from north of the Eight Mile River in Lyme petitioned the General Assembly in April 1723 to join with others from the southern part of Haddam east of Connecticut River to form a new parish. They stated that most of them lived twelve miles from the meetinghouse in the First Society and faced the additional burden of having to ford the Eight Mile River. On April 30, 1723, the town appointed two agents from the portion of town that had previously received permission to form a separate society to oppose this new petition.[20] Eleven men signed a remonstrance arguing that granting the East Haddam-Lyme petition would be extremely detrimental to all those living in the northern part of Lyme since they had already secured permission from the town to form a separate society, had been granted one hundred acres of land to support the ministry, and discussions had already begun about building their own meetinghouse.

No action was taken on the East Haddam-Lyme memorial, so the petitioners renewed it in September.[21] This forced the hand of the rest of the residents of the northern part of town and they formally petitioned the legislature for parish privileges in October 1723. In a document signed by forty-two men, about "fortey fameleys," they affirmed that they lived between four and nine miles from the meetinghouse and agreed to pay their proportion of the salaries of Noyes and an assistant pastor provided they were given the privilege of having the "publick Worship of god amongst us." The legislature ordered that notice be given to the inhabitants of the First Society to determine their feelings on the proposed separation. The society voted on February 24, 1723/4 to endorse the petition of the northerners and the General Assembly incorporated the new parish in May. The northern boundaries of the new society were "partly Colchester and part by East Haddam lines."[22] A militia company was established in October 1723, when the legislature appointed John Colt, captain; Daniel Sterling, lieutenant; and Richard Ely, ensign "of the north company or train-band in the town of Lyme." The society hired the Reverend George Beckwith (1703-1794) who was ordained in January 1729/30 shortly after the death of Moses Noyes.[23]

The landlocked town of Colchester, originally called Jeremiah's Farm,[24] was

---

[20] Hadlyme Society from parts of Lyme's Third Society and East Haddam was established by the General Assembly in October 1742. Stark, *Lyme*, 12-13.

[21] Stark, *Lyme*. 10-12; Burr, ed., *Lyme Records*, 165-66.

[22] CA, Ecclesiastical Affairs, Series 1, III, 42-46; *Colony Records*, VI, 457.

[23] CA, Militia, Series 1, I, 205, CSL; *Colony Records*, VI, 412.; Stark, *Lyme*, 12. Beckwith, Yale College Class of 1728, gained the approval of the New London County Association of ministers in August 1729 and ministered to the flock in Lyme North Society until his death, although an associate minister was ordained in 1787. Dexter, *Yale Graduates*, I, 366-68; New London Association, 1708-1788, General Association of Connecticut Records, August 19, 1728, 42, nehh-viewer.s3-website-us-east-1.amazonaws.com The author thanks John Van Epps of the Connecticut Conference of the United Church of Christ for the information that Association records had been digitized.

[24] From Jeremiah Adams who was granted some 340 acres by the Connecticut General Court in March 1661/2 where he kept cattle. Hughes and Allen, *Connecticut Place Names*, 84.

established a generation later than Lyme.[25] The Connecticut General Court granted a "petition of divers of the inhabitants in the county of Hartford" to form a new plantation in October 1698. The bounds were outlined as "beginning at the north bound of Twentie Mile River, and so to extend southward, to a river called Deep River, and to extend eastward from the bounds of [East] Haddum seven miles."[26] The following spring the legislature passed "An Act for the enlargem[en]t of the new plantation lately granted at or near Jeremies Farme, upon the roade to New London." The north bounds were unchanged, but the west bounds were delineated as the east boundaries of Middletown and Haddam, the south bounds to "joyn the north bounds of Lyme," and the east and northeast on Norwich and Lebanon.[27]

After a 1699 complaint of Colchester residents that they were "obstructed in the improvem[en]t" of their plantation because several persons claimed considerable tracts of land within" the township, the legislature appointed a committee to try to resolve all these claims.[28] One year later the inhabitants argued that settlement was discouraged "by Owaneco and the Moheags" who claimed land within the township.[29] The Assembly asked the governor and council to mediate the dispute "with the Moheags and to aggree with them to quitt their claim to the lands within the township, upon as reasonable termes as may be obtained" with all expenses to be borne by Colchester. At the same session, an agreement on the boundary between Colchester and Lebanon was endorsed.[30] The legislature granted permission to the people of the new town to organize a church in October 1703 and it settled John Bulkley/Bulkeley (1679-1731) as the town's first minister in December.[31] Bulkley, Harvard College Class of 1699, came from distinguished ecclesiastical lineage and was a scholar of considerable note, thus It seems

---

25 The first Connecticut towns formed along navigable bodies of water - Long Island Sound, Connecticut River, and Thames River. The initial inland town was Farmington (1645), followed by Simsbury, (1670, then Wallingford (1673), Woodbury (1673), Derby (1675), Waterbury (1686), Danbury (1687), Windham (1692), Colchester (1698), Plainfield, (1699), and Lebanon (1700). Four of these towns were located on streams of secondary importance - Farmington and Simsbury on the Farmington River, Wallingford on the Quinnipiac, and Woodbury on the Housatonic. *Connecticut Register and Manual*, 43, 415, 437, 466, 549, 579, 583, 603, 610; Bruce C. Daniels, *The Connecticut Town: Growth and Development, 1635-1790* (Middletown: Wesleyan University Press, 1979), 15-16, 25.

26 Colchester had an area of 64.1 square miles and the name came from Colchester in Essex County, England. Daniels, *Connecticut Town*, 183; Hughes and Allen, *Connecticut Place Names*, 82.

27 *Colony Records*, IV, 29192

28 The committee returned its report concerning the boundary between Colchester and Lebanon to the General Assembly in October 1699. *Colony Records*, IV, 305.

29 From the perspective of the Mohegans, the settlers "were an unsavory lot" and members of the tribe from "time to time" had been "threatened by them of Colchester who are settled upon our land without our consent." The Colchester men burned wigwams and, as the sachem proclaimed, his followers could not "goe hunting upon our own land for feare of being killed by them." Quotations from Michael Leroy Oberg, *Uncas: First of the Mohegans* (Ithaca, NY: Cornell University Press, 2003), 205-06.

30 The boundary line between Colchester and Lyme was surveyed in May 1705 by county surveyor John Plumbe. Perkins, *Connecticut Farm*, 186-87.

31 Florence S. Marcy Crofut, *Guide to the History and Historic Sites of Connecticut* (New Haven: Yale University Press, 1937), II, 671-72, 674; *Colony Records*, IV, 281, 291-92, 298-99, 305, 333, 334, 445; *Contributions to the Ecclesiastical History of Connecticut* (New Haven: William L. Kingsbury, 1861), 364.

surprising that he would come to such a rural backwater community. Perhaps he looked forward to the challenge.[32]

In May 1704 during Queen Anne's War, the legislature ordered eight frontier towns, including Colchester, not to be "broken up or voluntarily deserted" without its approval.[33] The first militia officers for the new town were appointed in May 1707, Samuel Gilbert, captain; Samuel Loomis, lieutenant; and Israel Wyatt, ensign. Due to its inland location and concerns about valid title to lands because of Mohegan claims, the town grew relatively slowly. It did not send its first representatives to the General Assembly until September 1708 and is first noted in the "Lists of Persons and Estates" in October 1708 when its total list was £2,497 for eighty-one males.[34] At the same session, the legislature released the new and struggling town from paying "country rates," made it part of Hartford County, and appointed Michael Taintor as Colchester's first justice of the peace. In 1711, when the town's lists of estates had grown to £3,911, the town was required for the first time to pay colony taxes of two pence per pound.[35] The new town gradually grew and one indication is seen in an October 1723 petition to the General Assembly in which twenty-seven young men from Colchester, including James Harris, Jr. and Jonathan Harris, asked for permission to form a troop in horse in the town.[36]

A generation passed before any effort was made to form a second parish from outlying areas of the town and it came from a tiny group of inhabitants in the southeastern part of Colchester and northeast section of Lyme at Paugwonk.[37] The General Assembly endorsed a petition sent by inhabitants of the region in May 1725 and established New Salem Society, a subject that will be discussed in detail in Chapter 5.

The third parish, called Westchester, had its origins with a May 1728 petition

---

[32] His father, the Reverend Gershom Bulkeley (1656-1713), was a minister in New London and Wethersfield, a physician, and opponent of charter government after 1688. Grandfather Reverend Peter Bulkley (1583-1659) was a Cambridge University graduate and minister in Concord, Massachusetts. John Bulkey married Patience Prentiss, daughter of John Prentiss of New London, in 1701. The Bulkleys were the most prominent family in eighteenth-century Colchester and the largest slave owning one. Reverend John left at least one slave and in 1790 seven descendants possessed sixteen slaves, six lived in Colchester and one in Lyme. Clifford K. Shipton, *Biographical Sketches of the Graduates of Harvard University* (Boston: Harvard University Press, 1933), IV, 450-54; 1790 United States Census, Connecticut, New London County, microfilm, 83-101, CSL.

For information on Gershom and Peter Bulkeley, see, Robert Charles Anderson, George E. Sanborn, Jr., Melinde Lutz Sanborn, *The Great Migration: Immigrants to New England 1634-1635*, Vol I, A-B (Boston: New England Historic and Genealogical Society, 1999), 459-65; Donald Lines Jacobus, *The Bulkeley Genealogy* (New Haven: The Tuttle, Morehouse & Taylor Company, 1933), 92-111, 116-26; *Sibley's Harvard Graduates*, I, 389-402.

[33] *Colony Records*, IV, 463. The other towns were Danbury, Mansfield, Plainfield, Simsbury, Waterbury, Windham, and Woodbury.

[34] Neighboring Lebanon was incorporated in 1700, grew much more rapidly, and sent its first representatives to the General Assembly in May 1705. Its 1705 lists of estates and persons was £3,736 and with ninety males. *Colony Records*, IV, 499, 521; V, 71.

[35] Ibid, V, 24, 66, 71, 80-81, 277. The list of estates in 1711 for Lyme was £7,677 and for Lebanon £5,828.

[36] CA, Militia, Series 1, I, 213.

[37] By way of contrast, Lebanon ordained its first minister in November 1700, three years before Colchester, its Second Society (Lebanon Crank) was established in 1716, and Goshen Society settled its first minister in November 1729. *Ecclesiastical History*, 365, 391, 414.

by inhabitants from the western portion of Colchester and the extreme eastern portion of "Haddam East," later East Haddam. The thirty-six memorialists noted that the total taxable list for Colchester, excluding "Paugwonk" Society, stood at £9,218-16-0, more than enough to support a third parish in the town and they reiterated the usual arguments for parish privileges. The petitioners affirmed that "for Diverse Years" they had "been under great Difficulty in Attending the public worship of Almighty God" and they lived four to five miles from the nearest church. The legislature appointed Thomas Kimberly of Glastonbury and Samuel Lynde of Saybrook to consider the memorial.[38] The two men endorsed the petition after going to the area on June 25, 1728 and seeing the conditions the memorialists had to endure.[39] The new parish was established in October 1728 and one year later the General Assembly granted permission for them "to be imbedded in church estate, and to call and settle an orthodox minister.[40] Westchester ordained its first minister, the Reverend Judah Lewis (1703-1739), in December 1729.[41]

By the end of the 1720s when Colonel Samuel Browne had completed his purchases, population had grown and expanded to encompass almost the entire geographic limits of Lyme and Colchester. Lyme was divided into three vigorous church societies, while Colchester, a generation younger than Lyme had been similarly divided, although two of its parishes, New Salem and Westchester, were still in the process of organization. Westchester had just ordained its first minister, while struggling New Salem Society established four years earlier had still not succeeded in doing so. In 1718, however, when Browne first began acquiring land in Connecticut, virtually the entire area of his purchases consisted of uninhabited wilderness, although perhaps a handful of Native Americans lived in the region.

---

[38] Samuel Lynde was a nephew of Benjamin Lynde of Salem, Massachusetts who married a sister of Colonel Samuel Browne. F. E. Oliver, ed., *Diaries of Benjamin Lynde and Benjamin Lynde, Jr.* (Boston: Privately Printed, 1880), vii-ix.

[39] CA, Ecclesiastical Affairs, Series 1, III, 209-11.

[40] *Colony Records*, VII, 158-59, 203-05, 257-58.

[41] Lewis graduated from Yale in 1726 and died in office ten years after ordination. *Ecclesiastical History*, 499; Dexter, *Yale Graduates*, I, 329.

Chapter 3

James Harris, Land Speculator

James Harris (1673-1757) is unknown today, but he played a significant role in the early history of Salem and Montville. He left numerous traces of his presence in New London County, particularly in court and land records.[1] The sole monuments to Harris that exist today, however, consist of Harris Brook, a small stream that crosses Route 82 west of Salem Four Corners before it flows into the east branch of the Eight Mile River, and Harris Road in the same town.

Harris was born in Boston on April 4, 1673, eldest son of James (1642-1714) and Sarah Eliot Harris (b. 1647), of modest middle-class origins.[2] The family was not prominent or wealthy like, for example, such early New Londoners as those of the Christophers, Rogers, Saltonstall, Wetherell, and Winthrop families.

James's father was also born in Boston and it is not known who his parents were, although several adult males with the same surname settled in the Massachusetts Bay Colony in the 1630s.[3] He spent most of his life in Boston and is thought to have married Sarah Eliot, daughter of Deacon Jacob and Margery Eliot, in 1667.[4] The elder James may have learned about the Lyme area when he lived near Twelve Mile Island on

---

[1] To distinguish him from others with the same name, he is sometimes referred to as James Harris, Jr. and much more often as Lieut. James Harris.

[2] For information on the history of the Harris family, see Nathaniel Harris Morgan, *Harris Genealogy: A History of James Harris of New London, Conn. and his Descendants from 1640 to 1878* (Hartford: The Case, Lockwood & Brainard Co., 1878), 3-30; Gale Ion Harris, "James and Sarah (Eliot?) Harris of Boston and New London," *The New England Historical and Genealogical Register*, 154 (January 2000), 3-27.

[3] Gale Ion Harris states that possibly James was the son of a John Harris who came to Massachusetts in 1635 on the *Christian*, but Robert Charles Anderson found no evidence for that conclusion. Harris speculates that four Harris males; William of Block Island and Lyme, John of Boston and Glastonbury, Thomas of Twelve-Mile-Island in Lyme and East Haddam, and James the elder may have had the same father. Harris, "James Harris of New London," 14, fn 58; Anderson, *Great Migration*, 225-27. A number of Harrises migrated to Massachusetts during the 1630s – Joshua, Thomas, Walter, John, and Parnell – but no record of any James Harris has been found. Robert Charles Anderson, *The Great Migration Begins: Immigrants to New England, 1620-1633*, II (Boston: New England Historic Genealogical Society, 1995), 863-66; Gale Ion Harris, "Thomas Harris, Merchant of New England," *National Genealogical Society Quarterly*, 80 (1992), 36-56; Gale Ion Harris, "Thomas Harris, Sawmiller of Hartford, Connecticut," Ibid, 78 (1990), 182-203.

[4] Nathaniel Harris Morgan, author of the first genealogy of the family, wrote that James Harris, Sr., married Sarah Denison of Boston in 1666. Gale Ion Harris on the other hand presents convincing circumstantial evidence that his wife was Sarah Eliot. Morgan, *Harris Genealogy*, 17; Harris, "James Harris of New London," 5-9.

the Connecticut River in the 1660s with Thomas Harris, although he returned to Boston by the early 1670s. He became a tavern keeper in Boston's South End in the 1690s and removed with his wife to New London around 1704, probably to live with his son's family. "Old James Harris" died at his son's home in Mohegan [later the North Parish of New London, now Montville] on June 9, 1714.[5] Five days earlier his will was drafted in which he left his entire estate to his wife Sarah for her lifetime and then after her death to be divided equally among his surviving children.[6]

James the younger was the third of twelve children, only four of whom appear to have survived to adulthood.[7] Nothing is known about his childhood, although he probably learned the weaving trade in Boston. He may have known about Connecticut from his father, but it is also possible that he learned about the New London area from relatives who were among the earliest settlers of the town, one of whom was Walter Harris (1590s-1654). Walter sailed on the *Speedwell* to Massachusetts in 1637 with his wife and children and lived in Weymouth before moving to New London in 1653. Among his six children were sons Gabriel (1629-1684) and Thomas (1635-1691).[8] Gabriel, a second-generation resident of New London, inherited the "house, land, cattle and swine, with all other goodes reall and personell" of his relatively prosperous parents.[9] When Gabriel died, he also left a substantial estate that included real property valued at some £670.[10] His younger brother Thomas, a merchant in the Barbados trade, died on June 9, 1691. His estate was valued at £927-09-09 and included three slaves.[11]

James married Sarah Rogers (1676-1748), daughter of Samuel Rogers (1640-1713) of New London and a woman above his station, in 1696 not long after he arrived

---

[5] Joshua Hempstead, *The Diary of Joshua Hempstead, 1711-1758* (New London: The New County Historical Society, Inc., 1901, 1999), 35. Republication of 1901 work with improved index.

[6] He appointed his son James and daughter-in-law Sarah as executors of his estate and signed with a mark. Harris, "James Harris of New London," 3, 5, 9-11; Morgan, *Harris Genealogy*, 17-19.

[7] The eldest child Sarah (b. 1668) lived in Boston and probably married twice. Eighth child Asa (1680-1715) had four children. The youngest Ephraim (b. 1689) witnessed a deed in New London in 1706, but is not found in any additional records. Harris, "James Harris of New London," 15-16, 27-31.

[8] The inventory of the estate of Walter and Mary Harris was taken on April 14, 1656. It included "one negro" valued at eight shillings and "two Indians" at two shillings. New London Land Records, III, 47-49, microfilm, CSL.

[9] He was chosen ensign of the New London "Train Band" in May 1665 and enrolled as a freeman of the colony in October 1669. *Colony Records*, II, 17, 116.

[10] Gale Ion Harris, *Harrises of Connecticut: Scattered Descendants* (Salina, MI: McNaughton & Gunn, Inc., 2012), 223-27; Frances Manwaring Caulkins, *History of New London, Connecticut From the First Survey of the Coast in 1612, to 1852* (New London: The Author, 1860), 269-71; Gabriel Harris, New London, 1685, New London Probate District Records, no. 2454, microfilm, CSL. He was survived by six children; Thomas (26), Peter (23), John (22), Samuel (20), Mary (16), and Joseph (12). Gale Ion Harris has been unable to positively connect James Harris with the man of the same surname who came to New London in 1653. Despite the lack of evidence regarding the known Harrises studied by Anderson and the fact that Walter arrived in Massachusetts after the ending date of the *Great Migration* study, a connection between the Walter and James branches of the family is believable.

[11] Thomas Harris, New London, 1691, NLPR, Volume A, 70-71, CSL. A number of other Harrises lived in the area, all descended from Gabriel. At least one other James Harris lived in New London. He was born around 1718 and married in 1744. Joshua Hempstead called him Ensign James Harris. Kathryn Harris Burkley, *The Walter Harris Family of New London, Connecticut* (privately published, 1991), not paginated.

in town.[12] His father-in-law was one of the wealthiest and most prominent inhabitants of the town and owner of extensive tracts of land in the Mohegan section of New London, later New London North Society, and still later Montville.

Since Harris likely got an immense boost from marriage, it is useful to briefly discuss the probable influence of Samuel Rogers and his daughter Sarah had on his subsequent career as a land speculator.[13] Samuel married Mary Stanton (b.c. 1643) in 1662, daughter of Thomas Stanton of New London and Stonington, the well-known Indian interpreter.[14] At the time of the marriage, the two fathers gave the young couple the princely sum of £400 sterling and James Rogers also gave his son a stone house and bakery at Winthrop Cove in New London. He demonstrated his mettle in 1675 by serving along with his father on a committee to fortify the town after the outbreak of King Phillip's War.[15] By 1680, Samuel moved to Mohegan becoming the first white settler on these Native American lands. He was close to Uncas, sachem of the Mohegans, and his son Owaneco, both of whom donated land to him in compensation for the friendship and services he provided for the tribe.[16] Samuel Rogers owned vast quantities of real estate in the region and ranked as one of the largest property owners in southeastern Connecticut.[17] He was a grantee or grantor on close to 150 New London deeds between 1662 and 1713, including nine from Uncas and Owaneco.[18]

Before his death on December 1, 1713, he drafted a will in which he made bequests to his second wife Johanna, daughter Mary Gilbert, son Samuel Rogers, daughter Sarah Harris, son Daniel, daughter Elizabeth Harris, granddaughter Elisabeth Stanton, and son Jonathan. To Sarah Harris, he gave ten shillings and directed his son Daniel pay her £10. This modest inheritance was due to the fact that he had already "given her the rest of her portion alre[a]dy."[19] Despite being the eldest son of one of the leaders of early New London, Samuel Rogers never held the public offices commensurate with his pedigree due to the fact that his younger brother was founder and leader of the infamous Rogerenes.[20]

---

12 Harris, *Harrises of Connecticut*, 247.

13 Samuel Rogers was the eldest son of James (c. 1615-1687) and Elizabeth Rowland Rogers (d. 1709), one of the most prominent of the early settlers of New London and father of John Rogers (1648-1721), founder of the Rogerenes. The other children consisted of Joseph (1646-1697), Bathshua (1650-1711), James (1652-1714), Jonathan (1652-1714), and Elizabeth (1658-1714). James Swift Rogers, *James Rogers of New London, CT, and his Descendants* (Boston: Published by the Compiler, 1902), 27-47; Anderson, *Great Migration*, VI, 72-84.

14 On Thomas Stanton, see Anderson, *Great Migration*, VI, 467-79.

15 Susan Lim, *Sola Scriptura and Sectarianism: The Rise of the Rogerenes in Colonial New Londaon, 1664-1721* (Cheshire, CT: The Connecticut Press, 2019), 12.

16 Uncas and Owaneco made their first transfers of land to Rogers in October 1676 and March 1677. A third early deed is dated April 1679. Oberg, *Uncas*, 201, 255.

17 Rogers, *Rogers Descendants*, 39-40.

18 Samuel and Mary had six children who lived to adulthood. Mary, the oldest surviving child, married Captain Samuel Gilbert and Elizabeth, the third, married Asa Harris, brother of James, Ibid, 41.

19 Ibid, 39; Samuel Rogers, New London, 1713, NLPR, no. 4590. The date of the will was February 20, 1712/3 and his probate record contains a will but no inventory.

20 No evidence exists to believe that Harris had any association with the Rogerenes except through marriage

Within two years of marriage, James settled in Mohegan, probably on a fifty-acre plot sold by Owaneco to Sarah Harris in November 1698 for forty shillings "Currant mony of New England."[21] Sarah was also grantee on three other deeds between 1706 and 1710. In August 1706, Samuel Rogers "in Consideration of his naturall Love and Great Affection" for Sarah Harris deeded her and husband James a "Tract of Land and meadow Lying near & Adjoyning to the Greate pond [Gardner Lake] as Lyeth betwixt New London and Collchester" encompassing about 170 acres.[22] Then came two deeds from Samuel to Sarah in 1709 and 1710, both due to the affection the father had for his daughter. By the first gift, Sarah Harris received "A Tractt of Land and meadow Lying near & Adjoyning to the Greate pond as Lyeth betwixt New London and Collchester." By the second, his "beloved Daughter Sarah Harris" and husband James received 100 acres.[23]

Harris first bought and sold land in the Mohegan section of New London, then Lyme, followed by Colchester. He often purchased and disposed of it at a rapid pace and was grantee and grantor on about 95 New London deeds, around 25 from Lyme, and almost 60 more from Colchester. The extent to which Harris depended upon his wife can be ascertained by the number of sales in which Sarah Harris was a co-signer.[24] Her signature appears on 9 New London, 8 Lyme, and 13 Colchester land sales, on properties she owned, came to her from her father, were originally purchased with money she helped furnish, or to which she held dower rights.[25]

His first transaction consisted of an exchange of one hundred acres with Thomas Jones of New London in 1699. Harris was grantee or grantor on six additional deeds prior to 1710.[26] He became a major landowner at Mohegan on May 10, 1710 when Owaneco, "Sachem of Mohegan," sold John Livingston, Robert Denison, Samuel Rogers, Jr., and James Harris a large tract of land totaling well over 4,000 acres for £50.[27]

---

and his father-in-law had no strong connections with the sect. Lim, *Sola Scriptura*, 76, 118.

[21] Oweneco to Sarah Harris, November, 11, 1698, NLLR, VI, 4, 48; Harris, "James Harris of New London," 17.

[22] Samuel Rogers to Sarah Harris and James Harris, NLLR, June 25, 1709, VI, 138.

[23] Samuel Rogers to Sarah Harris, June 16, 1709; Samuel Rogers to Sarah Harris, Ibid, May 29, 1710 VI, 183, 213. The second deed specifically stated that Sarah gave the land "unto her husband James Harris."

[24] Under the legal principle of coverture, a married woman was allowed access to the courts "only through the personality of her husband." Husbands, therefore, generally controlled the property brought to marriage by their wives. *Black's Law Dictionary*, Seventh edition (St. Paul, Minn.: West Group, 1999) 373.

[25] NLLR, VI, 31, 48, 291; VIII, 275, 289, 337, 371; XI, 96; Lyme Land Records, III, 182, 360; IV, 176, 312, 322, 335, 336, 337. To give just one example of how essential Sarah was, the first sale of 4,000 acres to Colonel Samuel Browne in August 1718 contained Sarah's signature after that of husband James, plus two additional notations. First, on August 21, 1718, "Sarah Harris ye wife of the abovesaid James Harris consents to the Sale of the aboves'd Lands and doth hereby give up her Power of Thirds and Rights of Dower in the same." Second, on March 23, 1734, she again acknowledged that she was "one of the Subscribers to this Instrument [and] personally appeared and acknowledged the same to be her free Act and Deed." LLR, III, 74, 199.

[26] NLLR, VI, 19, 47, 48, 48, 69, 138.

[27] NLLR, VI, 205-06, 210-11; Henry A. Baker, *History of Montville, Connecticut* (Hartford: Press of The Case, Lockwood & Brainard Company, 1896), 80-83. The first deed was dated April 13, 1710 and the second May 10, 1710. Joseph Stanton, "Interpreter," witnessed the second deed. Two fifths of the land went to Colo-

Surveyed by John Plumb in 1713, the first division totaled around 2,900 acres with each lot encompassing 500-600 acres. The second division made at the same time was three-quarters of a mile in length.[28] At virtually the same time, Harris purchased 104 acres from Thomas Angel of Providence, land that Angel had earlier bought from Samuel Rogers, Jr., and Samuel Rogers, Sr. gave another 100 acres to his "beloved daughter Sarah Harris," both properties bordering on Sawmill Brook.[29]

James and Sarah became the parents of nine children between 1697 and 1720, all except the youngest born in New London and all except the fifth and ninth children, both named Alpheus, survived the rigors of childhood, married, and had children of their own.[30] On September 10 1700, New London awarded Harris a cattle mark of "a half Crop on the hind Side of both Earrs and a Cross slit on the hind Side neare Ear."[31] In January 1707/8, John Livingston, Samuel Rogers, Jr., James Harris, and Daniel Stebbens sent a petition to the New London County Court protesting the proposed route of a new country road between New London and Colchester.[32] Harris became a militia officer when the legislature established the first trainband in what later became New London North Society. In May 1715, it appointed Robert Denison, captain; James Harris, lieutenant; and Samuel Avery, ensign of the company "living to ye North."[33] He retained this position until he moved to Colchester and held the courtesy title for the rest of his life, an indicator of his prominence in the community.

New London County Court Records cast light on other aspects of Harris's life, not all favorable, and reveal a constant struggle with debt. Over the course of more than

---

nel John Livingston and one fifth each to the remaining three grantees. A certain amount of uncertainty exists concerning this purchase from the Mohegans. One source states that the purchasers had to return the land to the tribe, but when the Connecticut General Assembly passed an act in May 1721 establishing New London North Society, it confirmed the 1710 purchase by Colonel John Livingston, Robert Denison, Samuel Rogers, Jr., and James Harris. Paul Grant-Costa, "The Last Indian War in Southern New England: The Mohegan Tribe of Indians v. The Governour and Company of Connecticut, 1703-1774" (Unpublished Ph.D. Dissertation, Yale University, 2008), 116; CA. Towns and Lands, Series 1, III, 187, CSL; *Colony Records*, VI, 256.

[28] Baker, *Montville*, 81-83.

[29] NLLR, VI, 212-13. Sawmill Brook Brook flowed from Opsobosket or Little Pond into the Thames River at Uncasville, a section of what became Montville. Both brook and pond are now called Oxoboro. Hughes and Allen, *Connecticut Place Names*, 331-32

[30] The children were: Sarah (1697-c. 1742), James (1699-1780), Mary (1702-1761), Jonathan (1705-1761), Abigail (b. 1711), Lebbeus (b. 1713), and Delight (1720-1783). Sarah married Pelatiah Bliss (1697-1763) of New Salem and he witnessed several James Harris deeds. James married Ann Gilbert, daughter of Captain Samuel and Mary Rogers Gilbert, his first cousin, and spent most of his adult life in Saybrook. Mary wed John Holmes, Jr. of Colchester and the couple moved to Salisbury. Jonathan spent most of his life in Colchester and married Mary Vibber of New London. Abigail married Samuel Fox, Jr. of New London and they resided in the North Parish. Lebbeus served as agent for the Browne family, settled his father's estate, was granted Susquehannah Company lands in 1754, and moved to Horton, Nova Scotia in the early 1760s. He wed Alice Ransom of Colchester. The youngest child Delight married Alpheus Rogers of New London. Harris, "James Harris of New London," 21-27.

[31] New London Town Records, Record of Ear Marks, 1691-1807, 12, New London City Hall. The mark was later assigned to William Wheeler, 2d.

[32] RG 003, New London County Court Records, Papers by Subject: Travel, January 15, 1707/8, Box 91, folder 8, CSL.

[33] CA, Militia, Series 1, I, 57, CSL.

fifty years, James Harris was a plaintiff or defendant in some 300 court cases tried before the Hartford, New London, and Windham county courts. He was the defendant in about 80% of all lawsuits.[34] They show that he faced considerable difficulties in paying his bills and keeping his head above water. Thus, despite whatever aspirations he might have had to achieve the economic success of some of his New London merchant contemporaries, Harris always struggled. He first appeared in his normal role as a defendant in June 1699 when the New London County Court found him guilty in a debt by bill for £3-18 plus £0-19-8 costs of suit.[35] Between 1702 and 1710, he was defendant in five cases and plaintiff in one lawsuit that was withdrawn, probably because he was paid the debt.[36] The pace of lawsuits for nonpayment increased rapidly in the next decade when James became much more heavily involved in buying and selling land. While the lawsuits filed up to 1710 were for modest sums, like £1-5, £9-12, and £14, the plaintiffs thereafter often sued Harris for more significant amounts.[37]

Court records for the same decade show that James engaged in the horse trade and not always in a legal manner. Seven lawsuits from 1700 to 1708 document this chapter of Harris's life. In the first, a question arose over the ownership of a horse that Harris planned to sell to Daniel Stebbens, an animal in the possession of a third party, and uncertainty existed as to whom the horse belonged. Was Harris attempting to sell a horse that did not belong to him? We do not know because the suit was withdrawn.[38] Three months later the colony prosecuted Harris who lived "neere the bounds of New London" for stealing seven horses from Samuel Gager, Joshua Able, Samuel Calkins, and John Johnson and also "of Cutting a horses Ears Illegally."[39] The court convicted him on both charges and sentenced him to pay a fine of £10 and "be whipt 20 lashes" for the illegal cutting of ears and treble damages plus thirty-six more lashes for theft of the horses. Harris "submitt[ed] himself to the Mercy of this Hon[ora]ble Court"

---

[34] See Appendix A for a more detailed breakdown.

[35] RG 003, *Richard Steer v. James Harris*, NLCC, Trials, June 1699, Vol. 7, 229, CSL. A second debt lawsuit filed against Harris in September was withdrawn. *Benjamin Brewster, Jr. v. James Harris*, September 1699, Ibid, Vol. 7, 245.

[36] He confessed judgment in one, two were withdrawn, one was classed as a nonsuit, and the determination on the last is not known. *Jeremiah Chapman v. James Harris*, NLCC, Trials, June 1702, Vol. 7, 340; *Hezekiah Woolworth v. James Harris*, NLCC, Files, June 1706, Box 3, folder 7; *William Lee v. James Harris*, Ibid, September 1707, Box 4, folder 1; *William Billings v. James Harris, Jr.*, Ibid, September 1709, Box 4, folder 18; *Matthew Griswold v. James Harris, Jr.*, Ibid, September 1710, Box 5, folder 8; *James Harris, Jr. v. Robert Stodar*, Ibid, September 1710, Box 5, folder 8.

[37] In addition, he signed two bonds to certify that a party in a lawsuit would appear when the case was called. Henry Merrow recognizance bond, June 1706, NLCC, Files, Box 3, folder 9; Samuel Waller, Jr. surety bond, June 1707, Ibid, Box 3, folder 18.

[38] *Daniel Stebens v. James Harris*, NLCC, Trials, March 1700, Vol. 7, 270.

[39] The victims lived in the nearby towns of Norwich and Lebanon. The fact that Harris lived in the northern and largely uninhabited section of town at Mohegan "neere the bounds of New London" provided what proved to be an imperfect cover for illegal activity.

In another lawsuit that may or may not have been related, Samuel Calkins and one other Lebanon man sued Thomas Stodder of Norwich for illegally transporting five horses out of the colony. The defendant confessed and the court sentenced him to be whipped thirty stripes and pay a fine of £20. *Samuel Calkin and Nathaniell Dewey v. Thomas Stoder*, NLCC, Trials, June 1700, Vol. 7, 275.

and it remitted £5 in fines and the corporal punishment provided he "Give Security to make Sattisfaction to the persons wronged."[40]

The June 1701 court heard a case in which Robert Stodder of New London sued James Harris for slander because he had accused the plaintiff of stealing two horses from him. The same court heard a countersuit in which Harris accused Stodder of taking "a Gray and a bay horse" away. The defendant was fined £5.[41] In a fourth lawsuit, Robert Denison of Stonington sued Harris over a white horse in the latter's possession. The horse was returned to Denison and he recovered costs of suit £0-19-0.[42] One year later Stodder again sued Harris for the recovery of a black horse stolen from him and in the defendant's possession. The court ruled that the horse belonged to Stodder but that Harris had not stolen it. The defendant, was, however, forced to pay court costs.[43] Lastly, Nathaniel Niles of Kingstown, Rhode Island sued in 1708 over a July 1697 contract to exchange horses and the court ordered that Harris pay the plaintiff fifty shillings.[44] Two other lawsuits involving horses occurred in the next decade. A partial record from November 1711 contains a reference to a possible lawsuit between Harris and Ephraim Culver and John Culver of Lebanon concerning the theft of a horse belonging to Colonel John Livingston. In another 1713 case, the colony charged John Pike of Norwich with stealing three horses from Harris, but found the defendant not guilty.[45]

Despite Harris's legal problems, he was selected to serve on a jury of inquest in May 1702 to investigate the death of the baby of Joanah Tub[b]s of New London. The jury determined that the child was stillborn.[46]

In the second decade of the eighteenth century, the lawsuits became much

---

[40] *Dom Rex v, James Harris*, NLCC, Trials, June 1700, Vol. 7, 283, 286, 287, 316; Ibid, NLCC, Files, June 1700, Box 1, folder 13. John Johnson of Lebanon testified that one of the persons who received a stolen horse was Harris's brother-in-law Samuel Gilbert, then of Hartford. The horse taken from Joshua Able was worth £3 and Harris paid treble damages.

[41] *Robert Stodder v. James Harris*, NLCC, Trials, June 1701, Vol. 7, 309. No verdict has been found, but Stodder sent a memorial to the court in which he discussed his "folly." *James Harris v. Robert Stod[d]er*, Ibid, June 1701, Vol 7, 315. At the same court session, a fragmentary record of another lawsuit exists, a summons to Samuel Waller, Jr., Henry Brooks, and Robert Stodder to give evidence against Samuel Waller, Jr. who was accused by Harris of "Stealing a bay horse and a Gray horse" on the night of March 3, 1700/1. "To Samuel Waller Junr," NLCC, Trials, June 1701, Box 1, folder 17.

[42] *Robert Denison v. James Harris*, NLCC, Files, June 1704, Box 2, folder 10.

[43] *Robert Stodder v. James Harris*, Ibid, June 1705, Box 2, folder 18.

[44] *Nathaniel Niles v. James Rogers*, Ibid, September 1708, Box 4, folder 10.

[45] *James Harris v. Ephraim Culver and John Culver*, Files, November 1711, Box 5, folder 16; *Queen v. John Pike*, NLCC, Trials, November 1713, Vol. 7, 159.
    The Harrises descended from Walter Harris also faced legal problems.In November 1713, the colony attorney sued Thomas Harris, Joseph Harris, Samuel Harris, William Harris and two others for assault, "naked dancing," and debauchery against several maids. The accused with that surname were the great-grandchildren of the first Harris to settle in the town. *Rex v. Thomas Harris, Joseph Harris, Samuel Harris, Gabriell Woodmancy, Richard Mitchell, and William Harris*. NLCC, Files, November 1713, Box 7, folder 3; Burkley, *Walter Harris*, unpaginated.

[46] Inquest, May 30, 1702, NLCC, Files, Box 1, folder 24.

more numerous and the amounts involved were often a good deal larger because of his difficulty in paying for the lands he had purchased.[47] The first two debts by bond cases were tried in November 1714. Colonel John Livingston of New London accused Harris of failing to pay two separate bonds for £100 each. Harris paid his debt in the first lawsuit and appealed the guilty verdict in the second.[48] In a similar lawsuit, Abigail Angel, widow of James, of Providence sued in a debt by bond dated May 18, 1710 by which Harris agreed to pay James Angel "four hundred ounces and an half ounce Troy Weight in [silver] Bullion" by May 1, 1713 in payment for three parcels of land near "Mohegan fields" in the north part of New London that the Providence man had earlier purchased for investment purposes.[49] Harris failed to discharge the debt, confessed judgment in February 1716, and agreed to pay the the sum owed by May together with interest and costs of suit.[50]

The records also show that even after Harris confessed judgment for debts he had incurred, sometimes he could not pay them until several months later.[51] One example, Colonel Samuel Browne sued Harris in November 1719 in a debt by bond for £1,000. Harris confessed that he owed £212 plus interest and £1-16-6 costs of suit and requested that the execution be suspended until March 15, 1720. The court granted execution on June 7, 1720, a second time on August 9, again on October 5, and a fourth occasion on January 17, 1720/1, thus postponing payment for almost one and

---

[47] For the period between 1711 and 1720, James was a defendant in thirty-eight cases and plaintiff in five, all except two were brought before the New London County Court.

[48] *John Livingston v. James Harris*, NLCC, Trials, November 1714, Vol. 8, 236; Ibid, Vol. 8, 244. On appeal, the Superior Court decided in Harris' favor and he was awarded court costs of £2-3-2. RG 003, *John Livingston v. James Harris*, March 1714/5, Early Records, Connecticut Superior Court, Vol. 1, 54, CSL No information exists on the nature of the bonds. The likelihood is that Harris borrowed money from the wealthy Livingston.

[49] Samuel Rogers, Jr. to James Angel, NLLR, May 19, 1710, VI, 209. Angel paid £213 in bills of credit for the land.

[50]*Abigail Angell v. James Harris*, November 1715, NLCC, Trials, Vol. 9, 42; *Abigail Angell v. James Harris*, February 1716, Ibid, Vol. 9, 95; *Abigail Angel v. James Harris*, February 1716, NLCC Files, Box 9, folder 17, no. 18; James Angel to James Harris, Jr., NLLR, May 18, 1710, VI, 212.

[51] Whenever a person borrowed money from another, the contract, usually in the form of a bond or note, specified the date on which the principal was supposed to be repaid together with lawful interest. When the debtor did not repay all that he owed by the specified time, the creditor could sue. Many creditors waited several months before taking this step and often a month or more elapsed from the time of the summons to appear until the date of the meeting of the court session to hear the case, thus giving the defendant more time to settle the debt. Not infrequently, court cases were delayed or continued from one court session to the next. Parties found guilty could delay execution by asking for a review at a subsequent session or by appealing to the Superior Court. Debtors, therefore, had a number of ways to play out the string and postpone paying back what they owed.

Illustration 1. James Harris Memorial to New London County Court.[52]

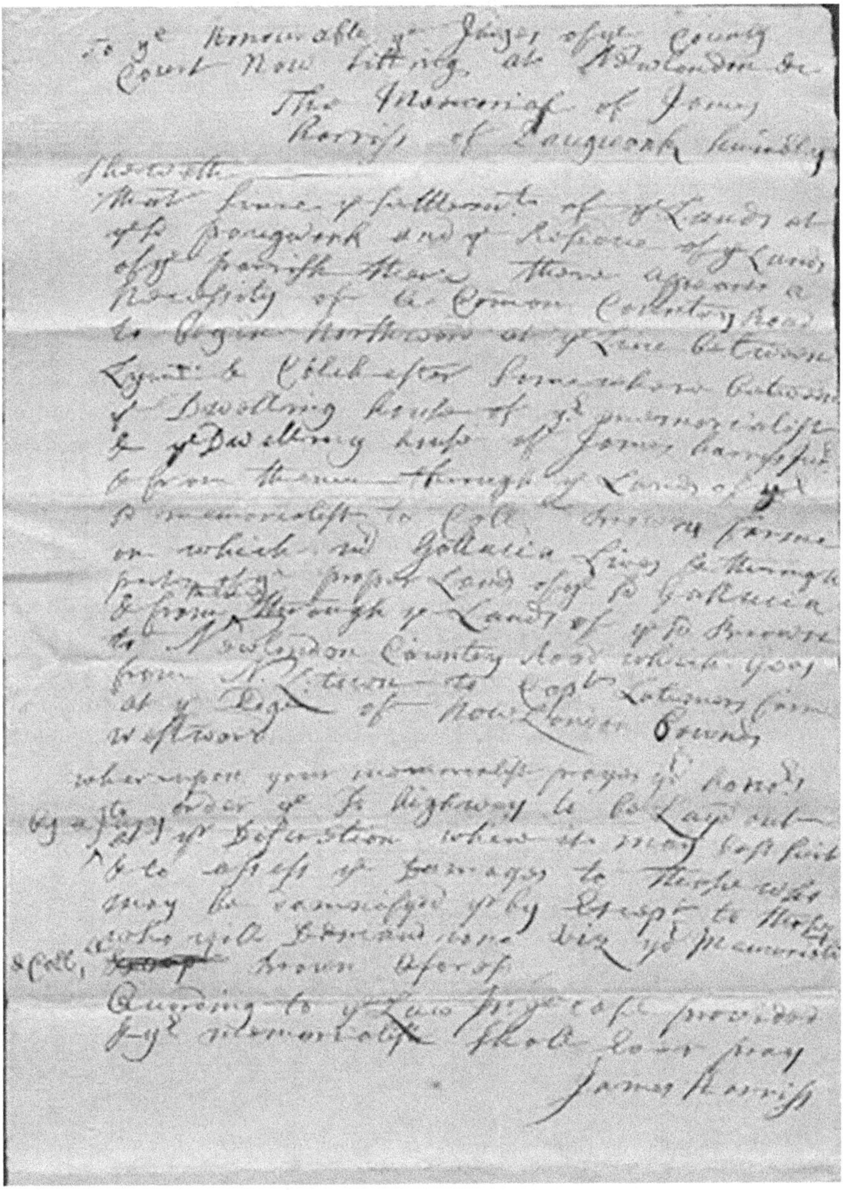
To ye honorable ye Judges of ye County Court now sitting at New London &c
The Memorial of James Harris of Paugwonk humbly sheweth
That since ye settlement of ye Lands at ye Paugwonk and ye settling of ye Land of ye parish there, there appears a necessity of a common Country road to begin northward at ye Line between Lyme & Colchester somewhere between ye Dwelling house of ye sd memorialist & ye Dwelling house of James Harris Junr & from thence through ye Lands of ye sd memorialist to Coll Browns farme on which sd Gallaua lives & through part of ye proper Land of ye sd Gallaua & from through ye Lands of ye sd Browne to New London Country road which goes from N London to Capt Latimers farme at ye Edge of New London Bounds westward
whereupon your memorialist prays yr honrs to order ye sd highway to be layd out by a Jury of Inspection where it may best suit & to assess ye damages to those who may be damnifyed thereby except to those who will demand none viz ye memorialist & Coll Brown aforesd
According to ye Law in yt case provided & ye memorialist shall ever pray
James Harris

one-half years.[53] Over the course of the decade, Harris was sued for unpaid debts that

52 Memorial of James Harris, 1726, NLCC, PbyS: Travel, Box 91, folder 17, CSL. A sample of his handwriting. Note the way the document was folded before being flattened during processing.

53 *Samuel Brown v. James Harris*, NLCC, Trials, November 1719, Vol. 11, 206. See also, *Jonathan Rogers v. James Harris*, Ibid, June 1720, Vol. 12, 85. Harris confessed judgment in a debt by note for £6-12 and costs

totaled £1,920.[54]

In addition, and like his father-in-law, James maintained close relations with the Mohegans, next to whom he lived. After a small group of Indians led by Cesar Sachem attacked the house of Jonathan Hill in April 1716 in response to white encroachments on their land, Harris acted as attorney for the tribe in the lawsuit that followed. The New London County Court heard the case in August and the jury found "for the Defendants Costs of suit" £1-6.[55] In a related case, Hill sued Harris accusing him of instigating the Indian attack on the "Mansion house" of Hill at Mohegan on April 9, 1716. Hill also sued the Mohegans who seized the property to regain the "peaceable possession" of the house and for £30 damages. Harris in his unsuccessful plea of abatement argued that the plaintiff had no right to the house because it was on Native American property. The court "over Ruled" the defendant and ordered Harris to pay court costs of £2-3-6.[56]

Purchases and sales of land increased rapidly after 1710, as Harris's land speculation career gained momentum. He was grantee on six more New London deeds between 1711 and 1719 and grantor on another nine during the same time frame.[57] His most significant transaction during this time period was the October 1711 sale of "one Moiety or half of the one fifth part of A Certain Tractt of Land purchased In Partnership . . . of Oweneco Sachem of Mohegan to Major John Merrett and Mrs. Mercy Raymond."[58] He sold the bulk of his land to men and women from the New London area. Presaging Harris's transactions with land speculators from outside the colony, he conveyed 650 acres together with a house and barn in 1717 to Joseph Otis of Scituate, Massachusetts at Mohegan.[59] Between 1720 and 1729, Harris disappeared from New London land records.[60] He moved to Colchester in the summer of 1718 and actively bought and sold land in that town and Lyme. Harris moved back to New London eleven years later after he sold his Colchester farm to Colonel Samuel Browne.[61]

---

of £0-12-2. The execution was delayed until September, delayed again until December, and a third time until March 28, 1721.

[54] Debts by bond were for twice the amount of the debt or the value of the service to be performed, the amount sued for was, therefore, divided in half to get an accurate figure of how much he borrowed.

[55] *Jonathan Hill v. Cezar Sachem and Ben Uncas*, NLCC, Files, August 1716, Native Americans, Box 1, folder 10; NLCC Trials, Vol. 9, 114.

[56] *Jonathan Hill v. James Harris*, NLCC, Ibid, Box 1, folder 10; NLCC, Trials, Vol. 9, 112. Harris appealed the adverse verdict and the Superior Court upheld the original one. *Jonathan Hill v. James Harris*, Early Records, CSC, September 1718, Vol. 2, 37.

[57] James Harris was grantee (purchaser) of seven parcels of land from James Angel, Owaneco, Samuel Rogers, Joshua Wheeler, Elizabeth Winthrop, Paul Wentworth, and Jonathan Rogers. He was grantor in sales to Major John Merrett (2), Merrett and Mercy Raymond, Abigail Lord, Jonathan Copp, John Nobles, John Livingston, Joseph Otis, and Joseph Bradford.

[58] James Harris to Major John Merrett and Mrs. Mercy Raymond, NLLR, October 14, 1711, VI, 245.

[59] James Harris to Joseph Otis, NLRR, April 27, 1717, VII, 135-36.

[60] Harris, "James Harris of New London," 19. In James Harris to Joseph Bradford, NLLR, July 2, 1718, VII, 224-25 and one other deed, he was styled "Gent[lema]n," otherwise he was called a yeoman.

[61] Evidence from New London County Court Records reveals that Harris moved to Colchester sometime be-

At some point during this time period, Harris became acquainted with several wealthy land speculators, the most noteworthy being Colonel Samuel Browne of Salem, Massachusetts and Colonel Thomas Fitch and John Dolbeare, both of Boston. Over a period of around a dozen years, he purchased and often quickly sold about 8,100 acres to Browne in Lyme, Colchester, and New London; 350 acres to Fitch in Colchester; and some 1,640 acres to Dolbeare in all three towns. Browne accumulated in total 9,646 acres, about half of the area of what later became the town of Salem, Fitch around 930, and Dolbeare some 3,260 acres, divided between New Salem and New London North Society. Why Browne and the others selected the New Salem area as a focal point for investment is relatively easy to explain. The region was virtually unsettled, distant from dangerous frontier areas, land was cheap, and much closer to navigable rivers than the properties Browne purchased during the 1720s in Stafford and Union.

It appears as if Harris acted as an agent to scout out, purchase, and resell mostly vacant land to Browne and the others. For example, on November 7, 1717, John, George, Sarah, Mary, and Deborah Griswold of Lyme sold Harris a tract of land totaling 4,550 acres in the northeast corner of the township to James Harris for £900 in New England bills of credit.[62] The following May Harris sold 4,000 acres of that huge parcel "Situate in ye northward part of ye Town of Lyme" for £1,600 in New England currency to Colonel Samuel Browne of Salem.[63] In May 1723, the Griswolds sold another tract of 2,871 acres "more or less" adjacent to the lands of Browne and Harris to James Harris for £2,080.[64] Within ten days, Harris resold the same property estimated at 2,865 acres to Browne for £2,350 in New England bills of credit.[65] Harris made a tidy profit on both transactions. Around 85% of the land purchased by Browne in the region came from Harris, the bulk in the two large adjacent parcels in 1718 and 1723. The remaining acquisitions were often not contiguous and were scattered throughout the central and northeastern sections of the parish. The third largest property totaled 626 acres (526 in Lyme and 100 in Colchester), a part of which was the Colchester farm on which Harris lived. Unlike most of the Browne purchases, this tract contained three houses, a sawmill, barn, and smith's shop and, therefore, sold for a much higher price, £3,450 in "Current money of New England."[66]

Harris also sold several properties to other absentees from Massachusetts and Rhode Island. The first such transaction occurred in April 1717, when he conveyed to Joseph Otis of Scituate, Massachusetts a house, barn, and 650 acres at Stony Brook in the northeast corner of New London that may have been where he lived before moving to

---

ween March and November 1718 and returned to New London between June and November 1729. NLCC, Trials, Vols. X, XI, XVI.

[62] John Griswold et al to James Harris, LLR, November 7, 1717, III, 184; IV, 301. The quitclaim for the property was dated July 5, 1718 and it consisted of all the land "Claiming by from or under the Title of their father mr mathew Griswold ye second Late of Lyme Deceased." LLR, III, 192.

[63] James Harris to Samuel Brown, LLR, July 5, 1718, III, 188, 198.

[64] John Griswold et al to James Harris, LLR, May 7, 1723, IV, 64-65.

[65] James Harris to Samuel Brown, LLR, May 16, 1723, IV, 66.

[66] James Harris to Samuel Brown, LLR, July 8, 1729, IV, 336. New England bills of credit had depreciated in value over the course of the decade. The signature of Sarah Harris appears on this deed.

Colchester.[67] Over the course of the next thirty years Harris sold lands in Lyme to Daniel Pearce of Kingston, Rhode Island; John Woodworth of Scituate, Massachusetts; and John Dolbeare.[68] He deeded lands in Colchester to Benjamin Ellery of Newport, Dolbeare, and Thomas Fitch and in New London to Dolbeare and Godfrey Malbone of Newport.[69]

The sale of lands in Colchester, Hebron, Lyme, and New London to Colonel Thomas Fitch (1669-1736) and John Dolbeare (1670-1740) deserve special mention.[70] These two extremely wealthy men invested heavily in Connecticut lands and Fitch had close connections with Browne.[71] They both joined the Governor's Council in Massachusetts in 1715.[72] The colonel's only surviving son John Fitch (1709-1735) graduated from Harvard in the class of 1727 and his classmates included Samuel Browne the younger and William Browne.[73] It is not unreasonable to believe that he heard about inexpensive and uninhabited lands in Colchester and Lyme from his Salem colleague. Between 1718 and 1730 in a dozen deeds, Fitch acquired almost 1,150 acres in the two

---

[67] James Harris to Joseph Otis, NLLR, April 25, 1717, VII, 135-36.

[68] James Harris to Daniel Pearce, LLR, May 22, 1718, III, 187; James Harris to John Woodworth, LLR, September 7, 1718, III, 201; James Harris to John Dolbear, LLR, May 14, 1725, III, 176.

[69] James Harris to Benjamin Ellery, Colchester Land Records, September 13, 1720, II, 363-64; James Harris to John Dolbear, CLR, May, 14, 1725, II, 587; March 21, 1727, II, 720; May 11, 1730; III, 132-33; James to Thomas Fitch, CLR, August 19, 1725, II, 588; 3, 32; James Harris to John Dolbear, NLLR, September 28, 1726, VIII, 337; March 24, 1726/7, VIII, 370-71; James Harris to Godfrey Malbone, NLLR, January 6, 1735/6, XI, 95-96; September 28, 1739, XII, 302; May 11, 1747, XIV, 68. In addition, in 1734 Harris mortgaged several tracts of land in New London North Society to James Bowdoin of Boston. NLLR, May 18, 1734, X, 173.

[70] See Map 1 on page 68 for the location of the Fitch and Dolbeare lands in New Salem.

[71] Colonel Thomas Fitch was a wealthy Boston merchant. In addition to real estate in Boston, including part of the "Common north of Boyleston Street," he acquired some 2,200 acres in Lunenburg, 2,346 in Dunstable, an equally large tract in Townsend, together with holdings in other recently organized towns, not to mention his land holdings in Connecticut. He married Abigail Danforth of Roxbury in 1694. At the time of his death, five of his six children had died, the only survivor being Martha who married James Allen. Another daughter Mary married Andrew Oliver. Fitch was described as "a Gentleman of great a valuable Accomplishments, remarkable for his Sagacity, Greatness of Mind, and substantial vital Piety" and "his Corpse was yesterday Interred with great Respect, the Regiment of the Town being under Arms." The funeral procession including the governor, "His Majesty's Council," the House of Representatives, and vast numbers of People." Ezra S. Stearns, "The Descendants of Dea. Zachary Fitch of Reading," NEHGR, 55 (1901), 291; New-England Weekly Journal, June 29, 1736, [2]; Sibley's Harvard Graduates, VI, 159, 164; VII, 383-84; VIII, 133-34.

Fitch owned the Three Mariners tavern at the head of Long Wharf and, like many prominent traders, was civic minded. He supported Boston's charity school, headed a list of subscribers to the town library, and served as a Trustee of the Charity of Edward Hopkins. Carl Bridenbaugh, Cities in the Wilderness: The First Century of Urban Life in America, 1625-1742 (New York: Oxford University Press, 1938, 1954), 266, 443, 453; Indenture, March 25, 1720, Trustees of the Charity of Edward Hopkins, Records of the Treasurer, Colonial North America at Harvard Library. With regard to his trading activities, see Thomas Fitch v. Edward Bainton, a 1721 complaint regarding a shipment of rice to London. Robert Auchmuty, Harvard Law School Library, Colonial at Harvard.

[72] Boston News-Letter, May 30, 1715, [1]. Fitch had previously served as a representative from Boston in the House of Representatives in 1709 and 1711-13. "Representatives of the Town of Boston in the General Court before the Revolution," Collections of the Massachusetts Historical Society, Second Series, X (1823), 27

[73] Sibley's Harvard Graduates, VIII, 133-34. Others in the same class included traitor Dr. Benjamin Church, Governor Thomas Hutchinson, Connecticut's Revolutionary War governor Jonathan Trumbull, and Israel Williams, "Monarch of Hampshire County." Ibid, 125-29, 149-217, 267-330, 301-33.

towns and another 780 acres in neighboring Hebron.[74] He purchased his first fifty acres at Paugwonk in Colchester from Israel Wyatt.[75] Approximately 350 acres in Colchester came from James Harris.[76] The other 800 acres came from ten other grantors and perhaps Harris assisted Fitch in finding these properties. Three hundred acres were situated in the Paugwonk section of Lyme and the rest in Colchester.[77] Fitch in total acquired some 1,930 acres of land, more than three square miles, in three eastern Connecticut towns.[78] Browne may have informed Fitch of the possibility of acquiring cheap land in Stafford because he also acquired 936.5 acres in that new town between December 1725 and March 1727.[79]

John Dolbeare, a wealthy brazier, pewterer, and ironmonger, had customers in southeastern Connecticut.[80] In 1716, for example, Joseph Peck of Lyme signed a receipt for £9-17 shillings for items purchased from Dolbeare.[81] His first purchase of land in

---

[74] Fitch's first Hebron purchase came in 1724, when he paid James Harris £357 for 650 acres in Hebron on the road from Colchester to Glastonbury, a deed that Sarah Harris also signed. Three years later he acquired another 230 acres in a quit claim from Nathaniel Dewey and Joseph Dewey. James Harris and Sarah Harris to Thomas Fitch, Hebron Land Records, December 12, 1724, II, 144; Nathaniel Dewey and Joseph Dewey to Thomas Fitch, March 7, 1727, Ibid, II, 230. Fitch's daughter Martha Brattle, widow of James Allen, and grandson Andrew Oliver, Jr. sold virtually all of the Hebron lands between November 1759 and August 1763. Ibid, V, 1, 11-12, 21, 92, 199, 201, 280, 291, 301, 303, 331, 343, 394, 406.

[75] Israel Wyatt to Thomas Fitch, CLR, January 17, 1717/8, II, 240.

[76] James Harris to Thomas Fitch, CLR, August 19, 1725, II, 580; James Harris and Sarah Harris to Thomas Fitch, CLR, November 19, 1728, III, 32.

[77] LLR, IV, 337; CLR, II, 240, 257, 580, 719, 770; III, 32, 115, 117, 134-35, 164. Fitch purchased these lots between January 1718 and March 1730. Fitch, like Colonel Browne, rented farms, two lessees were Daniel Galusha and Thomas Gustin. Perkins, *Connecticut Farm*, 54-55.
  The 300 acres the colonel purchased in Paugwonk had passed through several hands before he acquired them. James Harris sold the property to Daniel Pearce of Kingstown, Rhode Island in May 1718. Pearce sold the land to Joseph Powers of Kingstown one year later and he conveyed the tract to Jonathan Rogers, son of James in 1725. The latter transferred the same 300 acres to Jonathan Rogers, son of Samuel in August 1726. The second Jonathan sold the property to Colonel Thomas Fitch in January 1726/7. Perkins, *Connecticut Farm*, 192-93.

[78] Colchester bordered both on Lyme and Hebron. The two surviving daughters of Colonel Fitch, Martha and Mary, inherited his Connecticut lands. Martha married James Allen (1697-1755) of Boston in 1725 and Mary wed Andrew Oliver (1706-1774) in 1728. Martha had no children and after the death of her first husband married General William Brattle (1706-1776) who inherited her property after her death in 1763. Mary died in 1732 and her lands came to Andrew Oliver, Jr. Brattle and Andrew, Jr. made frequent appearances in Connecticut court and land records after coming into possession of Fitch's land. *Sibley's Harvard Graduates*, VI, 159-64; VII, 15, 383-84; XII, 455. As the map of the confiscated estate of William Browne shows, Brattle and Oliver still owned land in New Salem.

[79] Stafford Land Records, I, 118-19, 230, 231, microfilm, CSL.

[80] Dolbeare was born in Devon, England, moved to Massachusetts when he was about nine, and married Sarah Comer of Boston in 1698. He had customers in New London, so that may explain how he learned about investment opportunities in southeastern Connecticut. Some of his pewter is still extant and bears his mark. The inventory of his estate taken in 1740 totaled £17,000 and included 414 ounces of silver coin, 37.5 ounces of gold pistoles, and 644 ounces of household plate. Winifred Lovering Holman, "Early Dolbeares," *NEHGR*, 112 (1958), 176-77; Ellwood Count Curtis, *The Descendants of Edward Dolbeare, Sr. (c. 1644-1711)* (Cedar Falls, IA: Galactic Press, 2007), 3-5. He died on June 20, 1740 "at an advanced Age." Dolbeare was "an eminent Brazier of this Town, possessed of a very valuable Estate." *Boston Gazette*, June 23, 1740, [3].

[81] Joseph Peck receipt, LLR, June 14, 1716, II, 391.

the region took place in 1725 when he acquired some 220 acres at the Colchester and Lyme bounds from James and Sarah Harris for £400 in New England bills of credit.[82] Over the course of the next five years, he also purchased another 330 acres in Colchester, 200 acres in Lyme, and almost 2,100 more in the North Parish of New London, the bulk of which came from Harris at a total cost of some £4,580. The tracts ranged in size from twenty-two to 700 acres.[83] The lands remained undeveloped until his son George moved to New Salem in the mid-1730s. When John drafted his will in 1737, he gave his "son George that lives in Colchester, Conn., all the land he now lives upon . . . with utensils, negroes, etc. valued at £1,600."[84] To further demonstrate his wealth, he placed an advertisement in a Boston newspaper in 1736 offering to sell or rent a "Large House . . . with 3 Rooms upon a Floor and 3 Stories high, with 2 large Gardens and a large Yard, also a good Well and Pump."[85]

The fourth important absentee with whom Harris had significant dealings was Godfrey Malbone (1695-1768) of Newport.[86] Best known in Connecticut for his acquisitions in Windham County, he purchased more land in New London. In addition, Malbone loaned money to Connecticut farmers, as evidenced by a suit against Daniel Ely of Lyme in June 1733 in a debt by bond and six years later against Joseph Tallman of New London in another debt by bond for £4,000 secured by a "messuage," 450 acres of land, and livestock.[87] Malbone purchased over 1,900 acres in New London North Society.[88]

82 James Harris and Sarah Harris to John Dolbeare, CLR, May 14, 1725, II, 587.

83 CLR, II, 720; III, 132-33; LLR, IV, 176; NLLR, VIII, 275-76, 289, 290, 298-99, 337, 370-71; IX, 151.

84 Holman, "Early Dolbeares," 177. The difference between the cost of his land at £4,580 and the value as stated in John Dolbeare's will of £1,600 reflects the difference between valuation in colonial paper currency and pounds sterling. By the will of his mother Sarah, George Dolbeare was given all the lands in Connecticut and New Hampshire "belonging to me or whereof I have the disposal." Curtis, *Descendants of Edward Dolbeare, Sr.,* 6. Like Browne and Fitch, George Dolbeare rented farms. In 1759, he leased a 500 acre farm in Lyme and Colchester to David Dodge, Jr. *George Dolbear v. David Dodge,* NLCC, Files, June 1765, Box 138, folder 9, no docket.

85 *Boston Evening-Post,* March 2, 1736, [2].

86 Malbone had extensive commercial connections in Connecticut. He was plaintiff or defendant in around forty lawsuits in the colony. The first reference to him in court records comes from 1731 when he sued John Waterman, Jr. of Norwich in a debt by bond. NLCC, Trials, June 1731, Vol. 17, no. 109. The following year he sued to replevin a small vessel that had been seized by Charles Hazelton of New London. RG 003, NLCC, Papers by Subject: Summons for Evidence, August 17, 1732, Box 87, folder 3, CSL.

87 *Godfrey Malbone v. Daniel Ely,* NLCC, Files, June 1733, Box 37, folder 14, no. 204; *Godfrey Malbone v. Joseph Tallman,* Ibid, June 1739, Box 58, folder 2, no. 304.

88 He purchased 1,781 acres from James and Sarah Harris and 130 from Samson Houghton. NLLR, XI, 95-96; XII, 302; XIV, 145, 168, 173, 181; XVI, 98. The largest piece of land of some 1,020 acres was mortgaged to James Bowdoin of Boston in 1734 before being sold to Malbone in 1749. James Harris to James Bowdoin, May 18, 1734, NLLR, X, 173; XV, 181; James Bowdoin to Godfrey Malbone, NLLR, December 18, 1749, XV, 182.
The large estate he purchased was in Pomfret, now Brooklyn, containing some 3,000 acres. When he transferred the lands to his sons, the estate contained twenty-seven slaves. Leonard Byrne, "The Wayward Squire of Kingswood Manor," *The League Bulletin,* 30, no. 2 (May 1978), 27; Lorenzo Johnston Greene, *The Negro in Colonial New* England (New York: Atheneum, 1942, 1969), 29, 107; Howard W. Preston, "Godfrey Malbone's Connecticut Investment," *Rhode Island Historical Society Collections,* XVI, no. 4 (October 1923),

The single most noteworthy New London purchase by Harris after his one-fifth share of the huge tract at Mohegan in 1710 was the August 1726 acquisition from Major John Merrett of New London at a cost of £5,000 all his lands, "Tenements & heriditements," servants, horses, livestock, and swine in New London, Norwich, and Colchester owned solely by the Major or in partnership with Mrs. Mercy Raymond.[89] By agreement between Harris and Mrs. Raymond, the servants were divided with Harris acquiring slaves Rose, Caesar, Joe, Sampson, and Fillis [sic]; "Andrew a Mustee; and George an Indian." It is not known how long the seven servants remained with Harris.[90] With regard to the livestock owned by the Merrett-Raymond partnership, Harris received 70 sheep, 30 lambs, 40 goats, 20 kids, 5 cows, 2 heifers, 2 calfs, a bull, and 15 horses.[91]

Harris spent about a decade in Colchester living in a house just over the Lyme line that he sold to Colonel Browne in 1729. During that time, he served as agent for the Massachusetts magistrate.[92] He held no public offices in that town except for being appointed in April 1723 to a committee to seat the meetinghouse, although he also served on a twelve-man jury of inquest to determine the cause of death of Stephen Tyler of Colchester in January 1719.[93] He was, however, a leading figure in nascent New Salem parish, first, in the effort of its small number of settlers to gain parish privileges, and, second, to promote its development.

He appeared just as frequently before the bar while residing in Colchester during the 1720s as when living in New London, being plaintiff on nine occasions and

116-17.

[89] John Merrett to James Harris, NLLR, August 24, 1726, VIII, 311, 332.

[90] This complicated agreement led several lawsuits. At the February 1728 session of the New London County Court, Mercy Raymond sued Harris for the return of a mare and colt that the defendant had unlawfully seized at the time of the partition. *Mercy Raymond v. James Harris*, NLCC, Files, February 1728, Box 26, folder 20, no. 25. The court also heard a case in which Mrs. Raymond sued Harris for £30-4-0 damages for illegally keeping a Negro woman called Filus [sic] for fifty-three weeks and Mustee boy Andrew for fifteen weeks. The case was withdrawn and no more details exist. Filus and Andrew had been assigned to Harris by the August 1726 agreement. Perhaps Harris transferred them back to Raymond and retained their services for too long a time. *Marcy Raymond v. James Harris*, Ibid, February 1728, Box 27, folder 3, no. 74. In addition, when the Merrett-Raymond partnership was terminated, a debt of £35-15-6 owed to Joseph Bradford of New London remained unpaid. Merrett had overpaid his one third share of the debt by £6-0-7 and Harris sued Raymond to collect the overpayment and £30 damages. The suit was withdrawn. *James Harris v. Mercy Raymond*, Ibid, June 1728, Box 27, folder 11, no. 77. Raymond also sued Harris four times for debt during this time frame. The defendant was found guilty in each case and he asked for reviews at the next court in two instances at which time they were withdrawn. *Mercy Raymond v. James Harris*, NLCC, Trials, June 1727, Vol. 16, 57 (two cases); November 1727, 92; February 1728, 162; June 1728, 191.

[91] John Merrett to James Harris, NLLR, August 24, 1726, VIII, 311; Agreement James Harris and Mrs. Mercy Raymond, Ibid, October 10, 1726, VIII, 339. Raymond received Negroes "Will, Buscoe, Sharper, Harrie, Silvia & Grace; "Felix and Cate Mustees;" plus Indian servants Robin and Judith.

How long he retained the livestock and servants is unknown. Considering his financial condition, the chances are that it was not for long.

[92] See letter of attorney February 17, 1723/4 in *Samuel Brown v. Samuel Gilbert*, NLCC, Files, February 1728, Box 27, folder 2, no. 54.

[93] Colchester Record of Births, Marriages, Deaths, 1713-1801, 173, Colchester Town Hall. His son James, Jr. was selected as a lister in November 1726 and surveyor of highways one year later. Ibid, 178; CA, Miscellaneous, Series 1, II, 275, CSL. Daniel Galusha also served on the jury.

defendant in thirty-three lawsuits before the New London County Court. As a general rule, when Harris was plaintiff, he sued for collection of modest debts by note or bill, but when a defendant in suits of bond for much larger amounts. The court found Harris guilty in twenty-four lawsuits, while the other nine cases were withdrawn. He also appeared nine times before the Hartford County Court and once at the Windham County Court. Although James devoted the bulk of his time purchasing and selling land, he, like most landowners, farmed with labor furnished by his sons and, perhaps, servants of color. The only existing evidence for this activity is four court cases between 1721 and 1734 involving the buying and selling of horses.[94]

Harris returned to New London North Society in 1729 and was admitted as a freeman on April 28, 1730.[95] The question remains, why did he decide to sell his large Lyme-Colchester farm to Colonel Browne and move back to New London North Society?[96] From all appearances, he had considerable status in the new community and owned a prosperous farm of 526 acres in Lyme with "a Small Dwelling house and a sawmill," together with another 100 acres in Colchester "with two small . . . Dwelling Houses, a Barn, & smiths shop."[97] The likelihood is that he was weighed down by debt and had to sell.

Colonel Browne died in 1731 and Harris had little contact with the Browne family thereafter. He continued, however, to buy and sell land in New London North Society. In one sale worthy of note, James sold his sons Jonathan and Lebbeus three pieces of land in New London North Society in February 1738/9 amounting to 650 acres for £400 together with all his remaining property in Colchester.[98] At some time during the 1730s, he joined the North Society Congregational Church.[99] In addition in January 1735/6 after the New London County Court selected its usual tavern keepers, he and eighteen other were appointed as retailers of strong drink, the only year that such

---

[94] *Benjamin Atwill v. James Harris*, NLCC, Trials, June 1721, Vol. 13, 43; *James Harris v. John Waterman*, Ibid, June 1727, Vol. 15, 32; *James Harris v. Marcy Raymond*, Ibid, February 1728, Vol. 16, 15; *James Harris v. Return More*, June 1734, Ibid, Vol. 18, no. 231.

[95] New London Town Records, Freemen, 1730-1775, 42, New London City Hall.

[96] As evidence of his intention to make Colchester his permanent home, James Harris "of Paugwonk" petitioned the New London County Court in June 1726 on the need for a new highway from Lyme to Colchester to run from his house and that of his son James through the Browne lands upon which Daniel Galusha lived to the New London country road. James Harris Memorial, NLCC, PbyS: Travel, June 1726, Box 91, folder 7. See Illustration 1 on page 43.

[97] LLR, IV, 336.

[98] The deed was not recorded until May 1757, three months after the death of James. Given the long delay, the likelihood is that the sons did not pay for the land and that Harris used this device to transfer property that otherwise might have been at risk, although the deed stated perhaps truthfully that the two sons had £400 "Currant Money to me paid." The first 100 acre tract of land adjoined "Massapeag" included a "Mansion house." The second farm of around 250 acres was called the "Bakers farm" and third plot was probably 250 acres of woodland. No specifics were given for the Colchester lands. James Harris to Jonathan Harris and Lebeus Harris, NLLR, February 14, 1738/9, XVI, 168.

[99] Both he and Sarah were listed as members of the church in 1739 at the time the Reverend David Jewett became its minister. Montville Congregational Church Records, 1722-1827, Vol. 3, 20, 21, 27, CSL. Jewett provided more information on the entire family in another section of the same volume that was separately paginated, one that included the dates of death of "Old Mr Harris" and his two wives. Ibid, 15.

were chosen.[100]

His name appears in a number of New London records, showing that he was a man of some note in the community. Within three years of his return to the town, the inhabitants elected him selectman for the North Society.[101] In May 1733, James and more than twenty merchants and entrepreneurs sent a memorial to the General Assembly urging it to issue £25,000 in "Bills of Credit to encourage trade" because of the scarcity of currency in the colony.[102] He signed this petition because, despite the profits that James apparently accrued from land sales to Browne and others, he had serious cash flow problems.[103] Three months later he mortgaged fifty acres at "Massageauge" in New London's North Society to the colony of Connecticut in return for £100 in newly minted bills of credit.[104] The loan was supposed to be repaid on or before May 1, 1741, but Harris did not do so until December 28, 1747.[105]

He was among several men summoned to testify in lawsuit involving Jonathan Rogers and the Reverend James Hillhouse, first pastor in New London North Society, in which Rogers accused the defendant of trespass on fourteen acres of land in the North Parish.[106] In 1736, Harris acted as agent for the town of New London in an unsuccessful memorial to the legislature urging repeal of an October 1734 act concerning the places for holding sessions of the New London County and Superior Courts.[107] In November 1740, he was one of two men chosen to serve as a juryman at the next county court session.[108] In February 1750, the New London County Court appointed James and one

---

100 NLCC, PbyS: Travel, January 21, 1735/6, Box 92, folder 4. Prominent inhabitants Joseph Coit, Solomon Coit, John Pickett, and Gurdon Saltonstall also served as purveyors of strong drink.

101 The seven New London selectmen signed an indenture in 1732 authorizing James Champlin of Lyme to run a ferry at "Niantick Gutt." Indenture between Selectmen of New London and James Champlin, August 1, 1732, RG 062:095, New London Town Records, 1674-1925, Box 5, folder 10, CSL.

102 CA, Trade and Maritime Affairs, Series 1, I, 101, CSL.

103 Harris was by no means unique in this regard. Connecticut lacked an adequate medium of exchange and in the late 1720s and early 1730s a number of aspiring merchants, most from the eastern part of the colony, sought to create a land bank. The New London Society United for Trade and Commerce was given legal sanction by the General Assembly in May 1732. The organization immediately and illegally turned itself into a land bank, issued bills of credit backed by mortgages, and was dissolved by the horrified legislature in February 1732/3. The Assembly, however, recognized the justification of their grievances and authorized the printing of £30,000 in colony backed bills of credit to be secured by mortgages in May 1733. CA, Trade and Maritime Affairs, Series 1, I, 162-63; *Colony Records*, VII, 390-92; Bruce P. Stark, "The New London Society and Connecticut Politics, 1732-1740, *CH*, no. 25 (January 1984), 1-21.

104 Massapeag/Massapeaug is in Montville on the Thames River two miles northeast of Uncasville. Richard Haughton purchased the tract of land from Uncas in 1658. Hughes and Allen, *Connecticut Place Names*, 330.

105 James Harris to Colony of Connecticut, NLLR, August 4, 1733, X, 88; Colony of Connecticut to James Harris, NLLR, December 18, 1747, XV, 102.

106 NLCC, PbyS: Summons for Evidence, November 21, 1733, Box 87, folder 5; *Jonathan Rogers v. James Hillhouse*, NLCC, Files, November 1733, Box 38, folder 3, no. 89.

107 CA, Civil Officers, Series 1, II, 250, CSL.

108 NLCC: PbyS: Jurors, November 1740, Box 75, folder 18, CSL. The wording of the warrant was as follows: "To Either of the Constables of the Town of New London . . . Greeting - In His Majesties Name You are hereby Required to Summon Two Able and Sufficient Men . . . to Serve as Jurymen att the County Court to be Held at Norwich . . . Hereof fail not and make due Return of this Writ, with the Names of the Persons

other man a committee to lay out a highway between "Elderkins bridge to Norwich Landing."[109]

Harris continued to interact with his Native American neighbors by support-ing Connecticut's side in the infamous Mohegan case, by which the majority of the tribe encouraged and sustained by the Mason family fought an unsuccessful three generation battle to recover lands in eastern Connecticut that they believed were unlawfully seized from them.[110] In November 1735, Harris informed Connecticut Governor Joseph Tal-cott that John Mason with the support of a faction of the tribe intended to appeal to the Crown in an attempt to overturn white ownership of a vast amount of land it sold over the previous forty years. Talcott asked Harris to travel to New London to search for records that would buttress the Connecticut case and to Rhode Island in order to convince the Rhode Island government not to support Mason's appeal. Harris was successful in both of these endeavors. In January and February 1736, however, he failed in an attempt to per-suade Sachem Mahomet not to join John Mason and his son Samuel on their journey to London to present the case of the Mohegan Indians against the Colony of Connecticut.[111] In August 1737, Harris was the first of five signatories to a statement affirming that Ben Uncas was the lawful Sachem of the Mohegans.[112] He and Ben Uncas traveled to Boston in March 1738 on behalf of the colony. They went to see "Col Brown, Mr Dolbeare & Mr Allen, to raise money in defence of the Gov[ernmen]t ag[ains]t Mason, & got a promise of £5 from the first, & 50s a piece from the other two." The writer of the letter went on to relate that Harris "hath been indefatigable in the affair & I doubt not but it has been very expensive."[113]

Harris again appears in the Mohegan case in May 1742 when Samuel Mason, having returned from his English sojourn and in negotiation with Connecticut au-thorities, demanded that the New London North Society speculator be removed from

---

Endorsed thereon As the Law Directs." On the verso of the warrant, constable Richard Burch wrote that he had summoned "James Harris and John Morgan to Serve as Jurors."

The justices of the peace, selectmen, constables, and grand jurors of each town met every January to nomi-nate lawful freeholders to serve on the juries of the county and superior courts. The names of those nominated were placed in a secure box held by the town clerk and the constable receiving warrants drew out the names of the number of men required by the court. *The Public Statute Laws of the State of Connecticut* (Hartford: Printed by Hudson & Goodwin, 1808), 426.

[109] CA, Travel, Highways, Ferries, etc., Series 1, II, 11, 18, CSL. We know about this appointment primarily because Samuel Griswold of Norwich, one of the landowners the highway was designed to pass through, protested and claimed that Harris should not have served in this capacity because he "was not at this time a Freeholder."

[110] The authoritative study of the long struggle between the Mohegan Tribe and the Colony of Connecticut is Paul Grant-Costa's, "The Last Indian War in Southern New England: The Mohegan Tribe of Indians v. The Governour and Company of Connecticut, 1703-1774," a work that deserves a wide audience.

[111] Grant-Costa, "Last Indian War," 165–67; Joseph Talcott, *The Talcott Papers: Correspondence and Docu-ments (Chiefly Official) During Joseph Talcott's Governorship* (Hartford: Connecticut Historical Society, 1892), I, 344-47. Mahomet led the pro-Mason faction of the tribe and Ben Uncas the pro-Connecticut one. Ma-homet and John Mason died of smallpox in London in the summer of 1736. Ibid, 180-81.

[112] *Talcott Papers*, II, 27-30.

[113] John Read to Governor Talcott, *Talcott Papers*, II, 98-99. The men referred to were Samuel Browne the Younger, John Dolbeare, and James Allen, husband of Martha Fitch Allen, daughter and heir of Colonel Thomas Fitch.

property that he leased from the tribe.[114] The following May the loyal portion of the tribe designated "our friend James Harris to assist" them in "prefering the memorial" to the General Assembly to confirm the choice they made for their own "Councelors."[115]

One of the high or low points in the long struggle by a portion of the Mohegan tribe and their Mason family allies to gain back their land took place in Norwich in the summer of 1743 when a court of commissioners convened to review the Indian claims.[116] The documentation mentions Harris on several occasions. They include listing him as one of the possessors of lands "in controversy in the north parish of *New London*," as one of four purchasers of a large tract in New London from Owaneco in 1710, as attorney for other possessors of lands in dispute, and as leaseholder granted by Ben Uncas in 1742.[117] A majority of the commissioners concluded that Connecticut had acted properly and they rejected the claims of the Masons and their Indian allies to be restored to their ancestral lands.[118]

The General Assembly in March 1745 authorized John Bulkley of Colchester to retrieve "firelocks" furnished James Harris for use by the Mohegans and a year and a half later the colony reimbursed Harris £100 for his expenses for his help in the Mohegan case.[119] He held one other position in New London after moving back to the North Society. In December 30, 1751, the town meeting appointed Daniel Coit, John Bradford, and Harris a committee "to take an Exact Account of all the Mohegan Indians now Liveing and Register all their Names in the Town Clerks Office."[120] Around two years later he moved back to Colchester to live with his son Lebbeus.[121]

When Harris reached his eighth decade, he became much less active in affairs, particularly after 1750, and hence the number of court appearances declined. He became a litigant in just nine cases, one of the last of which was tried before the New London County Court in June 1756, when he sued Gershom Breed of Norwich in a debt by bond for £600 in depreciated old tenor bills of credit to obtain a deed for "Two Carr rooms in ye City of London" conveyed in 1688 to Elisabeth Wheeler,

---

114 Ibid., 210. Ben Uncas, Sachem of the Mohegans, leased "one certain tract or parcel of land and buildings, *lying situate within the Moheagan fields,*" in said *New-London*" for twenty years to James Harris and his sons Jonathan and Lebbeus on March 25, 1742. *Governor and Company of Connecticut and Moheagan Indians, by their Guardians. Certified Copy of Book of Proceedings before Commissioners of Review, 1743* (London: W. & J. Richardson, 1769), 135-36. Thanks to Paul Grant-Costa for furnishing me with a partial copy of *Proceedings*, containing the sections with information on James Harris.

On May 8, 1745, a different group of tribal leaders sent a memorial to the General Assembly protesting against Harris who "Much abuses us" by forbidding them from any access to the land that he leased from the tribe in 1742. Jonathan Law, *The Law Papers: Correspondence and Documents During Jonathan Law's Governorship of the Colony of Connecticut, 1741-1750* (Hartford: The Connecticut Historical Society, 1907), I, 287-89.

115 Grant-Costa, "Last Indian War," 216; *Law Papers,* 85, 88.

116 For an extended discussion of the meetings of the court of commissioners, see Grant-Costa, "Last Indian War," 214-34.

117 *Proceedings before Commissioners*, 15-16, 30, 119-20, 122-23, 125,, 132-36, 182-84, 191.

118 Grant-Costa, "Last Indian War," 229-30.

119 *Colony Records.* IX, 96-97, 252. For other references to Harris, see Ibid, IX, 171-72, 360, 376.

120 New London Town Meeting Records, 1740-1789, 34, New London City Hall.

121 *Esther Richards v. James Harris*, NLCC, Trials, June 1754, Vol. 22, no. 136.

to Joshua Wheeler, and much later to James Harris. The court found Breed guilty, the defendant appealed, and he lost again at trial before the superior court in March 1757.[122] Unable to the last, however, to avoid controversy over land entanglements, Benjamin Uncas on behalf of the tribe sued Harris's executors in a suit for covenant broken over the lease of tribal lands "in Mohegan."[123] In two other instances during the 1750s, the court summoned him to give evidence.[124]

Sarah Harris died in November 1748 and James subsequently married Sarah Jackson, widow of Samuel Jackson.[125] He died in Colchester around February 10, 1757.[126] Despite his apparent prosperity and the buying and selling of so much land in three towns for more than fifty years, his estate was insolvent. The inventory was taken on April 13, 1757 and his estate was valued at just £52. He possessed no real property unless one counts "an old Negro Man . . . much Infirm" who had no monetary value. His library contained around twenty-five books, most of a religious character, including "Mr. Whitfields Sermons," a modest collection of household goods, some pewter, a feather bed with bolster, a looking glass, and such amenities as a tobacco box and tobacco tongs, "Waiters Bell," "a pair of Spectacles and Case," and "an old white Wigg." Luxuries consisted of silver spoons, a silver seal, gold rings, and a silver buckle. Harris owed £191-13-6 to creditors and the total paid out to them was just £43-9-9.[127] The estate was finally settled in 1763 when Lebbeus Harris, administrator of the estate, collected £14-7-4 plus £3-17-3 costs of suit from his brother James in a suit for a debt by note.[128] A modest end to an important life.

---

122 *James Harris v. Gershom Breed*, Ibid, June 1756, Box 104, folder 16, no. 104; *James Harris v. Gershom Breed*, Early Records, CSC, March 1757, Vol. 16, page 72.

123 *Benjamin Uncass "Sachem of the Mohegans" v. Jonathan Harris and Lebeus Harris*, NLCC, Trials, June 1760, Vol. 23, no. 35; Ibid, NLCC, PbyS: Summons for Evidence, June 1760, Box 90, folder 6. The court decided in favor of the plaintiff in June 1761, but the defendants appealed. *Uncass v. Harris and Harris*, NLCC, Trials, June 1761, Vol. 23, no. 59.

124 *George Richards v. Noah Hammond*, NLCC, PbyS: Summons for Evidence, November 1752, Box 89, folder 6; *Don Joseph v. Francis Po*, Ibid, June 1754, Box 89, folder 13.

125 Harris, "James Harris of New London," 17. The old Mohegan cemetery in Montville contains a double slate stone for his two wives. Morgan, *Harris Genealogy*, 20.

126 Harris, "James Harris of New London," 16. As Joshua Hempstead wrote, "Lt. James Harris was buried the 10th aged 80 odd. He formerly Lived in the North parish & Latterly with a Son Lebbeus att Poagwonk where he died." Hempstead, *Diary*, 663.

127 James Harris, Colchester, 1757, Colchester Probate District Records, no. 1574. Harris, "James Harris of New London," 20. The persons to whom Harris owed money included sons Jonathan, Lebbeus, and James, plus nephews Asa and Ephraim Harris. Harris, "James Harris of New London," 22-30. Three quarters of the total went to Lebbeus Harris.

128 *Lebbeus Harris v. James Harris*, NLCC, Trials, June 1763, Vol. 22, no. 19; Ibid, NLCC, Files, Box 127, folder 3, no. 19. The court stated that Lebbeus lived formerly in Colchester but then resided in Horton, Nova Scotia.

Chapter 4

Colonel Samuel Browne Buys an Estate

Colonel Samuel Browne (1669-1731) of Salem, Massachusetts, owner of about half of the land in what later became the town of Salem, Connecticut, was the grandson of William Browne (1608-1688), who migrated to Salem in the summer of 1635.[1] William and his wife Mary sailed on the *Love* to Massachusetts. His enrollment on the vessel listed him as a fisherman, perhaps due to his membership in the Fishmongers Company.[2] He settled in Salem, was literate and well read, ran successful fishing and trading businesses, and became an extremely wealthy man.[3] He joined the Salem church on November 26, 1648 and became a freeman the following May. Browne held numerous public offices, including those of grand juror, selectman, commissioner to hear small claims, deputy to the Massachusetts General Court, and assistant 1678-84.[4] Twice married, his first wife Mary probably died in 1638 and his second wife Sarah Smith was the mother of all his eleven children.[5] He was a generous benefactor to the Salem poor,

---

[1] The surname was spelled both with and without an "e," but for the sake of consistency, Browne will be used in the text except when written differently in direct quotations or as recorded in deeds. The name is invariably spelled with the final e in the diaries of Benjamin Lynde, Sr. and Benjamin Lynde, Jr. Oliver, ed., *Lynde Diaries*, passim.

[2] William Browne is reputed to have been the youngest son of Francis Browne (d. 1626) of Brundish or Brandon, Suffolk, England; grandson of Thomas Browne (d. 1608) of Brundish; and great-grandson of Simon Browne of Browne Hall, Lancashire, a barrister who removed to Brundish. "Browne Family Letters," 352-53; [Sidney Perley], "Descendants of William Browne of Salem," *The Essex Antiquarian*, XIII (Oct. 1909), 159; Anderson, *Great Migration*, I, 445; Ezra D. Hines, "Browne Hill and Some History Connected with It," *Essex Institute Historical Collections*, XXXII (1896), 211.

[3] Sources described him as "an opulent and public-spirited merchant of Salem," "a prominent Salem merchant," and overseas trader. Lawrence Shaw Mayo, *The Winthrop Family in America* (Boston: The Massachusetts Historical Society, 1948), 100; Richard S. Dunn, *Puritans and Yankees: The Winthrop Dynasty of New England, 1630-1717* (Princeton, NJ: Princeton University Press, 1962), 203. By his will, Browne left his Latin and English books to his son William. Anderson, *Great Migration*, I, 442.

[4] William H. Whitmore, *The Massachusetts Civil List for the Colonial and Provincial Periods, 1630-1774* (Albany: J. Munsell, 1870), 26. He was dismissed from his assistant post in 1684, because he was one of several political leaders who resisted the King and opposed the taking away of the Massachusetts Charter. Joseph B. Felt, *Annals of Salem*, second edition, II (Salem: W. & S. B. Ives, 1845), 539-40.

[5] Sarah's father Samuel Smith died in 1642. William Browne served as his executor and his family received a considerable proportion of Smith's substantial estate, one that consisted of home buildings, 234 acres of land, a substantial herd of livestock, and household goods valued at £395. These assets aided Browne in his economic advancement. George Francis Dow, ed., *Records and Files of the Quarterly Courts of Essex County* (Salem, MA:

the Salem church, and Harvard College.[6] He died, predeceased by Sarah, on January 20, 1687/8. In his will, made generous bequests to sons William and Benjamin and daughter Mary Winthrop, plus contributions to educational and religious institutions and small sums to more distant relatives and servants.[7] The prominence of the family was further attested by the fact that it had a coat of arms and owned a copy of an ancestor portrait painted by Hans Holbein during the reign of Henry VIII.[8] At the time of his death, he was the richest man in Salem.[9]

A paragraph summary fails to do justice, however, for the economic and political achievements of the founding father of the Browne family, for it is impossible to believe that his sons Major William and Benjamin or grandson Colonel Samuel could have accomplished as much without the firm foundation laid by the first settler. The town of Salem was about a decade old when Browne arrived in 1635 and neither by wealth nor lineage did he merit a position of leadership in the community.[10] William moved politically and socially upward due to his extraordinary economic acumen. The records of the Essex County Quarterly Court and the Salem town meeting provide a means for measuring this success and documenting his rise to political prominence.

One year after his arrival, Browne first appeared in the town records of Salem regarding land grants and husbandry and, by 1640, as a shopkeeper.[11] William served on a petty jury in 1648 and was elected to the first of twenty terms as selectman in

Essex Institute, 1911, I, 45-47; "Abstracts from Wills, Inventories, &c., on File in the Office of Clerk of Courts, Salem, Mass.," *EIHC*, I (April 1859), 3; "Will of Samuel Smith," *Essex Antiquarian*, I (March 1897), 44-45.

[6] He is reputed to have paid one tenth of the cost to construct the Salem church in 1673. On May 13, 1692, the Harvard College treasurer acknowledged the receipt "of one hundred pounds in money" for the support of "poore Scholars" from Major William Browne and Benjamin Browne, executors of the estate of William Browne. Benjamin F. Browne, "Youthful Recollections of Salem," *EIHC*, L (January 1914), 8; William Bentley, "A Description and History of Salem," *CollMHS*, First Series, VI (1799), 287; Receipt by John Richards, Records of the Treasurer of Harvard University, Colonial at Harvard Library.

[7] "Essex County Estates Administered in Suffolk County, Prior to 1701," *EIHC*, XLI (April 1905), 180. By his will, Browne gave the town's ministers £30, the church £20, £50 to the town poor, the same for the support of education in the town, and £100 to Harvard College.

[8] Anderson, *Great Migration*, I, 439-45; [Perley], "Descendants of William Browne," 159; Hines, "Browne Hill," 211-12, 235, 237; Sidney Perley, *History of Salem, Massachusetts*, I (Salem, MA: Sidney Perley, 1924), 366-68; Perley, *History of Salem*, II, 8, 10. For a sample of Browne's signature, see Perley, I, 366. The ancestor was Sir Anthony Browne.

[9] Despite his prominence, Browne merits just two mentions in Bernard Bailyn, *The New England Merchants in the Seventeenth Century* (New York: Harper Torchbooks, 1955, 1964). The first concerns the marriage of one of his daughters to Thomas Deane and the second as a signer of a 1665 petition, plus two general references to the prominence of the family. Ibid, 122, 125, 135, 137. A reading of Bailyn, however, can give one an idea of the probable outlines of Browne family trading enterprises. See chapter 4, "The Legacy of the First Generation," especially pages 76-91.

[10] For an overview of trade and commerce in early Salem, see William I. Davisson and Dennis J. Dugan, "Commerce in Seventeenth-Century Essex County, Massachusetts," *EIHC*, CVII (April 1971), 113-42. The Reverend Hugh Peter (1598-1660), minister of Salem, encouraged this growth. He established plans for a fishery and for promoting both coastal and international trade. Bentley, "Description and History of Salem," 251.

[11] Martha O. Howes and Sidney Perley, eds., *Town Records of Salem, Massachusetts* (Salem: The Essex Institute, 1868), I, 22, 37, 47, 87, 98, 100, 103. He was characterized as "a sopemaker" when admitted as a town inhabitant in July 1637. Ibid, I, 58.

1650.[12] By the time he had obtained an important town office at the age of forty-two, his name appeared a number of times in the records of the Essex County Quarterly Courts. Between 1638 and 1649, the Salem businessman was party to nine court filings, mostly as plaintiff in suits for debt, involved in seven other legal cases, including those as attorney and a foreman of a grand jury, and was mentioned on several other occasions.[13]

Court records for his entire career show that Browne was a very successful merchant and was plaintiff in more than sixty debt cases.[14] He was a party to several lawsuits involving the fishing industry, as well as iron mining and trade.[15] Court records also reveal that the first William Browne was not initially considered a leader in Essex County. Although generally styled "Mr.," a sign of respect, he never secured an appointment as a militia officer or judge of the county court until the time he was elected a member of the colony's council in 1678. Thereafter he was sometimes called the "Worshipful Wm. Browne, Esq."[16]

He achieved prominence in the community around 1650. In addition to near continuous service as selectman between 1650 and 1673, the town elected Browne deputy to the General Court three times between 1659 and 1673 and commissioner to hear small claims for seven terms between 1658 and 1679.[17] He also held a number of other positions of trust over the years: supervising the repair of the meetinghouse in 1656; membership on a 1659 committee to oversee the construction of a minister's house; on a 1670 committee to supervise the building of a new meetinghouse; being chosen in 1670 to deliver the votes for nomination of magistrates; and service on a 1673 committee to erect a new town house.[18] Court records contain further evidence of his new importance. In addition to tenure as judge while on the Massachusetts Council, he served as foreman of the grand jury in October 1649 and May 1650 and juror on several occasions between 1650 and 1665. He held a license to sell strong drink in 1651 and from around 1660 to 1679 at a time when such men were usually community leaders.[19] Moreover, Browne inventoried a number of estates and served as executor or administrator of several others, including that of his father-in-law Samuel Smith in 1642 and

---

[12] Ibid, I, 104, 165.

[13] *EssexQCR*, I, 7-182 passim.

[14] The breadth of his mercantile career is likewise revealed by his listing as a creditor in the inventories of estates of some forty Essex county householders.

[15] See, for example, *EssexQCR*, January 25, 1651/2, I, 216 and September 29, 1665, III, 210-11 on fishing industry; July 7, 1653, I, 293 and September 30, 1658, II, 127 on his iron industry investments; and May 25, 1650, I, 192 and June 29, 1658, II, 88 concerning his trading activities. In addition, Browne and two other men were granted permission by the town to build a gristmill in September 1659. *SalemTR*, II, 2. Since Browne became an eminent merchant, it is not surprising that he filed suits before the Middlesex and Suffolk county courts. The records of the Court of Assistants demonstrate these wider economic connections. *Records of the Court of Assistants of the Colony of Massachusetts Bay, 1630-1692* (Boston: Published by the County of Suffolk,1928), I, 38-39; III, 25, 236.

[16] *EssexQCR*, September 26, 1678, VII, 106; April 29, 1680, VII, 397.

[17] *SalemTR*, I, 223; II, 4, 24, 64, 158, 212, 224, 247, 275, 310.

[18] Ibid, II, 195; II, 2, 111, 125, 163.

[19] *EssexQCR*, I, 180, 191, 204, 238, 243, 270, 313; II, 370; III, 246; VII, 319. Prior to becoming a retailer of strong drink, the court charged him in 1644 and 1645 with selling wine without a license. Ibid, I, 75, 83.

brother-in-law of the same name in 1679.[20] Essex County Quarterly Court Records contain hundreds of entries to the merchant that attest to his importance in the region from the early 1650s to 1685.[21]

Six of the eleven children of William and Sarah Browne lived to adulthood and the second generation of the family was as prominent and wealthy as the first.[22] The eldest son, Major William, was born on April 14, 1639 and died on February 14, 1715/6.[23] Like his father, he lived in Salem and had a successful mercantile career.[24] Thanks to the achievements of his father the second William ascended the political ladder at a much younger age. Seventeenth-century records provide much useful information on his career. He took the freeman's oath in November 1662, was sergeant in the militia in September 1665 and had advanced to the rank of captain by 1679, was a retailer of "strong waters" for most of the period between 1667 and 1680, and was appointed to receive claims on the estates of Captain John Corwin and Captain George Corwin, Jr.[25] The town of Salem chose him to carry votes for magistrates to Boston in March 1666, as constable two years later, selectman on five occasions between 1670 and 1679, on the committee to oversee the building of a new meetinghouse in 1670, and deputy to the General Court in 1675 and 1677.[26]

In addition to serving in the General Court, he was on the Council, both during the time of Governor Andros in the Dominion of New England and under the Charter of 1691.[27] After news reached Boston of the success of the Glorious Revolution

---

[20] Ibid, I, 42, 47; VII, 205.

[21] They also reveal that he possessed at least one slave by the name of Black Dick who was involved in a 1683 theft from his warehouse. Ibid, IX, 110, 115, 149; Richard P. Gildrie, "'The Gallant Life': Theft on the Salem-Marblehead, Massachusetts Waterfront in the 1680s," *EIHC*, 122 (October 1986), 292, 296.

[22] William (1639-1716), John (1641-69), Joseph (1647-78), Benjamin (1648-1708), Sarah (b. 1649), and Mary (1657-1690). Anderson, "Great Migration," I, 443-44; [Perley], "Descendants of William Browne," 159-60; *Sibley's Harvard Graduates*, II, 206-09. The best overview of the daily activities of the three generations of descendants of William and Sarah Browne can be found in F. E. Oliver, ed., *Diaries of Benjamin Lynde and Benjamin Lynde, Jr.* A genealogical chart of the Browne and Lynde families located at the end of the book fills in several holes in the family history and the diaries of both father and son contain a good deal of information on their Browne relatives.

Additional information about the Salem Brownes is found in George B. Loring, ed., "Some Account of the Houses and Other Buildings in Salem, From a Manuscript of the Late Col. Benj. Pickman," *EIHC*, VI (June 1864), 93-99.

[23] The greater the prominence of a person the more elaborate the funeral. That for Browne on February 28, 1715/6 typifies such ceremonies. As Samuel Sewall reported, "I go to Salem invited to be a Bearer. Bearers were, William Tailor, esqr, Lt. Govr John Hathorn esqr, Saml Sewall, John Appleton, John Higginson esqr., Andrew Belchar. Was laid in a Tomb just about Sunset, at the Burying Point. Col. Lynde, Mr. Davenport, Major Fitch, Col. Winthrop had Scarvs and Rings; Mr. Speaker Burrill had a Scarf. A great many Men were at the Funeral, but few Women; twas very cold." Samuel Sewall, "Diary of Samuel Sewall," *Collections of the Massachusetts Historical Society*, Fifth Series, VII (1882), 74.

[24] One 1671 lawsuit concerned debts owed to "Mr. William Browne, jr. & Co." *EssexQCR*, IV, 384. Like his father, the younger William was owed money by a number of estates of deceased persons.

[25] Ibid, I, 29-30; III, 226, 428; VII, 226, 414; IX, 155, 487-88, 563; *SalemTR*, II, 294.

[26] *SalemTR*, II, 64, 93, 109, 114, 200, 221, 292. The town also selected him to acquire powder and to a committee to care for the poor. Ibid, II, 316, 318.

[27] Felt, *Annals of Salem*, II, 541-42, 563-64; Whitmore, *Massachusetts Civil List*, 31. Governor Andros ap-

on April 18, 1689, William was among fifteen prominent Massachusetts men, mostly land speculators and merchants, demanding that Governor Andros, a loyal supporter of deposed King James II, surrender. Two days later Browne and twenty-two others formed a "Council of the safety of the people and the conservation of the peace," a body that governed the Commonwealth until the arrival of first royal governor, Sir William Phips, in 1692.[28]

The Massachusetts legislature in May 1689 elected Major William Browne a justice of the peace for Essex County and four years later selected him as one of four persons on the Inferior Court of the Common Pleas for Essex County. He resigned both positions on December 9, 1715, due to ill health two months before his death. Elected to the Governor's Council in 1693, he retained that position until 1714.[29] Married twice, his first wife Hannah Curwen of Salem was the mother of all his children. Their oldest surviving child was Colonel Samuel Browne.[30] "William Browne was a man of great wealth, and munificent in his private charities and public benefactions" to education in Salem, the church, care of the poor, and to Harvard College.[31]

Major William had three siblings worthy of mention. Joseph (1647-1678), the fifth child of the first settler, graduated from Harvard College in 1666, became a minister, married Mehetabel Brenton, daughter of the governor of Rhode Island, and died one year after taking charge of the church in Charlestown.[32] The sixth child, Benjamin (1648-1708) was predeceased by his wife and two minor children.[33] By his will, the wealthy merchant made generous bequests to Harvard College for the support of poor scholars from Salem, the Salem Congregational church, the local grammar school, and to the town of Salem to help build an almshouse, in addition to bequests to a number of

---

pointed Major William Browne to the forty-two member Second Commission on April 16, 1688.

28 They joined the revolt in order to eliminate a governor and council they could not control. Bailyn, *New England Merchants*, 174-76; Theodore B. Lewis, "Land Speculation and the Dudley Council of 1686," *WMQ*, 3rd Series, XXXI (April 1974), 269; David S. Lovejoy, *The Glorious Revolution in America* (New York: Harper & Row, 1972), 242.

29 Whitmore, *Massachusetts Civil List*, 46-49, 82, 132. The Council had thirty-six members.

30 William and Hannah Curwen/Corwin Browne had twelve children between 1666 and 1784, only three of whom reached adulthood; Samuel, Captain John (1672-1729), and Mary (1679-1753) who married Benjamin Lynde (1666-1745) of Salem. [Perley],"Descendants of William Browne," 159-60; *Lynde Diaries*, [240].

31 [Perley],"Descendants of William Browne," 159-60; Hines, "Browne Hill," 212-13; Benjamin W. Labaree, *Colonial Massachusetts: A History* (Millwood, NY: KTO Press, 1979), 122.
   The major's large residence burned in a conflagration on June 28, 1698 that started in a warehouse and destroyed five houses. Browne's loss was estimated at between three and four thousand pounds. He thereupon constructed a larger and more luxurious mansion. Samuel Sewall "Diary," *CollMHS*, Fifth Series, V (1878), 481. The Sewall Diaries contain a great deal of information on the Browne family.

32 Anderson, *Great Migration*, I, 443; *Sibley's Harvard Graduates*, I, 206-09. Joseph and Mehetabel had no children.

33 Benjamin was chosen justice of the peace for Essex County on May 27, 1692 and served on the Council from 1701-07. Whitmore, *Massachusetts Civil List*, 47-48, 132. Benjamin's estate was valued at around £30,000. Among his bequests were £1,000 each to niece Mrs. Ann Winthrop, niece Mrs. Mary Lynde, and brother William, and the residue of his estate to nephews Samuel and Captain John Browne. Lothrop Withington, "English Notes about Early Settlers in New England," *EIHC*, XLVII (January 1911), 63-64; Browne, "Youthful Recollections of Salem," Ibid, 9.

nieces and nephews. He gave the residue of his estate, "both real and personal, whether in Great Britain, Barbados, New England, or elsewhere, to my two nephews Major Samuel Browne and Captain John Browne of Salem," sons of William Browne, Jr.[34] Mary (1657-1690), the tenth child, married Wait Still Winthrop, son of Connecticut Governor John Winthrop, Jr.[35] Two of their five children survived the rigors of child-hood, one of whom was John Winthrop (1681-1747).[36]

Colonel Samuel Browne was born on August 8, 1669, the eldest surviving child of William and Hannah Curwen Browne, and baptized on September 12. Even more prominent than his father and grandfather, he held numerous offices in Salem and Massachusetts Bay and like his ancestors generously supported public causes. The positions of trust that Samuel held included selectman for six years between 1695 and 1703, town treasurer 1699-1710, representative to the Massachusetts General Court on four occasions, retailer of liquor in 1712, Governor's Council 1715-31, justice of the peace, judge of the Court of Common Plea for Essex County from 1715 until death, and militia colonel.[37] In addition, he served for many years as a leading proprietor of the "Common lands in Salem" and on a number of its committees.[38]

An opulent merchant, he lived in the finest home in Salem, a three storied structure of seventeen rooms. Like his father and grandfather, he had two wives. He married Eunice Turner of Salem on March 19, 1695/6 who died childless. His second wife was Abigail Keach of Boston whom Samuel married on February 21, 1705/6. They became the parents of seven children, four of whom died young.[39] She died on February 18, 1724/5 at thirty-eight and was the subject of a laudatory funeral sermon by New England's foremost theologian.[40] Extremely active in the affairs of the First Church of Salem, Samuel was admitted in full communion on July 6, 1697 and all his children

---

[34] Anderson, *Great Migration*, I, 443; [Perley], "Descendants of William Browne," 160; Elizabeth French, "Genealogical Research in England," *NEHGR*, LXIII (1909), 361-62. Captain John Browne's son Colonel Benjamin Browne (1706-1750) became prominent after the death of Colonel Samuel. [Perley], "Descendants of William Browne," 160, 162.

[35] Wait Winthrop sought to rebuild his fortune by marrying into a wealthy mercantile family. Dunn, *Puritans and Yankees*, 203-04.

[36] Anderson, *Great Migration*, I, 444; Mayo, *Winthrop Family*, 100, 107, 110, 118, 121, 137.

[37] Perley, *History of Salem*, III, 86, 251-52; Whitmore, *Massachusetts Civil List*, 82-83, 132. Browne held the rank of captain in August 1703. "An Order to Warn Soldiers, Salem," *EIHC*, II, (June 1860), 154.

[38] "Salem Commoners Records, 1713-1739," *EIHC*, XXXVI (April 1909), 161, 173; XXXVII (January 1901), 107-28.

[39] Felt, *Annals of Salem*, I, 441-443-47; *Ibid*, II, 64, 254, 398, 511, 564; [Perley], "Descendants of William Browne, 160; Hines, "Browne Hill," 213-14; Richard D. Pierce, ed., *The Records of the First Church in Salem, Massachusetts, 1639-1716* (Salem, MA: Essex Institute, 1974), 29; *Boston News-Letter*, May 30, 1715, [1]; Perley, *History of Salem*, I, 366-67; Ibid, III, 251-52.

[40] Cotton Mather, *Virtue in it's verdure. : A Christian exhibited as a green olivetree, in the House of God; with a character of the virtuous Mrs. Abigail Brown: (the amiable and memorable consort of the Honourable Samuel Brown, Esq;) who expired Feb. 18. 1724* (Boston: Printed by B. Green, 1725), 22-27. Mather praised her piety adding, "Rarely has one Died among us more *Universally Lamented*: Rarely one so Beloved by All" and a woman "So Affable, so Courteous, of such easy Access for the *Poor & Needy.*" Her elaborate funeral was held on Wednesday, February 24. The bearers included the lieutenant governor. Samuel Sewall, "Diary," *CollMHS*, Fifth Series, VII (1882), 349.

were baptized there.[41] He served on numerous church committees, including those for inspecting the accounts of the deacons in 1703, inviting the Reverend George Curwen to preach in 1711, serving as a church delegate to mediate a dispute in Wenham in 1719, and representing the church at an ordination at Boston North Church that same year.[42] As one might expect, the prosperous and public-spirited first citizen of Salem was also known as a leader of Salem society. Judge Samuel Sewall (1652-1730) wrote in 1729, "I humbly Thank your Honour for the Succession of Kindnesses wherewith you have been distinguishing me, and for the many bountiful Entertainments you have honored me with at your House; especially in the time of the Sessions of the Superiour Court."[43]

Browne strongly supported education in Salem, like other members of his family.[44] He served as member of the first grammar school board in 1712 and was by far the most generous supporter of education in his day.[45] His most noteworthy contributions occurred in 1729 and in his 1731 will. In 1729, he donated £240 divided among three schools, £120 to the grammar or Latin school, £60 to the English school, and a like amount to the women's school, all to pay tuition for poor scholars. By his will, he gave another £150 to the same schools.[46] His generosity extended to Harvard College. He donated £150 to the College in 1720, the income of which was to pay the tuition of his children or their posterity and poor scholars from Salem. By will, he gave another £60 to be used for the purchase of plate "with my Coat of Arms on it" and a farm of around 200 acres in Hopkinton.[47] The income and rents were to be dedicated

---

41 Browne's first wife joined the church at the same time and his second wife Abigail in May 1712. Pierce, *First Church in Salem*, 50, 51, 54, 56, 178, 222.

42 Ibid, 191, 212, 268, 270; Sidney Perley, "Evidence Relative to the Authenticity of the 'First Church' (So-Called) in Salem," *EIHC*, XXXIX (July 1903), 245-52, 265. He and his father and grandfather donated expensive silver to the First Church. The colonel gave a 13" silver flagon engraved as "The Gift of Saml. Browne Esqr. to the First Church of Christ in Salem 1731." His grandfather donated five two-handled 5" cups and his father an oval dish. John H. Burt, "The Early Church Plate of Salem," *EIHC*, XLIII (April 1907), 99-101.

43 Samuel Sewall to Samuel Browne, May 26, 1729, "Letter-Book of Samuel Sewall," *CollMHS*, 6th Series, II (1888), 267-68. He wrote the letter upon hearing the news of the death of Browne's daughter Abigail. For further information on the Browne family in Salem society, see "James Jeffrey's Journal for the Year 1724," *EIHC*, XXXVI (October 1900), 332-33.

According to Gilbert Burnet Lewis, "Records of Browne Family Portraits," *EIHC*, LXXXVI (July 1950), 285-87, the Honorable Samuel Browne had his portrait painted by John Smibert. The portrait was in fact of his son Samuel and painted in 1734 at the same time as one of his brother William. This portrait and a copy of English ancestor Sir Anthony Browne were owned by Mrs. Mary Deans (Mayer) Wallis of Philadelphia in 1950.

44 The entire Browne family were generous benefactors. William Browne, Sr., Reverend Joseph Browne, Benjamin Browne, William Browne, Jr., and Captain John Browne all donated significant sums. Between 1678 and 1731, donations and bequests totaling £745 were made to the Salem schools and all except for £45 came from members of the family. John Duncan Phillips, *Salem in the Eighteenth Century* (Boston: Houghton Mifflin Company, 1937), 123.

45 Sidney Perley, compiler, "Extracts from Salem School Committee Records, *EIHC*, XCI (January 1955), 33-45.

46 Felt, *Annals of Salem*, I, 444-47; Phillips, *Salem in the Eighteenth Century*, 123-26.

47 Browne initially conveyed the lands in a ninety-nine year lease to the Trustees of the Charity of Edward

"for bringing up some poor scholar or scholars."[48]

Colonel Samuel Browne was an extremely eminent and wealthy man and, as such, participated in a number of civic functions. When news was received on August 25, 1713 of the peace treaty that ended Queen Anne's War, he read the proclamation of peace to the assembled multitudes from Salem and neighboring towns.[49] Three years later Massachusetts Governor Samuel Shute traveled to New Hampshire. Colonel Browne and the Salem troop of militia met him at a neighboring town and "escorted him to this place, whose principal gentlemen met him on the line." As he entered the town he was saluted by a discharge of cannon. He was conducted to Colonel Browne's where he lodged and "had a splendid entertainment that night and next morning."[50] On September, 10 1727, Browne held a dinner at the leading tavern in town to proclaim George II the new King of England, an event attended by all the leading men in Salem.[51] Two years later, at the funeral of Governor William Burnet, Browne served as one of six pallbearers.[52]

Relatively little evidence exists to document the economic successes of the first three generations of the Brownes, although much can be learned from a close analysis of land records. What follows provides a hint of activities of the wealthiest family in Salem. William Browne, Sr., called a shopkeeper in 1640 and merchant by 1655, participated in Salem's land divisions and bought and sold much property. For example, the town granted him 20 acres in 1636, 10.5 acres in 1637, 80 acres in January 1639/40, plus later grants at "North River" and the "North Field," and 275 acres on the Ipswich River in 1650.[53]

The Brownes, particularly the first one, had long and intimate connections with the Essex County fishing industry. He along with several other men outfitted fishing voyages with the stipulation that the entire catch be sold to the financiers.[54] To cite

---

Hopkins in March 1720. The twenty-one trustees included Jonathan Belcher, Thomas Fitch, Cotton Mather, and Governor Samuel Shute. Indenture, March 25, 1720, Trustees of the Charity of Edward Hopkins, Records of the Treasurer, Colonial at Harvard.

[48] *Harvard College Records, Parts I and II*, in *Publications of the Colonial Society of Massachusetts*, 15-16, (Boston: The Society, 1925), 282, 449, 454, 843.The College hired silversmith John Burt of Boston to craft a two-handled cup. William C. Lane, "Early Silver Belonging to Harvard College," *Publications of the Colonial Society of Massachusetts*, 24 (Boston: The Society, 1923), 173-74.

[49] Felt, *Annals of Salem*, II, 511; Perley, *History of Salem*, III, 402.

[50] Felt, *Annals of Salem*, II, 64.

[51] Phillips, *Salem in Eighteenth Century*, 129.

[52] "The Pall was supported by his Honour Governour Dummer, the Hon William Tailer, Esq; Thomas Hutchinson, Esq; Samuel Brown, Esq; Thomas Fitch, Esq; and Isaac Winslow, Esq;." *New-England Weekly Journal*, September 15, 1729, [4].

[53] Anderson, *Great Migration*, I, 440; Perley, *History of Salem*, I, 313-15. For a good overview of the land transactions of William Browne, Sr., see Anderson, *Great Migration*, I, 440-41.

[54] Daniel Vickers, *Farmers & Fishermen: Two Centuries of Work in Essex County, Massachusetts, 1630-1850* (Chapel Hill: University of North Carolina Press, 1994) provides an excellent overview of the business. For more detail on the relationship between merchants and fishermen, see pages 102-03. In addition to Browne, the other prominent fish dealers in the first decades of settlement were Edmund Batter, George Corwin, and Moses Maverick. Ibid, 157.

just one example, he outfitted four men in 1674 "with 'Beefe and nett,' a shallop, and room to dry their fish on condition that at the end of the voyage he would receive all their fish and oil and credit them with equal shares of the profits."[55] Some additional documentation can be found in court records, for example, two 1665 lawsuits in which Mordecaie Creford sued Browne and others for illegally seizing eight quintals of fish from his boat.[56] In 1710 in the midst of Queen Anne's War, a number of fishermen and their merchant supporters, including William Browne, petitioned the Massachusetts General Court stressing the importance of this activity at that critical time.[57]

As far as the mercantile careers of the Brownes are concerned, the record is sparse, although it is apparent that the first William Browne engaged in international trade. As early as 1652, he and two other Salem merchants signed an agreement for a voyage to Barbados.[58] In June 1655, carpenter Francis Berry of Barbados acknowledged that he owed William Browne of Salem, merchant, £7 sterling, to be paid "at some convenient storehouse near Indian Bridge" in this Lesser Antilles island. Four years later Samuel Randall of Boston on a ship sailing to London "bound himself to pay a £30 debt to to 'Mr. William Browne of Salem' at London."[59] In 1661, Browne was one of four purchasers of the cargo of a ship owned by a French Huguenot from La Rochelle. By the next year, he was half-owner of a warehouse.[60] William's sons John and William secured rights to build a wharves on South River in Salem in 1663 and William, Sr. purchased an interest in the town wharf in 1681.[61] Evidence also exists that Browne shipped cargo on the *Blessing* in 1652 and together with his son William was owner of the *Dolphin* in 1685 that sailed on a voyage from Boston to Barbados and then across the Atlantic. He was also part owner of a man-of-war sent out in 1677 to combat pirates.[62] William Browne, Jr. owned shares of the *Salem Galley*, a privateer, that captured the *William*, a French ship, off Newfoundland in August 1696. Browne purchased the lawful prize in November for £155. At the same time, the privateer captured the *Light*, 140 tuns burthen and, that, too, was sold as a prize. Six Salem merchants, including John and Samuel Browne, purchased the ship and rechristened it as the *Salem Merchant*. John and Samuel each acquired one-eighth of the vessel. Some twenty years later Samuel Browne bought

---

[55] Ibid, 103.

[56] *EssexQCR*, II, 210-11.

[57] Harriet Silvester Tapley, "The Province Galley of Massachusetts Bay, 1694-1716, Part 1," *EIHC*, LVIII (January 1922), 87-88.

[58] "Suffolk County Deeds. Volume I," *Essex Antiquarian*, IX (July 1905), 103. Specifically, the agreement was between Edward Prescot of London, owner of the *Blessing*, with "william Browne, George Corwin & Walter Price merchants of Salem to lade and dispatch the said Ship out of New-England by the first day of this Instant July which Goods for Loading the said Ship having bin ready but the said ship being neither rig[ge]d nor Graved" and, therefore, was unable to sale for Barbados.

[59] Anderson, *Great Migration*, I, 440.

[60] Perley, *History of Salem*, I, 351; II, 358.

[61] Ibid, II, 352-53, 357.

[62] Ibid, II, 362, 370.

one-fourth of two saw mills near the town bridge from John Trask.[63]

The best available evidence of his successful mercantile career comes from a detailed December 1727 letter of instructions to John Touzell, whom Browne had appointed master of the sloop *Endeavor*. The colonel directed that the vessel sail to the West Indies with permission to stop at up to four British islands to dispose of his cargo and then "Purchase a Loading of good Mollasses, Some Rum, good Cotton wool, good Cocoa, Nutts & good Indigo, and any other thing you may bring herewith Safety, that will turn to advantage." He also authorized the master to sail elsewhere if the English markets were too low. Browne followed with further instructions to pack the cargo carefully, pay all port charges, and "to use the greatest Prudence, Diligence & good Husbandry you Can in all my affairs."[64] The letter makes clear that Browne vigorously pursued his mercantile endeavors.

Colonel Samuel Browne was the leader of the political, social, and economic elite that dominated Salem, a coterie of four closely related families that became wealthy through trade. The wealthiest resident in town, his personal estate and income surpassed by two and one half times that of his closest rival, brother-in-law John Turner, and ten times that of the third wealthiest man Timothy Lindall.[65] To say that the family enjoyed strong connections with the Massachusetts social and money elite is an understatement. The Colonel's aunt Mary Browne married Wait Still Winthrop in 1678 and Wait Still Winthrop's only son John married Ann Dudley (1684-1776) in 1707, daughter of Massachusetts Governor Joseph Dudley. Their eldest daughter Mary (1708-1767) married future Rhode Island Governor Joseph Wanton (1705-1780).[66] Colonel Browne's two wives, Eunice Turner and Abigail Keach, were relatively well connected, but not to the extent of some other members of his family. His younger sister Mary married Benjamin Lynde (1666-1745), Harvard College Class of 1686, also a prominent Salem politician.[67] The colonel's eldest son married Katherine Winthrop, third daughter of John and Ann Dudley Winthrop. Second son William married Mary Burnet, daughter of another

---

[63] Ibid, III, 318, 322; James Duncan Phillips, *Salem in the Seventeenth Century* (Boston: Houghton Mifflin Company 1933), 287; "Essex County Notarial Records," *EIHC*, XLI (April 1905), 183, 185. Notarial records provide additional information on the mercantile careers of the second William Browne and his son Samuel. Ibid, XLI (April 1905), 185, 188, 192; (October 1905), 391; XLII (April 1906), 161-62; XLIV (October 1908), 330.

[64] "Sam'l Browne - Merchant in Salem - His Instructions to Capt. John Touzell - Voyage to the West Indies," *EIHC*, I, 66. In a P.S., Browne also asked that the captain bring him limes and oranges. Touzell described his difficulties on this voyage in selling his cargo of fish and shingles in a letter to Browne that he wrote from St. Kitts on February 14, 1727/8. "To Coron'll Samuel Brown Esq.," *EIHC*, I, 83-84.

[65] Richard J. Morris, "Social Change, Republican Rhetoric, and the American Revolution: The Case of Salem, Massachusetts," *Journal of Social History*, 31, no. 2 (Winter 1997), 420. The fourth person was another brother-in-law Benjamin Lynde.

[66] [Perley], "Descendants of William Browne," 159-60; Mayo, *Winthrop Family*, 100, 121, 137; *Sibley's Harvard Graduates*, IV, 535-49. The fourth Winthrop daughter Rebecca married Gurdon Saltonstall of New London, son of the Connecticut governor of the same name and fifth daughter Margaret married Jeremiah Miller, a prominent New London merchant.

[67] Benjamin Lynde and his elder son Benjamin, Jr. (1700-1781) owed their wealth and political positions to Colonel Samuel Browne. *Sibley's Harvard Graduates*, III, 356-57; VI, 250-57.

Massachusetts governor, in 1737.[68]

Befitting a man of his political eminence, social standing, and wealth, Browne owned two mansions on Main Street in the center of Salem. The first consisted of a house built by his father on the north side of the street that was inherited by Samuel's second son William. The second was constructed by Colonel Browne on the south side of Main Street, the "Homestead where I now live," and was devised to his eldest son Samuel.[69] When the Commonwealth of Massachusetts confiscated the Salem estate of grandson William, the mansion was described as a "very handsome House in the centre of the town" measuring "52 feet by 37" that together with garden, orchard, and offices was worth £2,000 sterling."[70]

In addition to maintaining an expansive lifestyle and engaging in conspicuous consumption, Colonel Browne devoted considerable attention to the acquisition of vast quantities of land, for real proerty represented assets that could not be destroyed by fire or the perils of the sea. Like precious metals, land represented true wealth that could provide income to the owner and be passed on to later generations. Colonel Browne purchased a number of parcels of land, a handful containing dwellings and outbuildings, in Lyme, Colchester, New London, Hebron, Stafford, and Union, Connecticut between 1718 and 1730. The bulk consisted of vacant woodland, much of such poor quality that it was unsuitable for anything except for the grazing of livestock and swine and the harvesting of timber. These lands could be acquired extremely cheaply, often for as little as ten shillings per acre in depreciated New England paper currency. With the rapid expansion of population in southern New England, however, even the poorest land could find a buyer, or, if the purchaser wished to hold on to it for benefit of future generations, as did the Browne family, discrete sections could be divided into farms, improved by the owner, and then rented. Rentals could then yield a modest income to the landlord.[71]

Why, however, were the almost totally uninhabited lands of southeast Colchester and northeast Lyme deemed to be worthy of interest? Location provides the answer. All lands in southern New England on navigable waterways had long since been settled, yet what became the Browne estate had development potential due to its proximity to the Connecticut and Thames Rivers. The properties were "Ten Miles from New London" and "Ten Miles from Norwich Market Towns and Seaports." The western boundary was just five miles from Connecticut River.[72]

The question remains, however, how and under what circumstances did the

---

68 Ibid, VIII, 120. William Browne was twenty-eight when he married. The diary entry of Benjamin Lynde, Jr. (1700-1781) has the following entry for September 13, 1737. "My Coz. W. Browne set out for New York, where in November he married Miss Mary Burnet, ye lat[e] Governor Burnet's only daughter, then about 14 yrs 1/2 old, and bro't her home in May." *Lynde Diaries*, 152.

69 Phillips, *Salem in the Eighteenth Century*, 169; "Col. William Browne House," *EIHC*, LXXII (1936), 283; Will of Samuel Browne, Essex County Probate Records, Vol. 321, 234-38, microfilm, Massachusetts State Archives.

70 "Essex County Loyalists," *EIHC*, XLIII (1907), 294.

71 Samuel's grandfather started the family practice of buying and renting farms. See *EssexQCR*, II, 137 (1658); VII, 206 (1679).

72 Memorial of William Browne, AmLC, AO 12/10, 227, NAUK.

Colonel decide to purchase land in southeastern Connecticut? Could he have learned about the uninhabited woodland close to traditional Mohegan lands directly from James Harris? After all, the New London landowner grew up in Boston and spent considerable time in the city of his birth in 1707-08, perhaps to help settle the estate of Connecticut Governor Fitz-John Winthrop who died in 1707, and he had acquaintances there, but Browne and Harris traveled in widely separate social circles, so this connection seems doubtful. The common denominator was their mutual relationship with the most eminent and once powerful family in New England, the Winthrops. Wait Still Winthrop married Mary Browne in 1678, aunt of Colonel Samuel, and the Winthrops had strong connections with the New London area. John, the only son, moved to backwater Connecticut in 1711 to take over management of the family estates, became aware of and likely knew James Harris, and may have recommended him to the Colonel as a proper agent to acquire land for him.[73] Harris also had dealings with Colonel John Livingston, whose wife Mary was the only child of Wait's brother Fitz-John Winthrop.[74]

Whatever the circumstances, Harris was the grantor for most of the land that the Salem magistrate acquired in southeastern Connecticut. The Colonel's first purchase of what became a huge absentee estate occurred in 1718 when he bought 4,000 acres in the northeast quarter of Lyme from Harris. As noted in the previous chapter, Harris had purchased 4,550 acres in "the northeast Corner of ye Township of Lyme from the heirs of Matthew Griswold for £900 and resold the bulk of that uninhabited parcel of woodland, rocks, and boulders to Browne for £1,600.[75] The deed, like virtually all conveyances, provided a series of specific markers to delineate the bounds, including phrases like, "the stump of an old Tree" and "an old Red oak tree marked with a heap of stones around it," but was also described in more general terms as east on the New London boundary, south on lands that had already been partially laid out, west on lands belonging to the "heirs of mr mathew griswold Decd" and those of James Harris, and north on the Colchester line.[76] Browne's second purchase in May 1723 also consisted of property that the Griswold heirs had sold to Harris. It contained 2,865 acres and was located west of the 1718 purchase. Beginning at the northeast corner at "an ash Tree marked with Stones about it," the property extended south some 900 rods bordering on lands of Harris and Browne, then west and around land owned by Samuel Peck of Lyme to the [East] Haddam line, north on the Haddam line to the Colchester line, and then east on the Colchester-Lyme line to the ash tree.[77]

Lands often passed through two or three buyers over a relatively short time frame before they ended up in the hands of Browne, showing the extent of land speculation in early eighteenth-century Connecticut. Take, for example, his third major purchase of some 635 acres at a cost of £1,400 from absentee William Gardiner of South Kingstown, Rhode Island in October 1724. This parcel was situated on the west shore

---

[73] Mayo, *Winthrop Family*, 97, 100, 108, 110, 121-22, 136-37.

[74] Harris, "James Harris of New London," 18-19; Mayo, *Winthrop Family*, 95-96.

[75] LLR, III, 184, 188, 192, 199.

[76] James Harris to Samuel Brown, LLR, May 27, 1718, III, 188. Browne purchased the 300-acre Peck property in 1728. LLR, March 14, 1728, IV, 299.

[77] James Harris to Samuel Brown, LLR, May 16, 1723, IV, 66.

of what was then called Great Pond, Twenty Mile Pond, or Mason's Pond, now Gardner Lake, in the northeastern section of what was shortly to become New Salem Society and near the New London bounds. Gardiner purchased the property from Aaron Stark in May 1724 and Stark had acquired the land two years previously in two separate transactions from Benjamin and Anna Gorton of Warwick, Rhode Island and James Harris.[78] The Gortons in turn had purchased the "mantion house & five hundred acers of upland & meadow & swamp land" from Peter and Mary Mason in 1717 for £500, while Harris bought his 150 acres near "20 mile pond" from John Hobart of New London in October 1721.[79] Going back further, Daniel Mason acquired the five hundred acre parcel from Owaneco in 1686, while the smaller plot was laid out to Hobart by the proprietors of Colchester in January 1710/11.[80] One other example. Colonel Browne purchased 145 acres from Daniel Galusha in March 1729 for £300 at the Lyme-Colchester line.[81] Galusha had purchased the same 145 acres from James Harris on June 1722 in exchange for thirty acres of land that formerly belonged to Josiah Church and £30, the property "lying by the Rhoade to new london Commonly Called the Governors Rhode."[82]

Over the course of eleven years the Salem magnate accumulated an estate of 9,664 acres in two blocs, each made up of several purchases. After the donation of twenty acres for a minister's lot, the net amounted to 9,644 acres. The Colonel purchased 18 separate plots of land ranging in size from 20 to 4,000 acres, 9 from Harris and 9 from eight other men. One section encompassed the bulk of the property and totaled some 8,579 acres and was located primarily in the Lyme portion of what became New Salem Society. The second portion of around 1,065 acres mostly bordered on the south and west shores of Gardner Lake in the northeast section of the parish. The vast preponderance of the estate consisted of uninhabited woodland, but five conveyances made reference to dwellings and outbuildings.

In a 1724 deed, Browne purchased 635 acres in Colchester from William Gardiner that contained "houses, barns, orchards, &c." Three years later Daniel Davis conveyed 80 acres to Browne containing "one Messuage or Tenement." This was followed by 300 acres from Samuel Peck of Lyme "with a small mansion house" in 1728. In 1729, Harris sold the Salem man 526 acres in Lyme containing "a Small Dwelling house and

---

[78] William Gardiner to Samuel Brown, CLR, October 30, 1724, II, 533; Perkins, *Connecticut* Farm, 31, 244. Gardiner purchased the farm for £1,200 six months before he sold the property to Browne. The first purchase from Gorton for £800 consisted of "a Certain Messuage or tenement of housing & lands Containing a Dwelling hows or mantion hows & five hundred acres of upland & meadow & swamp land" west and north of "twenty mile pond." The second track "lying by the great pond" was "by Estimation one hundred & fifty acres be it more or less" and was acquired at a cost of £54. Aaron Starke to William Gardiner, CLR, May 2, 1724, II, 517-18; Benjamin and Anna Gorton to Aaron Stark, CLR, January 22, 1722, II, 428; James Harris to Aaron Stark, CLR, November 15, 1722, II, 437.

[79] Peter and Mary Mason to Benjamin Gorton, CLR, September 20, 1717, II, 371; John Hobart to James Harris, CLR, October 6, 1721, II, 419.

[80] Perkins, *Connecticut Farm*, 242-44.

[81] Galusha, a carpenter, was of Dutch ancestry and born in Chelmsford, Massachusetts. He moved to Lyme in 1719. Stark, "Myth and Reality," 172.

[82] Daniell Galusiah to Samuell Brown, LLR, March 1, 1728/9, IV, 333; James Harris to Daniel Galutiah, LLR, June 2, 1722, IV, 223.

a sawmill," plus another 100 acres in Colchester "with two small mantion or Dwelling Houses, a Barn, & smiths shop." Lastly, Robert Staples sold Brown the 40 acre "farm which I now live on."[83] The total quantity for these lands was 1,601 acres and the bulk even of these four purchases consisted of unimproved and virgin woodland, rocks, and ledges.

Map 1. New Salem Lands of Samuel Browne[84]

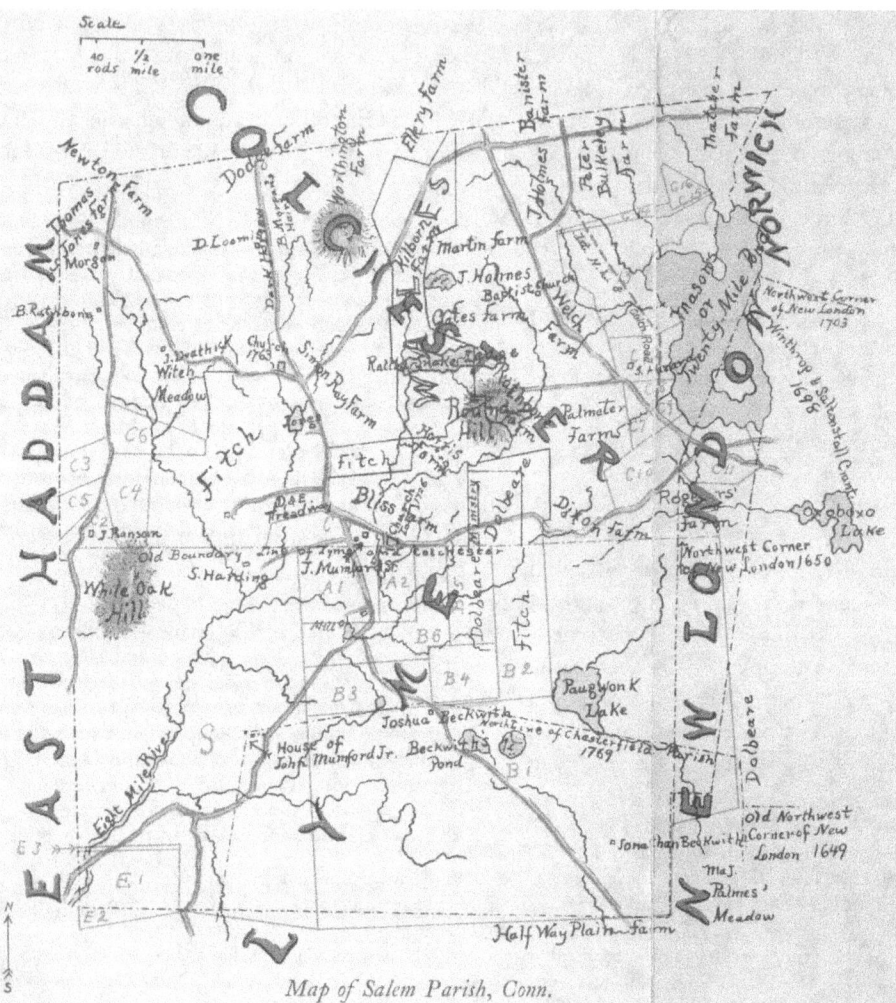

Map of Salem Parish, Conn.

---

[83] William Gardiner to Samuel Brown, CLR October 30, 1724, II, 533-34; Daniel Davis to Samuel Brown, CLR, December 27, 1727, II, 760; Samuel Peck to Samuel Brown, LLR, March 14, 1728, IV, 299; James Harris to Samuel Brown, LLR, August 25, 1728, IV, 336; Robert Stapels to Samuel Brown, CLR, March 11, 1729, III, 31.

[84] Perkins, *Connecticut Farm*, map between pages 55 and 56. The numbered lots represent Browne purchases, except for B2 and B5. All of the Lyme section of New Salem was Browne property except for sales to Dolbeare and Fitch. Map reproduced courtesy of The Connecticut Historical Society.

Table 1. Browne Estate[85]

Lot[86]	Grantor	Date	Acres	Town	Source
B1	James Harris	May 22, 1718	4,000	Lyme	LLR,III, 188
S	James Harris	May 16, 1723	2,865	Lyme	LLR, IV, 66
	Will. Gardiner	Oct. 30, 1724	635	Colchester	CLR, II, 533
C14	Aaron Stark	Jan. 15, 1725/6	45	Colchester	CLR, II, 633
C16	James Harris	Feb. 8, 1725/6	37	Colchester	CLR, II, 625
C2	Daniel Davis	Dec. 27, 1727	80	Colchester	CLR, II, 760
C7[87]	James Harris	Apr. 10, 1728	176	Colchester	CLR, II, 790-91
C11	James Harris	Apr. 10, 1728	172.5	Col.- NL	NLLR,IX, 63
B4	Daniel Galusha	Mar. 1, 1728/9	145	Lyme	LLR, IV, 333
C3	Robert Staples	Mar. 11, 1729	48	Colchester	CLR, III, 31
E1-3	Samuel Peck	Mar. 14, 1728	300	Lyme	LLR, IV, 299
C4-5	Aaron Gillet	Mar. 14, 1729	165.5	Colchester	CLR, III, 35
B3	James Harris	July 4, 1729	200	Lyme	LLR, IV, 337
	James Harris	July 4, 1729	20	Colchester	CLR, III, 61[88]
A1[89]	James Harris	July 8, 1729	526	Lyme	LLR, IV, 336
	James Harris	July 8, 1729	100	Colchester	LLR, IV, 336
C3	Samuel Tubbs	Sep. 22, 1729	21	Colchester	CLR, III, 29
C6	Aaron Gillet	Sep. 22, 1729	128	Colchester	CLR, III, 67-68
Total			9,664		

While buying huge quantities of land in southeastern Connecticut, Browne also acquired equally large holdings in what would become the towns of Stafford and Union in the northeast part of the colony near the Massachusetts border. The Connecticut General Assembly sold the territory called the Union lands, then part of Stafford,

---

85 Copies of all these deeds are also located in Perkins, *Connecticut Farm*, 190-99, 238-45.

86 The lot number designations come from Perkins.

87 Lots C7, C9, and C10 sold by Harris to Browne.

88 Colonel Browne donated this lot to New Salem Society for the use of the ministry. Perkins, *Connecticut Farm*, 29.

89 The 526-acre Browne purchase consisted of Lots A1, A2, B6, and C.

to twelve proprietors from Windsor in July 1720 for £307, the funds to be used for the benefit of Yale College. Hoping to make a quick profit, some proprietors soon sold their shares. In April 1723, John Arnold of Mansfield conveyed to Browne "a thirteenth part of the Land known by the name of Union" for £180 and the next year James Marjerous [McJerom] of Windsor sold him another thirteenth part of the "Union Land" for the same price. Each portion contained around 1,300 acres. In December 1729, the proprietors or their representatives, including Samuel Browne, met to divide the area into lots and distribute them to the proprietors. The General Assembly established the town of Union in October 1734.[90]

Stafford was incorporated in 1719 and at sixty square miles was one of the largest towns in the colony. Located in the hill country, the land, like that of Lyme and Union, was rocky with thin soil of extremely poor quality.[91] Thus, the lands cost relatively little to buy and could be easily retained without a great deal of tax liability. Between 1725 and 1730, the Salem merchant purchased around 8,020 acres in Stafford, primarily from Joseph Orcutt, but also from Gershom Hall, John Pasco, Daniel Pease, John Warner, and the Town of Stafford. The parcels ranged in size from forty-five to 3,500 acres.[92] Browne bought the largest tract from Joseph Orcutt in 1725 for just £650, less than four shillings per acre.[93] His second son William inherited the Stafford and Union lands.[94]

In October 1729, Browne made another Connecticut purchase, a tract of 311 acres in Hebron.[95] The Salem merchant's property in Connecticut, divided among five towns, amounted to around 20,575 acres,[96] but this impressive total represented only a minority of his total holdings in Massachusetts, including its Maine portion, New Hampshire, and Rhode Island. Browne may have been the richest man in the Bay Colony, but he was hardly alone in his purchases of large amounts of unsettled land in New England. Several wealthy oligarchs of Massachusetts and Rhode Island acquired extensive land holdings. As noted in the previous chapter, Colonel Thomas Fitch and John Dolbeare, both of Boston, purchased significant quantities of land in New Salem and New London and James Harris sold additional parcels to other absentees, the most notable of whom was Godfrey Malbone of Newport. These men also rented farms to

---

[90] Early General Records, Connecticut Colonial Records, Vol. 49, 451-52; Vol. 50, 110, CSL; Harvey M. Lawson, *The History of Union* (New Haven: Press of Price, Lewis & Atkins Co., 1893), 38-40; *Colony Records*, VII, 527-28. Union encompasses 28.7 square miles and in 2010 had a population of just 854, the smallest for any town in the state. The community, together with neighboring Stafford and Willington and a handful of towns in northwest Connecticut had the poorest land quality in the colony. Daniels, *Connecticut Town*, 187-88.

[91] William P. McDermott, *Stafford, Connecticut, 1719-1740: From Farm to Factory* (Tolland, CT: Kerleen Press, 2010), 3-15.

[92] Stafford Land Records, I, 105-398 passim, CSL.

[93] Joseph Orcutt to Samuel Brown, Stafford Land Records, September 3, 1725, I, 177-78.

[94] These legacies are unmentioned in the standard biographical sketch of the third William Browne. *Sibley's Harvard Graduates*, VIII, 120-24.

[95] Joseph Dewey to Samuell Brown, HLR, October 9, 1729, II, 149-50. His grandson William sold the property almost forty years later. William Brown to Samuel Gilbert, HLR, December 28, 1768, V, 185.

[96] This total amounted to almost to six-tenths of one per cent of the entirety of Connecticut.

tenants, but not on the same scale as the Brownes. The practice was not an uncommon one, although renters formed a relatively small minority of all Connecticut farmers. Speculators from Connecticut, like Harris, were equally active in buying and selling land, albeit on a considerably smaller scale. They lacked the resources of the wealthy magnates from Massachusetts and instead of purchasing land for long term investment purposes, like Browne, Dolbeare, and Fitch, often turned over their properties on a fairly rapid basis.

Absentees needed to manage their lands and the Brownes hired a series of agents/overseers to care for and help develop their properties in New Salem. In order to generate income for the owner, the lands had to be cleared, divided into farms, and rented to tenants. These efforts were well under way by the time Colonel Browne died in 1731 and, befitting a man of his character and substance, his funeral on May 21, 1731 attracted much attention. The *"Funeral* of the late Honourable *Samuel Browne* Esq; of *Salem,* was attended with great Solemnity" by the governor, lieutenant governor, "and a great Number of Persons of *Distinction,* both of the Civil Sacred and Military Order; a Multitude of People following the *Hearse."* The newspaper death notice praised him for his "ancient and honorable Family and his Superior worldly *Estate,"* for his eminent service in a number of public offices, his being a *"faithful* Assertor of the true Interests of his Country," and for being a "hearty *Friend* to the Religion and Liberties of it." He was also praised for his generous support of education, the church, and for "his Attendance on the *Public Worship* on the Lord's Days . . . even when his Bodily Weakness was *visible* great upon Him."[97]

Browne left a huge estate. His numerous bequests, in addition to those already mentioned to educational institutions, included £70 to the First Church of Salem for the "purchase [of] a Silver flagon &c," £45 to be divided among the four ministers in town, £100 to aid the poor, and gifts to many members of his family.[98] In addition and unlike so many of his merchant contemporaries, he left behind a great deal of silver coin.[99]

He divided his real property among his three sons.[100] To eldest son Samuel

---

[97] *New-England Weekly Journal,* May 31, 1731, [2]. The *Lynde Diaries* do not contain any entries for 1731.

[98] He gave £150 went to his mother, £100 to cousin Sarah Woodward in England, £25 to cousin Ann Lechmere, the same amount to cousin Lucy Green, £20 to James Jeffry, Jr., £10 to Daniel Epes, Jr., and £5 to John Cox. In addition, Browne granted his brother-in-law Benjamin Lynde, Sr. two small plots of land in Salem, "Sister Lynde" £200, nephew Benjamin Lynde, Jr. £150, nephew William Lynde £50, and niece Sarah Plaisted £20. Will of Samuel Browne, Vol. 321, 234-38, MSA.

[99] Six years after his death a newspaper article provided additional information on his great wealth. "We hear from Salem, that on Friday last William Brown, Esq; the youngest surviving Son of the Hon. Col. Brown, deceased, having had Information of some Money conceal'd in a Place which he owned, caused a search to be made for the same, where was found five or six Jarrs full of Silver, containing about one thousand ninety-three Ounces of Silver of several Species, among which was found about six thousand New-England Shillings, scarcely discolored." *Boston News-Letter,* July 21, 1737, [2].

The fact that he possessed such a large supply of coin provides further evidence of his prosperity since most merchants had little hard currency. As one prominent scholar noted, "the balance of trade was so heavily weighted in favor of the home country that only by ingenious or complicated devices" could a merchant hope to accumulate coin. Bailyn, *New England Merchants,* 183.

[100] Abigail, the only daughter of Colonel and Mrs. Abigail Browne, died on April 16, 1729 at age nine. "She was a Child who by her dutiful behavior very much endeared her to Father, and her Death discover'd a pious

Browne went "all my Lands, Houses, Buildings, Fences whatsoever which I have lying in Lyme, Colchester and New London Townships in the Colony of Connecticut." Other property devised to Samuel consisted of lands at Stage Point in Salem with marsh and "wharfing," "my Homestead" together with "the warehouse, wharfing, and my Said Land Joining to it." All these properties were entailed to his "Son Samuel . . . and the Heirs of his body lawfully begotten." Other lands bequeathed to him consisted of all lands and houses in Lynn, Manchester, Attleboro, Oxford, Brookfield, Plymouth, Plympton, Massachusetts and Hebron, Connecticut. In addition, the eldest son received his father's one-eighth share of an iron works and £1,000 in "Bills of Credit or good Bonds."[101]

Second son William received all lands in Stafford and Union, plus those in Providence, Rhode Island, together "with the Houses and Buildings . . . that were formerly my Hon[ored]d Father's" and his part of warehouses, wharfing, a cooper's shot, and land owned by the Colonel's father including some additional real estate in Salem, plus property in Gloucester and Uxbridge, some of which was entailed.[102] Third son Benjamin inherited a farm in Salem, a second one in Newington, New Hampshire, plus lands and buildings in Stoughton, all entailed. Benjamin also received unentailed lands and part of a wharf in Salem, plus more land and tenements in Ipswich, Springfield, Hadley, and Middlesex County.[103] Personal property bequeathed to Benjamin consisted on one-third "of my Plate," some furniture, and £10,000 "in Publick Bills of Credit and good Bonds." All the shipping and the remainder of the Colonel's estate was divided equally between the two older brothers.[104]

In the career of Colonel Samuel Browne, grandson of the first Browne of Salem, the political and economic fortunes of the family reached its zenith. The first family of Salem may not have monopolized all the public offices in the town, but was its dominant political force and virtually all the time from the 1670s to the American Revolution at least one Browne served in high public office.

---

inclination to depart to be with Christ." *Boston Gazette*, April 21, 1729, [2].

[101] Will of Samuel Browne, MSA.

[102] William sold the Union lands he inherited during the 1750s and his son William Burnet the Stafford properties in 1770-71. Union Land Records, II, 110, 116-29, 140, CSL; Stafford Land Records, IV, 74-78, 88, 113-14, CSL.

[103] Benjamin died not long after graduating from Harvard. "Sometime the last Week died at Salem, and on Friday last was Enterred Mr. *Benjamin Brown*, youngest Son of the Late Hon. Col. *Brown* of that Town. A young Gentleman just arriv'd to Age, and possessed of a very plentiful Fortune left him by his Father, all of which we hear he has given equally between his two surviving Brothers, *Samuel* and *William Browne*, Esqrs. *Boston Evening-Post*, May 2, 1737, [2].

[104] Will of Samuel Browne, MSA.

Interlude

Browne Family Portraits

Many prominent and wealthy New Englanders memorialized themselves by sitting for portraits and the Brownes were no exception.

The well-known and talented British artist John Smibert (1688-1751), the first professionally trained artist in North America, came to the colonies in 1728 and settled in Boston two years later. He painted the portraits of numerous Massachusetts worthies.[1] He opened a shop in 1734 from which he sold artist supplies and kept a studio above the store where he displayed copies of Old Masters that he had painted in Europe.[2] That same year he executed a series of three portraits of members of the Browne family - William Browne, Samuel Browne, and Samuel's wife Katherine Winthrop Browne, all then in their twenties.[3]

These individuals personified the aristocracy of Massachusetts.[4] The possibility exists that the artist rendered them in his Boston studio, but it is far more likely that Smibert painted them on a trip to Salem because of the time required for their completion. Collectively they express confidence in their right to rule and to be given deference by the common herd.

It is difficult to avoid taking what one already knows about a person and then using the portrait to reinforce those traits, but here is a rank amateur's analysis of the three paintings. William Browne had passed his twenty-fifth birthday when he sat for the Scotland born artist. Although a year younger than Samuel, William had the look of a man of substance, unlike his older brother. Indeed, only a man of great social reputation and confidence would seek the hand of the teenage daughter of a former Massachusetts governor. Compare the two portraits. William wore a rich-looking maroon outfit that projected power. Samuel looked like a pleasure-seeking young man who was happy to enjoy the fruits of the labor of his father. He was already putting on weight, probably due to the joys of the cup and table, and was luxuriously dressed in a green coat with gold braid and gold buttons, the picture of a gentleman who enjoyed the good life. His visage did not project strong character. Samuel's wife Katherine was the daughter of one governor on her mother's side and the descendant of two Winthrop governors on her father's side. Her portrait projects the self-assurance of a woman who knows that she is important.

---

[1] One can go online to see reproductions of many of Smibert's works.

[2] See, https://www.britannica.com/biography/John-Smibert, accessed March 7, 2022.

[3] Unfortunately, no known portraits exist for the two most important members of the family, Colonel Samuel Browne and his grandson Governor William Browne.

[4] The images of William, Samuel, and Katherine Wintthrop Browne on the following pages appear courtesy of Wahoo Art. See, en.wahooart.com.

William Browne (1709–1763), by John Smibert ca. 1734.

Samuel Browne (1709–1742), by John Smibert ca. 1734.

Katherine Winthrop Browne (1711–1781), by John Smibert ca. 1734.

Chapter 5

New Salem Society and the Browne Family

When Colonel Samuel Browne began purchasing land in northern Lyme and southeastern Colchester, the area consisted primarily of unpopulated wilderness. His first two acquisitions in 1718 and 1723 totaling some 6,850 acres were entirely uninhabited. The first residents of the region lived in the northern Colchester section of what was to become New Salem Society several years before anyone settled on the Browne lands.

The clear leader of the handful of inhabitants in the area was Captain Samuel Gilbert (1664-1733).[1] His association with the region dates back to January 1708, when the New London County Court appointed him one of three surveyors to lay out a country road four rods wide from Colchester to New London.[2]

The residents in the region asked the General Assembly that they be annexed to New London's newly constituted North Society in May 1722. Just eight names were listed, the first being Colonel Samuel Browne who signed "for his Lands There." These first stirrings of an identity apart from that of Colchester and Lyme occurred when the Massachusetts land magnate was in his nascent efforts to develop and bring farmers to his lands. The fact that he signed the initial memorial indicates that he was visiting the region at the time. Gilbert's name comes second and the remaining signatories probably constituted the bulk of the landowners in the region and demonstrated just how tiny the population of the area was.[3] The "humble Petition" of "Severall Inhabitants" of Lyme and Colchester asserted that they lived so far from any place of public worship in their

---

1 Born in Hartford, Gilbert married Mary Rogers, daughter of Samuel and Mary Stanton Rogers in 1684. James Harris was his brother-in-law. The Connecticut General Court commissioned him as ensign of the North Train Band of Hartford in 1698, he moved to Colchester by 1706, and made captain of its militia company in May 1707. He served as captain of a company in Colonel William Whiting's regiment in the 1709 Canadian expedition. Gilbert sold his 280-acre farm in Colchester in 1724 shortly after he moved to the Paugwonk section of Lyme. He possessed one slave that his son Daniel inherited. Homer Worthington Brainard, Harold Simon Gilbert, and Clarence Almon Torrey, *The Gilbert Family: Descendants of Thomas Gilbert, 1582-1650* (New Haven: A. C. Gilbert Co., 1953), 77-78.

2 NLCC, PbyS: Travel, January 15, 1707/8 Box 91, folder 8. On June 5, 1708, Colonel John Livingston, Samuel Rogers, Jr., James Harris, and Daniel Stebens living near the north boundary of New London protested the way of new road was laid out. Ibid.

3 The other signers of the petition were Samuel Allen, Richard Tozer, John Pearshall, William Chapman, Pelatiah Bliss, and James Harris, all residents of Colchester. CA, Ecclesiastical Affairs, Series 1, III, 131.

own towns that it was virtually impossible for them to do so. They requested, therefore, that they be annexed to the new North Parish of New London where a meetinghouse was soon going to be built. The General Assembly took no action.[4] In November 1724, Captain Gilbert petitioned the county court for a highway to be constructed from New London to Colchester by way of "Land Commonly Called Pawgank."[5] He was also the first tavern keeper from New Salem, serving in that position in 1727.[6]

The following spring seventeen "Inhabitants of the northerly part of Lime [sic] bordering upon the aforesd southerly part of Collchester," probably the bulk of the adult males living in the area, petitioned for parish privileges. In a letter dated Salem, [Massachusetts], March 12, 1724/5 addressed to the "Inhabitants & Livers In ye South Part of Colchester and the North Part of Lyme," Browne stated that he had learned of their intention to build a meetinghouse on the land of Lieutenant James Harris in Colchester near the Lyme line. He promised to donate £50 in "Bills of Creditt" to help defray construction costs "as Soon as the meeting House Is Raised & Covered the Top & Sydes." He understood that the proposed location stood near the center of the "Intended Parish or Town." "I Pray God to Give you Councell & a good Agreement and to Prosper you In so Good an undertaking."[7] The petition was dated May 7, 1725 and the signers set forth the standard arguments for parish privileges. They lived too far from established places of public worship in Colchester and Lyme to be able to attend church services without "grate Difficulty" and were "theirfore very Desiaras to Erect an house . . . [for] publick Worship of God." They stated that they already had the support of the town of Colchester and asked that the General Assembly favorably consider their memorial.[8] Colchester had previously voted on April 27, 1725 to endorse the efforts of the inhabitants of the "South East part" to form a separate parish, provided they continued to pay the minister's rate in the old society until they settled their own minister.[9] The inhabitants of the new North Lyme Parish on the other hand urged on May 3 that the memorial be rejected because it was still organizing and could ill afford the loss of even a handful of taxable estates.[10]

---

[4] Ibid, III, 131. The North Parish was established in 1721. *Ecclesiastical History*, 429.

[5] NLCC, PbyS: Travel, November 1724, Box 91, folder 15. Gilbert resided in Colchester in 1722, but had moved to Lyme by 1723. NLCC, PbyS: Summons for Evidence, November 27, 1723, Box 86, folder 4. The New London Court summoned Captain Samuel Gilbert on two other occasions in 1724 and 1725. Ibid, Box 85, folders 6, 10.

[6] NLCC, PbyS: Travel, January 10, 1726-27, Box 91, folder 18. The Lyme selectmen nominated him for that position and Gilbert's son Daniel later served in the same capacity. Ibid, Box 92, folders 6, 9.

[7] CA, Ecclesiastical Affairs, Series 1, III, 121.

[8] Seventeen men signed the memorial - Captain Samuel Gilbert, Lieutenant James Harris, Lieutenant John Holmes, James Treadway, Thomas Jones, Daniel Galusha, Ensign Ephraim Wells, James Harris, Jr., Pelitiah Bliss, Elisha Mirick, George Holmes, William Dickson, Robert Staples, Richard Tozer, Thomas Jones, Jr., Daniel Palmeter, and John Holmes, Jr. The bulk of the signatories lived in Colchester. CA, Ibid, III, 132. Note that Gilbert comes first and he is followed by Harris. Gilbert and Galusha may have been the only Lyme residents.

[9] ColchesterBMD, Vol. 1, 174., CTH.

[10] CA, Ecclesiastical Affairs, Series 1, III, 132.

Illustration 5. Samuel Browne's Letter of Support, March 12, 1724/5[11]

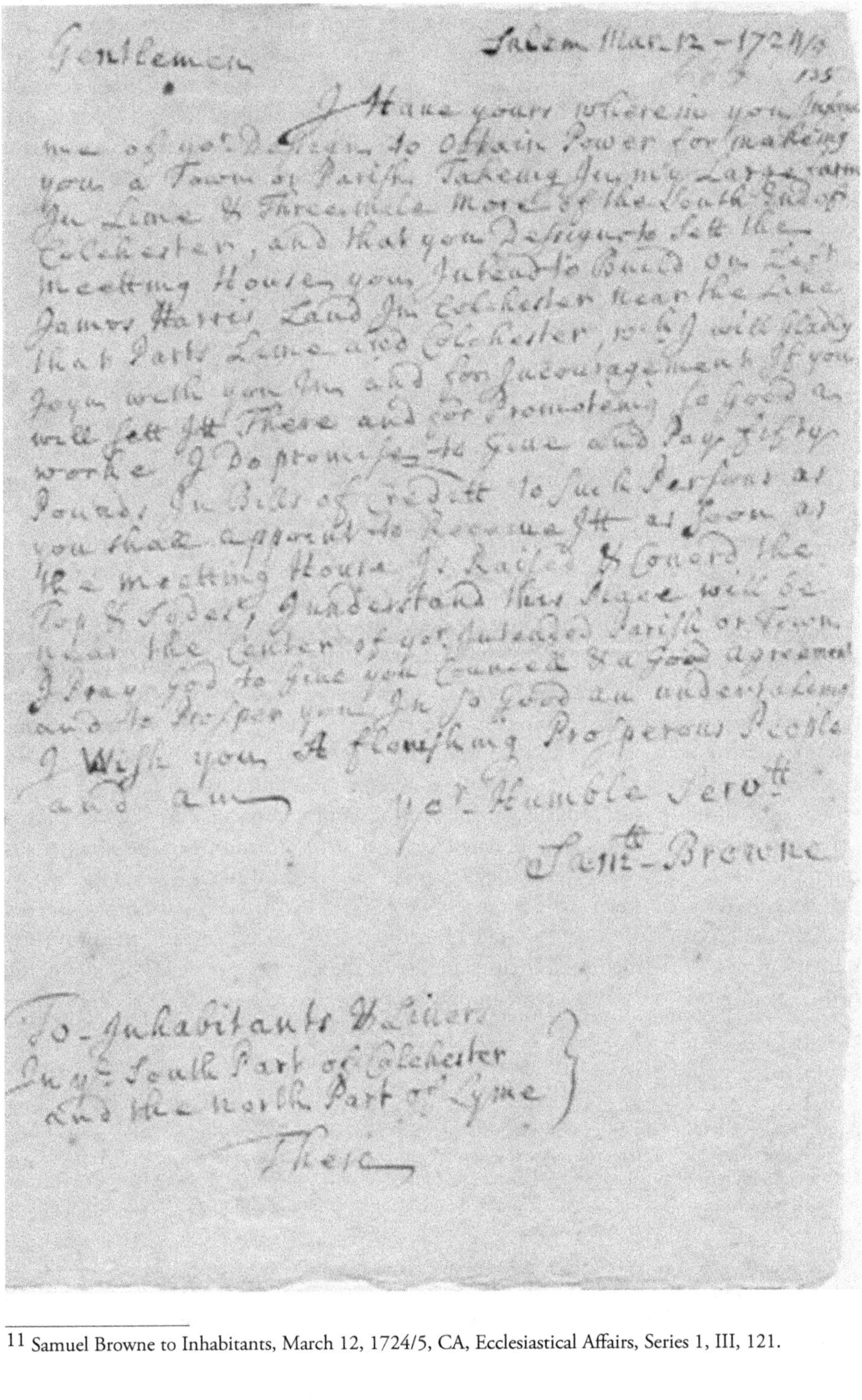

Despite the opposition of North Lyme Parish, the General Assembly immediately approved the petition and voted to establish the new society. The legislature set the bounds as recommended by the petitioners, beginning at the southeast corner of Haddam, then east to the New London line, north by the New London boundary to the Norwich line, by Norwich bounds to tree where Colchester and Lebanon meet, then west to northeast corner of the farm of Thomas Jones straight to the Haddam line, and then south to the Lyme line. Perhaps the fact that the number of signatories had doubled in just three years helped persuade the legislature that the new parish would continue to grow. In addition, the support the petitioners received from the wealthy Salem absentee was likely a strong factor. In his honor and in the hope of further support, the parish was named New Salem. The following year Harris donated two acres of land in Colchester for a meetinghouse, burying ground, and training field for the militia.

From any objective standard, the legislature made a serious mistake in establishing New Salem Society. Its residents were poor, the area sparsely settled, and absentees Samuel Browne, John Dolbeare, and Thomas Fitch owned more than half the land. In 1728, for example, the parish list of polls and rateable estates totaled just £1,900, insufficient to support the gospel ministry. The struggles of the people to organize after 1725 demonstrates the erroneous good intentions of the General Assembly in allowing them to gain parish privileges.

The paltry number of inhabitants of the new society met on October 11, 1725 and voted to petition the General Assembly to be released from colony taxes for four years, yet allow that all lands in the parish to be taxed at the rate of one penny per acre for four years. They selected James Harris to represent them before the legislature.[12] The memorial, however, did not ask for a release from colony taxes and instead requested that the General Assembly allow them to tax unimproved lands and that "Country Raits be levied and Applyed" to defraying parish expenses for four years. The General Assembly granted the petition in part by authorizing the inhabitants of the parish "Called New Salem" to levy a tax of one penny per acre on "the unimproved land within the said parish" for four years after the ordination of its first minister.[13] At the same time, another petition from eighteen men dated October 19, 1725 addressed the new parish's militia problem. They stated that they labored under great difficulties due to the fact that they lived in two towns whose centers were "fare Distant from our homes," served in three militia companies, and some had to travel eight to ten miles to perform their military duties.[14] The memorial included a list in the hand of James Harris giving the names of fifty-one men eligible for military service, plus the names of sixteen others

---

12 CA, Ecclesiastical Affairs, Series I, III, 134. The memorial was in the hand of Society Clerk Thomas Gustin.

13 Ibid, III, 136; *Colony Records*, VI, 576-77. The parish was first called New Salem in October 1725. The formal designation of the society as New Salem came from the draft in May 1726 of "An Act in favor of New Salem." The first sentence began as follows: "Be it Enacted . . . That the People of ye North Part of Lime [sic], and South part of Colchester be Named, Called and known by the Name of New Salem, and that the sd Parish of New Salem, be and hereby is, Annexed to the County of New London. CA, Ecclesiastical Affairs, Series 1, III, 138. This act was never passed.

14 CA, Militia, Series 1, I, 292. Petition signers: James Harris, James Treadway, Thomas Jones, Daniel Galusha, Isaac Fox, Daniel Davis, James Fox, Robert Staples, James Cutting, Thomas Jones, Jr., James Treadway, Jr., John Holmes, Sr., William Dixon, Robert Dixon, James Harris, Jr., John Lord, Richard Tozer, and John Brown.

who were in the process of settling in the parish.[15] The General Assembly took no action until May 1734 when it appointed John Holmes, Jr. captain, Pelatiah Bliss lieutenant, and Samuel Rogers ensign of the militia company in New Salem.[16]

Harris presented two additional petitions in 1726, the first to the New London County Court and the second to the colonial legislature. In the memorial to the court, he asked the body to appoint "a Jury" to lay out a road in Paugwonk. "Since ye Settlement of ye Lands at ye sd pauwonk," the need had arisen for a "Country Road to begin Northward of ye Line between Lyme & Colchester . . . between ye Dwelling house of yr memorialist & ye Dwelling house of James harris Jun[io]r," through the lands of the petitioner, the farm of Colonel Browne "on which mr Gallusia Lives," land owned by Daniel Galusha, through more Browne land to the "New london County Road."[17] (See Illustration 1, Chapter 3, page 43) The second petition from James Harris on behalf of the "Parish of New Salem" came to the May 1726 session of the legislature. The New Salem parishioners noted that with respect to military service, they lived in two towns in two different counties, were part of three militia companies, and had to travel from six to twelve miles to perform their duties. Harris stated that the society contained enough inhabitants to form a captain's company and requested three indulgences from the General Assembly. First, they again asked to be released from "Country Rates" for four years; second, that they may be set apart as a distinct military company; and, third, that the company be in New London County. The legislature granted their second and third requests.[18]

While this May 1726 petition was being considered, Samuel Gilbert and forty others from the "Southerly part of Colchester and Northerly Part of Lyme Called New Salem" asked the legislature for relief. Citing the inconvenience of performing military duty and attending town meetings in Lyme and Colchester, they prayed to be made into a separate township because of the great difficulties they endured by living in two different towns, two counties, and three separate militia companies. In addition, the petitioners asked to be released from taxes for four years. The General Assembly took no action.[19]

One indicator that the area's population was growing, albeit slowly, occurred in June 1727, when the New London County Court gave a license to Captain Samuel

---

15 Ibid, I, 293.

16 *Colony Records*, VII, 488. Captain John Holmes married Mary Harris, third child of James Harris, and Lieutenant Pelatiah Bliss married Sarah Harris, eldest child of James. Harris, "James Harris of New London," 21-24.

17 The Memorial of James Harris of Paugwonk, NLCC, PbyS: Travel, Box 91, folder 17. The court declined to take action.

18 CA, Ecclesiastical Archives, Series 1, III, 137.

19 CA, Ecclesiastical Archives, Series 2, I, 98, CSL. The memorial was dated May 30, 1726. The petition contained the names of Samuel Gilbert, John Holmes, Ephraim Wells, William Worthington, William Chapman, Jr., Daniel Palmeter, John Pendall, Richard Tozer, Thomas Jones, John Lambart, Daniel Galusha, Jonathan Daniels, Thomas Gustin, John Dethick, James Treadway, William Dixon, Robert Staples, James Treadway, Jr., John Dixon, Thomas Fox, James Harris, Jr., Pelatiah Bliss, Daniel Davis, William Treadway, Edward Palmeter, John Holmes, Jr., George Holmes, Josiah Treadway, John Lord, Thomas Jones, Jr., John Brown, John Gilbert, John Randall, Jr., Daniel Gilbert, James Jones, Daniel Daniels, James Tozer, John Gustin, John Douglas, Jonathan Harris, and Isaac Fox.

Gilbert, the most prominent inhabitant of the new society, to keep a house of public entertainment.[20] Upon the recommendation of the civil authority of Colchester, the Hartford County Court occasionally appointed others from New Salem to serve as tavern keepers.[21] In April 1749, for example, the court appointed "Mr. Stephen Gardner for paugwonk," plus Deacon Ebenezer Palmeter on the New London Road and Ichabod Chapman on the Lyme road.[22]

The religious situation in the new parish was also unfavorable and it experienced great difficulty in settling a minister. In August 1727, the inhabitants of New Salem requested assistance from the New London County Association of Ministers. Eliphalet Adams of New London and Benjamin Lord of Norwich petitioned Governor Joseph Talcott to provide encouragement for the new society by either refunding their taxes for three or four years or giving them money out of the public treasury so that they could hire a minister and finish their meetinghouse. "They have lost two very Hopeful preachers already only for want of an Ability to give Them just Encouragement to Stay among them." The ministers also feared that unless some action took place soon to assist the society, the people who lived at remote distances from other churches would turn to "The Sectaries" who already lived among them.[23]

At a society meeting on April 28, 1728, the parish voted to ask permission of the General Assembly to settle the Reverend David Deming as its minister.[24] This action finally prompted the legislature in May to grant "liberty unto the inhabitants of the parish, partly in Colchester and partly in Lyme, called New Salem, to embody into church estate . . . and to settle an orthodox minister amongst them."[25] The New London Association, however, upon receiving news of legislative action, sent a letter on May 29, 1728 to Deming asking him to appear at their next meeting in August to answer questions that had arisen concerning "a Lightness of Carriage unbecoming a Minister of the Gospel & also Drinking to Excess." He failed to respond and the Association wrote to the committee from New Salem "for Settling a Minister" chaired by John Holmes

---

[20] NLCC, Trials, June 1727, Vol. 16, 71. The granting of the license took place one year after Gilbert successfully sued Daniel Galusha in a case of defamation and slander. Galusha claimed that Gilbert was drunk. The jury ruled in the plaintiff's favor and awarded him £5-1-8 in damages and costs. *Samuel Gilbert v. Daniel Galusha*, NLCC, Trials, Vol. 15, 189.

[21] The civil authority consisted of justices of the peace, selectmen, constables, and grand jurors. They met in early January of each year to nominate tavern keepers and the county court generally officially appointed these individuals for one year at its next court session.

[22] Hartford County Court, PbyS: Travel, Box 539, April 1749 packet, CSL. Gardner also served as tavern keeper in 1751. Ibid, April 1751 packet. Lebbeus Harris held the position from 1754 to 1759. Daniel Gilbert and John Gilbert, lived in the Lyme section of the parish, held the position of innkeeper for several years between 1738 and 1755. NLCC, PbyS: Travel, Boxes 92-93 passim.

[23] CA, Ecclesiastical Affairs, Series 1, III, 144. The memorial was dated August 16, 1727 "New London North Parish."

[24] Deming had previously preached for three years beginning in April 1725 without receiving a call from Lyme North Society and the disappointed man sued the "Committee for ye North Society" demanding £210 damages. *David Deming v. Daniell Sterling, Richard Eley, and Daniell Eley*, November 1728, NLCC, Files, Box 28, folder 4, no. 23.

[25] CA, Ecclesiastical Affairs, Series 1, III, 143; *Colony Records*, VII, 182-83.

that they "Cannot advise ye Inhabitants to Settle him Among them."[26] Deming did not become their minister and it took another five-and-a-half years before a permanent one came to the society.[27]

The Reverend Mr. Joseph Lovett finally "was Ordained Pastor of a Church in New-Salem in Colchester, Connecticut" on Wednesday October 10, 1733.[28] Born in Beverly, Massachusetts, Lovett graduated from Harvard in 1728, came to Connecticut in 1731 to preach at Pomfret-Mortlake Parish, and in November gained a license to preach the gospel from the Windham County Association of Ministers. He married Anne Holmes, daughter of John and Elizabeth Gates Holmes of Colchester, in 1734.[29] At around the same time, he purchased fifty acres of land "att a place Called Paugwonk" and built a house upon it.[30]

The troubles of the parish, however, were by no means over. The tax list for 1738 still amounted to just £1,900 and the society at a May 4, 1739 meeting voted to petition the General Assembly for permission to tax "all our unimproved Lands" at a rate of one pence per acre.[31] A memorial dated May 10, 1739 and presented to the legislature by

---

[26] New London Association, May 28-29, 1728, August 20, 1728, 36, 38-39.

[27] David Deming (1681-1745/6) was born in Wethersfield, graduated from Harvard in 1700, farmed in Middletown, served as minister in Medway, Massachusetts 1715-22, preached briefly at Block Island, and moved to Lyme where he preached on occasion and worked as schoolmaster. *Sibley's Harvard Graduates*, III, 518-19; Judson Keith Deming, *Genealogy of the Descendants of John Deming of Wethersfield, Connecticut* (Dubuque, Iowa: Press of Mathis-Mets Co., 1904), 29-30. Deming was sued for debt on six occasions between February 1729 and November 1733, but most infamously charged with "lascivious carriage . . . by Exposing his Most Secret parts" in June 1736, an act that occurred two years before when he was teaching at a school in the First Society of Lyme. The jury found Deming not guilty and dismissed him upon paying court costs. *William Roe v. David Deming*, NLCC, Files, February 1729, Box 29, folder 1, no. 97; *Lawrence Wessels v. David Deming*, Ibid, June 1729, Box 29, folder 19, no. 252, 253 (two cases); *Daniel Sterling v. David Deming*, Ibid, November 1729, Box 30, folder 16, no. 208-09; *Joshua Champion v. David Deming*, Ibid, November 1733. Box 38, folder 15; *Dom Rex v. David Deming*, Ibid, June 1736, Box 46, folder 16, no. 370.
The New London Association took formal action against Deming in both 1734 and 1737. In June 1734, the Association noted that he had not replied their 1728 letter, that charges of "Some Lascivious and Immodest Actions" had been made by a young woman, and it suspended him from preaching. Three years later, the Association voted to formally censure him. New London Association, June 4, 1734, June 1737, 60-61, 71.

[28] *Boston Weekly News-Letter*, October 18, 1733, [2]. He died in April 1786 and his death notice reported that "Some Years since, he was a settled Minister at *New Salem* in *Colchester*." *Connecticut Gazette* [New London], April 22, 1786, [3].

[29] *Sibley's Harvard Graduates*, VIII, 1726-1730, 446-47; General Association of Connecticut Records, Windham Association 1723-1814, November 16, 1731, 43.
Joseph and Anne Lovett became the parents of daughters Elizabeth in April 1737 and Anne in March 1739. Mrs. Anne Lovett died on May 13, 1739. ColchesterBMD, Vol. 1, 130. The *Harvard Graduates* sketch mentions that he "married again, but to whom is not known." The second marriage ended in divorce. In a petition presented to the Hartford County Superior Court, Lovett wrote that had married Eleanor Bugbee of Woodstock on February 6, 1739/40. She deserted him on February 20, 1742/3 and "hath ever since continued Willfully to absent herself from & totally Neglect all her Dutys of her Marryage covenant." The court granted the petition in September 1746. Early Records, CSC, Vol. 12, 47, 98.

[30] Perkins, *Connecticut Farm*, 27; William Worthington to Joseph Lovit, CLR, October 25, 1733, III, 260. He purchased two other lots in Colchester, one of which he sold back to the original owner. Daniel Brown to Joseph Lovett, CLR, September 24, 1736, III, 403; Joseph Lovett to Daniel Brown, CLR November 27, 1739, V, 215-16; Joseph Wright to Joseph Lovet, CLR, October 28, 1749, VI, 332.

[31] CA, Ecclesiastical Affairs, Series 1, V, 238. The lister was Jabez Jones and society clerk Pelatiah Bliss.

their agent Israel Newton noted that a "Land Tax" had expired in October 1737 and that due to costs for building their meetinghouse, settling a minister, and paying his salary, "which Burthen should have been Insupportable without the Benefit of the Tax aforesaid." They had great difficulty in supporting the minister because "two thirds of the Land in said Parish belongs to Non resident Prop[rietor]s Gentlem[e]n of great Wealth & fortune [living] in other Governments the Value of whose Lands has been vastly advanced by our Settlements as afors[ai]d)." They requested, therefore, in light of their low circumstances that the legislature "Grant a Land Tax of a penny p[e]r Acre on all Unimproved Lands in said Society" for four years. The General Assembly agreed and passed an act "Towards the Support of the Gospel."[32] The bulk of the population consisted of freeholders who lived in the north and west portion of the parish and the petition provides a strong indicator of how much absentee landownership proved to be a drag upon development because tenants were far fewer in number than were permanent residents.

Another effort to tax unimproved lands occurred in 1743. The society meeting voted on April 25, 1743 to appoint George Holmes agent to petition the legislature "to have our unimproved Lands Taxed at one half-penny pr Acre." Holmes noted that in 1739 the General Assembly had authorized the collection of a tax of one penny per acre on unimproved lands and urged a renewal of this provision at the lower rate of a half penny per acre. That body responded favorably and appointed Holmes to collect this tax "on all unimproved lands" in the parish for the next four years.[33] In a remonstrance dated October 10, 1743, Katherine Browne, widow of Samuel Browne the younger and mother of six-year old William Browne, argued that the unimproved lands in the society had twice previously been taxed to support the gospel ministry, that Colonel Samuel Browne had donated twenty-six acres to support the church, and helped pay for the construction and furnishing of a house for the minister. The levy enacted by the legislature was too burdensome to be paid by the estate of the minor who now owned the lands. In response, the General Assembly abated one half of the tax rate on unimproved lands in the parish.[34]

A discouraged Joseph Lovett resigned his pastorate in 1744 and removed around a decade later to New London and the society could not find anyone to replace him.[35] Perhaps the desertion of his second wife a year earlier had an impact on this decision. If this personal problem was not serious enough, however, the Great Awakening wreaked havoc on the small parish. The Reverend Jonathan Parsons of the First Society in Lyme, a controversial proponent of the revival of religion, "preached for Mr. Lovett of New Salem, at his desire" in June of 1741 or 1742 and was followed by lay exhorters.[36] The

---

32 Ibid, V, 238-40.

33 Ibid, IX, 208, 210; *Colony Records*, VIII, 533.

34 CA, Ecclesiastical Archives, Series I, IX, 211; *Colony Records*, VIII, 566.

35 Lovett remained in New Salem until at least 1752 and had moved to New London by 1755. Although he never permanently filled another pulpit, Lovett continued to preach and evidence exists that he did so in both the Lyme First and Second Societies. *Joseph Lovett v. Samuel Tubbs*, NLCC, Files, June 1752, Box 94, folder 5, no docket; *Joseph Lovett v. Thomas Manwaring*, NLCC, PbyS: Executions, 1755, Box 42, folder 8; *Joseph Lovett v. Moses Noyes* et al, NLCC, Files, February 1769, Box 148, folder 11, no docket; *Joseph Lovett v. Benjamin Lee et al*, Ibid, February 1770, Box 153, folder 11, no. 225.

36 Joseph Tracy, *The Great Awakening: A History of the Revival of Religion in the Time of Edwards and White-*

parish became overrun with religious dissenters, a not illogical occurrence as Baptists and Separatists who did not depend on an educated clergy or expect public support for their preaching found strong support among those who lived far away from town centers and were generally less wealthy than those living in more established regions.[37] Religious dissent spread rapidly in the society during the Great Awakening, as it did in many New England communities.[38]

New Salem's difficulties had begun during "the time the Great Religious Commotion prevailed," according to a deposition made by Colonel Elias Worthington of Colchester on May 12, 1792.[39] Until 1742, "good harmony & agreement Subsisted between the Minister & people there."[40] At that time, Jabez Jones, Sr., who lived in northwest corner of the society, became head of a faction that "opposed Mr. Lovett" and he accused the pastor of being "an unconverted man."[41] Soon Jones began holding Separate meetings in his house and his exhortations "so inflamed the minds of the people against Mr. Lovett that he sought for & obtained a Dismission." Jones continued to preach in his own home until a group of New Light radicals from Colchester joined them and they built a Separate meetinghouse with him as pastor. Zebulon Waterman, brother-in-law of Jones, led a second schism. He "separated from the Church & Congregation in the Old Society in Colchester," became a Baptist, and was ordained minister over a church that was constructed in the eastern part of New Salem Parish. The two of them maintained the only preaching in the society after the resignation of the Reverend Joseph Lovett.[42]

Concern about dissenters first found expression in a May 14, 1747 memorial to the General Assembly by Thomas Gustin on behalf of the society. He stated that the total for New Salem's taxable estates stood at £4,140 in depreciated paper currency. Of that total, Baptist estates amounted to £1,005 and those of New Lights who had separated from the established church another £640. This left estates worth just £2,506 "of which Residue also a very Considerable Proportion are but Tenants."[43] Gustin sought

---

field (Boston: Tappan and Dennet, 1842), 152-53; William G. McLoughlin, *Isaac Backus and the American Pietistic Tradition* (Boston: Little, Brown and Company, 1967), 32.

37 Separatists or Separate Congregationalists were people who left (separated from) established Congregational churches due to the feeling that their ministers were unregenerate, disputes about the propriety of infant baptism, and a greater openness to adult baptism by immersion. Separatism became especially strong in New London County.

38 Charles C. Goen, *Revivalism and Separatism in New England, 1740-1800* (Middletown, CT: Wesleyan University Press, 1962, 1987).

39 Worthington's statement is not correct in all details, particularly with regard to dates, but he provides important information on what happened in New Salem between 1740 and 1790.

40 Only three dissenters lived in the parish; Josiah Gates, Jonathan Rathbun, and James Welch "who professed themselves of the Baptist or Quaker order."

41 Jabez Jones, son of Thomas Jones, lived in the Thomas Jones house in the extreme northwest corner of New Salem Society. See Map 1, page 68.

42 William G. McLoughlin, *The Baptists and the Separation of Church and State*, Vol. 2 (Cambridge, MA: Harvard University Press, 1971), 953; CA, Ecclesiastical Affairs, Series 2, I, 128. Two Separatists, later Baptists, Isaac Backus and Jedidiah Hide, preached in Colchester and Lyme in 1747. McLoughlin, *Isaac Backus*, 32.

43 CA, Ecclesiastical Archives, Series 1, IX, 215.

relief from the legislature, but it took no action.

One year later came a petition signed by twenty-three men who emphasized that since the Reverend Mr. Lovett had left four years earlier, they had been "Destitute of a minister" and this had led to "great profanation of the Sabbath."[44] They had attempted in vain to hire a new "Orthodox" minister in large measure due to "Differing Sentiments in matters of Religion" and prayed that the General Assembly would help them in their time of need.[45] In response, the legislature passed an act in May 1748 granting the memorialists the right and any others who wished to join them, but no others, permission "to call and settle an orthodox minister among them." The Assembly also granted the memorialists the right to tax the unimproved lands in the parish for the next four years and exempted them from paying "Any Publick Tax to this Government" for four years "provided they Call and Continue a Minister among them."[46]

The next act in the saga took place in May 1750, when Charles Bulkley, agent for the society, sent a memorial to the Assembly in which he made reference to the Dixon et al petition of May 1748 and averred that the "Inhabitants have Obtained a Worthy orthodox young Gentlemen to Preach" the gospel to them, but that New Salem was still unable to formally settle a minister.[47] He prayed on behalf of the parish that it be enabled to collect the taxes authorized by the act of 1748 and that Simon Tubbs be collector of these rates. The legislature negatived the petition.[48] Another memorial by new agent Thomas Gustin on October 10, 1750 stated that the parish had preaching since April 1749, although it was still unable to formally settle a minister, and had begun to assess a tax in 1749, one that "Some of the Proprietors" disputed. They concluded by requesting that the Assembly authorize the collection of taxes as per the 1748 legislation and it responded by passing another act decreeing that the May 1748 taxes be "laid, Assessed, and Collected" on unimproved lands.[49]

Collector George Holmes then asked the General Assembly in May 1751 for permission to tax the lands of nonresident proprietors.[50] This proposal prompted Epes and Katherine Sargent, step-father and mother of William Browne, to send a four-page petition to the General Assembly on May 6, 1751 asking for a redress of grievances. This memorial provides an excellent overview of the deplorable religious conditions in New Salem at mid-century. The Sargents discussed at considerable length the 1748 petition

---

[44] Signers of the memorial: John Dixon, Elnathan Palmeter, William Carr, Benjamin Lothrop, Solomon Wickwire, John Holmes, Thomas Gustin, George Dolbeare, William Dixon, Ebenezer Palmeter, William Chapman, Clement Daniels, Elijah Staples, Thomas Gustin Jr., Thomas Tozer, Robert Staples, Simon Tubbs, Thomas Collett, Jonas Hamilton, George Holmes, William Dodge, Jonathan Hungerford, and Samuel Dodge. This list likely consisted of all the male adherents to traditional Congregationalism in the parish.

[45] CA, Ecclesiastical Archives, Series 1, IX, 216.

[46] Ibid, I, IX, 217; *Colony Records*, IX, 371-72. The memorialists wanted to tax unimproved lands at the rate of two pence per acre, but the legislature reduced that amount to one pence.

[47] Perhaps Simon Ely of Lyme who was licensed to preach by the New London Association on June 3, 1746. New London Association, 124-25.

[48] CA, Ecclesiastical Archives, Series 1, IX, 218.

[49] Ibid, IX, 219-20; *Colony Records,* IX, 577.

[50] CA, Ecclesiastical Archives, Series 1, IX, 222.

of John Dixon, Elnathan Palmeter, and twenty-one others to settle a minister and levy taxes on the themselves plus any others who "enter their Names with the Clerk" of the Society, one that the legislature had granted. In addition, it granted them permission to tax "the unimproved Lands in sd. Parish for the space of 4 Years." The parish hired a minister to preach at the rate £3-10 per Sabbath, but were not "yet able to setle a Minister amongst them." The society meeting took advantage of the fact that it had hired a minister to preach among them, although they had not settled one, to lay a tax on the unimproved lands in the parish, a tax that was suspended due to the opposition of the "Proprietors," but the legislature the last October renewed the taxation provision. The Sargents argued that these measures were "obtained by Surprise" and doubted not that they would be set aside once the legislature knew the true situation. Further, they related that Colonel Samuel Browne had given the inhabitants of New Salem £50 to help them in settling a minister, had promised another £30 per year to help pay a minister, rented a house for him, and donated thirty acres of land near the meetinghouse for support of the church.[51] They further affirmed that on two previous occasions taxes had been levied on unimproved lands.

The grand list of New Salem Parish, continued the Sargents, amounted to around £5,000 and the number of householders about seventy-eight, of which John Dixon, Elnathan Palmeter, and their supporters numbered just twenty-six. Their list of polls and ratable estates totaled just £1,274, only half of them were "Freeholders," and their "List doth not amount to £700." A tax on the unimproved lands of absentee proprietors they claimed would yield about £170. The present pastor earned £3-10 per "Sabbath" or £180 per year. The design of Dixon and the others, therefore, was "only to collect the Taxes on the unimproved Lands of the Nonresident Proprietors, which will be near enough to pay the Hire of the Minister."[52] How, then, could the General Assembly allow such a miscarriage of justice as a "Tax to be Levy'd on the unimproved Lands of sd. William Browne, Orphan?"

They specifically requested that the Assembly appoint a committee to go to New Salem Society, "view ye Circumstances thereof," and report back to the next session of the legislature. The Assembly postponed consideration of the memorial until October 1751.[53] At that time and as a temporary expedient, the Assembly gave permission for Holmes to collect the tax on unimproved lands "for the first of said four years only."[54] In addition, the legislature appointed Jonathan Trumbull of Lebanon and Hezekiah Huntington of Norwich a committee to go to New Salem to consider the matters brought up by the memorials of the Sargents and George Holmes[55] No report was ever issued and the following May the Assembly refused a request from Holmes that the recalcitrant non-resident proprietors be required to pay their back taxes.

On May 26, 1752 former minister Joseph Lovett reported that the parish was in a state of total disarray because "there is four societys in sd parish and there is four

---

51 Twenty acres.

52 The Sargents further charged that only six to eight persons attended parish meetings.

53 CA, Ecclesiastical Affairs, Series 1, IX, 221.

54 Ibid, IX, 223; *Colony Records*, X, 63-64.

55 CA, Ecclesiastical Affairs, Series 1, IX, 221, 224.

ministers or persons that preach Every Sabbath."[56] Religious order in the society had totally collapsed.[57] Still, the situation in New Salem likely would not have been so dire had not such a large proportion of its lands been controlled by absentees. If the parish had not been so burdened by unoccupied lands owned by nonresidents, the population would have grown much more rapidly and, with a larger tax base, it would have been in a better position to support and maintain regular orthodox preaching.

The long and depressing tale of New Salem's difficulties in securing and main-taining orthodox preaching is instructive. The population of the parish was too sparse to maintain a settled minister and it lacked the tax base to pay the costs of settlement and to properly compensate him. The rapid expansion of religious dissent, the result of the turmoils produced by the Great Awakening, made matters worse and its spread demonstrates the desire of ordinary men and women to hear the word of God preached on a regular basis among them. Congregational Separatists and Baptists did not require that their ministers be college educated snobs who often looked down their noses at their ill-educated flock. Elders of dissenting congregations may not have been had col-lege degrees, but they made up for their lack of formal religious training by their zeal to preach the Gospel and their insistence that they be supported solely by believers rather than all taxpayers as in established church parishes. They were cheaper and often provid-ed a better level of preaching than generally given by the educated clergy.[58] A win, win situation for ordinary inhabitants.

*****

Colonel Samuel Browne supported established religion in New Salem both out of conviction and as a way to encourage settlement in the wilderness, not dissimilar to the ways that good schools and low taxes encourage people to move into communi-ties today. Nevertheless, with his extensive mercantile and political interests and living in another colony, he had relatively little direct contact with his holdings in southeast Connecticut. He made at least one trip to his property in May 1722 when he signed a petition asking that the area be added to New London's North Society.[59] Browne offered

---

[56] Ibid, IX, 256. New Salem Society remained without a permanent minister until the parish was reorganized in 1813. *Ecclesiastical History*, 401-02, 472. David Huntington who became minister in Lyme North Parish in 1792 preached in New Salem during the 1780s. He was admitted to the Colchester freeman's rolls in 1788. Colchester BMD, Vol. 2, 1751-1894, 351, CTH.

[57] New Salem represents the worst-case scenario of religious orthodoxy torn asunder in the wake of the Great Awakening, although other towns like Lyme also experienced the rapid growth of religious dissent and the concomitant decline of the established church. Goen, *Revivalism and Separatism in New England*, 78-79; Franklin Bowditch Dexter, ed., *Extracts from the Itineraries and Other Miscellanies of Ezra Stiles, D.D., LL.D. 1755-1794 with a Selection from his Correspondence* (New Haven: Yale University Press, 1916), 266-67. In his one comment on New Salem, Stiles wrote that "New Salem Parish made about 1726, partly out of Lyme & part Colchester. Rev. Joseph Lovet ord[ained] 1729 or 1730, dism[issed] about 1745, no Pastor since; all became Bapt[ist] but four." Stiles, Ibid, 311.

[58] For an excellent overview of the growth of religious dissent in Connecticut, see, Charles C. Goen, *Revival-ism and Separatism in New England, 1740-1800*. Discussions of events in Colchester and Lyme can be found on pages 6, 22, 60, 77-78, 84, 101, 169, 302-04.

[59] CA, Ecclesiastical Affairs, Series 1, III, 131.

to donate £50 to help build the meetinghouse in 1725 and four years later he purchased a narrow twenty-acre strip bordering on the south at the Lyme border from James Harris for £50 that he donated to the parish for the use of the ministry.[60] This concern to promote religion, however, represented only a small part of his goal to develop his properties so that they could be rented and provide income.

He acted to improve his estate through agents like James Harris and Captain Samuel Gilbert. We do not have a great deal of evidence on the extent of his efforts, but some hints remain. After his first purchase of 4,000 acres of wilderness, rocks, and trees from Harris in 1718, Gilbert hired house-wright Daniel Galusha to build a house near the country road from New London to Colchester.[61] In January 1723/4, Colonel Browne signed a contract with Ephraim Tiffany of Lyme by which in return for £100 in New England paper money he agreed to "subdue" at least sixty acres, build a house, and dig a well within seven years on part of the 2,865 acre tract that Browne had recently purchased from Harris.[62] By 1729, at least three houses and a saw mill had been constructed for Colonel Browne in South Salem, e.g. the Lyme portion of New Salem Society, the work superintended by Samuel Gilbert.[63]

Browne lived more than one hundred miles from New Salem and made only rare trips to examine his Connecticut lands. Several agents or overseers over the years managed them and we know most of their names, although their terms of service cannot be determined with any precision. The total number from the 1720s until Colonel Samuel Browne's grandson fled Massachusetts with the British evacuation of Boston in March 1776 was probably eight, six prior to the arrival of John Mumford, Sr. in 1759. The men in the approximate order of their service to the absentees were Samuel Gilbert, James Harris, Jeremiah Chapman, Jr., Samuel Chapman, Jr., Stephen Gardner, and Lebbeus Harris. Jeremiah Chapman, Jr. filled the role at the end of the 1730s.[64] Stephen Gardner held the position in the late 1740s and early 1750s and Lebbeus Harris succeeded him.[65]

---

[60] Perkins, *Connecticut Farm*, 29, 195.

[61] Perkins, *Connecticut Farm*, 48. In November 1731, Galusha sued the estate of Samuel Browne for £100 damages asserting that on March 6, 1718/9 he covenanted with Browne to build a house and barn after receiving a loan of £100 on his property. He had constructed both at a cost of £180-01-06 and was, therefore, owed the difference. The suit was withdrawn. This may have been the dwelling occupied by several of his overseers. *Daniel Galusiah v. Estate of Samuel Brown*, NLCC, Files, November 1731, Box 33, folder 13, no. 50.

[62] Ephraim Tifeny [sic] to Colon[e]l Brown, LLR, January 21, 1723/4, V, 257; Perkins, *Connecticut Farm*, 47. The deed was called an indenture and, as surety to ensure completion on schedule, Tiffany mortgaged his 324-acre farm in "Joshua Town" in Lyme to Browne.

[63] George N. Bates, "History of Salem, Connecticut" (unpublished manuscript, 1935), 7-8, CSL.

[64] When Chapman was called to testify in a debt dispute between Matthew Stewart and Gilbert Melilly, he wrote on September 13, 1739 that he was "obliged to Settle Some Affairs this day Between Mr. Samll Brown and Severall of his Tenants So that I cannot Possibly come down and give my Evidence." *Matthew Stewart v. Gilbert Melilly*. NLSC, Files, Box 15, folder 10, no. 13, CSL.

[65] Perkins, *Connecticut Farm*, 48-51; NLCC, PbyS: Travel, Box 539. Fragmentary evidence for Hartford County tavern keepers' licenses shows that Gardner operated an inn for "paugwonk" from around 1749-52 and Harris for the years 1755-59. The evidence from court records reveals that Lebbeus moved from New London to Colchester in the early 1750s. *Lebeus Harris v. James Brown*, NLCC, Files, June 1748, Box 85, folder 6, no docket; *Lebeus Harris v. James Wentworth*, NLCC, Trials, August 1752, Vol. 21, no. 74.

Not a great deal of other information exists on the development of the Browne New Salem lands. A handful of the properties he acquired had already been at least partially cleared and had houses on them and these could immediately be rented. As previously mentioned, the Colonel purchased 635 acres in Colchester from William Gardiner in 1724 that contained "houses, barns, orchards, &c"; 300 acres in 1728 from Samuel Peck of Lyme with a small house; a James Harris property in 1729 that contained 526 acres in Lyme with a small house a sawmill and 100 acres in Colchester with two small dwellings, a barn, and smith shop; and forty acres from Robert Staples, the "farm which I now live on."[66] Thus, by the time of his death, Browne had at least a half dozen properties that could be rented and the likelihood exists that the number was higher because court records, in particular cases of debt by bond, provide some indication of further efforts to develop his properties, although they typically offered no specific information.[67] As can be seen from Table 5, Tenants in 1774 and Chapter 10, many of those who leased farms were required not only to pay rent, but also to make improvements on their farms so that the rent could be increased for the next tenant.

The records of the New London and Hartford County Courts include a number of suits for debts by bond, some for loans that were not repaid and others from renters who failed to fulfill the conditions of their leases. Normally the bond was for twice the amount of the money borrowed or the value of the service to be performed. The New London County Court heard its first case involving the Salem land baron in November 1719 when Colonel Browne sued James Harris in a debt by bond of March 13, 1718 for the defendant's failure "to Execute a Deede of mortgage and Record ye same." Harris confessed judgment and agreed to pay Colonel Browne £212 principal and interest together with costs of suit.[68] In a second loan secured by bond, Ephraim Tiffany of Lyme borrowed "Sixty pounds in Currant money of New England" on September 6, 1725 to be repaid in one year plus six percent interest.[69] By the time the New London County Court heard the case in June 1734, both of the original parties had died and the court determined that the heirs of the defendant still owed £31-10 plus court costs.[70]

The first bond involving the lease of a farm is dated March 4, 1718/9 and was between Daniel Galusha and Samuel Gilbert on one part and Samuel Browne on the other.[71] The New London County Court heard the case in November 1730. Colonel

---

[66] William Gardiner to Samuel Brown, CLR, October 30, 1724, II, 533-34; Samuel Peck to Samuel Brown, October, LLR, March 24, 1728, IV, 299; James Harris to Samuel Brown, LLR, August 25, 1728, IV, 336; Robert Stapels to Samuel Brown, March 11, 1729, CLR, III, 31.

[67] Bonds were common legal devices by which one party promised to perform a service or deliver a good within a specified time period and the surety was secured by a bond.

[68] *Samuel Brown v. James Harris*, NLCC, Files, November 1719, Box 15, folder 6, no. 78; *Samuel Brown v. James Harris*, NLCC, Trials, November 1719, Vol. 11, 206.

[69] James Harris and James Treadway witnessed the bond and the following January Harris turned over the bills of credit to Tiffany and promised to bring Browne his receipt.

[70] *Samuel Brown and William Brown v. Caleb Bennit, Bethiah Bennit, and Samuel Tiffany*, NLCC, Files, Box 40, folder 1, no. 153.

[71] As already noted, not all bond debts involving the Browne family concerned leases. For example, in February 1727/8 the New London County Court tried a case between Browne and Samuel Gilbert of Lyme for a debt by bond for £50. The defendant had borrowed £25 from Browne on October 27, 1719 on the promise

Browne sued for £300 damages for the failure of the defendants to fulfill the terms of their lease of 300 acres in Lyme. The court found the defendants guilty, they appealed to the Superior Court, and the court dismissed the case because the plaintiff was deceased and "this action cannot proceed."[72] In another example of a bond for a lease, Katherine Browne, widow of Samuel Browne the younger, sued Jonathan Read of Lyme and John Read of Norwich. The defendants had leased a farm with a house in Lyme for seven years from Colonel Samuel Browne on October 27, 1731 and had failed to pay the agreed upon rent, so one brother was brought to court in 1744. The widow collected £77-13.[73]

Samuel Browne was not the only absentee to rent lands in New Salem. Records exist for two 1729 leases by Colonel Thomas Fitch to Thomas Gustin and Daniel Galusha. Gustin rented 187 acres for eight years for which Fitch paid him £100. In return, Gustin promised to bring twenty-four acres "of unbroken upland to English grass, to fence in and plant 3 acres of good ap[p]le trees," plus keep twenty goats on the land and turn over half of the increase to Fitch and within eight months "to erect a dwelling house, and barn, and to dig and stone a seller [sic] under half of said house." Fitch leased Galusha 200 acres under similar conditions.[74] Another who rented farms was George Dolbeare of New London, son of John Dolbeare. In June 1765, he sued David Dodge of Colchester for £200 for his failure to pay rent for seven years on a 500-acre farm situated both in Lyme and Colchester.[75]

Although the Browne family did not bring slaves to New Salem before 1759, slavery existed in the region prior to that time. Captain Samuel Gilbert purchased a "negro man Named Peter" from Gilbert Bant of Boston in September 1723 and deeded him to his son Daniel "after my Decease and his mother's" on February 20, 1732/3 six months before his death.[76] James Harris acquired six slaves and an Indian servant from Major John Merrett in 1726 and it is likely that some of them worked on his Colchester farm before he sold it to Browne in 1729. Still, since most of the first tenants lacked the resources to purchase their own farms, it is unlikely that slaves worked to tame and farm the lands while Colonel Samuel and his son controlled the property.

New Salem Society lost its chief benefactor when Colonel Samuel Browne died in May 1731. His oldest son Samuel inherited his southeast Connecticut lands and replaced his father as the wealthiest man in Salem. Samuel, Jr. (1708-1742) and

to repay the sum plus interest the following year. The defendant confessed judgment and paid the plaintiff £34-7-10 plus court costs of £1-2-0. *Samuel Brown v. Samuel Gilbert*, NLCC, Files, February 1727/8, Box 27, folder 2, no. 54. For another similar case, see *Sam[ue]ll Brown. v. Samuel Gilbert*, Ibid, February 1727/8, Box 27, folder 2, no. 55. Harris served as agent for Browne to collect these and other debts during the 1720s.

72 *Samuel Brown v. Daniel Galusiah and Samuel Gilbert*, NLCC, Files, November 1730, Box 32, folder 19, no. 8; *Samuel Brown v. Daniel Galusiah and Samuel Gilbert*, NLSC, Files, September 1731, Box 10, folder 16, no. 9. The records are unclear whether the lawsuit was caused by a failure to pay rent and/or to make improvements to the property.

73 *Katherine Brown v. John Read*, NLCC, Files, November 1744, Box 78, folder 7, no. 1. For a transcript of this case, see Appendix V: Tenant Contracts.

74 Perkins, *Connecticut Farm*, 54.

75 *George Dolbear v. David Dodge*, NLCC, Files, June 1765, Box 138, folder 9, no docket.

76 Brainard et al, *The Gilbert Family*, 79-80.

his brother William (1709-1763) graduated from Harvard in 1727. Samuel, Jr. suffered from poor health throughout his short life. The Harvard Corporation, no doubt eager to show its respect for the generous family, released him from all "Errands" first year students were obliged to engage in due to a "bodily Infirmity which disables him." He married Katherine Winthrop (1711-1781) of New London in 1732.[77] In addition to suffering from poor health, he was considered to be an indolent wastrel who squandered much of the personal property he inherited.[78]

The second Samuel, unlike his father, brother William, and son left relatively few historical traces.[79] He suffered the total loss of one vessel and gradually withdrew from mercantile pursuits.[80] He died on November 26, 1742 leaving a wife and minor children Abigail and William. His estate was appraised at £21,000 and contained some 104,000 acres of land, much of it entailed, but no shipping. The inventory listed all his Connecticut lands and from whom they were purchased. The total amounted to 9,642 and one-half acres.[81]

Younger brother William followed the family tradition of engaging in foreign trade and holding high public office, although not on a continuous basis like his father and grandfather. He devoted much more of his life to pleasure. Browne served in the Massachusetts House in 1739, three terms in the Council in 1740-41 and 1744-46, and was appointed a justice of the peace on March 1, 1743/4. He enjoyed society, built a mansion in what is now Beverly, and entertained lavishly. Scottish born Dr. Alexander Hamilton visited William on July 30, 1744. Hamilton described the unfinished mansion Browne was constructing and thought him "narrow and avaricious" with "a strange taste for theologicall controversy."[82] A second visitor in October 1750, Captain Francis

---

[77] Her father John Winthrop who had moved to London 1726, never met his son-in-law, but disliked him anyway. This characterization should not be given much value since Winthrop was a man who combined ancestral pride with incompetence. Mayo, *Winthrop Family*, 130, 156; *Sibley's Harvard Graduates*, IV, 537, 546.

[78] Loring, "Manuscript of the Late Col. Benj. Pickman," 94; Morris, "Social Change," 421. Pickman wrote in 1793 that Samuel, Jr. "was concerned in mercantile affairs, but his indolence preventing his giving much attention to business, most of his personal property was spent."

[79] His name infrequently appeared in public prints. In one known April 1735 reference, Browne is found among a long list of merchants who affirmed that they would no longer "accept bills of credit for payment of bills." Among others on the same list were James Bowdoin, John Dolbeare, Thomas Fitch, Eliakim Hutchinson, and Joseph Prince. [Boston] *Weekly Rehearsal*, April 14, 1735, [2]. Seven years later and two months before death, Governor William Burnet "breakfasted at *Samuel Browne's* Esq: at *Salem*" after having stayed the previous night at the house of his uncle. *Boston Post-Boy*, September 13, 1742, [3]. For other newspaper references, see the *Boston Post-Boy*, March 29, 1736, [3]; *New-England Weekly Journal*, January 20, 1741, [2].

[80] Benjamin Lynde, Jr. noted in a diary entry for March 16, 1733 the "news of the Spaniard's taking Mr. Browne's ship and Capt. B. Browne's brig; ship new and cost about £7000, and brig, 2500, also two brigs of Boston." *Lynde Diaries*, 138. Captain, later colonel, Benjamin Browne, was Samuel Browne's, Jr.'s first cousin, as was Benjamin Lynde, Jr.

[81] Samuel Browne, 1742, Essex Probate Records, Vol. 325, 448-55, MSA; *Sibley's Harvard Graduates*, VIII, 118-19; Morris, "Social Change," 421-22. Despite his wealth, his lack of any political status was demonstrated by the fact that Boston newspapers printed no obituary, merely a short death notice. "And last Friday died at Salem, Samuel Browne, Esq;." *Boston News-Letter*, December 2, 1742, [2].

[82] *Sibley's Harvard Graduates*, VIII, 120-24; Whitmore, *Massachusetts Civil List*, 57, 133; *Boston News-Letter*, May 29, 1740, [1]; Carl Bridenbaugh, ed., *Gentleman's Progress: The Itinerarium of Dr. Alexander Hamilton 1744* (Pittsburgh: University of Pittsburgh Press, 1948), 120-21.

Goelet, had a more favorable impression. He called on Browne, stayed for tea, walked around town with him, climbed the tower of St. Peter's church to view Browne's new dwelling then in construction in Beverly in the shape of a block letter H with wings eighty feet long, dined with him, and rode with him to visit his new country house. The third William is the best known for the building of his "pleasure palace" in Beverly.[83]

Another Browne who took the mantle of political leadership after the death of the colonel in 1731 was Samuel, Jr.'s cousin Benjamin Browne (1706-1750). Placed at the head of the Harvard class of 1725, the trader married the Eunice Turner, thus uniting the two wealthiest mercantile families in Salem, and, like his uncle, held a number of offices of trust.[84]

The second Samuel traveled to New London on at least three occasions, the first time when he visited Madame Ann Winthrop. She gave a barbecue in the young man's honor in December 1731 when he was wooing her daughter; the second time in the spring of 1732 when he married Katherine Winthrop; and a third occasion in September and October 1739, an extensive stay with his mother-in-law.[85] During the 1739 visit, diarist Joshua Hempstead accompanied "Mad[a]m Winthrop, Mr Saltonstall & his wife & 2 Children, Colln Brown & his wife & Child" on a day sail to Fishers Island."[86] Browne likely made a quick trip to his New Salem lands because on October

---

83 "A Stately Pleasure-House," *EIHC*, XXXI (August-December 1894), 205-12; Browne, "Youthful Recollections of Salem," 9.

An early newspaper reference to the second son occurred in May 1738 when a Boston weekly reported from Salem that "one day last Week William Browne, Esq; of that Place, with his Lady, a Daughter of his late Excellency Governour Burnet, arrived there in prefect [sic] Health from *New-York*." Mary died of consumption on August 1, 1745 at age twenty-two. Some three years later he married Mary French of New Brunswick, New Jersey. The second Mary died on August 10, 1761 at their home in Beverly and was "interred in the Family Vault in Salem" three days later. By his two wives, he had nine children, most of whom died young and only William Burnet Browne, married. *Boston Evening-Post*, November 11, 1737, [2] May 8,1738, [2]; August 17, 1761, [3]; *Lynde Diaries*, 152, 165-66; [Perley], "Descendants of William Browne," 159-62.

Other references to the third William included a 1738 advertisement for the return of his runaway servant called Maximus, "a short Negro fellow . . . who can play Well upon a Violin." Upon the 1743 victory of British and allied forces over the French at the Battle of Dettigen, a celebration attended by a "Number of the Principal Gentlemen of the Town met at the Hon. William Brown Esq., (whose house was illuminated)," where they toasted the royal family, the English and Austrian generals, and the "Victories" of "the Army of the Allies." When the royal governor traveled to Salem in September 1742, he stayed overnight with William Browne and in December 1745 he signed a letter of appreciation to General William Pepperell, one of the heroes of the capture of Louisbourg. He also signed a merchants' petition concerning the manning of the state ship *Province Sloop* in April 1760, advertised to rent his old home in Salem that same month, and offered a $20 reward for the return of Massachusetts Province Note No. 443 lost in the mail between New York City and Massachusetts. *Boston Evening-Post*, July 31, 1738, [2]; September 13, 1742, [2]; October 17, 1743 [3], April 7, 1760, [3]; April 14, 1760, 3]; October 20, 1760, [1].

84 The offices included selectman, service in the Massachusetts House of Representatives from 1732 to 1740, justice of the peace, judge of the quorum, militia officer, and leader of the proprietors of "New-Salem (so called)" lying in the county of Hampshire." *Sibley's Harvard Graduates*, VII, 462-63; Whitmore, *Massachusetts Civil List*, 133; *Boston Evening-Post*, September 27, 1742 [2].

85 The wedding banns were published on Sunday, March 26, 1732, they married in a private ceremony on March 28, and the nuptials celebrated by "a great Entertainment" at Madame Winthrop's on April 13, 1732. Hempstead, *Diary,* 240, 244-45, 351-53.

86 While on Fishers Island, the travelers stayed with George Mumford, a wealthy slaveowner and half-brother of John Mumford who some twenty years later was hired by Samuel's son William to take care of his New Salem properties. Perkins, *Connecticut Farm*, 76-77.

12 he purchased thirty-four acres and 110 rods in Colchester from John Dodge.[87] The Browne family left New London on October 30, 1739.[88] Samuel was the elephant in the New Salem closet, an absentee who rarely, if ever, made a personal appearance in the parish, yet controlled half of its lands.

After Samuel, Jr.'s death, his widow Katherine and her second husband Epes Sargent also evinced relatively little interest in their Connecticut lands aside from collecting rents and sending a series of petitions to the General Assembly requesting that taxes on the unimproved lands of nonresidents be abated or disallowed.

The agriculturally productive parts of New Salem were known for their wheat and tenants on the Browne and Fitch lands sent large quantities of it to Boston. A part of one farm, Lot A1 comprising some 589 acres in Lyme and purchased by William Winthrop in 1783, was called the Wheatfield Hill farm as early as 1717.[89]

Since absentees owned such a significant proportion of the land in New Salem, this situation proved to be an insuperable obstacle to normal population growth and development. As can be seen from Map 1, about two thirds of New Salem was owned by absentees Samuel Browne, Thomas Fitch, and John Dolbeare. And, not all absentees controlled large quantities of land. Joshua Hempstead, the New London diarist, for example, owned some 245 acres in three lots in Colchester north of the Fitch lands that he rented to tenants.[90] Many tenants were required to improve the lands during the terms of their leases, but renters did not have the incentive to make the improvements that homeowners had and New Salem permanently suffered the results from this lack of investment.

The three societies in Lyme and two in Colchester grew rapidly, a clear contrast to the situation in New Salem where absentee landownership provided an unfortunate counterpoint to the neighboring parishes.

87 Ibid, 352; John Dodge to Samuel Brown, CLR, October 12, 1739. IV, 78. New Salem residents Palatiah Bliss and Samuel Tubbs witnessed the deed. He offered £90, but failed to pay for the property, so the inventory of his estate did not include it. Stark, "Myth and Reality," 175 n34.

88 Hempstead, *Diary*, 353.

89 William S. Bartlet, *The Frontier Missionary: A Memoir of the Live of the Rev. Jacob Bailey, A. M.* . . . (Boston: Ide and Dutton, 1853), 25; Perkins, *Connecticut Farm*, 56, 203-04.

90 Patricia M. Schaefer, *A Useful Friend: A Companion to the Joshua Hempstead Diary, 1711-1758* (New London: New London County Historical Society, 2008), 75, 78; Bates, "History of Salem, Connecticut," 12; Affidavit of Elijah Backus, Jr., June 29, 1786, AmLC, AOP, AO 13/50, NAUK.

Chapter 6

Slavery in Eastern Connecticut

William Browne, the third owner of the New Salem lands, brought slaves to his absentee estate. He did not do so in a vacuum because slavery had long existed in southeastern Connecticut, the rest of New England, and the Americas as a whole, but it needs to be emphasized that the northern American colonies were a society with slaves and not a slave society as were the southern colonies.[1]

No certainty exists as to when slavery came to Connecticut because we cannot know for certain that the first Negroes in the colony were enslaved. Standard sources state that Negro slaves could be found in New Haven as early as 1644 and Hartford by 1653.[2] One of the first persons in the region with servants who may or may not have been slaves was Walter Harris of New London. The inventory of his estate taken in April 1656 listed "one negro" valued at 8 shillings and "two Indians" at 2 shillings.[3] In 1670, the New London County Court summoned Mr. [Richard] Ely of Lyme for profaning the sabbath, together with John Sampson and his "negroe servant Moses" who were "Instrumental therin."[4] According to Governor William Leete in answer to a questionnaire sent by the British Committee for Trade and Foreign Relations dated July 15, 1680, the colony had "but fewe servants amongst us, and less slaves, not above 30, as we judge, in the Colony," a figure that at best represented only an informed estimate and almost certainly a conservative one.[5]

Political leaders grappled with the concept of perpetual servitude in the sev-

---

[1] James J. Gigantino II, *The Ragged Road to Abolition: Slavery and Freedom in New Jersey, 1775-1865* (Philadelphia: University of Pennsylvania Press, 2015), 1. Both New York and New Jersey had far stronger ties to the institution than did Connecticut. Ibid, 84-85.

[2] Lorenzo J. Greene, "Slave-Holding in New England and Its Awakening," *Journal of Negro History*, 13 (October 1928), 495; Bernard C. Steiner, "History of Slavery in Connecticut," *Johns Hopkins University Studies in Historical and Political Science* (Baltimore: The Johns Hopkins Press, 1893), 12, 23. Another historian wrote that the colony had slaves as early as 1639. Edgar J. McManus, *Black Bondage in the North* (Syracuse: Syracuse University Press, 1973), 6.

[3] Walter and Mary Harris, NLLR, April 14, 1656, III, 47-49. The higher worth of the Negro may reflect his/her status as a servant for life.

[4] NLCC, Trials, Vol. 3, 21.

[5] The inquiry of the Committee on Trade to the governor of Connecticut asked twenty-seven questions. Question 16 was as follows: "What number of Merchants and Planters, English or Foreigners, Servants and Slaves; and how many of them able to bear Armes?" *Colony Records*, III, 293, 298, 300.

enteenth century and, following the examples of legislative action in the Caribbean and southern colonies, began to pass laws concerning the status of the blacks among them. The first slaves in New England and Connecticut consisted of Native Americans captured in the Pequot War of 1636-37.[6] Some were kept as servants in the region and others were sold into slavery in the West Indies.[7] The Massachusetts General Court in its 1641 Body of Liberties passed the first legislation that allowed for the legal enslavement of Indians and Negroes, a law endorsed by the delegates of the New England Confederation two years later.[8] "There shall never be any kind of slavery, villinage, nor captivitie amongst us, unless [they] be captives taken in just warres, and such strangers as willingly sell themselves or are sold to us." The phrase "or are sold to us" is the critical one.[9]

Regulations respecting Indian servitude came from provisions passed by the New England Confederation in 1643 and 1646, ones that were repeated in the Connecticut Code of 1650 in the section relating to Indians.[10] The Code made no specific reference to slaves in its provisions for "MASTERS; SERVANTS; SOJOURNERS," although the section concerning the capture of runaways applied to servants of all races.[11] The first act passed by the General Court that specifically concerned Africans dates from May 1660 when it decided "that neith[e]r Indian nor neger serv[an]ts shalbe required to train, watch or ward, in" in the colony.[12] One scholar believes that the 1660 act may

---

[6] For a revisionist account of Indian slavery in New England, see Margaret Ellen Newell, *Brethren by Nature: New England Indians, Colonists, and the Origins of American Slavery* (Ithaca, NY: Cornell University Press, 2015. The introductory chapter provides a good overview of the author's thesis.

[7] Guocun Yang, "From Slavery to Emancipation: The African Americans of Connecticut 1630s-1820s. (Unpublished Ph.D. Dissertation, University of Connecticut, 1999), 30-31. Indian servitude in New England did not generally pass from generation to generation. The colonists rationalized enslaving Native Americans "under the doctrine of 'just war' which permitted enslavement of enemies captured in a defensive conflict." Newell, *Brethren by Nature,* 10.

[8] The New England Confederation, established in 1643, was composed of representatives from Connecticut, Massachusetts Bay, New Haven, and Plymouth colonies, primarily for the purpose of securing a joint response in dealing with what they regarded as the Indian menace. It met in Boston.

[9] Greene, *Negro in Colonial New England,* 125; Greene, "Slave-Holding in New England," 501; Winthrop D. Jordan, "The Influence of the West Indies on the Origins of New England Slavery," *WMQ,* 18 (April 1961), 244. Perhaps as early as the 1640s and definitely by the 1650s, Africans in New England were being held in servitude for life, a concept borrowed from the West Indies. Jordan, "Influence of the West Indies," 246.

[10] Ralph Foster Weld, *Slavery in Connecticut,* Tercentenary Pamphlet XXXVII (New Haven: Yale University Press, 1935), 2-3, *Colony Records,* I, 531-32. The provision concerned recaptured Indian prisoners who would either serve "or bee shipped out and exchanged for neagers."

[11] *Colony Records,* I, 538-39.

[12] Steiner, "Slavery in Connecticut," 382; Yang, "From Slavery to Emancipation," 37; *Colony Records,* I, 349. The Connecticut law was preceded by a 1639 Virginia statute that allowed all persons except Negroes to bear arms.

Steiner, Weld, and Yang provide the best overviews of the history of slavery in the colony, but a number of other works, some of a more general nature, are of considerable value. They include, Robert K. Fitts, *Inventing New England's Slave Paradise: Master/Slave Relations in Eighteenth-Century Narragansett Rhode Island* (New York: Garland Publishing Inc., 1998); William Chauncey Fowler, "The Historical Status of the Negro in Connecticut," in *Local Law in Massachusetts and Connecticut, Historically Considered* (Albany: Joel Munsel, 1872), 111-48; Gigantino, *Ragged Road to* Abolition; Greene, "Slave-holding New England," 492-533; Greene, *Negro in Colonial New England*; Leon Litwack, *North of Slavery: The Negro in the Free States, 1790-1850* (Chicago: University of Chicago Press, 1966); McManus, *Black Bondage in the North*; Edgar J. McManus, *A History*

have been prompted in part by a 1657 fire attributed to Africans that destroyed a house in Hartford, but he is in error.[13] All additional restrictive legislation enacted by the General Court between 1660 and the Glorious Revolution concerned Native Americans. Two acts of October 1669 limited the sale of lead and powder to Indians and prevented the sale of alcoholic beverages to them, while a May 1677 law passed just after King Philip's War aimed at preventing enemy Indians who had been captured or had submitted "to mercy" from running away.[14]

The colony published its second compilation of laws in 1673 and, although it had sections on "Indians" and "Masters, Servants and Sojourners," the code made no mention of slavery.[15] In October 1690, however, in order to assist the "many persons of this Colony [who] doe for their necessary use purchase negroe seruants" and these servants often ran away, the legislature passed a law which forbade the servants from "wandring out of their towne bownds or place to which they doe belong" without a ticket or pass.[16] Any servant breaking this law was to be apprehended, brought before a justice of the peace, and then returned to the owner after he paid all necessary costs.[17] Another act in May 1702 was passed in response to the situation in which purchasers of "Negro or Malatta Servants or Slaves," after "they have spent the principall part of their time and strength in their masters service" were set free without being able to care for themselves. The General Court directed, therefore, that all freed servants must be financially supported by their former masters. A follow-up law in May 1711 permitted selectmen to sue former masters if the freed people became impoverished.[18] This legislation demonstrates that some slaves were being freed by their masters at a time when the institution was becoming much more prevalent.

A 1703 act prohibited tavern keepers from selling strong drink to "apprentices, servants, or negroes."[19] Two additional laws passed in May 1708 specified the punish-

---

of Negro Slavery in New York (Syracuse: Syracuse University Press, 1966); Frederick Calvin Norton, "Negro Slavery in Connecticut," The Connecticut Magazine 5 (1899), 320-28; Bruce P. Stark, "Slavery in Connecticut: A Re-examination," Connecticut Review, 9 (November 1975), 75-81; David O. White, Connecticut's Black Soldiers 1775-1783 (Chester, CT: Pequot Press, 1973; Arthur Zilversmit, The First Emancipation: The Abolition of Slavery in the North (Chicago: University of Chicago Press, 1967).

13 Yang, "From Slavery to Emancipation," 37. An examination of the records of the Particular Court shows that on May 11, 1657 an Indian named Wigmagub confessed that he had been hired by two other Native Americans to burn down the house of a Mrs. Howell. Records of the Particular Court of Connecticut 1639-1663 (Hartford: The Connecticut Historical Society, 1928), 175.

14 Colony Records, II, 119, 271 308-09, 352.

15 The General Laws For the People of Connecticut (Cambridge, MA: Printed by Samuel Green, 1673).

16 This act provides the first evidence that the colony contained a considerably greater number of Negro servants than Governor Leete reported to the English government ten years earlier.

17 Colony Records, IV, 40. This law marked the beginning Connecticut's black code according to one scholar. Weld, Slavery in Connecticut, 9.

18 Titled "An Act for Negro and Malatta Servants to be Maintained by their Masters." Colony Records, IV, 375-76, 408. The 1711 "Act relating to Slaves, and such in particular as shall happen to become Servants for Time" specifically mentioned "negro, malatta, or Spanish Indians, who are servants to masters for time." Ibid, V, 233; Weld, Slavery in Connecticut, 10.

19 Colony Records, IV, 438.

ment of whipping for theft by "any Indian, molato or negro servant or slave" and whipping upon conviction for the striking of a white person.[20] An October 1715 law that prohibited the importation of any "Indian Servants or Slaves" had the effect of limiting slavery to Negroes.[21] This was followed by a May 1723, "Act to prevent the Disorder of Negro and Indian Servants in the Night Season," that forbade servants and slaves from leaving the places in which they dwelled after 9:00 PM. The act also prohibited these persons from entertaining anyone after the same hour. Conviction of the first misdemeanor by a justice of the peace could result in a public whipping of up to "ten stripes" and a second by the master being fined twenty shillings.[22]

All previous legislation concerning "Indian, Negro, and Molatto Servants and Slaves" was brought together and summarized in the law code of 1750, one section of which had its origins in 1702 and 1711 legislation which stipulated that "all Slaves set at Liberty by their owners" and all Negro, Mulatto, or Spanish Indians "who are Servants to Masters for Time" must be supported by their former owners if they ever fell into poverty.[23] Legislation in Connecticut respecting the status of African Americans generally followed the pattern of neighboring Massachusetts and was relatively mild in comparison to legislation passed in other colonies.[24]

Despite these restrictions upon the enslaved, their condition was far superior to that of their counterparts in the southern colonies and the West Indies and they were generally much better treated.[25] Like indentured servants and apprentices, they could sue their masters if they were unfairly treated and could testify in court. In addition, if Madame Sarah Kemble Knight in 1705 can be believed, Connecticut slaveowners were "too Indulgent . . . to their Slaves, suffering too great familiarity from them, permitting ym [them] to sit at Table and eat with them."[26] In a similar report fifty years later, Jacob Bailey noted on a trip to Lyme that the entire family he visited sat down to dinner to-

---

[20] Ibid, V, 52-53.

[21] Ibid, V, 534-35; Weld, *Slavery in Connecticut*, 3.

[22] *Colony Records*, VI, 390-91.

[23] *Acts and Laws of his Majesty's English Colony of Connecticut in New-England in America* (New-London: Timothy Green, 1750), 229-31. The 1750 code devoted more space to Indians than to slaves in sections called "An Act preventing Foreiners [sic] Trading with, and Corrupting the Indians . . ." and "An Act for Ordering and Governing the Indians in this Colony; and Securing their Interests, and Lands Therein." In addition, sections pertaining to "Masters, and Servants, or Apprentices" and preventing "Unseasonable Night Walking" applied to all persons "under the Government of Parents, Guardians, or Masters" and made no specific mention of slaves. Ibid, 79, 95-99, 152-53, 172. For a good summary of the legislation, see Greene, "Slave-holding in New England," 515-18.

[24] Robert C. Twombly and Richard H. Moore, "Black Puritan: The Negro in Seventeenth-Century Massachusetts," *WMQ*, XXIV (April 1967), 238-42; William M. Wiecek, "The Statutory Law of Slavery and Race in the Thirteen Mainland Colonies of British America, *WMQ*, XXXIV (April 1977), 258-80. Wiecek mentions Connecticut only three times in footnotes in his overview of slave laws. Ibid, 267-68, 274.

[25] For the differences between Connecticut and southern slavery, a good place to start is with the classic of Kenneth M. Stamp, *The Peculiar Institution: Slavery in the Ante-Bellum South*, although it focuses on nineteenth-century slavery.

[26] Weld, *Slavery in Connecticut*, 8-9.

gether, "both white and black."[27]

Lest one think, however, that slavery in Connecticut was entirely beneficent and tame, abuses always occur when some have complete or almost complete control over others, whether the individuals were spouses, apprentices, servants, or slaves. Perhaps the most notorious case in New London County took place in 1755 when the colony attorney prosecuted James Rogers of New London for the cruel assault on his slave Sharper for "in a forceable manner drove a Nail . . . Thro one of his Ears of . . . Sharper and Nail'd the Same fast to the Wall."[28] The jury, however, found Rogers not guilty.[29] In another case two years earlier, the same James Rogers sued Dr. Giles Goddard for the mistreatment of his Negro man Abner, age about twenty-five, who was sound and healthy except for two sores "one on his Left Elbow and the other Near his Private Part." Dr. Goddard, a "Physition and Surgeon," in April 1751 undertook to cure the Negro, but instead mangled the surgery and left Abner maimed and wounded. Rogers sued for £400 damages, but the jury found Goddard not guilty.[30]

Only four probated and inventoried estates in New London County between 1675 and 1700 noted the existence of slaves. When James Rogers of New London, grandfather of Sarah Harris, died in 1687, his substantial estate included four servants, one of whom was a slave for life.[31] The estate of John Liveen of New London inventoried in March 1690/1 listed one slave.[32] Thomas Harris, a Barbados trader, died in June 1691 and his estate was appraised a year later. The inventory of his estate was valued at £927-09-09 and listed two male Negro adults, both presumably slaves, and one male youth.[33] The wealthy New London trader Alexander Pygan died in 1700 and his estate included four slaves - a Negro man Yorke, woman Juda, Negro boy Mintus, and girl Bess.[34] By the early 18th century, then, slavery was well embedded in the New London area, although free people of color also lived in the region.[35]

---

27 Bartlet, *Frontier Missionary*, 25.

28 One indicator of the importance of the case is that the court summoned seven men to provide testimony. NLCC, PbyS, Summons for Evidence, February 11, 1755, Box 89, folder 11.

29 *Dom Rex v. James Rogers*, NLCC, Files, African Americans, February 1755, Box 2, folder 19. Called James Rogers of Great Neck, formerly James Rogers the Third.

30 *James Rogers v. Giles Goddard*, Ibid, June 1753, Box 2, folder 18. The court summoned seven men to give evidence in this lawsuit. NLCC, PbyS: Summons for Evidence, June 9, 16, 1755, Box 89, folder 9.

31 The servants were identified as an "Indian servant [William Wright] and his wife [Hagar] a Negro woman, to be free [in] about 3 years," "Adam [Rogers] a Molatos servant," and a "Negro woman deaf and dumb" [Maria], a slave for life. James Rogers, New London, 1709, NLPR, Volume A, 454-55, 463-64, microfilm, CSL; Allegra di Bonaventura, *For Adam's Sake: A Family Saga in Colonial New England* (New York: Liveright Publishing Corporation, 2013), 17-19, 34-35. *For Adam's Sake* is an outstanding study of slavery and freedom that focuses a great deal on African Americans in early Connecticut with most of the emphasis on Maria, her daughter Joan, and Joan's children with John Jackson.

32 John Liveen, New London, 1691, NLPR, Volume A, 155-58.

33 Thomas Harris, New London, 1692, NLPR, Volume A, 70-71.

34 Alexander Pygan, New London, 1700, NLPR, Volume A, 94-99.

35 Free people of color in the early eighteenth century included Robert Jacklin, John Jackson, Adam Rogers, Hagar Wright, and Samuel Wright. Barbara W. Brown and James M. Rose, *Black Roots in Southeastern Connecticut, 1650-1900* (New London: The New London County Historical Society, Inc., 2001), 196-97, 201,

No population figures for African Americans exist prior to the first official Connecticut census in 1756, yet court and probate records document their existence throughout the county. Inventories of estates list all real and personal property owned by the recently deceased, including servants and slaves.[36] Between 1701 and 1720, five New London estates listed servants or slaves.[37] The first person from Lyme with slaves in his inventory was William Ely whose 1718 estate included "one negro lad Called nero" valued at £45.[38] Slavery was much more common in urban New London than in rural Lyme. The second Lyme estate with slaves was that of John Noyes who died in 1733. His inventory included "one Negro youth called Warrick and one negro Girl called Grace."[39]

Slavery existed in Colchester almost from the time of its founding, although good documentation only dates from the 1740s. In 1745 and 1746, the estates of three men recorded slaves. The inventory of the estate of Major Asahel Newton listed servants Dave, Nero, and Cloe; that of Jonathan Kellog, Jr. an unnamed Negro man; and the one of Ebenezer Kellog a male named Cesar.[40] One more estate from the 1740s contained slaves, five from the 1750s, and seven from the 1760s. Three men left three slaves each, Major Asahel Newton, Captain John Smith, and Ichabod Lord.[41]

Court records document both the existence of slavery and the presence of free people of color in the region in the early eighteenth century.[42] The majority of court cases involving African Americans for the first four decades of the century concerned either free people of color or those whose status was contested. To cite the most conspicuous examples, Dr. Peter Tappan of Newbury, Massachusetts emancipated Robert Jacklin and he moved to New London.[43] He was a plaintiff or defendant in thirty-two lawsuits between 1718 and 1732. Free Mulatto Adam Rogers, his white wife Katherine, and their children are represented in eighteen lawsuits and the Rights/Wrights, a free family

---

349, 451.

36 Not all persons had probated estates and females were underrepresented. In addition, not all estates included inventories. It is possible, therefore, that inventories underestimated slavery in Connecticut, as age, changes in economic circumstances, and the passing on of property to heirs prior to death contributed to a situation in which the number and percentage of householders who owned slaves was likely lower among the deceased than the living.

37 Joseph Coit, Benjamin Shapley, Fitz John Winthrop, Samuel Gray, and Nicholas Hallam. NLPR, Volume A, 242-43, 349-50, 419-21, 454-55, 683-87; Volume B, 106-12.

38 William Ely, Lyme, 1718, NLPR, no. 1713. William Ely was a son of Richard Ely referred to above.

39 John Noyes, Lyme, 1733, NLPR, Volume C, 598-600. Another decade passed before the inventory of a third person from Lyme, Joseph Noyes, listed any slaves, a "Negro man servant Jube." Joseph Noyes, Lyme, 1743, NLPR, Volume E, 179-82.

40 Major Asahel Newton, Colchester, 1745, CPR, Vol. 1, 103; Jonathan Kellog, Jr., 1745. Ibid, 1745, Vol. 1, 104; Ebenezer Kellog, 1745, Ibid, Vol. 1, 144.

41 Ibid, Vol. 2, 50, 148, 184, 445; Vol. 3, 8, 24, 108, 152, 166, 198, 265, 275, 389-90.

42 New London County County Court Records and New London County Superior Court Records contain 179 records between 1701 and 1740 involving Negroes and other people of color, excluding Indians, as plaintiffs, defendants, subjects, and witnesses. People of color from New London are represented in 129 cases, Lyme 9, and Colchester 6.

43 Brown and Rose, Black Roots, 196.

of color, in seventeen. John Jackson, a free black man, his wife Joan, a slave, and their children filled court dockets with thirty-seven cases between 1701 and 1736. Most, but not all, concerned the question about the status of Joan and her children. John Jackson unsuccessfully claimed that Joan was free and a number of additional lawsuits revolved around the status of their children. If one eliminates double counts in debt lawsuits between Robert Jacklin and Sarah and Samuel Wright, 101 of 179 court records involving African Americans between 1701 and 1740 concerned these four families.[44]

The first lawsuit involving a Lyme slave was *John Rayner v. Edward Dewolf* tried by the New London County Court in November 1704. Rayner charged that Dewolf's slave Mingo threatened to kill his son Josiah and twenty-seven Lyme men signed a testimonial attesting to Mingo's good character.[45] Town and county records contain other references to slaves in the first third of the eighteenth century, for example, the marriage of Oxford Negro and Temperance "Molata" on January 12, 1725/6, both servants of Richard Lord.[46] To give an indication of the spread of slavery in southeastern Connecticut, three court cases from 1717 and 1724 provide good examples. The New London County Court heard the first in June 1717, *Jonathan Rogers v. William Rogers*, in which the New London plaintiff accused the defendant of throwing a stone through the window of his house, abusing his Negro man and his Negro woman who was riding on a horse. The "said Negro woman was flung of[f] from sd horse and being bigg with Childe [and] was in danger of Miscarrying."[47] Seven years later Andrew Morris of Lyme sued Zachariah Sill for assaulting his Negro servant.[48] The same court session heard a case in which the "Negro woman Bess," the servant of Joseph Talman of New London, was charged with being the receiver of goods stolen from the shop of Edward Robinson by a transient man called Merry. In her testimony, Bess tried to mitigate her guilt by implicating Will, the Negro man of Mr. Latimer, Christopher Sambo, and Dinah, a servant of Mr. Rogers. The court ordered Bess jailed and Will transported to a "Neighbouring Government."[49]

No way exists to know precisely the total number of those enslaved in Lyme, Colchester, or New London County in the first third of the eighteenth century. Still the evidence from a variety of sources clearly indicates that slavery was not uncommon. In terms of both number and percentage, however, far fewer slaves and free people of color lived in the region in the first third of the century than in the later period. If one can believe reports sent by Connecticut governors to the British government, only about

---

[44] During the same time period, the courts heard 165 cases that involved Indians. In the first third of the eighteenth century, then, it is likely that the Native American and African American populations in New London County were roughly equivalent.

[45] *John Rayner v. Edward Dewolf,* NLCC, Files, November 1704, Box 2, folder 14. Josiah Rayner had previously been charged with "Lascivious Carriage and behavior with a young woman." *King v. Josiah Rainer,* Ibid, June 1701, Box 1, folder, 18.

[46] LLR, IV, 170.

[47] *Jonathan Rogers v. William Rogers,* NLCC, Files, African Americans, June 1717, Box 1, folder 8.

[48] *Andrew Morris v. Zachariah Sill,* Ibid, June 1724, Box 1, folder 16.

[49] *Dom Rex v. Joseph Talman,* Ibid, June 1724, Box 1, folder 17.

30 Negro slaves lived in the colony in 1680, 700 in 1730, and 1,000 in 1749.[50] These numbers were almost certainly too low and the same is true for the estimates for whites in these returns - 39,300 in 1730 and 71,500 in 1749.[51] According to the 1756 Connecticut census, the number of white inhabitants totaled 126,976 and that for Negroes 3,019.[52] With regard to the African American population of the colony, the figures supplied to the Board of Trade by Connecticut governors almost certainly underestimated the true totals by around one third.

Colchester experienced the most dramatic increase in its number of Negroes between 1756 and 1774, the time that young William Browne brought slaves to his New Salem lands. In 1756, Colchester counted 84 Negroes, the number jumped to 154 just six years later, a figure that may have included Indians, and to 173 Negroes and 28 Indians in 1774. The Bulkleys, descendants of the first minister, were the chief slaveowners in the town. According to the 1790 Federal census, Colchester had thirty-six slaveowners with a total of sixty-four slaves. Six Bulkleys held fifteen of them.[53]

It needs to be emphasized that not all those called Negro in census records were slaves, for free people of color lived in the area almost from the beginning, but it is impossible to know their number and what percentage of the African American population they represented. Based upon the author's research, he estimates that somewhere between seven and ten percent of Negroes in the county were free, many, but not all, of mixed race. In the early part of the eighteenth century, free people of color in the New London region included the aforementioned Robert Jacklin, John Jackson, Adam Rogers, and Hagar Right/Wright. Robert Jacklin obtained his freedom in 1711, moved to New London, and purchased land in 1716. He sold it three years later, moved to Colchester, bought and sold property there, and later moved to Norwalk where he died.[54] The first Negro to buy land in New London, this action was deemed so controversial that the town's freemen protested and unsuccessfully urged the General Assembly to pass a law preventing land ownership by blacks.[55] John Jackson married Joan, a slave to James Rogers, and devoted himself to trying to gain freedom for his wife and children.[56]

---

[50] By way of contrast, Massachusetts with at least twice the population of Connecticut counted around 2,000 African Americans in 1715. Twombly and Moore, "Black Puritan," 224.

[51] Greene, *Negro in Colonial New England*, 89-91; *Colony Records*, VII, 584; IX, 596. His figures are around 38,000 for 1730 and 70,000 for 1749. A modern and more reliable estimate reckons the 1730 total at around 68,000 and the 1750 one at 113,000. Daniels, *Connecticut Town*, 46-48.

Until the first official census in 1756, all figures provided to the Board of Trade underestimated the population of the colony. The first to closely study Connecticut's population was Albert E. Van Dusen whose numbers for 1701 were 30,000, 47,500 in 1715, and 99,000 for 1749. Albert Edward Van Dusen, "The Trade of Revolutionary Connecticut" (Unpublished Ph.D. Dissertation, University of Pennsylvania, 1948), 12-14.

[52] *Colony Records*, X, 617-18.

[53] John Bulkley of Lyme had one slave. 1790 Census, 84, 91-92, 95, 123.

[54] Brown and Rose, *Black Roots*, 196-97.

[55] After he bought his New London lot, the New London Town Meeting on April 4, 1717 voted that "this Town to utterly oppose and Protest against Robart Jacklin a Negroe man's buying Land in this Town, or being any Inhabitant with Said Town." The town's representatives were instructed to ask the General Assembly to act. It did not. CA, Miscellaneous, Series 1, II, 33; Brown and Rose, *Black Roots*, 196.

[56] di Bonaventura, *For Adam's Sake*, passim. He never owned property.

Adam Rogers, originally a mulatto servant of James Rogers, married a white woman, Katherine Jones, had eleven children, nine of whom reached adulthood, but never owned any land.[57] Hagar Wright, also a servant of James Rogers, obtained her freedom three years after his death, and married Indian William Wright. Wright became a Rogerene, refused to recant, and was banished from the colony, leaving Hagar and four children behind.[58] A number of the free children, grandchildren, and great-grandchildren of Hagar and William lived in New London County throughout the eighteenth century.

Unless, however, a free person of color purchased land or became involved in the court system, little information exists on this relatively small number of people. In examining court records for the mid-eighteenth century, however, one finds a scattering of cases involving free people who did not belong to the Jackson, Rogers, or Wright families. They include Cezar Freeman (New London),[59] Sambo Negro (Lyme), Cezar Mulatto (Norwich), Hector Negro alias Throope (New London), Phillis Still (Saybrook), and Ishmael Powers (New London).[60] Court records also mention Jack Wake (New London) and Thomas Boham (Norwich).[61]

The 1790 Federal Census provides the first benchmark to measure free Negroes. In the town of Lyme, fourteen heads of family were called Negro, like Negro Pomp and Negro Wright. At least six were born free and a seventh purchased land in Lyme in 1773.[62]

William Browne brought slaves to Connecticut at the high tide of the institution in the colony. According to colony census data, the number of persons called Negroes jumped from 3,019 in 1756 to 5,101 in 1774, an apparent increase of sixty-nine

---

57 Brown and Rose, *Black Roots*, 349; George Waller-Fry, *Adam and Katherine Rogers of New London, CT* (Storrs, CT: Spring Hill Press,1977), 5-9. The only time he appeared in land records was in 1720 when Adam and Katherine Rogers quit claimed all their rights to the estate of Katherine's father to her brother Thomas Jones. They both signed the quit claim with an X. Adam Rogers and Katherine Rogers to Thomas Jones, NLLR, November 23, 1720, X, 179.

58 Brown and Rose, *Black Roots*, 452. Hagar, "a negro woman" and four children traveled to Hartford in February 1696 to visit her husband in prison. NLCC, Trials, Vol. 7, 174.

59 The estate of John Rogers owed money to Cesar Freeman of New London. John Rogers, New London, 1753, NLPR, no. 4543.

60 The author has supplied surnames like Negro or Mulatto to those who were so identified in court records. *Cezar Freeman v. John Richards and George Richards Jr.*, NLCC, Files, African Americans, November 1742, Box 2, folder 6; *Benjamin Colt et al v. Daniel Ely*, November 1748, Ibid, Box 2, folder 13; *Cezar Mulatto v. Jubee Negro*, February 1750, Ibid, Box 2, folder 14; *Ichabod Robinson v. Hector Negro*, Ibid, February 1753, Box 2, folder 17; *Stephen Nott v. Phillis Still*, February 1762, Ibid, Box 2, folder 31; *Ishmael Powers v. Samuel Bill*, February 1763, Ibid, Box 2, folder 33. Daniel Ely of Lyme freed Sambo, but he was unable to support himself and the selectmen sued Ely to get reimbursement for what they spent on his care.

61 *Governor and Company v. Jack Wake*, NLCC, Files, June 1746, Box 82, no docket; *Peter Wickwire v. Thomas Boham*, November 1749, Ibid, Box 88, folder 3, no docket; Brown and Rose, *Black Roots*, 33, 439. The selectmen of New London bound out Grace and Stephen Wake, children of John Wake, "a poor man." New London Town Records, Box 3, folder 11.

62 George Jeffery, Joseph Pumham, Solomon Scipio, Daniel Wright, Phineas Wright, and Samuel Wright. Caesar Freeman bought land in Lyme. Bruce P. Stark, "Decoding the 1790 Census for New London County African Americans," *Connecticut History Review*, 54, no. 2 (Fall 2015), 300-02. At least eight of the fourteen were of mixed race. It is not known if the Caesar Freeman in Lyme just before the Revolution was the same man who lived in New London at mid-century. David O. White notes that many African Americans who were already free served in the American Revolution, White, *Connecticut's Black Soldiers*, 19-20.

percent in eighteen years, but people of color had been seriously undercounted at the earlier date because several towns with a significant number of African Americans in 1774 did not include them in the first census. The true total for 1756 was probably around 4,000 and, thus, the bulk of the growth in slave population likely occurred between 1720 and 1755.[63] Both the 1762 and 1774 censuses more accurately counted people of color than did the 1756 one. Had it not been for the crisis with Great Britain after the end of the French and Indian War, however, slavery probably would have faced few challenges to its legitimacy for the foreseeable future.[64]

Table 2. Slavery and Freedom in New London County[65]

1756	White	Negro[66]	%N	Indian	Total
Connecticut	126,976	[4,000]	[3.0]	617	[131,593]
New London County	22,015	[1,000]	[4.2]	617	[23,642]
New London[67]	3,171	[150]	[4.5]	—	[3,321]
Colchester[68]	2,228	84	3.6	—	2,312
Lyme	2,762	100	3.4	94	2,956
1762					
Connecticut	141,076	4,503	3.1	940	146,519
New London County[69]	23,284	1,042	4.0	745	26,071
New London	4,800	200	3.9	160	5,160
Colchester	2,249	154	6.4	—	2,403

---

[63] The 1756 census did not count Negroes in the important slaveholding communities of Greenwich, Milford, New Haven, New London, and Wallingford. In addition, no totals were included for Canaan, Derby, and Hebron, all of whom counted more than fifty Negroes eighteen years later. These first five towns contained 984 Negroes in 1774 and another 228 lived in the other four. The census counted Indians in only in a handful of towns.

[64] For an excellent analysis of the beginnings of the antislavery movement in Connecticut, see Rupert Charles Loucks, "'Let the oppressed go free': Reformation and Revolution in English Connecticut, 1764-1765," (Unpublished Ph.D. dissertation, University of Wisconsin - Madison, 1995). See chapters 10-17. Loucks believes that antislavery sentiment commenced in 1767 with passage of the Townshend Acts. Ibid, 558-604.

[65] *Colony Records,* X, 617-18; XIV, 485, 487, 491; Christopher P. Bickford, "The Lost Connecticut Census of 1762 Found," *Connecticut Historical Society Bulletin,* 44 (April 1979), 37-38; *Heads of Families at the First Census of the United States Taken in the Year 1790* (Washington: Government Printing Office, 1908), 9. Indians were counted in the towns of Groton, Lyme, and Stonington in 1756, ten towns in 1762, and forty eight in 1774.

[66] The 1756 census gives a total of 3,019 Negroes for the colony as a whole and 829 for New London County. The estimates in brackets more clearly reflect reality.

[67] New London whites were also probably undercounted and, as already indicated, the census did not include the numerous Indians and Negroes in the town.

[68] Colchester was part of Hartford County until after the American Revolution.

[69] Killingworth did not distinguish between whites and blacks. Its total population was 1,587, so the estimate made was that the town had 1, 570 whites and 17 Negroes.

1762	White	Negro	%N	Indian	Total
Lyme[70]	2,477	88	3.3	100	2,665

1774					
Connecticut	191,392	5,101	2.6	1,363	197,856
New London County	1,542	1,194[71]	3.6	842	33,578
New London	5,366	316	5.4	206	5,888
Colchester	3,057	173	5.3	28	3,258
Lyme	3,860	124	3.0	104	4,088

1782[72]					
Connecticut	202,597	[5,200][73]	2.5	[1,073]	208,870
New London County	30,831	[1,200]	3.7	[720]	32,751
New London	unknown				
Colchester	3,169	196	5.8		3,366
Lyme[74]	3,576	[120]	3.2	[96]	3,792

1790					
Connecticut	232,558	5,569	2.3	—	238,127
New London County	31,884	1,316	3.96	—	33,200
New London[75]	4,410	204	4.4	—	4,614
Colchester	2,947	200	6.4	—	3,147
Lyme	3,734	125	3.2	—	3,859

As one can see, the number of persons classified as Negroes increased by more than 25% between 1756 and 1774, from around 4,000 to 5,101. County boundaries changed between 1774 and 1790, so if one uses the same towns as in the 1790 Federal census, the

70 The 1762 census total for Lyme has to be incorrect. Either one section of town was uncounted, part of the town was included with New London, or someone made a transcription error. The likelihood exists that the total for whites was 2,877, not 2,477.

71 New London County had the highest number of Negroes and Indians in the colony. Fairfield County had a higher percentage of slaves at 4.0 percent.

72 Connecticut's census of 1782 contains only totals for county and state. The summary for New London County is as follows: Towns - 8; males above 50 - 1,685; males between 16 and 50 - 5,884; males under 16 - 7,528; females - 16,034; total whites - 30,831; Indians and Negroes - 1,920. *A RETURN of the number of INHABITANTS in the State of CONNECTICUT, February 1, 1782; and also of the Indians and Negroes*, Broadside, CSL. More detail for Colchester, however, exists. It showed that the town's total populations was 3,365; white males 1,591, white females 1,578, black males 84, black females 112. ColchesterBMD, Vol. 2, 34, CTH.

73 Total for Negroes and Indians was 6,273 for the state, 1,920 for New London County, and 196 for Colchester. The 1782 census did not separately count them. The figures above represent interpolations based upon the 1774 and 1790 censuses.

74 Van Dusen, "Trade of Revolutionary Connecticut," 31. The total for Negroes and Indians was 216.

75 New London's population declined because Montville, formerly New London North Society, was incorporated as a separate town in 1786. In 1790, 3.6 percent of the new town's population of 2,053 consisted of people of color. Stark, "Decoding the 1790 Federal Census," 302.

percentage of Negroes in New London County in 1774 was 4.1 percent and had slightly declined by 1790.[76] Colchester experienced the most dramatic growth in Negro population, from 84 in 1756 to 173 in 1774, an increase of 106 percent, and no other town in the colony came even close to matching this growth. The bulk of the jump took place between 1756 and 1762 at the time William Browne brought slaves to Connecticut.

If newspaper slave sale notices can be believed, most of the increase was due to natural population growth, e.g. children born of slave women living in the colony.[77] The overwhelming majority of slaveowners possessed one to three slaves who served primarily as house servants and farm laborers that supplemented the work performed by family members and white servants.[78] One well documented example is that of Adam [Jackson], servant to Joshua Hempstead.[79] And, as inventories of estates show, a significant number were minors whose labor was of minimal importance.

*****

One question to consider, however, is whether any farmers in southeastern Connecticut practiced a form of commercial agriculture like that sustained in the nearby Narragansett region of Rhode Island, one based largely on slave labor?[80] Ronald K. Fitts believes that the Narragansett country shared many characteristics with the plantation South and has defined slave plantations as having four important commonalities. First, they were capitalistic enterprises; second, they produced agricultural products and raised livestock for international markets; third, slaves performed most of the labor; and, fourth, the owners and their families did not work in the fields.[81]

The Narragansett area formed part of what was then called King's County, now Washington County, and consisted of the towns of North Kingstown, South Kingstown, Narragansett, and Charlestown.[82] It comprised "a slave society within a so-

---

[76] Stark, Ibid, 290, 302, 306.

[77] New London County newspapers (*Connecticut Gazette, New London Summary,* and *Norwich Packet*) contain sixty-seven separate slave sale advertisements for the years between 1758 and 1779, most being for one slave. Just eight records state that the persons being sold were imported and the two advertisements offering the largest number of such slaves for sale were placed by merchants from Middletown. The sellers generally noted the ages of the Negroes and all were either adults in the prime of work life or children. Just six had reached thirty, the oldest was thirty-eight. She was described as a "likely Negro Wench" being sold "for want of Employ." *New London Summary,* August 7, 1761, [4]; October 8, 1762, [4]; *Connecticut Gazette,* March 10, 1769, [3].

[78] In 1790, 336 slaveowners in New London County held 586 slaves. Eight men and one woman held five or more slaves and twenty-three had four. Ten lived in Stonington, 6 in New London, 5 in Lyme, 4 in Colcheter, 4 Groton, and 3 Norwich. 1790 Census, passim; Stark, "Decoding the 1790 Federal Census," 294-95.

[79] Hempstead *Diary,* 188-692 passim; di Bonaventura, *For Adam's Sake,* passim.

[80] Peter Hinks suggested that I pursue this inquiry.

[81] Fitts, *Inventing New England's Slave Paradise,* 69-73.

[82] South Kingstown, the epicenter of slavery in New England, was the richest town in Rhode Island in 1730. Its population consisted of 965 whites, 333 Negroes, and 223 Indians. At the time of the 1748 census, the town had 1,405 whites, 380 Negroes, and 183 Indians. Greene, "Slave-holding in New England," 513. Another source set the slave population of South Kingstown in 1730 at 498, a figure that may have included Native Americans. Christian McBurney, "The South Kingstown Planters Country Gentry in Colonial Rhode Island," *Rhode Island History,* 45 (August 1986), 86.

ciety with slaves."[83] These four towns made up the slave center of New England and had a total population of 7,127 in 1774. The total for Colchester, Lyme, and New London that same year was 13,234, 613 being Negroes, 4.6% of the population. According to the Rhode Island census of 1748, these four towns contained 622 Blacks, 13% of the total population, while in 1774 the numbers were 702 Blacks, 10% of the population.[84] For better comparative purposes, twenty-two Narragansett country probated estates between 1751 and 1774 listed between ten and nineteen slaves.[85] The number for the three Connecticut towns was two, one of whom, George Mumford, only moved to New London shortly before his death. Given the fact that slave density was much lower in southeastern Connecticut than in Rhode Island, it cannot be legitimately claimed that a slave economy existed in the region.[86]

One important factor in comparing the two regions is land quality. Southern Rhode Island featured a great deal of extremely productive farm land, southeastern Connecticut not so much.[87] The Narragansett area was extremely fertile, "covered with luxuriant grass, and well adapted for grazing" and considered the best quality for agriculture in the North. The dairy and cheese center of New England, the region also raised large numbers of horses and sheep. A small landed aristocracy prospered on farms ranging in size from 600 to 1,000 acres.[88] With regard to Connecticut, geographer Mont Morgan divided the land into thirteen soil types, ranging from XX for "very stony and

---

[83] Christy Clark-Pujara, *Dark Work: The Business of Slavery in Rhode Island* (New York: New York University Press, 2016), 25-27.

[84] Fitts, *Inventing New England's Slave Paradise*, 12, 71-83. See also, Greene, *Negro Colonial New England*, 106; Bruce C. Daniels, *Dissent and Conformity on Narragansett Bay: The Colonial Rhode Island Town* (Middletown: Wesleyan University Press, 1983), 57-60; Sydney V. James, *Rhode Island: A History* (New York: Charles Scribner's Sons, 1975), 253-56; *Colony Records*, XIV, 487. Rhode Island had the highest percentage of slaves for any New England colony.

[85] Sixteen lived in South Kingstown, three in North Kingstown, and three in Charlestown. Fitts, *Inventing New England's Slave Paradise*, 85. In total, seventy-four probated estates listed slaves.

[86] Richard Archer in his recent book on the *Jim Crow North* asserted without providing any detail that eastern Connecticut resembled the Narragansett country in Rhode Island. The author disagrees. Richard Archer, *Jim Crow North: The Struggle for Equal Rights in Antebellum New England* (New York: Oxford University Press, 2017), 24, 37, 225.

[87] According to one of the most detailed studies of Narragansett planters, "the natural advantage of the Narragansett Country, its soil, its climate, its situation by the sea and the proximity to the port and town of Newport, were the underlying causes of the creation of the wealth of the community, and this material success was in turn responsible for the social and cultural development it attained." William Davis Miller, "The Narragansett Planters," *Proceedings of the American Antiquarian Society*, 43 (1933), 50.
Although Connecticut was a major participant in both the legal and illegal West Indian trade and the largest supplier of horses, oxen, cows, sheep, poultry, and onions to the islands and also a significant supplier of dairy products, the goods came from farms located throughout the colony and not from a limited number of towns as in Rhode Island. The colony, for example, supplied 74% of horses exported to the sugar islands in the decade before the American Revolution, most raised by farmers in the northeastern Windham County region. For the authoritative study of the importance of the West Indian trade to the colony, see Joseph Avitable, "The Atlantic World Economy and Colonial Connecticut" (unpublished Ph.D. dissertation, University of Rochester, 2009). See especially chapters 1 and 2. See also, Van Dusen, "Trade of Revolutionary Connecticut," chapters 4, 5, and 10.

[88] Greene, "Slave-holding in New England," 513; McBurney, "South Kingstown Planters," 85-87; Miller, "Narragansett Planters," 50-87.

mountainous land" to L for "valley land, level surface, of medium-textured soils over sand or gravel."[89] Lyme had the lowest percentage of blacks among the three towns per-haps due to the fact that seventy-five percent of its territory was XX. New London's soil was thirty percent XX and twenty percent X ("stony, hilly land of light-textured glacial till soils") and Colchester had thirty-five percent X and XX. On a scale of 0 to 12, the overall productivity level for Lyme was 2, New London 3, and Colchester 5.[90] Superior soil helps explain why Colchester had the largest percentage of slaves in the county.

Nevertheless, the possibility exists that a handful of eastern Connecticut farm-ers practiced a form of commercial agriculture similar to that in Narragansett Rhode Island, one based largely upon slave labor.[91] But whom and does William Browne fit into this pattern?

The estate containing the largest number of slaves at mid-century belonged to Captain George Mumford, half-brother of John Mumford of New Salem. His real and personal property valued at some £2,670 included fifteen slaves, six adult males, three women, and six children. Mumford spent twenty years as lease holder of Win-throp-owned Fisher's Island, entering into it in the spring of 1736 and leaving in May 1756, one month before he died in New London.[92] These slaves did not labor in south-eastern Connecticut, but on a New York island owned by absentee members of the Winthrop family and managed by Mumford.[93]

Another person to consider is Captain Nathan Jewett (1710-1761) of Lyme.[94] Browne and his Harvard classmate Jacob Bailey visited him in July 1754. He was the father of nine sons, one daughter, and possessed five to six slaves. Bailey reported as follows: "After dinner I went out with Mr. Jewett and his sons, to see them work at a little distance from the house. Here I beheld an abundance of good land, cleared and well brought to, upon which grew the finest grass, wheat, and Indian corn, I have seen anywhere this year."[95] Jewett had two adult male slaves, but his sons furnished the bulk

---

[89] This information comes from Daniels, *Connecticut Town*, 186-90. Appendix V of Daniels called "Land Types by Town" contains the data used here. He gathered and organized the information from Mont Morgan, *The Soil Characteristics of Connecticut Land Types* (New Haven: Yale University Press, 1939).

[90] Daniels, *Connecticut Town*, 186-88, 190. Soil type D was rated as fair for grain, grass, and pasture and type E was considered favorable for all three. Lyme had fifteen percent D soil, New London had thirty percent D, and Colchester forty percent D and twenty-five percent E.

[91] William Gardiner of South Kingstown, Rhode Island, the man who sold Colonel Browne 635 acres in Col-chester, for example, owned over thirty horses and 164 head of cattle, more than any farmer in southeastern Connecticut. Miller, "Narragansett Planters," 77, 82.

[92] Fishers Island, having an extent of around four square miles, was wholly owned by six generations of the Winthrop family who raised livestock there. The Massachusetts General Court conferred the island to John Winthrop, Jr. in 1640 and both Connecticut and New York respected his right to it. "A Brief History of Fish-ers Island Since European Discovery;" FishersIsland.net, accessed July 17, 2017; Henry L. Ferguson, *Fishers Island, N.Y., 1614-1925* (New York: privately printed, 1925), 12-67 passim.

[93] George Mumford, New London, 1756, NLPR, Vol. G, 81-82; Perkins, *Connecticut Farm*, 76-77. The wealth and number of slaves that Mumford acquired demonstrate that people without land could gain great prosperity.

[94] Born in Rowley, Massachusetts, Jewett moved to Lyme and married Deborah Lord in 1729. Frederic Clarke Jewett, *History and Genealogy of the Jewetts in America* (New York: The Grafton Press, 1908), 104-05.

[95] Bailey added that the place was still unpleasant "on account of its being encumbered with rocky and moun-

of the labor.[96] Thus, Jewett fails to meet at least two of the four distinguishing markers of a slave plantation.

Captain Richard Durfey, a merchant, died in 1757. The inventory of his substantial estate was taken on October 10th and it was valued at £6,926. His 550 acres of land and buildings were worth £5,000. He also owned two-thirds of a still house [distillery] worth £160. The livestock consisted of 3 yoke of oxen, 19 cows, 15 yearlings, 16 calves, 16 cattle, 330 sheep, and 6 horses, plus 8 Negroes valued at £220.[97] The strong likelihood exists that most of the livestock was raised for export purposes. The inventory gives no information on the slaves, not names, sex, or age, and the distribution of the estate to the four heirs made no mention of them.[98] Given the fact that he owned considerable landed property, enough livestock for export, and perhaps enough slaves to handle most of the farm work, Durfey, who gained his wealth through trade, likely practiced a form of agriculture that came close to mimicking that of Rhode Island and shipped his own livestock to the sugar islands.[99]

Three other New London area men with substantial numbers of slaves died between 1763 and the beginning of the American Revolution, only one of whom, Joshua Raymond (1697-1763) of New London North Society, possessed enough adult male servants for the pursuit of large scale agricultural production.[100] Joshua, a justice of the peace and well-to-do farmer, was the youngest of seven children of Joshua and Mercy Sands Raymond of Block Island and New London. By the will of his father, he inherited a homestead on Block Island, 100 sheep, 20 cattle, and the homestead farm in Mohegan fields. His mother partnered with Major John Merrett and purchased some 1,500 acres in the same region.[101] From his parents, then, Joshua Raymond possessed the founda-

---

tainous land." Bartlett, *Frontier Missionary*, 25-26. The farm was in the northern section of Lyme in the Eight Mile River watershed close to the East Haddam border. It was probably near or part of what is known today as the Raymond Farm on Route 156. Some of the most productive land in Lyme lies along the Eight Mile River north of Beaver Brook and along the Beaver Brook watershed. Much is still farmed in the twenty-first century.

[96] The Jewett estate included five slaves, a Negro girl, two Negro boys, and two men. His land, divided among his four sons, was valued at £1,650. He also owned two horses and around twenty-eight cows, steers, heifers, and oxen, some of which may have been intended for shipment to the sugar islands. Nathan Jewett, Lyme, 1761, NLPR, Vol. G, 589-94.

[97] In June 1741, Ebenezer Howard of New London sued Durfey for trespass by his slave Quokoo whom he accused of stealing and killing a swine. *Ebenezer Howard v. Richard Durfey*, NLCC, Files, June 1741, Box 66, folder 13, no. 45.

[98] Captain Richard Durfey, New London, 1757, NLPR, Vol. G, 166; Richard Durfey, New London, 1757, Ibid, no. 1,855. Joseph Lovett, former minister at New Salem Society, served as one of the three appraisers of the estate and also was one of three "Freeholders under Oath" who distributed the estate to his widow Sarah, sons Richard and Thomas, and daughter Sarah Wanton. Elder son Richard, Jr. received a double portion of the estate.

[99] One cannot assume that most of the labor was provided by the enslaved for the most commercial farmers relied chiefly on family and hired men.

[100] Joshua Raymond, New London, 1763, NLPR, Vol. H, 346; Nathaniel Green, New London, 1764, Ibid, Vol. G, 342; Thomas Mumford, Groton, 1766, Ibid, Vol. H, 407. Raymond had ten slaves, four of whom were adult males. Green possessed seven slaves, one a Negro man about sixty-five years old and five women and children, while Thomas Mumford's inventory listed seven slaves, only one of whom was a healthy male.

[101] Samuel Raymond, *Genealogies of the Raymond Families of New England, 1630-1 to 1886* (New York: Press of J. J. Little & Co., 1886), 6; Samuel Edward Raymond, *Raymond Genealogy*, Vol. 1 (Seattle: 1969), 35-37.

tion for export driven agriculture. Mercy possessed eight Negro and Mustee slaves and two Indian servants in 1726.[102] On her death in 1741, however, she owned no land and possessed no slaves.[103] The inventory of Raymond's estate taken on December 14, 1763 showed that he possessed eleven enslaved persons, at least five of whom were healthy adult males. He no longer owned any land, had a relatively modest supply of livestock, and the value of his estate was just £927.[104] Joshua had previously, however, given his four sons Joshua, John, Christopher, and Edward farms that totaled almost 1,000 acres "in Consideration of the Natural Love, favour, and affection" he held for them, so they were not part of his inventoried estate.[105] Considering the profile of his servants, the amount of land he owned in what is now Montville, and the number of farms he controlled, it is likely that he practiced a form of agriculture similar to that in Rhode Island, albeit on land of lesser quality.

Richard Durfey, Jr. of New London died in 1780 and left fourteen slaves. His farm of 382 acres with house, barn, and outbuildings was worth £2,292.[106] The inventory did not give the ages of the nine males and five females, but three of them appear to have been males in the prime of life. When the distribution was made in June 1786, widow Sarah received eight slaves and her five daughters, three of whom were unmarried, received one each, making a total of thirteen. The quantity of livestock was much less than that owned by his father, but the trials of the Revolution may help explain some of the differential. His estate contained 6 horses, 2 yoke of oxen, 32 cows and steers, and 8 sheep.[107] According to the 1790 census, Sarah possessed six slaves.[108]

James Rogers (1717-1790) of Great Neck in New London could well fit the picture of Rhode Island slave-based agriculture.[109] Rogers was the owner of Abner and Sharper in the 1750s, an unidentified Negro man in 1761, had a substantial estate, and

---

[102] Agreement James Harris and Mrs. Mercy Raymond, NLLR, October 10, 1726, VIII, 339.

[103] The inventory of her estate was taken on May 3, 1742 and her property was valued at £482-7-8. She had disposed of all her land, owned no slaves, but possessed one yoke of oxen, 13 head of beef, seven horses, 72 sheep and lambs, plus turkeys and geese. Mercy Raymond, New London, 1742, NLPR, no. 4308.

[104] The monetary value assigned to slaves provides the best indicator as to their health and use. Negroes Sippio, Pompey, Jack, and Eber were each assigned a value of £60, and Jumbo £45. A sixth adult "Nero & his wife Fillas" were worth a total £40, an indication that they were elderly. By his will, Raymond divided them among his wife and children. Joshua Raymond, New London, 1764, NLPR, no. 4300. His silver plate was valued at £38-12-6.

[105] Fitts points out that the landholdings of most Rhode Island planters were dispersed with the owner typically managing the home farm and the others by relatives or overseers. Raymond owned four farms. Fitts, *Inventing New England's Slave Paradise*, 73; NLLR, XVI, 236-37, 243-44; XVII, 104; XIX, 63.

[106] The appraisers set the worth of the entire estate as £3,225 about half of that of his father. The quantity and quality of his household goods indicated that he was well-to-do.

[107] Richard Durfey, New London, 1780, NLPR, Vol. 1, 64-65; Richard Durfey, Jr. New London, 1783, Ibid, no. 1856. The three were Hercules, Prince, and Cuff "now run away." The 1786 distribution still listed Cuff as a runaway.

[108] 1790 Census, 153. Between 1787 and 1789, she advertised to hire a farm manager. *Connecticut Gazette*, February 16, 1787 [3]; March 14, 1788, [3]; February 27, 1789, [3].

[109] Great Neck is part of Waterford and borders on Long Island Sound. The best known area of Great Neck is Harkness Park.

possessed four slaves in 1790.[110] He also advertised for the return of a runaway in the 1770s.[111] The land was of good enough quality to sustain commercial agriculture, but it is not known how many adult slaves he had in his possession. According to the family genealogy, he "owned a large plantation and many slaves" and bought a large number of farms. The inventory of his estate was taken on May 5, 1790 and his real and personal property was valued at £6,068.[112]

Several well-to-do merchants lived in the region, the three most important being Nathaniel Shaw (d. 1784) and Nathaniel Shaw, Jr. (1735-1782) of New London and John McCurdy (1724-1785) of Lyme. All owned slaves, but they derived the bulk of their wealth from international trade. Nathaniel Shaw, Jr. died tragically in April 1782 after a fatal accidental discharge of a gun. No inventory of his estate has been found, but in his will written just before death, he affirmed "I do hereby Emancipate & Set at Liberty all my Negro Slaves except Selah who is to be set free at twenty-one years of Age."[113] The inventory of the estate of his wealthy father taken in June 1784 amounted to more than £31,100 and contained some twenty plots of land. The estate did not include any slaves, but it is likely that he possessed some because sons Daniel and Thomas each had one in their households in 1790.[114] McCurdy's estate inventoried at £37,118 was among the largest in New England. He owned over twenty plots of land that the appraisers valued at £3,367, but the bulk of his estate consisted of liquidated state and federal notes worth £24,645 and private debts of £6,249. He never possessed a significant number of slaves.[115] We can, therefore, exclude the three wealthiest merchants from consideration.

In 1790, 6.4 percent of the population of Colchester consisted of African Americans, the highest for any town in New London County. Sixty-four were enslaved, eighty-four lived in black households, and fifty-two free blacks resided in white households. The persons with the largest number of slaves were Pierpoint Bacon (1724-1800)

---

110 Abner was around twenty-five and Sharper may have been about twenty. The third male was healthy except for a rupture and died after an operation. *James Rogers v. Giles Goddard*, NLCC, Files, African Americans, June 1753, Box 2, folder 18; *Dom Rex v. James Rogers*, Ibid. February 1755, Box 2, folder 19; *James Rogers v. Joseph Perkins*, June 1762, Ibid, Box 2, folder 32; 1790 Census, 156

111 Sy Mustee or Mulatto ran away twice and Piggen Negro once. *Connecticut Gazette*, July 7, 1775, [4]; May 16, 1776, [3]; *Norwich Packet*, December 12, 1773, [3]. Yet it is probable that the James who advertised in the *Packet* for the return of Piggen was Dr. James Rogers (1714-1783) of the North Parish. *James Rogers v. Noah Hammond*, NLCC, Files, June 1743, Box 75, folder 16, no. 246; Rogers, *Rogers Descendants*, 80.

112 His land holdings consisted of the Homestead, Goshen, Lester, and Miner Hill farms and also Wigwamps, the Crocker Lot, Picket Lot, Coit Lot, Lyme farm, Nathaniel farm, plus "other lands and houses." The livestock holdings of the elderly Rogers were not particularly impressive. The inventory recorded that he owned "Neat Stock" worth £226-6-4, plus one old mare, sheep valued at £16-6, and swine at £18-15-8. Rogers, *Rogers Descendants*, 87-88; James Rogers, New London, 1790, NLPR, no. 4526.

113 *Connecticut Gazette*, April 9, 1782 [3]; Nathaniel Shaw, New London, 1782, NLPR, Vol. 1, 24.

114 The estate included the "Mumford farm & 2 small pieces of Land at Pagwanck." Nathaniel Shaw, New London, 1784, NLPR, no. 4785; 1790 Census, 142, 154.

115 John McCurdy, Lyme, 1786, NLPR, no. 3327; John McCurdy, Ibid, Vol. 2, 3. Jackson Turner Main, "The Economic and Social Structure of Early Lyme," in Willauer, ed., *A Lyme Miscellany*, 44-45. Slave Humphrey purchased his freedom in 1778. The inventory listed a "Molatto Boy [Corrydon] about 12" years who his son Richard emancipated in 1813. LLR, XIV, 163; XXV, 229.

with 6, Joshua Bulkley (1741-1821) with 5, and Abigail Bulkley, the widow of Gershom (1709-1788) with 4.[116]

One of the wealthiest men in town before the American Revolution was David Day (1710-1775) of Westchester Society who died without issue.[117] He owned 17 pieces of land valued at £4,021, "7 Negro Servants" valued at £208, and livestock consisting of hogs, sheep, cattle, yokes of oxen, and horses worth more than £381. His estate also contained substantial quantities of Indian corn, cheese, potatoes, flax, wheat, rye, and oats. He practiced a form of commercial agriculture designed for the export trade.[118]

Gershom Bulkley, son of the Reverend John Bulkey, was another well-to-do Colchester farmer.[119] His estate papers do not account for all the slaves his widow Abigail possessed in 1790, but between his will and inventory of the estate three are mentioned, Caesar, Flora, and Jack.[120] Gershom owned seven farms, plus several hundred additional acres of land in Colchester. His real estate was valued at £8,515 and personal estate at £1,196, but no listing has been found of his livestock.[121]

Joshua Bulkley, son of Gershom Bulkley, freed three of his five slaves after 1790 - Tab in June 1798, Primus in November 1801, and Comboo in April 1807. When his estate was appraised in 1821, it was valued at $21,000.[122]

Pierpoint Bacon was the largest slaveowner in Colchester in 1790.[123] When he died without heirs in 1800, his estate was worth more than $37,000. He owned 816 acres of land valued at almost $18,000 and his livestock included 60 sheep, 11 cows, and 7 horses. In his will, he freed all seven slaves still in his possession and directed that the bulk of his estate be given to the First Society "for the purpose of supporting and maintaining a School" [Bacon Academy].[124]

---

[116] Stark, "Decoding the 1790 Federal Census," 302; 1790 Census, 91, 99.

[117] *A Genealogical Register of the Descendants in the Male Line of Robert Day, of Hartford, Conn.,* 2nd edition (Hartford: J. & L. Metcalf, 1848, 1913), 90, 92. According to the tax list for Colchester in 1762, Day had the second highest assessment in town, £345-15. 1762 Colchester Tax List, CTR, 1708-1784, folder 10, CHS.

[118] The inventory recorded that Day possessed 37 cows, 3 heifers, 3 yoke of oxen, 10 fat cattle, 16 calves, 1 bull, 12 horses, 11 two-year-olds, 28 colts, and 51 sheep. He also possessed 220 bushels of Indian corn, 7 bushels barley, 60 bushels wheat, 50 bushels rye, 200 bushels oats, 30 pounds wool, and 200 pounds of flax. David Day, Colchester, 1775, Colchester Probate Records, no. 1008; David Day, 1775, CPR, Vol. 4, 158-59.

[119] Gershom had the highest list of polls and ratable estates in 1762, totaling £393-10. 1762 Colchester Tax List, CTR, folder 10, CHS. His older brother Colonel John Bulkley (1705-1753) was a prominent political leader who served in the colony's Upper House, judge of probate, and on the Superior Court. John had three slaves, extensive land holdings, and a good supply of livestock, including 11 cows, 5 calves, 6 oxen, and 40 sheep. John Bulkley, Colchester, 1754, CPR, no. 489; Jacobus, *Bulkeley Genealogy*, 139-40, 172-73.

[120] Abigail emancipated the fourth slave Eliphalet in 1794. ColchesterBMD, II, 370. The Bulkeley genealogy gives the names of Caesar, an unnamed Negro woman, perhaps Flora, and her twin boys born in 1783, Jack and Peg. Jacobus, *Bulkeley Genealogy*, 173-74.

[121] Gershom Bulkley, Colchester, 1788, CPR, no. 484.

[122] ColchesterBMD, II, 360, 363, 375; Jacobus, *Bulkeley Genealogy*, 173-74, 292.

[123] Bacon had the third highest assessment in Colchester in 1762, £300. 1762 Colchester Tax List, CTR, folder 10, CHS.

[124] Pierpoint Bacon, Colchester, 1801, CPR, no. 118. The slaves were Sip, Cato, Jenny, Zilpah, and three children. The two boys, Araunah and Frank, were to be freed at age twenty-one, and the girl Mehitabel at

What about the slaves that William Browne brought to New Salem, a rural parish located in the middle of nowhere? Around 1759, he purchased "3 Negroes & 1 Woman" whom he left on the estate of his agent [John Mumford, Sr.] in Colchester and "afterwards purchased 3 or 4 [more] which were sent to" his farm in Lyme on "which his agent's Son [John Mumford, Jr.] was in Possession" because he "thought of improving his Farm in Connecticut."[125] We do not know the ages of the seven or eight slaves, how many were female, and how many from the two purchases lived on the estate when it was seized by the State of Connecticut in 1779.[126] Then the question presents itself, how were the slaves employed and by whom? The fragmentary evidence that exists shows that some were retained by agents John Mumford, Sr. and John Mumford, Jr. and that others were leased to tenants on other Browne farms and outsiders.[127] Assuming the adult males were initially divided between the two Mumfords, they together with whatever servants the agents possessed could well have led to the expansion of the home farms by clearing more land and constructing additional stone walls to the ultimate economic benefit of the absentee. Yet this scenario does not fit the image of a Narragansett slave plantation.[128] The terms of the only known Mumford lease in 1774 for seven years specified that he pay £20 per year rent for the first four years and £30 for the last three, build 30 rods of stone wall the first year and 20 rods per year thereafter, and clear 70 acres of land.[129] Mumford would have needed assistance to accomplish these goals and slave labor would have been essential, but we do not know how many slaves might have been available and how much labor may have been performed by his own servants or hired men.

If one uses 1779 inventory information, at most John Mumford, Jr. had three

---

eighteen.

Despite his importance and wealth, existing biographical information provides little insight on his economic activities except for comments on his land acquisitions. Pierpoint Bacon Files, Town Historian's Notes, Colchester Town Hall. Thanks to Peter Hinks for supplying the author with a copy of these files.

[125] "Essex County Loyalists," 298; Memorial of William Browne, AmLC, AOP, AO 12/10, 234, NAUK; Stark, "Myth and Reality," 167.

[126] According to confiscation documents, Browne possessed twelve slaves on his Connecticut lands. Six were adult males ranging in age from 22 to over 50, one was an adult female age 36, and five were children. The three oldest males ranged in age from around 42 to 53, another was 33, and the remaining two were in their twenties. The possibility exists, and it is only a possibility, that these seven Negroes made up the two lots that he purchased around 1759. If so, the two groups consisted of three adult males, two teenagers, and two youths, assuming that none had died in the interim, none were sold or permanently ran away, and the number purchased was seven and not eight. William Brown[e], Salem, Mass., confiscated, 1779, Norwich Probate District Records, no. 1760, CSL.

[127] Vicki S. Welch, "The Keys to the Shackles," *CH* 40, no 2 (Fall 2001), 230; CA, Revolutionary War, Series 1, XXXIV, 462; XXXVII, 233, CSL; CA, Miscellaneous, Series 2, I, 93, CSL. For more information on the leasing of slaves, see chapters 8 and 9.

Browne may have intended from the outset to rent out the slaves he brought to New Salem. This practice was widespread in Rhode Island. Clark-Pujara, *Dark Work*, 44, 47.

[128] It is, of course, conceivable that all the slaves originally acquired by Browne were adults, then around three to four each could be allocated to the two farms to enhance commercial possibilities.

[129] The terms for the leases are found in the documents that Browne gathered to support his Loyalist claim and we only have a summary of them and not the contracts. William Browne Tenants 1774, AmLC, AOP, AO 13/50, 142. For additional information on his leases, see chapter 10.

adult Browne slaves at his disposal, one of whom was a female with young children, and the number could have been less.[130] Moreover, since Browne did not directly employ the slaves, but parceled them out to others, and the profits he earned from his Connecticut lands came from rents and improvements and not from livestock or agricultural products produced for the export trade, this hardly fits the image of a slave plantation.

What, then, can we conclude? It is likely that several New London and Colchester area farmers, like Pierpoint Bacon, Gershom Bulkley, David Day, Richard Durfey, Sr., Joshua Raymond, and James Rogers practiced the kind of commercial agriculture described by Robert K. Fitts for King's County, Rhode Island, although on land that was neither as productive nor as large in scale.[131]

The large agricultural and livestock surpluses shipped from Connecticut to the sugar islands, however, did not come from an area like the bountiful Narragansett region with a comparatively small number of landowners, but from hundreds of farmers, many of modest means, scattered throughout the colony, including a couple of score in Colchester, Lyme, and New London. The foodstuffs, timber products, livestock, and draft animals exported were produced predominately by white farmers and their children.[132] The evidence, then, for the existence of slave plantations in the region is underwhelming and no convincing case can be made for William Browne's absentee estate.[133] Several farmers in New London County much more likely practiced a commercial agriculture than did Browne in New Salem, but none loomed as large as those in the Narragansett area, Fishers Island, or Shelter Island, Long Island.[134]

*****

Slavery reached its height in the colony in 1774, but with the crisis with Great Britain reaching the boiling point, the Connecticut legislature began taking steps to limit and restrict it. In October 1774, the General Assembly prohibited the further importation of slaves. Three years later in the middle of the Revolutionary War, it passed an act to encourage the emancipation of slaves.[135] The second act led to a flurry of manumissions, many because the men agreed to serve in the Continental Army, including twelve from Colchester and eleven from Lyme.[136] The gradual emancipation

---

130 According to confiscation documents, three adult male slaves lived in Colchester and not on the Mumford Lyme farm and two others, adult male Luke and infirm child Caesar, were leased to another farmer. William Brown[e], Salem, Mass., 1779, NPR, no. 1760; CA, Revolutionary War, Series 1, XXXVII, 233.

131 The substantial amount of cattle, horses, and other live animals in the inventories of their estates demonstrates that they practiced commercial farming for the export trade.

132 Avitable, "Atlantic World Economy," see especially pages 50, 80, 93-94, 107-27, 133, 155, 175.

133 The fact that a literature exists on the richness of Narragansett agriculture and the prominence of slavery there and nothing similar can be found for Connecticut is also revealing.

134 For a history of the Sylvester Manor provisioning plantation on Shelter Island, New York, see Mac Griswold, *The Manor: The Centuries of a Slave Plantation on Long Island* (New York: Farrar, Straus and Giroux, 2013) especially chapters 1, 9, and 10. When Nathaniel Sylvester, the first lord of the manor, died in 1680, his estate contained twenty-four slaves. Ibid, 164, 169.

135 *Colony Records*, XIV, 329; Charles J. Hoadly, ed., *The Public Records of the State of Connecticut* (Hartford: Press of Case, Lockwood & Brainard Company, 1894), I, 415-16.

136 ColchesterBMD, Vol. 1, 264-66; Vol. 2, 368-69; LLR, XIV, 139, 148, 163, 169; XV, 4, 6, 197, 216,

law of 1784 continued the process, although it did not free any slaves at the time.[137] By 1790, a majority of the people of color in New London County were free, 730 out of a total of 1,316. The figures for Colchester and Lyme matched that of the county as a whole, 136 of 200 Negroes in the first town and 74 of 125 for Lyme.[138] For the state as a whole, 49.5 percent of all persons classified as Negro had achieved their freedom. Whereas the bulk of Negroes in 1774 were enslaved, by 1790 the situation had greatly changed. A decade later over 80% were free, by 1810 some 95% had obtained their freedom, and by 1820 slavery was virtually extinct in the state. The enslaved population of Colchester in 1800 stood at thirty and that of Lyme at twenty-three. New London County counted just six slaves in 1820.[139]

226, 369; XVI, 322.

[137] David Menchel, "Abolition without Deliverance: The Law of Connecticut Slavery 1784-1848," *The Yale Law Journal*, 111, no. 1 (October 2001), 187-89.

[138] Specifically, Colchester counted 64 slaves, 84 free persons in African American households, and 52 other free people of color living with white families. The figures for Lyme were 51 slaves, 66 in African American families, and 8 other free people of color.

[139] Stark, "Decoding the 1790 Federal Census," 302, 306; Clark-Pujara, *Dark Work*, 80.

Chapter 7

John Mumford and Slavery Come to New Salem

William Browne, the third generation owner, was born in Salem, Massachusetts on February 27, 1736/7, the son of Samuel Browne and Katherine Winthrop.[1] After the death of his father in November 1742, he and his sister Abigail were raised by their mother and step-father Epes Sargent (Harvard Class of 1712) whom she married in 1744.[2] Sargent died on November 6, 1762, while Browne's mother lived until January 10, 1781.[3] William inherited more than 100,000 acres in New England and personal property valued at £5,000.[4] After going to local schools in Salem, he attended Harvard College. He held the Saltonstall Scholarship and was valedictorian of the Class of 1755. Not only was Browne a fine scholar, but also "a man of great Sobriety and free from every appearance of Vice." Classmate John Adams characterized Browne as a man of "a solid, judicious character."[5]

Jacob Bailey (1731-1808), a Harvard classmate and later an Anglican priest, provides information on William in 1754.[6] Bailey, a young man of modest means, ac-

---

[1] The young couple became the parents of five children between 1733 and 1738, three of whom died in infancy - Katherine (1733), Samuel (1734), and Ann (1738). *Lynde Diaries*, 37, 39, 138, 142, 143, 145, 154.

[2] Colonel Epes Sargent (1690-1762) was born in Gloucester, became merchant, and married Esther Maccarty of the same town. She died in 1743 and he married Katherine Browne on August 10, 1744. He moved to Salem to live in the Browne mansion and served in King George's War. Sargent and his first wife Esther were the parents of ten children and he fathered five more with Katherine. *Sibley's Harvard Graduates*, V, 645-46; Emma Worcester Sargent and Charles Sprague Sargent, *Epes Sargent of Gloucester and His Descendants* (Boston: Houghton Mifflin Company, 1923), 6-9. The National Portrait Gallery in Washington, DC has a portrait of Sargent.

[3] Katherine's obituary in the *Massachusetts Spy* praised her as a woman of "superior distinction which arises from worth and manners." "The pious were pleased with her exemplary virtue . . . her equals with her unassuming behaviour, and her inferiors with her condescension and benevolence." *Sibley's Harvard Graduates*, V, 646.

[4] William Browne is the subject of several biographical sketches. *American National Biography*, s. v. William Browne; *Dictionary of American Biography*, s.v. William Browne; *Oxford Dictionary of National Biography*, s. v. William Browne; Sydney W. Jackman, "William Browne, Governor, 1782-1788: A Study of his Early Life in his Native Massachusetts," *Bermuda Historical Quarterly*, XIII (Spring 1956), 17-24; S. W. Jackman, "Salem and St. George's, William Browne, Loyalist," *EIHC*, 118 (July 1982), 172-85; *Sibley's Harvard Graduates*, XIII, 551-60.

[5] *Sibley's Harvard Graduates*, XIII, 551; *ANB*, s.v. William Browne.

[6] For biographies of Bailey, see *Dictionary of Canadian Biography*, s.v. Jacob Bailey and *Sibley's Harvard Grad-*

companied the seventeen year old and sister Abigail on a journey from Boston to New London and back between July 9 and August 11, 1754, serving as a kind of chaperone for the student and his older sister.[7] Bailey recorded his impressions of the trip in his journal, one that devoted relatively little attention to the Brownes.[8] Bailey rode on a borrowed horse, while William and Abigail traveled in luxury in a chair pulled by a single horse. While in New London, they stayed with Winthrop relatives and on July 15 rode to "Paugwank, or North Salem, a place belonging entirely to my classmate Brown. Here we saw several fine fields of wheat and other grain" and some thirty tenants on "near twelve thousand acres of land." However, rather than staying on his property, the party traveled to Lyme and were invited to stay the night at the house of Captain Nathan Jewett where Bailey made his only reference to slavery on the trip. "In a few minutes, dinner was made ready and brought in, and set on a long table, round which the whole family gathered, both white and black. His family consists of nine sons and one daughter, two maids, and five to six negroes."[9]

Browne read law with Edmund Trowbridge, but never practiced because the management of his extensive lands, much entailed, took the bulk of his time except for public service. Nor did he engage in commerce, the foundation of his family's wealth, that his father had given up prior to his death in 1742.[10] When he accepted the temporary position of collector of the port of Salem in 1764, William forfeited any opportunity to enter the family business, because collectors were forbidden by Massachusetts law from engaging in trade.[11]

In keeping with the normal practices of elites, he married into another prominent New England family. His wife Ruth Wanton (d. 1799), a first cousin, was the daughter of Joseph Wanton (1705-1780), a prominent Rhode Islander, and Mary Win-

---

uates, XIII, 522-45. Clifford K. Shipton was notorious for his favorable treatment of Loyalists in his biographical sketches. The two longest for the Class of 1755 were for Bailey, twenty-four pages, and Governor Benning Wentworth of New Hampshire, thirty-two pages. Other prominent members of the Class of 1755 included President John Adams and Massachusetts Senator Tristam Dalton. Ibid, XIII, 513-20, 522-45, 569-78, 650-81.

[7] Abigail Browne was born on April 4, 1735, married Joseph Blaney in 1757, and died in December 1776. *Lynde Diaries*, 143; *Sibley's Harvard Graduates*, XIII, 4-5.

[8] The general impression one gets from reading Bailey is that Browne wanted to spread his wings by visiting friends and relatives, primarily in Connecticut.

[9] Bartlet, *Frontier Missionary*, 14-27; Stark, "Myth and Reality," 163-64.

[10] He may have toyed, however, with the idea of becoming a trader because a "William Browne of *Salem*" signed a merchants petition in 1760 and his uncle then lived in Beverly. *Boston Evening-Post*, April 7, 1760, [4].

[11] Morris, "Social Change," 421; *Boston Post-Boy*, October 8, 1764, [2]. According to one leading authority, those who sought or accepted port collector positions, as was done by several conservatives after the French and Indian War, demonstrated a propensity to be a supporter of British authority. The fact that Browne received this appointment at such a comparatively early age served as an indicator of his political leanings. Carl Bridenbaugh, *Cities in Revolt: Urban Life in America 1743-1776* (New York: Oxford University Press, 1955, 1970), 281-82.
    Browne held this position only for a short time in 1764-65. He was appointed by the Surveyor General and held it for a few months before being replaced by James Fisher. *Boston Gazette*, October 8, 1764, [3]; "The Bowdoin and Temple Papers," *CollMHS*, Sixth Series, IX (1897), 28, 44.

throp (1708-1767), daughter of John and Ann Dudley Winthrop.[12] He lived in the most opulent mansion in Salem, a three-story seventeen room house surrounded by gardens, orchards, offices, and stables. Worth at least £2,000 sterling, the large rooms were lavishly furnished and the mansion staffed by slaves.

Although raised a Congregationalist and a member of the First Church of Salem, he left it in 1769 to join the new North Church (Unitarian) where he owned several pews. He also rented a pew at St. Peter's Anglican Church.[13] A man of literary tastes, he actively participated in Salem's Monday Night Club made up of wealthy gentlemen, many of whom remained loyal to the crown.[14]

Young William Browne launched his political career in 1762, when the freemen of Salem elected him to represent the town in the Massachusetts legislature along with the scion of another prominent family, Andrew Oliver, Jr.[15] He remained in the good graces of the town's freemen until 1766, despite being an adherent of royal authority and belonging to the faction that generally supported Royal Governor Francis Bernard.

The freemen of Salem on October 21, 1765 adopted instructions for representatives Browne and Oliver opposing the Stamp Act and urging the legislature "do every thing you legally and prudently may, towards the repeal of the STAMP ACT." They also protested against the "riotous temper" that "has unhappily prevailed in several towns in this province - to the subversion of laws," to "vigorously to pursue all such measures as tend to suppress tumultuous proceedings" and "to prevent lawless outrage and violence." The two men helped secure their adoption by the Massachusetts legis-

---

12 Joseph Wanton of Newport, son, cousin, and nephew of Rhode Island governors, was a successful merchant and politician. He married Mary Winthrop in 1729 and they became the parents of eight children. He served as governor from 1769-75, but lost his post due to his failure to support American Independence. Ann, fifth and youngest daughter of Joseph and Mary Wanton, married Winthrop Saltonstall, another first cousin. *ANB*, s.v. Joseph Wanton; Charles Albert DuBosq and William Jones, "Descendants of Gov. John Cranston of Rhode Island, Addendum I, Joseph Wanton and His Descendants," *NEHGR*, 80 (July 1925), 252-53.

13 Browne was a proprietor St. Peter's. He probably purchased the pew for his wife who was an Anglican. Bruce E. Steiner, "New England Anglicanism: A Genteel Faith?," *WMQ*, XXVII (January 1970), 126n. Other members of the family had previously shown their support for the Church of England by donating to the purchase of a bell for the church. They consisted of his great uncle Benjamin Browne, uncle William, and father Samuel. Benjamin joined that church and William promised in 1736 to help pay the salary of its first priest. "A List of Subscribers Towards the Bell in St. Peter's Church, in Salem, 1741," *EIHC*, II (October 1860), 258-59; Harriet Silvester, "St. Peter's Church before the Revolution," *EIHC*, LXXX (July 1944), 245-46, 253-54.

14 *ANB*, s.v. William Browne; *Sibley's Harvard Graduates*, XIII, 551-52; Gilbert Streeter, "Salem before the Revolution," *EIHC*, XXXII (1896), 69-70. For a list of some of its members, see Fitch Edward Oliver, ed., *The Diary of William Pynchon of Salem* (Boston: Houghton, Mifflin and Company, 1890), 84-85.

15 Andrew Oliver, Jr. (1731-1799), son of lieutenant governor Andrew and Mary Fitch Oliver, graduated from Harvard in 1749 and married Mary Lynde, daughter of Benjamin Lynde, Jr. in 1752 and granddaughter of Colonel Samuel Browne. He and Browne were second cousins. The couple moved from Boston to Salem in 1760. He was chosen judge of the Court of Common Pleas in 1761 and to the legislature in 1762. He failed to gain reelection in 1766. Although generally a supporter of royal authority, he was the only member of his family who remained in Massachusetts after the beginning of hostilities. He inherited the Fitch lands in Connecticut while a student at Boston Latin and retained at least some of them until at least 1785. His New Salem property was then assessed at £99-13-3. *Sibley's Harvard Graduates*, XII, 455-61; 1785 Colchester Tax List, CTR, folder 3, CHS.

lature in October 1765 much to the dismay of the Act's most ardent opponents.[16] The following spring after its repeal the Boston Evening-Post listed the names of thirty-two men from thirty-one towns who "if they have in any shape discovered an approbation of the Stamp Act . . . they are justly . . . accounted [as] enemies to their country." The names included both Oliver and Browne.[17] The support of the two representatives for the Stamp Act ruined the political career of Oliver, but due to the Browne family's long leadership in Salem, young William was given a second chance.

The following year Royal Governor Francis Bernard told a British acquaintance that the Stamp Act crisis had produced a political realignment in the colony with anti-administration Whigs comprising close to two-thirds of the representatives. The friends of government were reduced to a rump and just thirteen of his allies retained their seats, two of whom were William Browne and Andrew Oliver, Jr. of Salem.[18] In early November 1766, Lieutenant Governor Thomas Hutchinson noted to a correspondent in England that among "my best friends [are] the two Salem members" who "were tied down by their towns." Two weeks later he informed William Bollan, former London agent for the colony, that he had presented copies of the English man's pamphlet *A Succinct View of the Origin of Our Colonies* to Browne and Oliver.[19]

The approbation of the Salem freemen for Browne ended, however, with the Massachusetts response to the Townshend Acts.[20] The legislature drafted a Circular Letter in February 1768 protesting against the new duties and the Earl of Hillsborough, secretary of state for the colonies, instructed Governor Bernard to demand that the General Court rescind its action. In June, the lower house by a vote of ninety-two to seventeen refused to do so. Browne and his Salem colleague Peter Frye voted with the minority and became known as "Rescinders."[21] Leading Massachusetts newspapers quickly publicized the betrayal of the infamous seventeen. On July 11, one journal listed "the Members of the late Honorable House of Representatives . . . who voted in favor of 'Rescinding' agreeable to His Majesty's Requisition, as signified in the Earl of Hillsborough's Letter."[22] Two weeks later a second reported the proceedings of a legal town meeting in the "ancient and populous Town" of Salem to show the world "the Sense they Had of the Late Conduct of their Representatives, William Brown and Peter

---

[16] "Newspaper Items Relating to Essex County, Massachusetts," *EIHC*, LI (April 1915), 135-36; *Sibley's Harvard Graduates*, XIII, 552; Colin Nicolson, ed., *The Papers of Francis Bernard: Governor of Colonial Massachusetts, 1760-69*, Vol. 2 (Boston: The Colonial Society of Massachusetts, 2012), 382.

[17] *Boston Evening-Post*, April 28, 1766 Supplement, [1].

[18] *Papers of Francis Bernard*, Vol. 3, 180-81.

[19] Thomas Hutchison to Unknown, November 11, 1766, in John W. Tyler, ed., *The Correspondence of Thomas Hutchinson*, Volume I: 1740-1766 (Boston: The Colonial Society of Massachusetts, 2014), 465-66; Thomas Hutchinson to William Bollan, November 22, 1766, Ibid, 477-79.

[20] Until his fall from grace, Browne was clearly the foremost citizen of the community. Gilbert L. Streeter, "Salem before the Revolution," *EIHC*, XXXII (1896), 71.

[21] Labaree, *Colonial Massachusetts*, 235; *Papers of Francis Bernard*, 4, 230; Morris, "Social Change," 424-25; Wallace Brown, *The King's Friends: The Composition and Motives of the American Loyalist Claimants* (Providence: Brown University Press, 1965), 20. Other loyal stalwarts included Timothy Ruggles (Marblehead) and Richard Saltonstall (Haverhill).

[22] *Boston Post-Boy*, July 11, 1768, [1].

Frye, Esqrs; who . . . gave their votes for *Rescinding.*" They voted to approve the act of the legislature in refusing to rescind and thanked the majority "for their firmness in defending the Liberties of the People." The majority also specifically condemned the minority who had shown their disloyalty to the colony.[23] The Salem freemen never again elected either of them to public office.[24]

Browne did, however, hold a number of appointive offices. The Massachusetts legislature chose him a justice of the peace for Essex County on November 19, 1761, judge of the Inferior Court of Common Pleas for Essex County on September 17, 1770, and colonel of the the the First Essex County militia regiment in 1771.[25]

According to both the standard biography and the authoritative work on the Boston Massacre, the Boston sheriff arrested Browne on September 6, 1769 for being a party to the beating of patriot James Otis, Jr. Such an action was totally out of character for him and, if one looks closely at the evidence, the two historians erred.[26] The Browne taken into custody was identified as being formerly of Salem, formerly of Beverly, and then of Virginia.[27] The only person fitting that description was William Browne's first cousin William Burnet "Virginia Billy" Browne (1738-1785), son of Samuel, Jr.'s younger brother, William.[28]

*****

Browne took over management of his extensive properties upon reaching his majority. His Connecticut estates had not been well managed since the death of his father and he quickly took steps to rectify the situation.[29] William had grown up with

---

[23] *Boston Gazette*, July 25, 1768, [3]. The minority included such prominent Salem citizens as Benjamin Pickman, Benjamin Pickman, Jr., Nathaniel Ropes, Benjamin Lynde, Andrew Oliver, Jr., Samuel Curwen, and Joseph Blaney.

[24] As Browne stressed in his memorial to the Commissioners for American Claims, "he lost his Seat, became an object of public Resentment, and in numerous Instances suffered in his Interest." Memorial of William Browne, AmLC, AOP, AO 12/10, 217, 219, NAUK.

[25] Whitmore, *Massachusetts Civil List*, 84, 134; *Sibley's Harvard Graduates*, XIII, 553; Ronald L. Boucher, "The Colonial Militia As a Social Institution: Salem, Massachusetts 1764-1775, *Military Affairs*, Vol. 37, No. 4 (December 1973), 127. The lieutenant colonel of the regiment was his former legislative colleague, Peter Frye. *Boston Gazette*, August 19, 1771, [2].

[26] John J. Waters, Jr. wrote that the assault on Otis was carried out by John Robinson, a member of the Boston Commissioners of Customs. John J. Waters, Jr., *The Otis Family In Provincial and Revolutionary Massachusetts* (New York: W. W. Norton & Company, Inc., 1968, 1975), 177.

[27] *Sibley's Harvard Graduates*, VIII, 124; XIII, 552; Hiller B. Zobel, *The Boston Massacre* (New York: W. W. Norton & Company, 1970, 148, 150, 350, 351.

[28] William Burnet Browne had moved to King William County, Virginia by June 1770. *William Burnet Brown v. Asa Houghton*, Windham County Court Records, Trials, June 1770, Vol. 14, 386, CSL; *William Burnet Brown v. William Williams*, Ibid, Vol. 14, 389. He had begun the process as early as 1766, when he advertised to sell a farm "within an Hour's Ride of three Sea-port Towns, *(viz) Salem, Marblehead*, and *Beverly*, containing about Four Hundred Acres of choice Land, with three Dwelling-Houses . . . one of them a genteel House, with a Kitchen, Stables, &c. calculated for a Gentleman of Fortune." "Newspaper Items Relating to Essex County, Massachusetts," *EIHC*, 295.

[29] To cite just one example, in 1757 the New London County Court heard a case in which Epes Sargent and his wife Katherine sued Daniel Brown of Lyme to collect an unpaid debt that dated back some fifteen years when Katherine was femme sole. *Epes Sergeant and wife Katherine v. Daniel Brown*, NLCC, Files, June 1757,

slaves, but the idea of bringing them to his lands in rural and underdeveloped New Salem first appears to have been expressed at a dinner with his future father-in-law Joseph Wanton of Newport Rhode, Island, a slaveowner, around 1758.[30] According to a third hand report written in 1900 by a descendant of the last overseers of the Browne properties, the engagement of John Mumford and the bringing of slaves to the region were the result of the following circumstances:

> Gov. Wanton of Rhode Island was entertaining Judge Brown at a dinner in Providence. Gov. W. was asked by his guest "if he knew of a young man of character and energy whose services could be secured by him for some time, to enter upon the subjigation [sic] of a large tract of land he owned in Salem, Connecticut, build a house and bring the land into cultivation." Gov. Wanton told him he knew just the man and at once arranged an agreement with Mr. [John] Mumford and Judge Browne. Mr. Mumford entered immediately upon his labor engaging a numerous gang of Blacks . . .[31]

Although what was written in the letter dates from some 140 years after the event described and is incorrect in important details, it speaks to a larger truth, of Browne's decision to bring slaves to his Connecticut lands.[32] Shortly after this purported conversation, the young man purchased seven or eight enslaved persons and shipped them to his Connecticut lands. One can speculate that Wanton played a significant role in this action as the family had long been active in the Guinea trade.[33]

John Mumford, Sr. (1712-1796), the man who moved to New Salem to oversee the Browne properties, was born and raised in South Kingstown, Rhode Island in a slave holding family in the slave center of New England.[34] John Mumford, Sr. and John

---

Box 107, folder 11, no docket.

[30] He married his first cousin Ruth Wanton, on March 19, 1761. *Sibley's Harvard Graduates*, XIII, 551-52; Perkins, *Connecticut Farm*, 58; Morris, "Social Change," 421; Sarah Deutsch, "The Elusive Guineamen: Newport Slavers, 1735-1774," *The New England Quarterly*, 55, no. 2 (June 1982), 233, 240, 245, 248, 252.

[31] Nathaniel Shaw Perkins to Alfred Mitchell, June 8, 1900, Mitchell-Tiffany Family Papers, Box 20, folder 105, Manuscripts & Archives, Yale University Library; Stark, "Myth and Reality," 168. Perkins heard the story from a daughter of John Mumford, Jr., Lucretia Mumford Thacher (b. 1785), and Alfred M. Bingham quoted the statement in his "Squatter Settlements of Freed Slaves in New England" article. Perkins called this story a family tradition and noted that John Mumford, Sr. could well have been known to Browne. John's grand-nephew David married Rebecca Saltonstall in 1758, a cousin to both William and his wife and as a child William Browne had sailed to Fishers Island and stayed at the house of John's half-brother George. This acquaintance could have served to help vet the Rhode Island man. Perkins, *Connecticut Farm*, 79.

[32] The conversation took place before William Browne became a judge and before Wanton became governor. The person hired was not "a young man," but the young man's father, John Mumford, Sr., and he did not bring a "numerous gang of Blacks" to Connecticut.

[33] James B. Hedges, *The Browns of Providence Plantations: Colonial Years* (Cambridge: Harvard University Press, 1952), xvi, 32, 81, 90. A number of Rhode Island merchants invested heavily into the African slave trade. Ibid, 70. The Wantons were also significant slave owners. Joseph, as an example, had an enslaved man called Venture in 1730. Elizabeth Donnan, *Documents Illustrative of the History of the Slave Trade to America, Vol. III, New England and the Middle Colonies* (Washington, DC: Carnegie Institution of Washington, 1932), 174, 183-84; *Thomas Williams v. John Winthrop and Joseph Wanton*, March 1731, Early Records, CSC, Box 10, folder 9, no. 18.

[34] Fitts, *Inventing New England's Slave Paradise*, 71-83.

Mumford, Jr. (1740-1825) came to the parish in 1759.[35] At around the same time that young William Browne engaged John Mumford, Sr. to manage his lands in New Salem, he began to purchase slaves to bring to his Connecticut properties. Some twenty-five years later in his memorial to the British commission tasked with examining claims for losses by Loyalists, he stated that when he began to improve his estate in Connecticut, he purchased "3 Negroes & 1 Woman, whom he left on this Estate." He later purchased "3 or 4 [more] which were sent to the farm on Claim[an]t's Estate which his agent's Son was in Possession."[36] The strong likelihood is that he acquired the slaves in Rhode Island and perhaps from a member of the Wanton family.[37]

John Mumford, Sr. was the son of Thomas Mumford II and his second wife Esther Tefft. They had one son and three daughters before Thomas died in April 1726 leaving an estate valued at £634-14-7. By will, the slaveowner gave his Negro girl, Morocco, to his son George by his first marriage and the remaining Negro slaves to his wife Esther. After her death, one slave girl went to daughter Sarah and Toby and Peg, to John Mumford. Although Thomas Mumford was quite well to do, John received a modest inheritance of a new house and five acres adjacent to the homestead farm.[38]

John married Elizabeth Perkins of North Kingstown in 1736. Called a cordwainer and yeoman, he and his wife sold his lands in 1737 and 1738, by the last he deeded all his property in South Kingstown to kinsman William Mumford for £300.[39] Mumford disappeared from the records until he arrived in New Salem and the first reference to him there occurs on June 20, 1759. At that time, the town urged the Hartford County Court to appoint him to "Keep a House of Public Entertainment."[40] John, Sr. became a Colchester freeman on September 18, 1759.[41]

---

35 James Gregory Mumford, *Mumford Memoirs: Being the Story of the New England Mumfords from the Year 1655 to the Present Time.* (Boston: The Merrymount Press, 1900), 63; Stark, "Myth and Reality," 168-69: Perkins, *Connecticut Farm*, 73-79.

36 "Essex County Loyalists," 298; Memorial of William Browne, AmLC, AOP. AO 12/10, 234.

37 Several family members, among them Edward, Evan, Joseph, and William Wanton had long connections to and active participation in the African slave trade. Jay Coughtry, *The Notorious Triangle: Rhode Island and the African Slave Trade, 1700-1787* (Philadelphia: Temple University Press, 1981), 37, 45-47, 49-50, 58, 87, 122, 132, 188-89.

38 Thomas first married Abigail (surname unknown) and they had six children, the two most important being George Mumford of Fishers Island and Thomas III of Groton. Mumford, *Mumford Memoirs*, 51, 54, 63, 81, 100.

39 Perkins, *Connecticut Farm*, 67, 73-74, 250-52.

40 As stated in its memorial, Lebbeus Harris had kept a tavern in that section of New Salem from 1754 to the end of 1758 and "Was about to Move out of the Town." When the civil authority and selectmen made their nominations in January 1759, they believed that "No other person Conveniently Scituate on that Rode [the Governors Highway from New London to Hartford] Which we thought proper to Nominate. But Since Mr. John Mumford is Moved into the house where Mr. Harris Kept the Tavern heretofore and is a person of Such Character that we think him a person fit and Sutable" to keep a tavern "where he lives for the Accomodation of the Traveller." HCC, PbyS: Travel, Box 539, April 1754-June 1759 packets, CSL. The clear import of this statement is that Lebbeus Harris served as agent for Browne throughout much of the 1750s and was replaced in 1759 by John Mumford, Sr. who moved into the house formerly occupied by Harris. Mumford continued to serve as an innkeeper until 1767 and again in 1773.

41 ColchesterBMD, Vol. 1, 155, CTH.

Illustration 6: Runaway Notice for Pharaoh[42]

October 9th 1764.
RAN-AWAY from Groton in Connecticut; a Spanish Molatto Slave, named PHAROAH, about 5 Feet 10 Inches high, well set, wore short Hair (but may have cut it off) considerably Talkative to appearance, artful and pleasant in his Manners and Behaviour, plays on a Violin, & had one with him; when he went away had on a stone grey Bearskin Coat, a strip'd Flannel Waistcoat without Sleeves, cloth colour'd Breeches, Stockings uncertain, as he carried a Variety with him in a Bag with other Cloathing, Brass Buckles in his Shoes. Whoever takes and secures said Slave so that the Owner may have him again, shall receive FIVE DOLLARS Reward with necessary Charges paid, by JOHN MUMFORD, of Colchester. N. B. All Masters of Vessels and Others, are forbid harbouring or carrying off said Slave, as they shall answer it at their Peril.

Despite his recent arrival in New Salem, the inhabitants of Colchester selected him as one of its surveyors of highways at the annual town meeting on December 24, 1759. Town meeting records also note that Mumford and Captain Henry Champion were chosen in November 1761 to meet with William Browne concerning a memorial to the legislature about a highway. He was selected again, on October 31, 1768, as agent for Colchester to meet with Browne and absentee Andrew Oliver, Jr. about building a highway through their lands. In addition, he witnessed a renewal of bounds between Browne and William Welch in April 1767 and acted as attorney for Browne in an execution for debt in October 1768.[43] A slaveowner, he advertised in October 1764 for the return of a "Spanish Molatto Slave" named Pharaoh who had run away from him in Groton.[44]

Although Mumford father and son did not own land in New Salem, the family was related to several prominent families in southeastern Connecticut and southern Rhode Island. They had connections with the Connecticut Winthrops

---

[42] *New London Gazette*, October 19, 1764, [3]. The advertisement contains a stereotypical image of a runaway African male.

[43] Perkins, *Connecticut Farm*, 253; ColchesterBMD, Vol. 1, 212, 219, CTH.

[44] *New-London Gazette*, October 19, 1764, [3]; *Thomas Mumford v. John Mumford*, NLCC, Files, June 1769, Box 151, folder 12, no. 325. John purchased Pharaoh from Thomas Mumford on September 25, 1764.

through John, Sr.'s more prominent half-brothers. Thomas Mumford, 3d (d. 1760) moved to Groton in 1720 and rented a farm from the Winthrops. Captain George Mumford leased a Winthrop farm on Fishers Island from 1736 to 1756. In 1755, he purchased a house on Main Street in New London from John Christophers and died there on June 22, 1756.[45]

John Mumford, Sr. lived in the house just north of the Lyme-Colchester line that the Browne agents generally occupied, a large mansion that had paneled walls and large beams. It faced west and was located on the main road from New London to Hartford. John brought his entire family with him, wife, two sons, and six daughters. Most of the children were near adulthood and soon married.[46]

Mumford left a relatively light footprint in Colchester town affairs, but was found more frequently in Hartford and New London court records. For example, the Hartford County Court in June 1760 found for Mumford in a case of debt by note for £7-10.[47] In a second lawsuit, Mumford sued William Potter of New London in 1767 for £20 damages after the defendant acting as his bailiff and receiver failed to deliver a shipment of pork, beans, and butter worth £13-10-6. Mumford eventually recovered £2-13-9 debt and £4-13-10 in court costs.[48] New London County Sheriff Christopher Christophers sued Mumford the next year for the recovery of two yoke of oxen, one heifer, three cows, one mare, seven hogs, and two calves worth £50 that the sheriff had attached and had temporarily put into Mumford's custody. The latter failed to deliver them to the signpost in Lyme on April 14, 1768, the court found in favor of the plaintiff, and Mumford had to pay more than £43 in damages and costs.[49]

According to Mary Perkins, John, Sr. remained as agent for the Salem magistrate until around 1769 at which time his son replaced him.[50] The evidence from court records, however, indicates that he remained in charge of the Colchester farm until at

---

[45] Captain George transferred the lease and livestock to Benjamin Brown. The livestock included of 1,350 sheep, 42 cows, and 33 calves. Perkins, *Connecticut Farm*, 76-77, 80; Stark, "Myth and Reality," 165. Mumford contemporaries in New London County included brothers David and Thomas, Jr. of Groton and merchant James Mumford. Douglas C. Conroy, "A Disputatious People: New London's Wartime 'Illicit Trade' with the French West Indies (1755-1763, unpublished manuscript, 2017), 18 -19, 41-42, 122, 124, 146, 148-59, and passim. David and Thomas, Jr. both married daughters of Colonel Gurdon Saltonstall of New London, the uncle of William Browne.

[46] Son Caleb, an invalid who never married, lived with other members of the family. He died on April 12, 1801 at age 47 and is buried in Salem's Woodbridge Cemetery. Sarah Mumford married Bliss Ransom. Hannah (b. 1747) wed Samuel Dolbeare, son of George and grandson of John Dolbeare. Elizabeth married John Gardner. Mary married George Hazard, son of Samuel Hazard and Abigail Mumford, daughter of Captain George Mumford. Lucretia married John Ransom, and youngest daughter Tabitha James Moffatt. Connecticut Headstone Inscriptions, Charles B. Hale Collection, Vol. 106, Salem, 1, CSL; Perkins, *Connecticut Farm*, 67, 80-82; Holman, "Early Dolbeares," 183-84.

[47] *John Mumford v. Joseph Woodworth, Jr.*, HCC, Files, June 1760, Box 158, no. 61. This was the first of eighteen court cases involving the senior Mumford.

[48] *John Mumford v. William Potter*, NLCC, Trials, June 1767, Vol. 24, no. 264; *John Mumford v. William Potter*, NLCC, Files, November 1767, Box 145, folder 10, no. 40.

[49] *Christopher Christophers, Sheriff v. John Mumford*, Ibid, June 1768, Box 147, folder 14, no. 105.

[50] His name disappears from town records after 1769. John Henry took over the farm in 1773. Perkins, *Connecticut Farm*, 83.

least 1772, regardless of whether or not he retained his management responsibilities. Mumford was defendant in three January 1772 lawsuits in which Colchester constable Elihu Clark sued for the nondelivery of Negro woman Patient, Negro man Tom, and a mare to him. They had been placed in his temporary possession after writs of execution had been secured by Peter Bulkley against Samuel Hazard and others and were to be sold to pay debts due the plaintiff.[51] When Colonel Gurdon Saltonstall of New London filed for bankruptcy in 1772, he listed several score of creditors from such places as Boston, Newport, New York, Providence, the City of London, and several Connecticut towns. Among the men to whom he owed money, was John Mumford of Colchester.[52] Around the time he retired as manager of the Browne estate, John, Sr. moved to the house of his son where he died in July 1796.[53]

John, Jr. resided on a thousand-acre farm in Lyme. A few years before John, Sr. retired, much of the southern section of New Salem was made part of Chesterfield Society. The parish also included the northern section of Lyme East Society and part of New London North Society. The northwest bounds of the new parish established in January 1769, one that proved to be no more successful than ill-fated New Salem, was four rods northwest from the northwest corner of John Mumford, Jr.'s recently constructed dwelling-house, called Elmgrove. Seventeen months later he married Lucretia Christophers (1750-1825), daughter of John and Jerusha Gardiner Christophers, thus directly connecting him with two of the more prominent families in the region.[54] Browne called Mumford his Connecticut agent, so the father and later the son probably took care to see that the leased estates were managed properly, collected the rents, and perhaps negotiated contracts with new tenants.

A snapshot exists for New Salem Society soon after William Browne launched his effort to introduce slavery on his Connecticut lands, thanks to the existence of a Colchester tax list for 1762.[55] Divided into three and a fraction parishes, the list of polls and ratable estates for the town amounted to £12,671 for the First Society, £6,313 for Westchester, £2,399 for Marlborough,[56] and £6,219 for the Colchester portion of New Salem, one that did not include additions, fourfold assessments, and faculty taxes which were assessed on those with non-farm income.[57] The town total was £27,591-6-6, with

[51] *Elihu Clark v. John Mumford*, HCC, Files, January 1772, Box 202, packet 1, no. 4,5,7. Bulkley recovered three judgments against Hazard for £68-5-9 debt and £1-12-1 costs in one case, twenty shillings damages and £7-4-4 costs in a second lawsuit, and twenty shills damages plus £6-8-5 costs in the third. Mumford signed receipts for having received the two slaves and the horse.

[52] CA, Insolvent Debtors, Series 2, X, 137, CSL.

[53] Perkins, *Connecticut Farm*, 155; Lyme Church Records, Vol. 1, 1787-1850, 89, CSL.

[54] Perkins, *Connecticut Farm*, 139-41. The father of the bride had earlier sold his house in New London to John's uncle George Mumford.

[55] Each town annually elected listers and collectors whose duty it was to assess all taxable property and to collect what was due to support the expenses of parishes, towns, and the colony government. Nothing similar exists for Lyme until 1781.

[56] The General Assembly incorporated Marlborough Society from parts of Westchester, Hebron, and Glastonbury in May 1736. *Colony Records*, VIII, 49.

[57] Houses, land, livestock and polls were all taxed. All males between sixteen and seventy years old with exceptions for college students, college tutors, school masters, ministers, and colony officials were assessed

£675-17 in additions and fourfold assessments of £704-12, making the grand total £28,971-15-6.[58] The New Salem list contained 104 names, five of whom were Browne tenants.[59] The value of the leases is evidenced by the fact that renters paid among the highest taxes in the parish. John Mumford, Sr. at £279 had the highest tax list and Joshua Ransom at £112-10 the sixth highest.[60] The average list for the five renters was £125.2, while that for all of New Salem was £59.8, a clear demonstration of the value of rented farms.[61]

*****

To the extent that we have any knowledge of William Browne's vast Connecticut estates and his management of them, it comes from court records. When William reached his twenty-first birthday, he began to make regular trips to Colchester and Lyme. As early as 1759 at around the same time he brought slaves to his farms, he began making loans to local farmers.[62] On August 17, 1759, for example, Jonathan Hamilton of Colchester borrowed "Eight pounds four shillings & four pence lawful Money" that he promised

a poll tax of £18. House lots up to three acres were assessed at twenty shillings per acre, e. g. one pound an acre. Land, depending on its fertility and use, was rated at between two and ten shillings per acre, except that meadow lands in Hartford County were assessed at fifteen shillings per acre. Livestock ranged from a high of £4 for a mature ox and £3 for a horse to a low of £1 for swine and yearlings. One hundred acres of woodland, as an example, at two shillings per acre were assessed at £10. Lawrence Henry Gipson, *Connecticut Taxation, 1750-1775,* Tercentenary Pamphlet, X (New Haven: Yale University Press, 1933), 2 3, 8; *Acts and Laws 1750,* 137-38.

58   Faculty rates, assessed on those with non-farm income, added another £356, with seventy per cent of the assessments coming from the First Society.

59 Stephen Harding £94-10, John Tenant £76, Samuel Tenant £59-04, plus John Mumford, Sr. and Joshua Ransom. John Mumford, Jr. lived in Lyme.

60 1762 Colchester Tax List, CTR, folder 10, CHS. The assessment on the property rented by John Mumford, Sr. was the fourth highest in the town of Colchester. Gershom Bulkey of the First Society had the highest assessment at £393-10, David Day of Westchester Society ranked second at £345-15, followed by Pierpoint Bacon in the First Society at £300.

61 1762 Colchester Tax List, CTR, folder 10, CHS.

62 Browne increased his income by providing banking services. In addition to lending money to Colchester farmers, facilitated by his New Salem agent, his reputation was such that in August 1765 future governor Jonathan Trumbull of Lebanon, a Harvard classmate of Browne's father, wrote "at the Request of Messrs. Jacob Eliot Junr & Oliver Buell both of this Town, who are desirous of Your Assistance in the Loan of One hundred pounds," £70 for Eliot and £30 for Buell. Browne replied a month later that he had made a loan of £80 for the benefit of Eliot. Jonathan Trumbull to William Browne, August 27, 1765, Jonathan Trumbull, Sr. Papers, Box 2, folder 8, CHS; William Browne to Jonathan Trumbull, September 28, 1765, Ibid.
  Evidence from Windham County Court Records shows that Jacob Eliot, Jr., the son of the Reverend Jacob Eliot of Lebanon Goshen, received this and one other loan from his Harvard friend. Browne sued Eliot to collect unpaid bond debts in June and December 1772. In the first instance, Eliot confessed judgment in a debt by bond for £131-14 debt and £1-1-3 costs. Six months later he confessed and was ordered to pay the plaintiff £95-12, £80 for the loan and £15-12 for accumulated interest, plus £1-14-6 costs of suit. *William Brown v. Jacob Eliot*, June 1772, WCC, June 1772, Vol. 14, 72, CSL; *William Brown v. Jacob Eliot*, Ibid, December 1772, Vol. 14, 190. Eliot (1734-1783), a classmate of Browne, died insolvent. His Harvard biographical sketch states that he was assisted "by the fact that the War effectively cancelled his indebtedness to his old friend and College Classmate William Browne." *Sibley's Harvard Graduates*, XIII, 586.

to repay with lawful interest by the following March.[63] Hamilton failed to pay off the loan, Browne finally sued, and the Hartford County Court heard the case in November 1766. The defendant defaulted, and Browne recovered £11-15-17 for debt and accumulated interest and £3-0-3 costs of suit.[64] At the same court session, Browne sued David Dodge of Colchester's First Society for the nonpayment of a bond dated November 1, 1760.[65] He also rented lands in Massachusetts.[66]

William filed several lawsuits in the Hartford County Court to gain back property that had been alienated, some during his minority. In the first, Browne sued Peter Bulkley of New Salem for "the Seisen and peaceable possession" of forty-five acres in Colchester that had been in the hands of the plaintiff in 1755.[67] The defendant pleaded that he was "not Guilty in manner and form . . . alleged," the court agreed, and Browne appealed to the superior court.[68] Before that body, Browne triumphed. He recovered his property, twenty shillings damages, and costs of suit £7-9.[69] Second, Browne sued William Welch of Colchester for the return of thirty acres that the defendant had seized sometime within the last fifteen years "without law or right." The defendant defaulted, but Browne only recovered damages of one shilling plus costs of suit.[70] Third, he sued Nathaniel Harris for the "Seisen and Possession" of eight acres in Colchester that the defendant took over in January 1762.[71] Finally, Browne sued Elisha Chapman of the First Parish in Colchester for violating the Connecticut statute, "An Act for Defeating

---

[63] John Mumford, Sr. drafted the document. It appears that Browne left a modest sum of bills of credit with Mumford for loan purposes. The interest borrowers paid on the loans served as income for the absentee and, indeed, for wealthy men throughout New England.

[64] *William Brown v. Jonathan Hamilton*, HCC, Files, November 1766, Box 183, packet 1, no. 14.

[65] The writ was read to Dodge on October 20, 1766, but he failed to appear at court. *William Brown v. David Dodge,* Ibid, Box 183, packet 2, no. 35. The bond required the defendant to pay the plaintiff £30 "in a reasonable time . . . with just costs" for money borrowed by Dodge. In June 1765, George Dolbeare of New London sued Dodge for not paying rent on a 500-acre farm in Lyme and Colchester. Dodge's taxable estate amounted to £88 in 1762. *George Dolbear v. David Dodge,* NLCC, Files, June 1765, Box 138, folder 9, no docket; 1762 Tax List, CTR, folder 10, CHS.

[66] Diarist William Pynchon noted the ill treatment of a tenant in April 1775. In addition, while in exile in England, Browne wrote on July 1, 1780 that about two months earlier, "I was decently accosted . . . by a man, about thirty years of age, who making himself known to me, proved to be the son of an old tenant, upon a farm, I once owned at Attleborough in the Massachusetts bay." Oliver, ed., *The Diary of William Pynchon,* 42fn; William Browne to Molly Carne, Sydney W. Jackman, ed., "Letters of William Browne, American Loyalist," *EIHC,* 96 (January 1960), 40.

[67] In the 1762 list of polls and ratable estates, the wealthy Peter Bulkey was rated at £266-10. 1762 Tax List, CTR, folder 10, CHS.

[68] *William Brown v. Peter Buckley,* HCC, Files, April 1768, Box 189, packet 2, no. 2. Samuel Huntington of Norwich served as one of his two attorneys. Huntington also represented John Mumford in a dispute over the ownership of slave Pharaoh. *Thomas Mumford v. John Mumford,* NLCC, Files, June 1769, Box 151, folder 12, no. 325.

[69] *William Brown v. Peter Buckley,* Early Records, CSC, March 1769, Vol. 19, 333.

[70] *William Brown v. William Welch,* HCC, Files, November 1768, Box 191, packet 1, no. 3. Samuel Huntington again represented Browne.

[71] *William Brown v. Nathaniel Harris,* HCC, Files, April 1769, Box 193, packet 1, no. 2. The case was not adjudicated because the clerk reported no appearance.

and punishing Trespasses." Sometime between September 1768 and January 1769 the defendant entered his land and cut down fifty trees of more than one foot in diameter and another fifty of smaller dimensions to the damage to the plaintiff of £37-10. The court found for the defendant, Browne appealed, and the Superior Court upheld the original verdict.[72]

Two memorials brought before the General Assembly, however, provide even better information on how Browne oversaw his lands and attempted to gain profit from rentals to tenants.

Ebenezer Tiffany of Lyme petitioned the General Assembly on March 25, 1767 claiming that William Browne had failed to honor an agreement with him. In March 1759, "your Petitioner hired a Farm of Wm Brown of Salem" for five years at the rent of £11 lawful money per year for the first two years and £12 for the next three, one third in bills of credit, one third in stone walls, and one third in clearing the farm.[73] Browne told him at the time of signing the lease that if he "improved said Farm" that after the expiration of five years "he would give your Petitioner a Lease of said Farm for as Long a Term as your Petitioner should then Chuse" at a reasonable rent.[74] Tiffany asserted that he had fulfilled the terms of the contract and, in addition, had built a large barn worth £50, a hog house valued at £5, erected sixty rods of fence, and sowed thirty acres of winter wheat and rye without any expectation of further profit except for the renewal of his lease, but Browne "utterly refus'd to give your Petitioner any further Lease of the Farm or to Suffer your Petitioner to remain any Longer thereon." Ebenezer thereupon asked Browne to pay him for the buildings and walls erected. The wealthy Massachusetts man declined to do so and did not allow the petitioner to reap and sell the grain he had planted without signing a surety bond. Tiffany concluded by asking the General Assembly "to take his unhappy Case into Consideration," appoint a committee to examine the situation, and grant him relief. Matthew Griswold of Lyme, one of the twelve members of the Upper House, received the petition and informed Browne's attorney Samuel Huntington of the necessity that the defendant appear to answer the charges at the May session of the legislature.[75] Despite depositions supporting Tiffany from Joseph Colt, James Gould, Elisha Ely, and Jasper Griffing, Jr., the legislature without comment declined to grant his petition.[76]

The second case had its origin on March 25 1767 when William Browne leased to Samuel Hazard of Colchester "a Farm of Land with a Dwelling House & other Buildings thereon" for seven years.[77] The terms required Hazard to pay Browne $100

---

72 *William Brown v. Elisha Chapman*, Ibid, April 1769, packet 2, no. 1. Samuel Huntington was Browne's legal counsel. *William Brown v. Elisha Chapman*, Early Records, CSC, Vol. 20, 77-78.

73 The farm was bordered on the west by the lands of James Gould, south on those of John Perkins deceased, and the other two sides by the lands of Browne. It totaled around 300 acres. The farm was almost certainly the property his grandfather purchased from Samuel Peck in 1728. See Map 1, Lot E1.

74 Tiffany's wording indicates that Browne was visiting New Salem at the time the lease was executed.

75 Petition of Ebenezer Tiffany, March 25, 1767, CA, Private Controversies, Series 2, XXVII, 179, CSL.

76 Ibid, XXVII, 179-82; *Colony Records*, XII, 605.

77 Samuel Hazard lived on Fishers Island in 1764 prior to his removal to Colchester, owned one male slave named Tom, and shared ownership of female Patient in 1772. *Samuel Hazard v. Samuel Bill*, NLCC, Files,

per year for the first four years and $140 for the last three. In addition, "your Petitioner Covenanted with sd. Brown to pay All Taxes arising on sd. Lands & to Erect every Year during . . . Thirty Six Rods of good double Stone Wall" wherever directed to do so by the owner. The farm contained 677 acres and was described as "the same Farm which was lately occupied by Samuel, John, & Caleb Tenant & was purchased" by William's grandfather "partly of William Gardner of South Kingston in the Colony of Rhode Island & partly of Aaron Stark & James Harris, both of Colchester."[78] Before occupying the farm, Hazard asked Browne to show him its boundaries "which he then did & especially direct[e]d your Petitioner to Occupy & Improve the Land to the Boundaries & Monuments then shewn him." Hazard took possession of the farm and "began to improve the Same to the Boundaries & Monuments shewn." Much to his surprise, however, he soon discovered that Peter Bulkley and Dudley Wright, both of Colchester, and "Sundry other Persons claim[e]d [a] great Part of sd. Farm within the Boundaries shewn as afores[ai]d." Browne brought an action of "Disseisin" against the complainants and recovered the disputed land, whereupon he directed "your Petitioner to continue his Improvements." Hazard cleared a large tract on the northern side of the farm, sowed it with wheat, and fenced it in "according to the Express Direction of sd. Brown." Then Bulkley sued Hazard in "four several Actions of Trespass against your Petitioner for the Cutting Timber, plowing, fencing . . . & Improving said Lands with his Claim & within the Boundaries shewn by sd. Brown."

Hazard asked Browne what he should do. The Salem man directed him "to go to Trial in all Said Suits" and stated that he spent "large Sums in defending the Title" to the lands in dispute. Bulkley, however, had recovered judgment on three lawsuits for "large Sums in Damages" against Hazard, he brought two other suits for trespass that were still in litigation, and Dudley Wright had recovered judgment against the petitioner for the surrender of forty acres of land and large damages. The "only Question" in all these trials "was the Extent & Boundaries of the Lands purchased by sd. Samuel Brown dec[ease]d of sd. Gardner, Stark, & Harris" and these suits determined that the bounds were "very far Short of the Boundaries & Monuments shewn by" Browne to Hazard by almost two hundred acres.[79] Hazard reckoned that his losses amounted to some £300 lawful money and that he had lost "the whole Benefit of his Lease." He asked the General Assembly to appoint a committee to examine his circumstances, that he be repaid for all his expenses, and be released from paying all rents.[80]

November 1764, Box 135, folder 6, no docket; *Elihu Clark v. John Mumford*, HCC, Files, January 1772, Box 202, packet 1, no. 4; *Peter Bulkley v. Samuel Hazard, Samuel Hazard, Jr., and George Hazard*, Ibid, January 1772, Box 202, packet 1, no. 17. As noted above, George Hazard, son of Samuel, married a daughter of John Mumford.

[78] The farm was located in the northeast quadrant of New Salem in the Gardner Lake area. Colonel Samuel Browne purchased the 635-acre property from William Gardiner on October 30, 1724, 45 acres from Aaron Stark on January 15, 1725/6, and the 37-acre plot from James Harris on February 8, 1725/6. The Hazard farm comprised most of these three purchases. CLR, II, 533, 625, 633.

[79]   For specifics on this series of lawsuits, see, *Peter Bulkley v. Samuel Hazard*, HCC, Files, April 1769, Box 193, packet 2, no. 2; *Peter Bulkley v, Samuel Hazard and Samuel Hazard Jr.*, Ibid, April 1770, Box 196, packet 2, no. 8; *Peter Bulkley v. Samuel Hazard et al*, Ibid, April 1770, Box 197, packet 1, no. 5; *Peter Bulkley v. Samuel Hazard*, Ibid, April 1770, Box 197, packet 1, no. 6, no. 7.

[80] Petition of Samuel "Hassard," April 21, 1772, CA, Private Controversies, Series 2, XIII, 166. The petition-

On May 2, 1772, eleven days after the date of the Hazard petition, Jabez Huntington of Norwich, one of twelve members of the Connecticut Council, ordered the sheriff of New London County to summon William Browne of Salem to appear before the next session of the General Assembly to give his reasons why the Hazard petition should not be granted. Huntington directed that the summons be given to Browne's attorney, Samuel Huntington of Norwich, and it was delivered to him on May 5th.[81] The matter remained in abeyance until May 1773 when Browne was in Colchester, traveled to Norwich to see Huntington and wrote him after discovering that his attorney had left for Hartford. In addition to mentioning that he had hoped that Huntington would have collected debts due him, he informed the lawyer that he had talked to Hazard the previous week. He discussed a dispute over the positioning of a stone wall, that arbitrators appointed by the county court had not yet met, and that Huntington should talk to John Mumford on the subject. "I have never been on the Farm since Mr. Hazard took it without him [Mumford] and I am persuaded he can afford great Light to the whole affair."[82]

Before the end of the month, the General Assembly appointed William Hillhouse of New London, William Whiting, and John Watrous of Colchester a committee to investigate the matter and report back to the legislature.[83] The committee met in Norwich, heard the parties on October 8, 1773, and decided in favor of Hazard. The legislature endorsed the report and resolved that "the Petitioner Be & he is hereby exonerated from the Payment of all Rents & fulfilment of all the Covenants Contained in Said Lease" due before March 25, 1773 and that Browne pay Hazard £45-9-1 "in full Satisfaction of the Matters alleg[e]d."[84] The monetary loss to Browne amounted to some £500. The following April the disgusted Salem man wrote Huntington and told him to "rescue my Farm by paying his Demand," but to make certain that Hazard paid the rent due for the past year.[85]

The New Salem properties of the Massachusetts adherent of royal authority represented close to sixty per cent of his wealth and he worked assiduously to improve and secure profits from them. Browne made regular trips to New Salem to oversee these lands,

---

er also noted that he lost all his "Considerable Estate." Perkins believed that the decision against Browne may have been caused by prejudice against Loyalists. Perkins, *Connecticut Farm*, 52, 142.

81 CA, Private Controversies, Series 2, XIII, 166.

82 William Browne to Samuel Huntington, May 12, 1773, Dreer Collection, Box 271, Historical Society of Pennsylvania. The author found out about this and three other letters in Larry R. Gerlach, *Samuel Huntington, 1731-1796* (Hartford: American Bicentennial Commission of Connecticut, 1976).

83 CA, Private Controversies, Series 2, XIII, 166.

84 Ibid, XIII, 167, 169. Hazard remained on the farm on the west shore of Gardner Lake rent free from March 1774 to October 1776, but the property was untenanted from then until the time Browne's estate was confiscated. He moved back to Rhode Island and was ordered to be expelled in 1779 for aiding the enemy. Perkins, *Connecticut Farm*, 52, 82; Caroline E. Robinson, *The Hazard Family of Rhode Island, 1685-1894* (Boston: Printed for the Author, 1896), 69. A Samuel Hassard of South Kingstown, Rhode Island advertised for the return of a runaway Negro called Jack in both 1775 and 1781. This may or may not be the same Samuel Hazzard. *Connecticut Gazette*, September 15, 1775 [3]; Ibid, March 9, 1781 [3].

85 William Browne to Samuel Huntington, April 5, 1774, Gratz Collection, Historical Society of Pennsylvania.

most undocumented, although two journeys related to the Hazard imbroglio are found in colony records. He came to Connecticut again in 1770 when he deeded two small strips of land to the town of Lyme for a new highway.[86] The deed dated September 9, 1770, was recorded October 10, and included the statement "there Personally Appeared the above Named William Browne and acknowledged the foregoing instrument."[87]

In spite of legal hurdles, the Connecticut lands of William Browne provided a modest income for the wealthy Salem man and he had every reason to feel optimistic about the future. The only cloud on the horizon was the fact that relations between the American colonies and the mother country were worsening and no one knew what the future might bring.

---

[86] The proposed highway located entirely on Browne lands in Lyme was delineated by a series of markers to piles of rocks, trees, and stone markers. The deed stated that "in Consideration of the interest there is for a Public Highway through my Lands in sd Lyme for all the Kings Subjects . . . begining at West ende of my sd Land about Ten rods Southwesterly from the Bridge that is over one of the Branches of the Eightmile river at a Large heap of Stones on a Rock . . . to a heap of Stones Said to be one of the Bounds of sd Brownes Land." LLR, XII, 422-24. Browne made certain to twice include the unnecessary phrase that the proposed road was for the use of "all the Kings Subjects," a subtle or not so subtle way of emphasizing his loyalty.

[87] The town clerk wrote that the instrument was "Signed & Delivered in the Presence of John Mumford, [and] Caleb Mumford." This document may be the only occasion in which Caleb's name is found in public records. Ibid, 424.
    Browne made additional trips to New Salem in 1761, 1768, and in 1773 as noted above.

Chapter 8

The Price of Loyalty: Confiscation and Sale

William Browne entered Massachusetts politics just before the beginning of the upheavals that culminated in the American Revolution. His career as an elected public official ended in 1768 with his support of the Crown in the Circular Letter controversy. His reputation was not improved by being one of four men publicly praised by merchant S. Hall of Salem in October 1770 for "the Favour [of] their Custom from Aug. 2, 1768 to Oct. 9, 1770" when the nonimportation agreements in protest of the Townsend Acts were in effect.[1] He had to depend upon the royal establishment in Massachusetts Bay for political preferment, although the legislature appointed him colonel of the first regiment of the Essex County militia in the summer of 1771.[2] He remained, however, the first citizen of Salem, lived in its finest house, and was known as a lavish entertainer.

His political sentiments were well known thanks to his acceptance of an appointment as collector of the port of Salem in 1764 and his legislative service on behalf of royal authority from 1765 to 1768. He could, however, have retained the friendship of his neighbors and sat out the war in peace had Browne not made himself universally hated, except among fellow Tories, after he welcomed the last royal governor and accepted positions from him in the wake of the Coercive Acts.

New Governor General Thomas Gage came to town on June 2, 1774, was escorted by the Salem regiment commanded by Browne, and later "was entertained in fine style at the elegant mansion of Colonel William Browne."[3] Some two weeks later "*the Merchants and Freeholders of the Town of Salem*" published a fulsome address "*to his Excellency Governor GAGE,*" lauding him on his appointment to his new office, one that "cannot fail to excite the most just Expectations that this Province will enjoy the happy Fruits of your Benignity" and Browne was among its numerous signers.[4] Soon thereafter

---

[1] *Essex Gazette* [Salem], October 16, 1770, 47.

[2] He had been chosen 2d Lieutenant Colonel in 1765. Even Putnam, "Militia Officers, Essex County Co., Mass. 1761-1771," *EIHC*, XXXIX (October 1892), 178-79.

[3] Streeter, "Salem before the Revolution," 71, 78; Robert S. Rantoul, "A Historic Ball Room," *EIHC*, XXXI (1894-95), 82-83.

[4] *Massachusetts Spy*, June 23, 1774, [2]. Another newspaper provided the names of those who signed the address. The forty-eight signatories included Browne, Joseph Blaney, Samuel Curwen, Benjamin Lynde, Benjamin Pickman, John Prince, William Pynchon, and John Sargent. *Essex Gazette*, June 14, 1774, [2];

on June 15, 1774 Gage appointed him to the five-member Supreme Court of Judicature to replace the deceased Nathaniel Ropes.[5]

Browne again demonstrated his loyalty to the new governor by endorsing an address of "his Majestie's Justices of the Court of General Sessions of the Peace" for Essex County. They hoped for "the restoration of the Province to that State of Domestic Peace . . . which has been for some years past interrupted by Feuds and Discord," the promotion of "good order and observance of the Laws," and wished his administration "Success which shall entitle you to the united applause of a grateful people."[6] Gage followed on August 9, 1774 by appointing Browne one of thirty-six men chosen as Mandamus Councillors for Massachusetts after the Massachusetts Government Act stripped the colony of its charter.[7] Not all of the men took the oath of office, but one who did was William Browne.[8] All who accepted office were deemed traitors by the patriot majority and the handful that refused to resign had to seek refuge in Boston.[9]

On August 30, the Superior Court attempted to hold a session in Suffolk County.[10] All persons designated to serve on the petit jury refused to do so, because

---

[5] *Boston News-Letter*, June 16, 1774, [3].

[6] The committee designated to relay the address to the royal governor consisted of William Browne, Samuel Curwen, Daniel Farnham, Peter Frye, and Andrew Oliver, Jr.. A large percentage of the signees belonged to the Anglican St. Peter's Church. "Gleanings from the Records of the County of Essex, *EIHC*, XIII (April 1877), 140-42; Silvester, "St. Peter's Church in Salem," 356. The Salem Oliver's father Andrew died in March 1774.

[7] From 1691 until 1774, the Massachusetts House of Representatives selected councillors subject to gubernatorial veto. This changed with Parliament's passage of the Massachusetts Government Act. The bill was introduced in Parliament on April 15, 1774, approved by the King on May 20, and the list of appointees sent to General Gage on June 3. One provision of the new law stipulated that its members were to be appointed by the Crown and those selected represented a who's who of supporters of royal authority in Massachusetts. They included Francis Green, Foster Hutchinson, Thomas Hutchinson, Jr., Joshua Loring, Andrew, Peter, and Thomas Oliver, William Pepperell, Timothy Ruggles, and Israel Williams. Peter Force, *American Archives, Fourth Series, Containing a Documentary History of the English Colonies in North America, from the King's Message to Parliament, of March 7, 1774, to the Declaration of Independence* (Washington: M. St. Clair and Peter Force, 1837), Vol. 1, 731. Accessed through archive.org/details/AmericanArchives-Fourth; Mary Beth Norton, *1774: The Long Year of Revolution* (New York: Alfred A. Knopf, 2020), 101-03.

[8] Whitmore, *Massachusetts Civil List*, 64, 70; *Essex Gazette*, August 16, 1774, [3]. Whitmore erroneously stated that only ten took the oath of office, but twelve took the oath in Salem on August 8, including Browne, and another thirteen did so in Boston on August 22, but several soon resigned. Browne's friend Andrew Oliver, Jr. took the oath as Mandamus Councillor, but resigned within ten days, hurried back to Salem, and worked to adhere to majority sentiment, a road not taken by Browne. Among the others who took the oath of office and then resigned were Francis Green, Colonel Abijah Willard, and Thomas Oliver. Governor Gage on September 2, 1774 reported on the turmoil in the Boston region and the resignation of several men appointed to the Mandamus Council, one of whom was Andrew Oliver of Salem who "upon the first rumour of disturbance . . . resigned his seat in Council." John Boyle who was living in Boston listed all members of the Mandamus Council. He reported that nineteen appointees resigned. *Sibley's Harvard Graduates*, XII, 458; Force, *American Archives*, Vol. 1, 731-32 764-69; Norton, *1774*, 161, 163-64; John Boyle, "Boyle's Journal of Occurrences in Boston, 1759-1778, *NEHGR*, 90 (1931), 377-78.

[9] A. C. Goodell, Jr., "The Centennial Anniversary of the Meeting of the Provincial Legislature in Salem, Oct. 5, 1774," *EIHC*, XIII (January 1877), 23-24

[10] Around the end of August, Browne left his home, never to return, and removed to Boston. A letter dated August 26, 1774 reported on or about that date that Governor Gage, in attempting to prevent the Committee of Correspondence from choosing delegates to meet at Ipswich on September 6, ordered a proclamation to be

three of the judges, Chief Judge Peter Oliver, Foster Hutchinson, and William Browne had "by taking the oath of Counsellors" of the Mandamus Court and "sworn to carry into execution all the late grievous Acts of the British Parliament, among the last of which is one . . . highly repugnant of every ideal of justice and common humanity . . . and oppressive to the good people of this Provence, and manifestly destructive of their natural, as well as constitutional rights."[11]

Illustration 7: Browne Affirming Acceptance of Council Position[12]

Laſt Friday, Jeremiah Lee, Eſq; Dr. Samuel Holten, and M. Elbridge Gerry, waited on the Hon. William Browne, Eſq; t Boſton, with the 5th Reſolve of the Delegates of this County, w received the following Anſwer, viz.

GENTLEMEN,

I Cannot conſent to defeat his Majeſty's Intentions and diſappt his Expectations by abandoning a Poſt to which he has been graciouſly pleaſed to appoint me;---an Appointment made without Solicitation or Privity, and accepted by me from a Senſe of Duty the King and the Hopes of ſerving my Country. I wiſh therefore give him no Cauſe to ſuſpect my Fidelity, and I aſſure you I will nothing without a due Regard to their true Intereſt. " As a Judge and in every other Capacity" I intend to act with Honour and In tegrity and to exert my beſt Abilities ; and be aſſured that neith Perſuaſions can allure me nor ſhall Menaces compel me to do an Thing derogatory to the Character of a Counceller of his Majeſty Province of the Maſſachuſetts-Bay.   WM. BROWNE.
          Boſton, September 9th, 1774.
To Jeremiah Lee, Eſq; Dr. Samuel Holten,
          and Mr. Elbridge Gerry.

In another response to the establishment of the new council, the patriot majority in Essex County met in convention on September 6-7, 1774 and issued stinging resolutions condemning all those who cooperated with Britain in suppressing American liberties, asserting that they "are and will be considered its unnatural and malignant enemies."[13] It demanded that Browne immediately resign his position on the Mandamus Council and the convention sent three representatives to meet with him in Boston.[14]

---

posted. He then "went to Coll Browns from whence he sent the High Sheriff to the Committee of Correspondence desiring them to wait upon the Governor at Coll Browns."

Browne was accompanied by his son when he left his native town, but his wife and daughter remained behind in Salem. In his memorial to the American Claims Commission, he certified that "when the tumult happened at Cambridge in August 1774, he was attending his duty at the Superior Court at Boston, and was from that time obliged to reside there until the Town was evacuated by the King's Troops in March 1776." John Jenks of Salem to Cotton Tufts of Weymouth, August 26, 1774, *EIHC*, XLVII (July 1911), 230-31; Jackman, "Salem and St. Georges," 178; Memorial of William Browne, AmLC, AOP, AO 12/139, 218.

11 Force, *American Archives*, Vol. 1, 747-49. One of the twenty-two jurors was Paul Revere.

12 *Essex Gazette*, September 13, 1774, [2].

13 Boucher, "Colonial Militia," 126; Edward Hake Phillips, "Salem, Timothy Pickering, and the American Revolution," *EIHC*, 111 (January 1975), 71-72.

14 One of whom Elbridge Gerry (1744-1814) of Marblehead signed the Declaration of Independence and

Councillor Browne rejected these demands, replying, "I Cannot consent to defeat his Majesty's Intentions and disappoint his Expectations by abandoning a Post to which he has been graciously pleased to appoint me." He added that he had not solicited the appointment and accepted it "from a Sense of Duty to the King and the Hopes of serving my Country."[15]

The *Essex Gazette* then published two fierce attacks on the man who once enjoyed almost universal respect in his home town in response to Browne's "Answer to a late Message from the large and respectable County of Essex."[16] The first letter "*To the Hon* WILLIAM BROWNE, *Esq; of* Salem, *now at* Boston," was dated September 15 by "JOHANNES IN EREMO," while the second author simply styled himself as "An AMERICAN." Both essays castigated Browne for accepting the appointment as Mandamus Councilor. In the first essay, the author stated that although he had "never had the Honor of any personal Acquaintance," he had a favorable opinion of him and hoped that his respect for "Liberty and a sacred Regard for constitutional Government" would have induced him to refuse this appointment "so universally abhorred by your fellow Subjects in America." Instead, Browne had chosen "to fasten the Yoke of Slavery upon your Children and Fellow Subjects of this Province." He concluded by entreating his former Essex County colleague to "*voluntarily, fully and speedily* abandon that Plan of Slavery, which you have taken up under."[17] "An AMERICAN" was much more harsh. He asserted in his first sentence that the Salem man's actions had "prove[d] your Title to the first Rank of its malignant Enemies." Browne was "a Man, *lost* to the Feelings of Humanity, the voluntary *Executioner* of the Iniquitous Designs of an unprincipled Ministry."[18] He remained in safety in Boston under the military protection of British troops rather than return to his hometown.[19] After hostilities commenced, he accepted the appointment as one of three leaders of an association to preserve order in Boston.[20]

The fact that Browne remained loyal to Great Britain should not be considered

---

later became vice president.

[15] *Essex Gazette*, September 13, 1774, [2].

[16] Ibid.

[17] "JOHANNES IN EREMO," Ibid, September 20, 1774, [4]. The name came from a book by Cotton Mather published in 1695 consisting of biographical studies of the Reverends John Cotton, John Norton, John Wilson, John Davenport, and Thomas Hooker. *Johannes in eremo: memoirs, relating to the lives of the ever-memorable . . .* ([Boston]: Michael Perry, 1695).

[18] "An AMERICAN," *Essex Gazette*, September 27, 1774, [1]. On October 4, 1774, the bulk of the commissioned officers of Browne's Essex regiment resigned their commissions. One month later at the urging of the Massachusetts Provincial Congress, the Lynn militia company previously commanded by the man who was "politically deceased of a pestilent and mortal Disorder, and now buried in the ignominious Ruins at Boston" elected new officers. Ibid, October 25, 1774, [3]; November 22, 1774, [3].

[19] A Salem mob burned the house of his former legislative colleague Peter Frye in October 1774. Brown, *King's Friends*, 35. Benjamin Pickman wrote on April 16, 1775 that "Col. Browne's tenant, Vining, and Mr. Hooper's tenant, at Danvers, are ordered by the committeemen to depart with their stock and effects, and to leave the farms to lie unimproved. None dares to build on Col. Browne's land where the fire was, viz; where Mansfield's shop stood. The church windows and Col. Browne's have repeatedly been broken by the rabble." Oliver, ed., *Pynchon Diary*, 42fn.

[20] Robert E. Monday, ed., *The Saltonstall Papers, 1607-1815*, Vol. 1 (Boston: Massachusetts Historical Society, 1992), 91-92, 468. The other two men were Peter Oliver and Foster Hutchinson.

surprising.[21] A number of men in his Salem social circle were Loyalists, including Andrew Oliver, Jr., although not all chose exile.[22] With regard to his family, brother-in-law Joseph Blaney (1730-1786) who married Abigail Browne in 1757, remained a passive Loyalist. Born in Marblehead, Blaney became a merchant in Salem. He refused to leave Massachusetts and remained uncomfortably in Salem until the death of his wife in December 1776. Joseph spent most of the remaining war years in Windham, Maine and then returned to Salem to lodge with the Sargents.[23] Epes Sargent, Jr. (1721-1779), the eldest child of Epes, Sr., was a Loyalist who intended to leave Boston with the British on March 17, 1776, but so dreaded the thought of abandoning his homeland that he returned to Gloucester and spent his remaining years living quietly there.[24] Epes and Katherine's youngest child John Sargent (1750-1824) evacuated with the British, served as an officer in the King's American Regiment, and died in Barrington, Nova Scotia.[25] Browne's uncle, the cautious and elderly Benjamin Lynde (1700-1781), whose friends were Loyalist leaning, remained neutral, and stayed in Salem.[26]

We catch one glimpse of William Browne after fighting began. In January 1776, he wrote to Salem exile Samuel Curwen giving him news from Boston, the names of a number of officers in the "rebel army," and reporting that inhabitants of Boston wishing to leave the city were quarantined by the colonials before crossing into the Massachusetts countryside. Browne also informed him that he had "sent a verbal message to Mrs. Curwen . . . informing her of your safe arrival and health," but felt that it was too dangerous to send the letter. He concluded by sending the regards of his wife and son Billy and "pray present mine to all friends with you."[27]

---

21 As Thomas C. Barrow noted, "within any colonial society there exists an establishment, a group of men whose orientation is toward the preservation of colonial status" because of their privileged position within society and these individuals generally "cast their lot with their colonial rulers." Thomas C. Barrow, "The American Revolution as a Colonial War of Independence, *WMQ*, XXV, (July 1968), 455-56. Carl Bridenbaugh reached a similar conclusion in his *Cities in Revolt* chapter on "The Twilight of the Aristocracy," pages 332-72.

22   Other Salem Loyalists included Samuel Curwen, deputy judge of the admiralty; Peter Frye, former legislator, judge, and register of probate; Colonel Benjamin Pickman; Samuel Porter; and Captain Thomas Poynton, all of whom went to Great Britain. Two older Salem political leaders, Benjamin Lynde and John Turner, resigned their offices and remained in Massachusetts. Marcus, "Social Change," 432, footnote 34; Phillips, *Salem in the Eighteenth Century*, 383-86.

23   *Sibley's Harvard Graduates*, XIII, 4-5.

24   Sargent and Sargent, *Epes Sargent*, 8, 10-11.

25 Ibid, 9, 307-08. John Sargent is reputed to have aided a British force under Colonel Alexander Leslie that marched to Salem to seize cannon stored there on February 26, 1775. Eric W. Barnes, "All the King's Horses . . . and All the King's Men," *American Heritage*, XI (October 1960), 58; Force, *American Archives*, Vol. 1, 1268.
   Another son of Epes and Katherine Sargent was Paul Dudley Sargent (1745-1827). After the death of his father in 1762, Joseph and Abigail Browne Blaney became his guardians. He became an officer in the American Army in the Revolutionary War. Sargent and Sargent, *Epes Sargent*, 9, 212-17.

26 *Sibley's Harvard Graduates*, VI, 254-56. A superior court judge at the time of the controversial trial of the British soldiers involved with the Boston Massacre, he attempted to resign, but Thomas Hutchinson persuaded him to remain. Robert McCluer Calhoon, *The Loyalists in Revolutionary America 1760-1781* (New York: Harcourt Brace & Jovanovich, Inc., 1973), 61.

27   William Browne to [Samuel] Curwen, January 8, 1776, American Revolution Collection, Box 10, Letters (Copies), folder 10N, CHS; Andrew Oliver, ed., *The Journal of Samuel Curwen, Loyalist* (Cambridge: Harvard University Press, 1971), 48-50.

Browne left with the besieged British troops in March 1776. With his departure, ended the history of this branch of the family that "was for several generations the richest and most munificent family in Salem."[28] He sailed directly to England on the packet *Lord Howe*, finding refuge in a nation that his great-great grandfather had left 140 years previously and leaving behind land and properties his family had worked for generations to accumulate and maintain. He brought with him "Sir William Howe's Dispatches to Government."[29] Whatever remote chance existed to retain these properties and the eminent position he held in Massachusetts society depended on the rapid success of British arms. Had his head, e.g. his economic circumstances, ruled his heart, William like Andrew Oliver, Jr. would have remained in the colonies. He no doubt realized, however, that he had burned all his bridges in the land of his forefathers and that little chance existed of returning to them, the huge price paid for his conspicuous loyalty to the British Crown.[30] His wife Ruth and daughter remained in Salem until March 1776 and then traveled to Newport where they stayed with relatives until late 1777 or early 1778.[31] After the British captured Newport, she sailed to England.

In May 1777 before any action was taken on his absentee lands, Zebulon Waterman, a Colchester attorney, sent a memorial to the General Assembly on behalf of clients Benjamin and Jedidiah Beckwith of Lyme. Jonathan Beckwith had recovered two judgments against William Browne "who is with the Enemies of the United States," one for book debt and the second for covenant broken. One judgment was levied on land belonging to Browne "Now Improved" by the two Beckwiths and "Taking from them a Great part of Said Farm which they held and Improved." The General Assembly set aside both judgments and "Declared [them] to be Null and Void."[32]

At around the same time, a large number of oaks on Browne property were cut down and transported to Norwich and used on the hull of the frigate *Confederacy* that was launched on November 8, 1778.[33] The earliest direct evidence that the estate

---

[28] The British evacuation fleet carried some 11,000 British soldiers and around 1,000 Loyalists, including about 100 officials like Browne. Christopher Ward, *The War of the Revolution*, Vol. 1 (New York: The Macmillan Company, 1952), 133; Browne, "Youthful Recollections of Salem," 8.

[29] Memorial of William Browne, AmLC, AOP, AO 12/10, 222, NAUK. According to Samuel Curwen, the *Lord Howe* left Boston on March 26, 1776, Browne sailed with Thomas Hutchinson, Jr., and Dr. Peter Oliver, Jr., and travelled on the only ship that sailed directly to England. The vessel arrived at Falmouth at the end of April. Oliver, ed., *Journal of Samuel Curwen*, 154; Mary Beth Norton, *The British Americans: The Loyalist Exiles in England* (Boston: Little, Browne and Company, 1972), 30.

[30] Despite the eminence and wealth of his family, Browne has received little attention in Massachusetts scholarly literature, in part due to the disappearance of his family papers. He is not cited, for example, in two of the most important works on Massachusetts Loyalists. Bernard Bailyn, *The Ordeal of Thomas Hutchinson* (Cambridge: Harvard University Press, 1974); Douglas Adair & John A. Schutz, *Peter Oliver's Origin & Progress of the American Revolution: A Tory View* (Stanford, CA: Stanford University Press, 1961).

[31] Their first child died in 1773. "On Thursday last died, at Bristol, in the 10th year of her age, Miss Cath Browne, only daughter of the Hon. William Browne, Esq; of Salem and grand-daughter of his Honour Governor Wanton." *Providence Gazette*, November 6, 1773, [3]; Oliver, ed., *Pynchon Diary*, 7.

[32] CA, Revolutionary War, Series 1, VIII, 195; *State Records*, I, 311.

[33] Perkins, *Connecticut Farm*, 145-46. For a study of the history of the *Confederacy*, see Damien Cregeau and Dayne Rugh, "USS *Confederacy*: The Life and Service of Connecticut's Continental Frigate," *Connecticut History Review*, Vol. 58, no. 2 (Fall 2019), 36-48.

furnished timber for the frigate came from a 1786 deposition by Ebenezer Backus, Jr. of Norwich before the Commissioners for Loyalist Claims in Halifax, Nova Scotia. He stated that the Browne estate "was of a Size and Quality superior to any in that Part" of Connecticut and "for that Reason most of the Timber used in Constructing the Continental Frigate Confederacy . . . was procured from said Estate."[34] The 32-gun *Confederacy* was one of two frigates ordered by Congress and built in Connecticut under the direction of the governor and Council of Safety. Major Joshua Huntington of Norwich superintended the project by securing workmen and materials, while Jedediah Willett oversaw the actual construction. The entire ship was built of Tory timber. The lands of William Browne furnished the oak for the keel, additional timber came from a Tory farm in New London, and the planks for the hull and deck from trees on lands owned by other "Enemies of the United States of America" in the region.[35]

*****

The story of the confiscation of the Browne estate needs to be examined from two perspectives; that of Connecticut and that of Browne's effort to gain compensation for his immense losses.

In May 1778 on the recommendation of the Continental Congress, the Connecticut General Assembly passed "An Act for confiscating the Estates of Persons inimical to the Independence and Liberties of the United States within this State."[36] Specifically, the act directed that the estates of all persons who had gone over to and joined the enemies of the United States "be forfeited, to and for the use of this State" and that the selectmen of the towns present the county court with evidence of the reasons for confiscating the property. If the county court judged that the facts alleged were true, then it was to make the decision "that all the estate, real and personal, of such person shall be forfeited." The court of probate for the district where the property was located was given responsibility for administering the confiscated estate.[37] After the Connecticut legislation, Massachusetts passed "An Act to prevent the Return to this State of certain Persons therein named, and others, who have left this State, or either of the United

---

34 Affidavit of Ebenezer Backus, AmLC, AOP, AO 13/50, 134, NAUK. Existing and incomplete records for the building of the *Confederacy* contain no information on timber taken from Browne lands. Extant accounts furnished to the author primarily give the names of persons from the Norwich area paid for getting timber. The single exception is a bill to pay William Dodge of Colchester £1-2-6 for four- and one-half days' work hewing "Ship Timber." Confederacy (Ship) Papers, Historical Society of Pennsylvania.

35 Frances Manwaring Caulkins, *History of Norwich Connecticut: From Its Possession by the Indians, to the Year 1866* (Hartford: Published by the Author, 1866), 404-05; CA, Revolutionary War, Series 1, VII, 271-72. As Joshua Huntington stated in his memorial, good timber "of the Proper Kind & Size" could be found on a farm in New London owned by either an Oliver of Boston or Thomas Moffat, both enemies of the country. The standard work on maritime Connecticut during the American Revolution makes a number of references to the *Confederacy*, but nothing about its construction except for stating that the ship was built by Willett under the direction of Major Huntington. Louis F. Middlebrook, *History of Maritime Connecticut During the American Revolution 1775-1783*, 2 vols. (Salem, MA: The Essex Institute, 1925), I, 54, 196, 213, 221; II, 260, 262.

36 For a complete list of actions taken by Connecticut against Loyalists, see Thomas N. Ingersoll, *The Loyalist Problem in Revolutionary New England* (Cambridge, UK: Cambridge University Press, 2016), 256.

37 *State Records*, II, 9-12.

States, and joined the Enemies thereof" in October 1778, a law that specifically named "William Brown, Esq;" of Salem. The measure was designed to prevent these enemies of the United States from returning to Massachusetts.[38]

In February 1779, pursuant to the act of the General Assembly, the Lyme selectmen petitioned the New London County Court.[39] They affirmed that sometime before March 1, 1778 "William Browne Esq. of Salem in the State of Massachusetts Bay" did "voluntarily go over to join with and screen himself under the Protection of the King of Great Britain." The Salem Tory was the "Owner and Proprietor of a Large Estate in Lyme aforesaid in Lands, Buildings and Negro Slaves." Browne's lands were "bounded Northerly on Colchester Town Line, Westerly on East Haddam Town Line, Easterly on New London Town Line and lands of Samuel Dolbear and others and Southerly on Lands of Jesse Beckwith, James Gould, and others." With regard to the slaves, they were in the possession of "John Mumford [and] Benjamin and Jedediah Beckwith Liveing on said Lands." The County Court declared the estate forfeit the same month and appointed Jabez Huntington, Esq., Judge of Probate for the Norwich District, to take responsibility for the property.[40]

The inventory for the Lyme portion of the estate bore the date of May 10, 1779. The document listed the names, sex, ages, and monetary value of slaves Great Prince, Little Prince, Prue, Cato, Phillis, Rose, Jimm, Luke and Ca[e]sar, the last named "of an Infirm Constitution." The three appraisers set the value of the "Twelve Thousand four Hundred & thirty Six Acres of Land" [sic] in Lyme and thirty-six acres in New London together with buildings and "appurtenances thereon under the Incumbrances of Leases for one Year and one Farm thereof for two Years" at £171,150-18-10 in depreciated "Continental Currency." The appraisers noted that all the lands had been entailed by William Browne's grandfather as documented by a copy of the will of Colonel Samuel Browne presented to them.[41] The inventory also included the following:

> There are a Number of Slaves apprized who beg for their Liberty. The Lease of Luke and Ca[e]sar are Expired and all the Rest may be at Liberty to be Disposed of as your Honors shall Direct. Mr. John Mumford who has had a Lease on them with a Farm being Desirous to be Released from the Negroes without Diminution

---

[38] Massachusetts Historical Society Trumbull Papers, XXIII, 102, CSL. The disposal of his Massachusetts lands can be traced in part in newspaper postings. The first in May 1782 authorized Essex County probate judge Benjamin Greenleaf "to receive and examine the Claims of the several Creditors to the estate of *William Browne*, late of Salem, Esq; Absentee" at the tavern of Captain Jonathan Webb one day per month for the next five months. A follow-up notice in November advised creditors of the necessity of submitting their claims by the end of the year. Lastly an August 1784 notice stated that the remaining portion of his Salem estate was to be sold on October 23 and it consisted of a "large mansion house with garden, out houses, and 1/4-acre land; [a] large dwelling house & 1/4 acre; [and] store with 1/4 acre." *Boston Gazette*, July 22, 1782, [1]; *Salem Gazette*, December 20, 1782, [4]; August 31, 1784, [3].

[39] Lyme selectmen in 1779: Richard Wait, Jr., Seth Ely, Abel Hall, Samuel Selden, Joseph Smith, and Daniel Lord.

[40] CA, Revolutionary War, Series 1, XXXIV, 462, CSL. Benjamin Huntington replaced Jabez Huntington as Judge of Probate by the time the inventory was taken. The court removed the case from the jurisdiction of the New London Probate Court in which Lyme was a part because Judge Gurdon Saltonstall was Browne's uncle.

[41] The records do not include a copy of the will.

of his Rent.[42]

The wording of the last sentence hints that Mumford thought that the slaves to be more trouble than they were worth.

At the same time the inventory was being taken, several of Browne's former slaves sent a memorial to the General Assembly asking for their freedom.

> The Memorial of Great Prince, Little Prince, Luke, Caesar, Prue and her three children, all Friends of America, but Slaves lately belonging to Col. Wm Brown now forfeited to this State Humbly Showeth that their late Master was a Torry and fled from his Native Country to Master King George where he now lives like a Poor Slave.
>
> That your Memorialists tho they have Flat Noses Crooked Shins and other Queerniss of Make Peculiar to Affricans are yet of the Humane Race free born in our own Country taken from thence by Man Stealers and Sold in this Country as Cattle in the Market without the least act of our own to forfeit Liberty but hope our Good Mistress the Free State of Connecticut Engaged in a War with Tyranny and will not Sell Good Honest Whigs and Friends to Freedom and Independence of America as we are to Raise Cash to Support the War because the Whigs ought to be free and the Tories Should be Sold.
>
> Wherefore your Memorialists Pray your Honors to Consider their Case and Grant them Freedom upon their Getting Security to Indemnify the State from any Expence of their Support in Case of Want or in Some other way Release them from Slavery Any your Poor Negroes as in Duty Bound Shall Ever Pray.

The petition was dated Election Day 1779 and signed by Great Prince, Little Prince, and Luke. At its May 1779 session, the Lower House approved the memorial, but the Upper House rejected it.[43]

This memorial was noteworthy for several reasons. First, the petitioners emphasized how different they looked because they were "Affricans." Second, they stressed that they were born free, had been captured by slave catchers, and then transported to "this Country" to be sold "as Cattle in the Market." It is highly unlikely, however, that all the adult slaves came directly from Africa, from the two groups that Browne brought to his New Salem lands around 1760. Caesar and several others had not yet been born, Prue and Luke would have been in their teens and Great Prince and Little Prince under ten. Browne, however, provided no information on the names or ages of the Negroes he brought to rural Connecticut. In addition, the petitioners, or perhaps the man who drafted the document on their behalf, used patriot Whig rhetoric to assert their right to be free.

Although the legislature failed to approve the petition, the Negroes soon gained their freedom. Judge of Probate Benjamin Huntington was asked if he intended to sell the slaves and "he answered in the Negative." Thus, they were left free to take

---

[42] CA, Revolutionary War, Series 1, XXXVII, 233, CSL. The appraisers were James Gould, Zebulon Waterman and Samuel Dolbeare. Probate Judge Benjamin Huntington paid the three men £27 lawful money for their services on May 12, 1779. William Brown[e], 1779, NPR, no. 1760.

[43] Vicki S. Welch, *And They Were Related, Too* (n.p.: Xlibris Corporation, 2006), 53; CA, Revolutionary War, Series 1, XXXVII, 234. That same year slaves in Fairfield and Stratford petitioned to gain their freedom. McManus, *Black Bondage in the North*, 169.

care of themselves, except for the children who were bound out. Specific provisions for the youths were made in 1784 when the legislature granted a memorial from Huntington who informed them that "Sundry small Negro Children belonging to said Estate" should "be Disposed of in some way to Prevent their being Chargeable to the State." He requested to be allowed to bind out "or otherwise Dispose" of the children and the legislature granted the petition.[44]

Katherine Sargent, widow of Samuel Browne and Epes Sargent, petitioned the Norwich Probate Court in March 1780 to be granted her right of "Dower and power of thirds" to all the land and buildings in Lyme and New London owned by her late husband. The judge ordered the petition filed.[45] Katherine then sent a memorial to the Superior Court saying that she was "Aggreaved by a Decree . . . of a Court of probate held at Norwich . . . Den[y]ing her Motion and Petition to her Right of Dower." The court affirmed the decision of Judge Benjamin Huntington because her son William had "Joined the Enemies of this & the United States of America."[46] In May 1780, the General Assembly, acting on a memorial from Probate Judge Huntington, told the listers of Lyme that their attempt to make a "fourfold assessment" on the confiscated lands "be rejected and not allowed to be brought into the general list."[47]

The Colchester portion of the estate was appraised on January 5, 1781 by John Henry, James Ransom, and John Douglass. That portion consisted of 1,132 acres of land valued at at £2,264 and three Negro men, Paddy, Pomp, and Old Fashion.[48] The Governor and Council of Safety meeting in Lebanon on July 4, 1781 directed the probate judges for each county "to sell the estates of inimical persons confiscated by law, at public vendue" and soon thereafter the land began to be sold.[49] Huntington divided the property into forty-six lots and gradually sold them between September 1781 and January 1787.

The process began with an announcement from Judge Huntington in the Connecticut Gazette on August 24, 1781. The advertisement stated, "To be SOLD at PUBLIC VENDUE, at the Dwelling-House of Mr. John Henry, in Colchester, on the 19th Day of September next, pursuant to an Act of the General Assembly in May last," about 9,000 acres "of excellent Land" in Lyme, Colchester, and New London, "with eleven Dwelling Houses and as many Barns, and a Number of Out Houses thereon," the confiscated estate of William Browne. A "Great Part of said Land is under good Improvement, and well supplied with Timber and Water." The property was divided into "suitable Lots" and buyers could make payment in "Bills of Credit" of Connecticut and orders "drawn by the Committee of Pay-Table." A second sale took place in January 1783 at John Henry's house for that "which yet remains unsold, consisting of about seven Thousand Acres of

---

44 CA, Miscellaneous, Series 2, I, 93; CA, Revolutionary War, Series 1, XXXVII, 241. No evidence exists to support the claim of Alfred Bingham that they were abandoned and forced to live in cellars. Bingham, "Squatter Settlements," 65.

45 William Brown[e], NPR, no. 1760.

46 Katherine Sargent Memorial, Early Records, CSC, March 1780, Vol. 22, 201.

47 State Records, III, 63.

48 William Brown[e], NPR, no. 1760.

49 State Records, III, 469. See also a supplementary act passed in May 1782. Ibid, IV, 162-63.

Land in Farms and Buildings, Orchards, &c. and some wild or uncultivated Lands."[50]

Illustration 8: Advertisement for the Second Sale of Browne Properties[51]

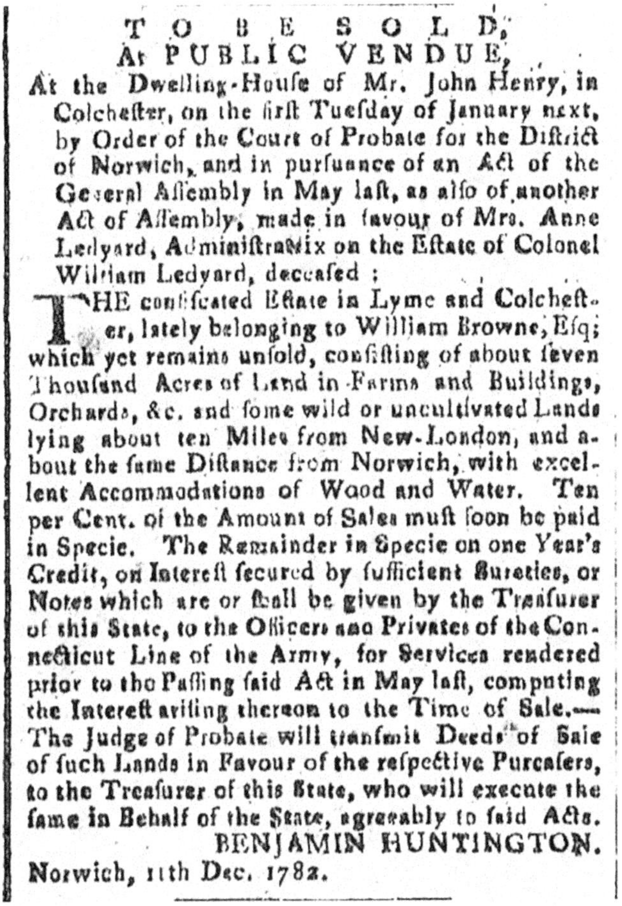

TO BE SOLD,
At PUBLIC VENDUE,
At the Dwelling-House of Mr. John Henry, in
Colchester, on the first Tuesday of January next,
by Order of the Court of Probate for the District
of Norwich, and in pursuance of an Act of the
General Assembly in May last, as also of another
Act of Assembly, made in favour of Mrs. Anne
Ledyard, Administratrix on the Estate of Colonel
William Ledyard, deceased :
THE confiscated Estate in Lyme and Colchest-
er, lately belonging to William Browne, Esq;
which yet remains unsold, consisting of about seven
Thousand Acres of Land in Farms and Buildings,
Orchards, &c. and some wild or uncultivated Lands
lying about ten Miles from New-London, and a-
bout the same Distance from Norwich, with excellent Accommodations of Wood and Water. Ten
per Cent. of the Amount of Sales must soon be paid
in Specie. The Remainder in Specie on one Year's
Credit, on Interest secured by sufficient Sureties, or
Notes which are or shall be given by the Treasurer
of this State, to the Officers and Privates of the Connecticut Line of the Army, for Services rendered
prior to the Passing said Act in May last, computing
the Interest arising thereon to the Time of Sale.——
The Judge of Probate will transmit Deeds of Sale
of such Lands in Favour of the respective Purcasers,
to the Treasurer of this State, who will execute the
same in Behalf of the State, agreeably to said Acts.
                        BENJAMIN HUNTINGTON.
Norwich, 11th Dec. 1782.

Since the State had seized the estate, Treasurer John Lawrence was listed as the grantor of the lands, but Probate Judge Huntington arranged the actual sales. By law, the lands were to be sold for the use and benefit of the state and the first occurred on September 19, 1781, when on the order of Connecticut's wartime Council of Safety, Huntington sold six acres of the forfeited estate to Captain Nathaniel Harris for £72.[52] By a second sale certified the same day, although not recorded until some four months later, Nathaniel Shaw of New London purchased two non-contiguous plots, lot 12 con-

---

50 *Connecticut Gazette*, August 24, 1781, [3]; December 27, 1782, [4].

51 Ibid, December 27, 1782, [4].

52 Nathaniel Harris (1743-1812), son of Jonathan and grandson of James, lived in New Salem, served in the Revolution, and was wounded in battle. Morgan, *James Harris*, 33-34, 41-42.

sisting of 62 acres and 32 rods and lot 21 containing 155 acres at a total cost of £379-13.[53] Although the specific evidence has not always been found, several sales represented payments for debt or services performed for the State of Connecticut.

Map 2. Confiscated Estate of William Browne[54]

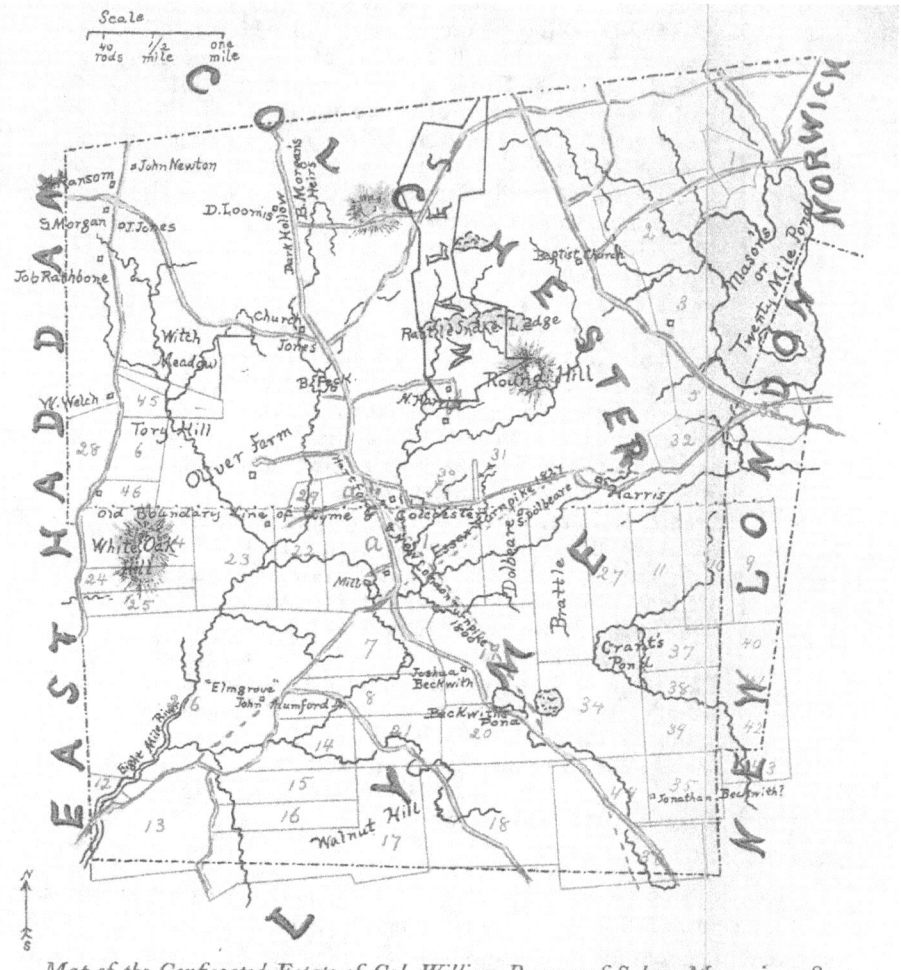

Map of the Confiscated Estate of Col. William Browne of Salem, Mass., in 1780

For the short period of time that the State controlled the Browne lands, it conscientiously maintained its ownership rights, as demonstrated when Judge Huntingon sued Daniel Beckwith, Jonathan Beckwith, Samuel Beckwith, and Stephen Beckwith, all of Lyme, for trespass. The State charged the Beckwiths in June 1785 with cutting and

---

53 CA, Revolutionary War, Series 1, XXXIV, 152, 158. The Council of Safety's order for Harris has not been found.

54 Perkins, *Connecticut Farm*, map between pages 64 and 65. Note the designations for Brattle, Dolbeare, and Oliver lands and the name of Tory Hill on Lot 6. Map reproduced courtesy of The Connecticut Historical Society.

taking away 300 trees on a large tract of land bordering easterly on the lands of Elijah Ransom westerly on a highway, southerly on the properties of Jonathan Miner, Jerusha Johnson, and Eleazar Mather, and on the north by the lands of James Ransom, John Loomis, and others.[55]

Table 3. Sale of Confiscated Estate[56]

Lot	Purchaser (Town)	Date	Price	Acreage	Town
31	Nathaniel Harris (Colchester)[57]	Oct. 23, 1781[58]	£72	6	Col.
7	Amasa & James Ransom (Col.)	Nov. 19, 1781	£1,017	194	Lyme
20	Daniel & John Loomis (Col.)	Dec. 5, 1781	£999	170.75	Lyme
14	James & Amasa Ransom (Col.)	Dec 6, 1781	£397	160	Lyme
12	Nathaniel Shaw (New London)	Jan. 28, 1782	£124	62	Lyme
21	Nathaniel Shaw (New London)	Jan. 28, 1782	£256	155	Lyme
6	Elias Peck (Colchester)	Apr. 11, 1782	£481	130	Col.
45	David Purple, Bond Bigelow (Col.)	Feb. 22, 1783	£157	45	Col.
28	Amos Jones (Colchester)	Feb. 28, 1783	£583	144	Col.
32	Ebenezer Rogers (Colchester)	Mar. 5, 1783	£62	62	Col.
26	Thomas Shaw (New London)[59]	Mar. 7, 1783	£3,938	1,094	Lyme
A1	William Winthrop (New London)	Mar. 26, 1783	£2,424	589	Lyme
1	Abner Chapman (Colchester)	Mar. 26, 1783	£151	62.5	Col.
2-3	Daniel Rodman (Norwich)[60]	Mar. 26, 1783	£1,59	494	Col.
5	Samuel H. Parsons (Middletown	Mar. 26, 1783		103.5	Col.
9	Stephen Billings (Lyme)	Mar. 26, 1783	£518	214	Lyme
10	Seth Phelps (Groton)	Mar. 26, 1783	£439	214	Lyme
11	Daniel Rodman (Norwich)	Mar. 26, 1783		214	Lyme
30	William Rathbune (Colchester)	Mar. 26, 1783	£2-10	50 rods	Col.
33	Samuel H. Parsons (Middle.)[61]	Mar. 26, 1783	£1,351	188	Col.
35	Samuel H. Parsons (Middleown)	Mar. 26, 1783		207	Lyme
36	Elijah Ranson (Colchester)	Mar. 26, 1783	£1,035	343.5	Lyme
37	Daniel Rodman (Norwich)	Mar. 26, 1783		111	Lyme
38-43	Nathan Allyn, 2nd (Groton)	Mar. 26, 1783	£306	611	Lyme, Mont.
44	Samuel H. Parsons (Middletown)	Mar. 26, 1783		125.5	Lyme

---

55 *State v. Daniel Beckwith, Jonathan Beckwith, Samuel Beckwith, and Stephen Beckwith*, NLCC, Files, June 1785, Box 192, folder 19, no docket. The suit was later withdrawn.

56 Perkins, *Connecticut Farm*, 203-22, 234-37, 246-50. Prices are generally rounded out to nearest pound, in sterling, public securities, or State money, and acreage to the nearest quarter acre. Deeds listed the totals in acres and portions thereof in rods. One hundred and sixty square rods comprise one acre.

57 Acquired by William Browne in 1767 by writ of execution on Jonathan Hamilton on a debt of £16-17. Ibid, 249.

58 The dates used are those listed in the land records of the towns. Several volumes of CA, Revolutionary War, Series 1, XXII, XXIV-XXVIII, and XXXIV contain additional information on the sale of these lands.

59 Farm on which John Mumford, Jr. lived. Nathaniel Matson of Lyme surveyed Lot 26 on June 27, 1781. Perkins, *Connecticut Farm*, 148, 222.

60 Daniel Roadham purchased lots 2, 3 11, and 37 at a cost of of £1,596 sterling. Ibid, 246. 246.

61 Revolutionary War General Samuel Holden Parsons, a native of Lyme, moved to Middletown just before the Revolution. Payment of 1,351 8s 7d was in Connecticut Securities given to men of the Connecticut Line for Lots 5, 33, 35, and 44. Ibid, 249.

Lot	Purchaser (Town)	Date	Price	Acreage	Town
23	Theodore Woodbridge (Glas.)[62]	Sep. 29, 1784	£1,154	288.5	Lyme
29	William Tarbell (Colchester)	Apr. 30, 1785	£60	30	Col.
25	Benajah Phelps (East Hartford)	June 8, 1785	£150	83	Lyme
15	James Ransom (Colchester)	Apr. 1, 1786	£184	147.5	Lyme
13	Ebenezer Tiffany (Lyme)	June 27, 1786	£92	513	Lyme
16	George Griffin (East Haddam)	June 27, 1786	£1,124	140.5	Lyme
19	Experience Robinson (Windham)	June 27, 1786	£689	27.75	Lyme
24	Gurdon Rogers (East Haddam)	June 27, 1786	£179	89.25	Lyme
27	Elisha Holmes	June 27, 1786	£131	238	Lyme
4	Thomas Shaw (New London)[63]	July 28, 1786	£1,378	230	Lyme
8	Thomas Shaw (New London)	July 28, 1786		209	Lyme
34	Thomas Shaw (New London)	July 28, 1786		258	Lyme
46	Thomas Shaw (New London)	July 28, 1786		60	Col.
17	Thomas Shaw (New London)	Sep. 9, 1786	£239	530	Lyme
22	John R. Watrous (Colchester)	Nov.30, 1786	£402	148.75	Lyme
18	Elizabeth Richards (New London)	Jan. 30, 1787	£430	480	Lyme

The 47 lots ranging in size from 50 rods to 1,094 acres were sold to thirty-one different individuals and several men made multiple purchases, most of whom lived in neighboring communities.[64] Prices per acre varied a great deal depending upon land quality and the medium of exchange, whether pounds sterling, public securities, or Connecticut lawful money. Thomas Shaw of New London made six purchases, the first on March 7, 1783, four on July 28, 1786, and the final one a month and a half later. His acquisitions totaled 2,381 acres. His first and largest purchase comprised 1,094 acres upon which John Mumford, Jr. lived for most of the rest of his life. General Samuel Holden Parsons paid £1,351 on March 26, 1783 for four lots totaling 624 acres. Others who acquired multiple parcels consisted of Daniel Rodman of Norwich with three; Nathaniel Shaw of New London, father of Thomas Shaw, with two; Amasa and James Ransom of Colchester, two; and John R. Watrous with two.[65]

Several recipients acquired their properties as a direct result of actions by the General Assembly. Lot A1, for example, came into the hands of William Winthrop because William Browne owed his cousin John Still Winthrop £2,338. John Still had long suffered from poor health and was "absent [from] Home in a long journey for the recovery of his Health" when he died abroad in April 1776.[66] William Winthrop, son of the

---

62 Woodbridge of Glastonbury and Dr. John R. Watrous of Colchester were joint grantees.

63 Thomas Shaw purchased lots 4, 46, 8, and 34 for a total £1,378 6s 7d. Ibid, 205.

64 Thirteen lived in Colchester; four in New London; two each from East Haddam, Groton, and Lyme; and one each from East Hartford, Glastonbury, Middletown, Norwich, and Windham.

65 James Ransom on his own right bought lot 15 in Lyme containing 147.5 acres on April 1, 1786.

66 An extract from a letter from Antigua of April 25, 1776 reported that, "Died here, JOHN STILL WINTHROP, Esq." Connecticut Gazette, June 14, 1776, [3]. The standard Winthrop genealogies mistakenly states that he died in New London on June 6, 1776. Mayo, Winthrop Family, 162; Robert C. Winthrop, Jr., A Short Account of the Winthrop Family (Cambridge, MA: John Wilson and Son, 1887), 12-14. When the large estate of John Still Winthrop was finally distributed among his many heirs in 1786, no mention was made of any land in New Salem Society because William had sold the property to William Stewart of New London in January 1784. John Still Winthrop, New London, 1776, NLPR, no. 5793; Perkins, Connecticut Farm, 204.
    John Still deserted the faith of his ancestors and became a member of St. James's Church in New London

deceased, petitioned in May 1782 to have his claim heard and the Assembly granted his request. In January 1783, the legislature directed the Norwich Judge of Probate to grant sufficient lands to Winthrop to satisfy the debt and he, therefore, acquired Lot A1.[67] At the same session, the Assembly granted the memorial of Major Theodore Woodbridge and Dr. John R. Watrous who were owed considerable sums for their Revolutionary War services by deeding them the 288-acre "Harding Farm" in Lyme then occupied by Robert Henry. This was Lot 23.[68] William Tarbell received Lot 29 as the result of another legislative act of October 1784. Tarbell had been badly wounded "in the Thigh at the Battle of Germantown," became an invalid, and the state granted him £60 worth of confiscated lands.[69] Benajah Phelps of East Hartford received Lot 25 comprising eighty-three acres as compensation for his losses in the Revolutionary War. As stated in his memorial, he had settled in Nova Scotia in 1766 but was forced to leave and return to Connecticut due to his "attachment to the Cause of his Country." The legislature granted him lands from the late property of William Browne to the value of £150.[70]

*****

Browne remained in England from 1776 until the fall of 1781 living in London, Cowbridge, Wales, and Cambridge.[71] His known exile correspondence began with a May 11, 1778 letter to his father-in-law, former Rhode Island Governor Joseph Wanton.[72] Other early correspondents consisted of people that he knew in Massachusetts; Lieutenant General Thomas Gage, Governor Thomas Hutchinson, Judge Peter Oliver, Richard Saltonstall, half-brother John Sargent, William Wanton, sister-in-law Mrs. Elizabeth Wickham, and Francis B. Winthrop. They all lived either in England or in British occupied Newport and New York City. Unfortunately, they provide little information about his Connecticut lands.

Browne wrote about mutual friends and told the former Rhode Island governor in his first letter that his wife had joined him and that she would be writing her father soon.[73] The next day he wrote his sister-in-law Mrs. Elizabeth Wickham, wife of

---

in 1759. Steiner, "New England Anglicanism," 129.

[67] *State Records*, IV, 205-06; V, 28.

[68] Ibid, V, 56-57.

[69] Ibid, V, 459,

[70] Ibid, V, 474-75.

[71] Exiled Americans congregated first in London, but began to disperse in 1778 after the disastrous news of Saratoga reached the home country. Norton, *The British-Americans*, 97-100. His time in the British Isles can be traced in George Atkinson Ward, *The Journal and Letters of Samuel Curwen, An American in England, From 1775 to 1783*, 4th edition (Boston: Little, Brown and Company, 1864). The exile noted in his diary on May 4, 1776, for example, that he "Called on my friend Browne" who "acquainted me with some facts relative to the unfortunate abandonment of Boston by the King's troops; which after all has the appearance of being forced." Ibid, 58.

[72] Wanton was deposed from office by Rhode Island patriots in April 1775, but he remained in Newport and was left alone because he had enjoyed a good reputation in the colony until fighting began. Two sons, however, chose exile and submitted claims for £18,000. Brown, *King's Friends*, 52.

[73] William Browne to Joseph Wanton, May 11. 1778, Letters of William Browne, Bermuda Archives.

Thomas Wickham, in Newport to tell her that his wife had arrived safely in England on March 14th and how he longed "to see your dear little Cath." This was followed by a letter to F. B. Winthrop in New York in which he asked to be remembered to family and friends in New London.[74] These early letters show that despite his relatively comfortable situation and a pension of £200 per year that he missed his New England home. He also discussed general information about the war and family news. He wrote one letter to his mother on August 22, 1780 in which he discussed mutual acquaintances from Salem in exile and concluded with "warmest wishes' to his friends in America, adding "as to my enemies, if I have any such, bid them, God speed."[75] In a letter to F. B. Winthrop on May 1, 1781, the only one in which he made a reference to his Connecticut lands, Browne regretted that he "had long before bid adieu to all expectations of ever seeing my dear Mother again," made a series of unclear statements of the relationship between her and "Mr. Sargent," one of her sons by her second marriage to Epes Sargent, followed with a vague mention of "his claim upon my estate in Colchester," and the news that "his majesty had been pleased to consider me in his appointment of a successor to the late Governor of Bermuda."[76] Two months later he wrote that he intended to travel to Bermuda by way of New York.[77]

Browne received the position of governor of Bermuda as a reward for loyalty.[78] He sailed for New York on the transport *John and Jane* and stopped for around a month in British occupied New York City, arriving on October 19, 1781 the same day that

---

[74] William Browne to Mrs. Wickham, May 12, 1778; William Browne to F. B. Winthrop, May 12, 1778, Letters of William Browne, Ibid.

  Joseph and Mary Winthrop Wanton had a number of children. Ruth married William Browne, Mary wed Captain John Coddington of Newport, Elizabeth married Thomas Wickham of Newport, and Ann to her first cousin Winthrop Saltonstall. DuBosq and Jones, "Descendants of Gov. John Cranston," 252-53.

[75] William Browne to Katherine Sargent, August 22, 1780, Jackman, "Letters of William Browne," 28-30. The friends mentioned were Samuel Mather, Jonathan Deuse, Reverend George Pigott, Samuel Porter, Thomas Poynton, and Benjamin Pickman. Jackman edited and published thirty-one letters written between May 11, 1778 and October 30, 1781. Katherine died on January 11, 1781 and was buried three days later. Oliver, ed., *Pynchon Diary*, 83-84.

[76] William Browne to F. B. Winthrop, May 1, 1781, Letters of William Browne, Bermuda Archives. In the same letter, he expressed regret at the death of F. B. Winthrop's brother who "had suffered so much, from a long, tedious, hopeless indisposition."

  Francis Bayard Winthrop (1754-1817), the second son of John Still Winthrop, was a businessman in New York City who remained on good terms with both the Americans and British during the American Revolution. The brother referred to was the eldest son John Winthrop (1751-1780). The third son was William Winthrop (1756-1827). Mayo, *Winthrop Family*, 197-206.

[77] William Browne to Molly Carne, July 1, 1781, Jackman, ed., "Letters of William Browne," 40.

[78] Benjamin Thompson (1753-1814), later Count Rumford, helped Browne secure this appointment, one that paid £750 per annum. *ANB*, s.v. William Browne; *DAB*, s.v. William Browne. The King granted him this position in May 1781 and Browne took his oath of office on May 18, 1781. *Pennsylvania Journal*, August 18, 1781, [1].

  From a twenty-first century perspective, Bermuda is important solely as a tourist destination, but in the eighteenth-century Atlantic World, the small island chain in the western ocean was "in the eye of all trade" and an extremely important place. Thus, contemporaries deemed the gubernatorial position a sinecure of considerable significance and of equal import to similar positions in Atlantic Canada. Michael J. Jarvis, *In the Eye of All Trade: Bermuda, Bermudians, and the Maritime Atlantic World, 1680-1783* (Chapel Hill, University of North Carolina Press, 2010). Jarvis mentions Governor Browne on several occasions. See pages 435-37, 439, and 449.

Cornwallis surrendered at Yorktown.[79] In November 1781, the Governor and Council of Safety granted William Winthrop of New London permission "to go to New York under the protection of a Flag" of truce "to transact business with William Brown, Esq, from whom a large sum is due his father's estate."[80] Soon thereafter "His Excellency William Brown, Esq; Governor of Bermuda, with his lady and family," sailed to Bermuda and "arrived safe at that island on the 22d of December last."[81] During his seven years as governor, two Loyalist lawyers from Massachusetts served with him, Andrew Cazneau from Boston as Judge of the Vice-Admiralty Court and member of the council, and Daniel Leonard from Taunton as chief justice. His capable leadership helped Bermuda navigate from war to peace and heal the divisions between the pro-American and pro-British factions.[82]

Sometime after the war ended, perhaps in 1784, the governor secretly returned to Rhode Island where a number of his Wanton relations lived to find out if any chance existed to retain at least part of his lands.[83] A member of the Mandamus Council, however, could not be forgiven. His estates in Massachusetts had already been sold and the same fate was occurring in Connecticut. Browne, therefore, returned to Bermuda until the end of his term of service.[84]

To get an understanding of Governor William Browne's quest to obtain compensation for his losses, it is necessary to begin with documentation gathered by Samuel Huntington (1731-1796) of Norwich, Signer of the Declaration of Independence, former president of the Continental Congress, and future governor of Connecticut. Browne hired the Norwich lawyer to represent him as early as 1768 and Huntington had served as his attorney in the important 1773-74 case against tenant Samuel Hazard, thus, he was the logical person to act on his behalf to help compute his losses and

---

79   In a letter written on board ship, Browne wrote, "By a line from Mr. [Francis B.] Winthrop at New York, I heard of the death of our dear mother." William Browne to Mr. [John] Sargent, September 18, 1781, Jackman, ed., "Letters of William Browne," 42.

80 Mayo, *Winthrop Family*, 205-06; *State Records*, III, 551.

81 *New-York Gazette and Weekly Mercury*, March 4, 1782, [3].

82 Cazneau returned to Massachusetts in 1788 and died there four years later. Daniel Leonard, like Browne a member of the Mandamus Council, never returned to his native land and died from a self-inflicted gunshot wound in 1829. E. Alfred Jones, *The Loyalists of Massachusetts: Their Memorials, Petitions and Claims* (London: The Saint Catherine Press, 1930), xiii, 78-79, 191-94; Force, *American Archives*, Vol. 1, 731.

Governor Browne is mentioned several times in Michael J. Jarvis, *In the Eye of All Trade: Bermuda, Bermudians, and the Maritime Atlantic World, 1680-1783*, 428-50. The author of this ground breaking study commits a mild pratfall in his information on Browne. Despite assertions to the contrary, the governor never pursued a mercantile career in Massachusetts and the author also made errors in a short biographical sketch located in a footnote. He again stated that after graduating from Harvard in 1752 [sic], Browne "became one of Salem's leading merchants." The biggest misstatement occurs in the following sentence: "In 1776, Massachusetts asked him to be the state's governor, but Browne declined the post and departed for England instead. Ibid, 435-36, 640 footnote 114.

83 The historical record is unclear with regards to the governor; however, his wife and daughter did spend several months in Salem and Newport in 1784. Oliver, ed., *Pynchon Diary*, 183, 189, 191, 196-98, 200-01.

84 Ingersoll, *The Loyalist Problem*, 283. Browne may have made a second back to the New England between 1784 and 1788. *Sibley's Harvard Graduates*, XIII, 559; *ANB*, s.v. William Browne.

provide documentation on the lands he had once owned.[85] The records consisted in large measure of copies of deeds to lands acquired by the governor's grandfather Colonel Samuel Browne.[86] With lawyerly precision, Huntington built the case for Browne beginning with the 1669 deed by which William Lord and his son Richard purchased a large tract of land from Chapeto in the northern section of Lyme, one that included much of the property that Samuel Browne would later purchase from James Harris. This was followed by a copy of the 1687 Lyme Patent and an excerpt from Lyme Town Records by which Matthew Griswold, Jr. was granted around 7,000 acres in the northeast quadrant of the town. Next came the April 1709 survey by Richard Lord and Joseph Peck of Lyme of the northeast bounds of the town from Haddam East to the "Nehantick River."[87]

Then came thirty-five deeds, plans, and surveys of lands purchased by Browne between 1718 and 1729, beginning with the August 1718 deed by which James and Sarah Harris conveyed around 4,000 acres in the northeast section of Lyme to Colonel Samuel Browne.[88] Next came two deeds by which the heirs of Matthew Griswold of Lyme sold 2,871 acres to James Harris in 1723 and his rapid resale of the property to Browne.[89] The transcripts also include William Gardiner's sale of 635 acres to Browne in 1724, a quitclaim from William Whiting of Hartford to Aaron Stark of Colchester and Stark's subsequent sale of 45 acres to the Salem magistrate in 1726, the sale of another 37 acres by Harris in 1726, 80 acres in Colchester by Daniel Davis of Lyme in 1727, and Samuel Peck's deeding of three tracts in "Paugunk" totaling 300 acres in 1728.[90] So continued the meticulous recording of deeds until all the properties that Colonel Samuel Browne acquired in Lyme and Colchester were documented.[91]

No date appears on the transcripts, but they had to have been created in time for the information to be used when Governor William Browne's claim was heard in

---

[85] Gerlach, *Samuel Huntington*, 22, 86.

[86] Thanks to Records Officers Andrew Bayley and Karla Ingemann of the Bermuda Archives and Government Records Centre for all their assistance in supplying copies of the original documents and transcripts of the same. The originals are difficult to decipher due to ink bleed through. The records copied by Huntington are in a 97-page booklet, while the transcripts fill eighty-eight pages. The "title page" states that "the following Deeds, Plans and surveys belonging to Wm. Browne are in the hands of Sam. Huntington of Norwich." The documentation also includes a memo listing materials in the possession of Huntington that consisted of 7 deeds, 2 plans, 2 surveys, and copies of 4 notes and bonds. Deeds and Plans of William Browne's Estate in the United States," Bermuda Archives and Government Records Centre.

[87] Transcripts of Deeds and Plans of William Browne's Estate in the United States, 1-9, Bermuda Archives. These documents were followed by a May 1703 act of the General Assembly which confirmed to the proprietors their rights to ownership of the lands in their respective towns. Ibid, 9-12.

[88] Ibid, 12-16. Huntington, as one would expect, meticulously transcribed all documents. The Harris deed not only included an exact citation to the location of the original, but also all signatures, witnesses, and attestation information.

[89] Ibid, 17-24.

[90] Ibid, 25-45.

[91] The Huntington transcripts often contain copies of deeds to plots of land sold to the men who thereafter deeded them to Colonel Browne. For example, in August 1716 the proprietors of Colchester laid out three plots of land totaling around eighty acres to James Newton, Jr. He sold them to Daniel Davis in 1722 and Davis transferred them together with "one Messuage or Tenement" to Browne in 1727." Ibid, 34-41.

June 1786. A letter from the governor to Huntington on March 1, 1786 indicated that Browne soon expected his case to be adjudicated. He specifically asked his lawyer to return six documents that "I left in your hands" when last in Connecticut. They consisted of the deed from "W. Gardner to S. Browne," the "plan of the same" by John Plumb, a deed from Aaron Stark to Browne, the plan made by John Skinner, and two deeds from James Harris to Colonel Browne, the first dated February 8, 1725/26 and the second July 8, 1729.[92] Although not all documentation Governor Browne accumulated to support his claim for reimbursement came from the Connecticut attorney, still it provided much of the documentary foundation for the memorial.

By the time the Commissioners for American Claims met to consider the Browne case, his Connecticut lands had been mostly sold and his Massachusetts properties worth more than £10,000 had also been sold with the proceeds paid into the state treasury.[93] Claims "against the estate of William Browne esqr a Conspirator and absentee" began to be submitted in January 1785 and they amounted to £3,843-5-1 1/4.[94]

With regard to Governor Browne's loyalist claim, the first document consisted of a copy of a May 17, 1786 letter from Peter Hunter, Secretary of the Office of American Claims, to Browne in Bermuda saying that the commissioners had never "Dispensed with the Personal Attendance of a Claimant . . . especially in one of such great extent as yours."[95] The governor sailed to Halifax, Nova Scotia where the Commission was meeting and formally submitted his claim on June 8, 1786.[96] The twenty-seven page memorial of William Browne "late of Salem in the Province of Massachusetts Bay" briefly recounted his political activities between 1762 to 1774, gave a summary of his losses totaling £33,256 pounds sterling, provided detailed documentation on his losses, and concluded with statements by acquaintances attesting to the accuracy of the claim.[97] Supplementary documents include a list of Massachusetts claims against the estate, a long affidavit by Ebenezer Backus, Jr. of Norwich concerning the value of the governor's Connecticut lands, and a summary of the claims allowed.

The claimant began with a three-page cover letter that demonstrated his loyal-

---

92 William Browne to Samuel Huntington, March 1, 1786, Gratz Collection, Case 3, Box 26, Historical Society of Pennsylvania. He directed Huntington to contact him by way of William Sheddon and John Ten Eyck in New York. The existence of this and one other letter indicates that the governor maintained a private correspondence not recorded in his letter-books.

93 British documents use pounds sterling, while those from Connecticut and Massachusetts valued Browne's real and personal estate in local currency that was worth much less than its British counterpart.

94 The Massachusetts General Court approved a resolve on March 15, 1786 empowering the judge of probate for Essex County to consider the claim of John Ewing. Another document listed twenty-four more claimants, including Paul Dudley Sargent and "Mrs. Ann Brown." "On the petition of William Ewing," William Browne, AmLC, AOP, AO 12/82, NAUK; "The Estate of William Browne Esqr. of Salem County of Essex an Absentee," William Browne, AmLC, AOP, AO 12/82.

95 Peter Hunter to Governor Browne, May 17, 1786, AmLC, AOP, AO 12/139. See Appendix F, for a transcription of this letter and other documents pertaining to Browne's claim.

96 *Sibley's Harvard Graduates*, XIII, 560. According to a newspaper report, Governor Browne sailed from St. George's, Bermuda on the sloop *Polly* for Halifax in early June. *Massachusetts Gazette*, July 10, 1786, [3].

97 To put Browne's claim in perspective, 2,908 whites submitted claims for their losses, 313 from Massachusetts, and royal officials like the Salem magistrate submitted 64 claims, about 20% of the Bay State's total. Brown, *King's Friends*, vi, 21, 23.

ty to the Crown while serving in Massachusetts office. Browne noted that between 1762 and 1768, as a "Member of the House of Representatives," that "he uniformly support- ed . . . those measures . . . best Calculated to maintain the King's Authority" and that his ability to retain an elected office was destroyed by his vote "to rescind an Obnoxious Vote of a preceding Assembly."[98] As a result of this courageous act, he "became an object of public Resentment and in numerous Instances suffered in his Interest." He thereafter held only appointive offices, including those of colonel of the Essex County militia reg- iment, justice of the superior court, and member of "His Majesty's Council." General William Gage, the last royal governor, chose him to the Mandamus Council in the sum- mer of 1774. He so feared for his safety that from August 1774 to March 1776 he lived under the protection of British troops in Boston. Massachusetts and Connecticut had seized all his property and he had lost a fortune that was "worth in 1774 at a moderate Computation Thirty three thousand two hundred and fifty-six Pounds Sterling."[99]

The cover letter was followed by a one-page inventory of his entire estate divid- ed into ten properties or sections. His Connecticut losses comprised about sixty percent of the total, £19,326 pounds sterling for his lands, £330 for his Negroes, and £500 for arrears in rent.[100] The evidence for the Connecticut portion of his losses dated Halifax, June 8, 1786, takes six pages and is called "Property No. 1." Browne produced both original deeds and copies of deeds to all the lands his grandfather purchased in the col- ony.[101] In order to account for the 500 percent increase in the value of these properties in a period of around fifty years, he emphasized that he had "laid out himself £7000 Sterling in Improvements" and that he valued the estate at forty shillings "Sterling" per acre. Thus, 9,663 acres at £2 per acre equals £19,326.[102] To buttress his case with regards to the worth of his Connecticut lands, the governor stressed that the estate was located between the Connecticut and Thames Rivers, therefore, "its Situation made it very Val- uable." Since, however, the property was divided into farms and the tenants were often required to make improvements, the estimate was not unreasonable. He concluded this section of the memorial by stating that some 1,000 acres were worth "£3.12 Sterling per Acre."[103] The governor also produced a copy of his grandfather's will "whereby he devized all his Lands &c in Lyme, Colchester and New London to his Eldest Son Sam- uel Browne in Tail Male."[104] Samuel's brothers William and Benjamin had died without male heirs and the claimant was the only son of Samuel who had died in 1742 without

---

[98] A reference to the infamous Circular Letter.

[99] Memorial of William Browne, AmLC, AOP, AO 12/10, 217-19, 222. He was one of twenty-one men from the Bay State whose claim amounted to more than £10,000. Browne, *King's Friends*, 24.

[100] Memorial of William Browne, AO 12/10, 220.

[101] Browne valued these lands at £3,883-13-8 sterling at the times of their purchase.

[102] Ibid, AO 12/10, 227. The governor noted that sales of 5,216 acres thus far had yielded £10,711 "Lawful Money."

[103] Three pounds and twelve shillings.

[104] Much of the rest of his estate was likewise devised "in Tail Male," e.g. entailed, to younger brothers William and Benjamin Browne.

drawing up a will.[105]

The governor then discussed his Salem, Massachusetts holdings. Property No. 2 consisted of "a very handsome House in the Center of the Town" measuring "52 Feet by 37" that with its garden, orchard, and offices was worth £2,000 Sterling. A second house on the premises, Property No. 3, that the claimant built for his mother after the death of Epes Sargent was valued at £750 Sterling.[106] Other properties included a dwelling house and wharf valued at £1,000 Sterling and a variety of other houses and lands worth £5,400. In addition, Browne owned the "Forrest River Farm" about four miles from Salem that was inherited by his uncle Benjamin "in Tail Male" and was worth £1,500 Sterling and a variety of other lands some £4,000.[107] The remaining eight pages of the claim consisted of depositions by Doctor Jonathan Prince about his Massachusetts property, copies of more deeds to his Massachusetts lands, and affidavits attesting to the truth of Browne's claim.[108]

Several additional documents in American Loyalist Claims provide more information. The first consisted of a sworn statement by Ebenezer Backus, Jr. a thirty-eight-year-old merchant from Norwich, taken at Halifax on June 23, 1786. He testified that the lands were situated close to "Norwich and New London, two Trading Towns scituate [sic] on a navigable River" and that his estate "was an extensive Tract of Land of several Miles in Length and Breadth" containing "a great Number of Valuable Farms." Moreover, "an excellent Growth of good Oak" covered much of the land "fit for the Purpose of Shipbuilding" and that of size and quality "superior to any other" so near the sea coast. Much of the timber used to build "the Continental Frigate Confederacy" came from Browne's lands. Backus characterized the land as well watered and productive, so much so that in 1781 he had purchased several hundred tons of English hay that he transported to Rhode Island for use by the French army. He testified, therefore, to the truth of Browne's statements about the quality and value of the Connecticut properties.[109]

The other documents consisted of a copy of the appointment of Benjamin Huntington as administrator of the confiscated estate to dispose of it "to the best advantage." They also included a detailed report on the sale of more than 5,700 acres through the end of January 1783 with the notation that the remaining 3,600 acres had a value of "a Guinea p[e]r Acre" and a listing of Browne's eleven Negro slaves.[110] Additional documents in another hand contained the names of the last thirteen tenants and the terms

---

105 Memorial of William Browne, AO 12/10, 223-28.

106 The two Salem houses were sold by "the Committee on the Sale of Confiscated Estates in the County of Essex" on October 23, 1784. The advertisement described the first dwelling as a "large and elegant Mansion House, Garden and Out Houses" and the second as "a large Dwelling-House and about one quarter of an acre of Land." *Salem Gazette*, August 31, 1784, [3].

107 Memorial of William Browne, AO 12/10, 220, 228-34.

108 Ibid, AO 12/10, 236-43. Ebenezer Backus, Jr., Joseph Chew, and Samuel Fitch testified to the extent and value of his Connecticut lands.

109 Affidavit of Backus, June 29, 1786, AO 13/50, 133-34.

110 Surveys taken in preparation for sale set the total at 9,454 acres and 107 rods. The estate was divided into three segments; 8,089 acres and 37 rods in Lyme, 464 acres and 29 rods for the Henry and Ransom farms in Colchester, and 911 acres and 41 rods "At the great Pond [Gardner Lake] in Colchester & New London." Report of Benjamin Huntington, April 11, 1783, AmLC, AOP, AO/13/50, 78-79.

of their leases and a compilation of bonds and notes due to Browne; Colonel Samuel Browne's lands in Charleton, Fitchburg, Ashby, Lincoln, Hadley, and Springfield, Massachusetts; and a complete inventory of his New Salem purchases.[111]

The Commissioners decided on Governor Browne's claim for £32,256 on July 15, 1786 and tentatively awarded him £7,658. The bulk, £5,000, represented the loss of his Connecticut lands. They also granted him £500 on the house in Salem "where Claimant lived," £200 on the house where his mother lived, £210 for his Negroes, and £200 for the house furniture and library.[112] They notified Governor Browne of their decision on July 20, 1786. "They have considered your Property in the Estates in Lime [sic], Colchester, New London [and] at Stage Point & Forest River Farm [in Massachusetts] only as Life Interest, as these Estates appear to have been entailed." They informed the governor that nothing further could be done on his claim unless more documentation was provided.[113] The result, then, was that Browne could collect only a fraction of the amount that he lost, just 23.7%.[114]

One might think that the entailment of so much of his property reduced the size of his claim, yet that may not to be the case because the Commissioners awarded him only 25% of the value of his house in Salem, 26.7% of the worth he set for the house where his mother had lived, and just 17% of price for a house and wharf in Salem. One authority on the subject states that claimants generally asked for a good deal more than what they ultimately received due to inaccurate or fraudulent claims as the value of property lost.[115]

After leaving Bermuda in 1788, Governor Browne retired to England and lived on Percy Street, Westminster.[116] Between 1792 and 1794, he sought unsuccessfully to collect £1,000 from Wanton relatives who had borrowed that sum in 1770.[117] His wife Ruth died in London on May 13, 1799 and the governor passed away on February 13, 1802.[118] An obituary published in a New York City newspaper noted that "WIL-

---

[111] Browne Tenants and Debts, AmLC, AOP, AO 13/50, 142-43.

[112] Award to Governor William Browne, AmLC, AOP, July 15, 1786, AO 12/61, 34-35, NAUK.

[113]   Peter Hunter to Governor Browne, AmLC, AOP, AO 12/139, 97, NAUK.

[114] The typical Loyalist who was awarded compensation for his losses received 37% of the claimed amount. Browne's was smaller perhaps because much of his property was entailed. Calhoon, *Loyalists in Revolutionary America*, 501.

[115] Eugene R. Fingerhut, "Uses and Abuses of the American Loyalists' Claims: a Critique of Quantitative Analysis, *WMQ*, XXV (April 1968), 252-53. The abuses were due to the fact that many petitioners inflated the value for property they had lost and because of inaccurate representations by men who endorsed the claims. My own view is that Browne attempted to accurately assess the value of all the property he lost in New England, but that the commissioners likely believed that as a general rule the memorialists inflated their claims and they adjusted their decisions accordingly, but they may as policy have only awarded a portion of the amounts sought.

[116] He was replaced by Henry Hamilton (c. 1734-1796). During the Revolutionary War, Hamilton was lieutenant governor and Superintendent of Indian Affairs at Fort Detroit and known as the "hair buyer." *The City Gazette* [Charleston, SC], April 28, 1790, [2]; "Henry Hamilton," *Wikipedia*.

[117] Sydney W. Jackman, "A Tory's Claim to the Wanton Estates," *Rhode Island History*, 19 (1960), 2-4.

[118] The couple had two children who lived to adulthood, William and Mary. His father purchased a commission for William in the 58th regiment of the British Army, but the emotionally troubled young man

LIAM BROWNE, Esq." had served on the Massachusetts Council until "he quitted at the commencement of the revolutionary war." After service as governor of "Bermuda Islands," he enjoyed an "honorable retirement" in London, "the rewards due to his loyalty as a subject, his services as a statesman, and to his benevolence as a man."[119] His passing was noted in Salem. "Gov. Browne was descended from one of the most antient [sic] and respectable families that lived in the town. He was a Justice of the Supreme Judicial Court in 1774, and Colonel of the first regiment of Essex."[120]

*****

In New England, the bulk of Loyalists belonged either to the minority Anglican Church, were recent immigrants from the old country, were dependent on royal authority for political advancement, or traveled in social and political circles dominated by those who were loyal to the crown.[121] Browne was one of several hundred people from Massachusetts who submitted claims to the British government seeking reimbursement for their losses. Well over fifty percent of applicants came from Boston. Nineteen former Salem residents petitioned for redress. Several, in addition to Browne, held prominent positions in the community, like Dr. Thomas Boulton (d. 1777), Samuel Curwen (1715-1802), Joseph Dowse (d. 1785), Peter Frye 1723-1820), John Mascarene (1722-1779), Benjamin Pickman (1740-1819), Samuel Porter, and Richard Routh (d. 1801).[122] As for Connecticut, the situation was similar, except that the colony contained far fewer recent immigrants, its royal establishment was much smaller, and both in number and percentage the number of Tories who left the state was lower.[123] Most of those who remained loyal to the crown were Anglicans from Fairfield County.[124] The standard study of Connecticut loyalism makes no mention of absentees.[125]

---

committed suicide in 1786. Mary married John Harvey Tucker (1777-1868), Yale Class of 1796, a Bermuda native, in 1803. *Oxford Dictionary of National Biography*, s.v. William Browne; Dexter, *Yale Graduates*, V, 231. They also had one other daughter who died in 1773. *Essex Gazette*, November 9, 1773, [59].

119 *DAB*, s.v. William Browne; *Sibley's Harvard Graduates*, XIII, 560; *New York Evening Post*, June 7, 1802,[3].

120 *Salem Gazette*, April 16, 1802, [3]. John Adams was not so charitable. Writing in 1815, he explained that the price of Browne's betrayal of his country was "the post of judge of the superior court." Quoted in Brown, *King's Friends*, 38.

121 William H. Nelson, *The American Tory* (Boston: Beacon Press, 1961, 1964), 3-18, 71-81. In reading the diaries of Benjamin Lynde and Benjamin Lynde, Jr. who discussed their eminent friends in high positions of government, one can hardly be surprised that the pull of loyalty should have been so strong among men like themselves. *Lynde Diaries*, passim.

122 Boulton was a physician; Dowse was Surveyor, Searcher, and Landwaiter of Customs at Salem; Curwen a merchant, justice of peace, and deputy judge of the Vice Admiralty Court; Frye served in the legislature with Browne, judge of the Court of Common Pleas, justice of the peace, Register of the Probate Court, and militia officer; Mascarene was Comptroller of Customs at Salem; Pickman a colonel in the Salem militia; Porter an attorney; and Routh a storekeeper and deputy collector of Customs. Jones, *Loyalists of Massachusetts*, 43-44,106-07, 120-21, 139, 212, 236-38, 249; Jackman, ed., "Letters of William Browne," 7, 29, 38, 42.

123 Ingersoll, *Loyalist Problem*, 258-59.

124 In Greenwich, Norwalk, and Stamford, seventy-five estates were confiscated, many of them owned by absentees. John W. Tyler, *Connecticut Loyalists: An Analysis of Loyalist Land Confiscation in Greenwich, Stanford and Norwalk* (New Orleans: Polyanthus, Inc., 1977), 76-95.

125 David Henry Villiers, "Loyalism in Connecticut, 1763-1783" (unpublished Ph.D. dissertation, Univer-

To consider what happened to the Loyalists, they can be divided into several broad categories. First, many hunkered down and quietly attempted to survive Revolutionary turmoils. They included such prominent acquaintances of Browne as Joseph Blaney, Benjamin Lynde, Andrew Oliver, Jr., Epes Sargent, Jr., and John Turner, plus the Connecticut Mumfords and several Rhode Island Wantons. Others chose exile and then returned to the United States after the war was over, such men as Samuel Curwen and Benjamin Pickman of Salem and Andrew Cazneau of Boston. Probably the largest number left the states and lived in exile in the Canadian Maritimes, Upper Canada, the West Indies, and the mother country. Finally, a handful of especially prominent Loyalists secured patronage positions from the British Crown, like William Browne and his Massachusetts colleagues Cazneau and Daniel Leonard.[126]

---

sity of Connecticut, 1975). He points out that almost all Loyalists of any position in society graduated from Yale and lived in Fairfield County. Ibid, 93, 100, 103.

[126] Wallace Brown, *The Good Americans: The Loyalists in the American Revolution* (New York: William Morrow and Company, Inc., 1969), 147-200, 217, 251.

Chapter 9

The Fate of the Browne Slaves

Given the great research interest on Connecticut African Americans, the subsequent lives of the slaves on the Browne estate merit serious attention. Documents in the Connecticut Archives list the names of twelve slaves. Nine lived on his Lyme lands and three in Colchester at the time the state seized the estate. Three had significantly less value than the others. Jimm was only six months old and was given a nominal value of just £10 and eleven-year-old Caesar the same, due to the fact that he was incapacitated. Paddy, an adult, likely had physical or mental impairments.

Table 4. Browne Slaves[1]

Name	Age[2]	Residence	Value
Great Prince	26	Lyme	£450
Little Prince	22	Lyme	£270
Prue	36	Lyme	£180
Cato	6	Lyme	£200
Phillis	10	Lyme	£250
Rose	3	Lyme	£100
Jimm	6 mo.	Lyme	£10
Luke	33	Lyme	£300
Cesar	11	Lyme	£10
Paddy	[53]	Colchester	1 shilling
Pomp	[42]	Colchester	£20
Old Fashion	[50]	Colchester	£20

Governor Browne's 1786 Loyalist claim provided the same information with one exception. He noted the existence of eleven slaves - Pompey, Paddy, Fashion, Great Prince, Little Prince, Luke, Caesar, Cato, Jimm, Prudence, and Phillis. It appears that Rose, age three, in 1779 had died sometime before 1786, although the remote possi-

---

1 Stark, "Myth and Reality," 164-65; William Brown[e], 1779, NPR, no. 1760. The inventory for the Lyme portion of the estate was dated May 10, 1779, while that for the Colchester part on January 5, 1781. The earlier inventory was valued in depreciated continental currency and the Colchester one in Connecticut's lawful money.

2 The ages for the first nine slaves come from the May 1779 inventory of the Lyme portion of the estate, while the estimates for the three Colchester slaves come from other sources.

bility exists that she had gone to another household and that Samuel Huntington was unable to find her.[3] Although Jimm was born three years after Browne had fled to Great Britain, the birth occurred before his lands were taken over by the state. Despite a thorough examination of Colchester, Lyme, and East Haddam records, little trace has been found on six of the twelve slaves listed in confiscation documents and for a seventh, Jimm, what can be pieced together is speculative.

Despite extensive research, several questions remain about the Browne slaves. First of all, we do not know where all of the slaves lived. Luke and Caesar may have been on the farm of Benjamin and Jedidiah Beckwith, perhaps Pomp Henry of Colchester worked for John Henry, and two others lived in Colchester, but whether or not the remaining seven Lyme slaves all lived on the Mumford farm is unknown. It is certainly possible that one or more could have been on other farms. Likewise, we do not know with whom the Colchester slaves lived. In addition, we do not know the mother of two of the children. According to the petition presented to the General Assembly by Great Prince and others, Prue had three children. Caesar and one other child had a different mother. Finally, we have no idea who fathered the five children. It could have been one of Browne's six adult male slaves, a male in the household of John Mumford, Jr., or a servant of another farmer in the area.[4]

Prue was the mother of three of the minor children.[5] No further conclusive evidence about her has been found. Probably, however, the "Negro Woman" Pru who died in the North Parish of Lyme in 1804 was the same person. The inquest for Pru[e] was held on January 21, 1804. Found dead in a field with no signs of violence on her body, the jury of inquest concluded that "her Death is Accidental by a Fit or Some cause unknown to us and by no act of Violence."[6]

Jimm, or James, was born in late 1778 and, except for an April 6, 1784 indenture, no further authoritative information has been found about him. The indenture, pursuant to an act of the General Assembly, directed Judge Huntington "to Bind out sundry Negroes Belonging to the Confiscated Estate of William Brown[e]." He indented James aged five and one half to Isaac Spencer of East Haddam for seventeen years and eight months until the boy turned 23.[7] According to the 1790 census, the household of Isaac Spencer, Jr. consisted of two males under 16, four males over 16, two females, and one other free person, almost certainly Jimm.[8] One can theorize that the James Brown associated with Prince Brown of Lyme and Fashion Freeman of East Haddam during

---

[3] Huntington Report, April 11, 1783, AmLC, AOP, AO 13/50, 79, NAUK.

[4] CA, Revolutionary War, Series 1, XXXVII, 233, 234, CSL.

[5] Ibid, Series 1, XXXVII, 234.

[6] NLSC, PbyS: Inquests, Pru, June 21, 1804, Box 45, folder 6, CSL. A Prudence Negro, aka Meribee, lived in East Haddam. She died in 1812 and numerous references to her are found in local records. It is unlikely that she was the former Browne slave. RG 062, East Haddam Town Records, 1762-1896, Boxes 6, 7, 26 passim, CSL.

[7] *State* Records, V, 303; William Brown[e], NPR, no. 1760.

[8] Bureau of the Census, *Heads of Families at the First Census of the United States Taken in the Year 1790: Connecticut* (Washington: Government Printing Office, 1908), 82. A number of Spencers lived in Millington Society, the section of East Haddam adjacent to the North Society in Lyme and New Salem.

the 1820s was the James who was indentured in 1784. He is found twice in Lyme land records, first in a mortgage deed of Prince Brown of June 26, 1820 in which James Brown and Ichabod Brown were co-signers of a debt by "Note of hand" and second four years later when Sylvia Freeman, who lived in the household of Fashion Freeman at the time of his death in 1821, and James Brown both of Lyme mortgaged seven acres of land in Lyme North Society in return for $18.00.[9] He also is found in court records in lawsuits that also concerned Prince Brown.[10] Strengthening the inference that James Brown of Lyme was the Jimm listed in confiscation documents is the fact that he was closely associated with two of the former slaves of William Browne, Fashion Freeman and Prince Brown. They shared the bond of servitude to the same master, a connection that may have lasted throughout their lifetimes. Indeed, the distinct possibility exists that one of these two men was Jimm's father.

Two other possibilities consist of a James Freeman found in the 1830 census for New London aged 36-55 and a second James, a colored man, who died in East Haddam on June 9, 1834.[11] Unless, however, additional information on James comes to light, it is impossible to know if Jimm survived childhood, if so, the James Brown of Lyme remains by far the most likely probability.

Rose was three years old in May 1779 and almost certainly died before her seventh birthday. No record of her life has been found, although it is remotely possible that the twenty-year-old female who ran away from Amasa Ransom of Colchester in 1800, one of the purchasers of the lands of Browne's confiscated estate, was the same person and that the Rose of Norwich who was accused of fornication four years later was also the same woman. Jesse Brown of Norwich sued Charles Lathrop of Windham in 1804 in a suit of trespass in New London County Court claiming $300 damages. Brown asserted that Lathrop had a "Negro Girl" Rose in his "Family & Service" who became the mother of a female child by reason of fornication in September 1803 and Brown sued to recover expenses "for doctoring & Nursing." In addition, Brown stated that Lathrop was responsible for the costs of maintaining the child to age 21. The court found the defendant guilty at the original 1804 trial, he appealed to the Superior Court, and the lawsuit was eventually withdrawn.[12] Rose, however, was a relatively common

9 Prince Brown to Samuel B. Mather and Nathan Griffing, 2nd, LLR, June 26, 1820, XXVIII, 557; Sylvia Freeman and James Brown to Henry Sisson, LLR, September 30, 1824, XXX, 539. He signed the deed with an X. By his will, Fashion Freeman designated "Silva a black Woman that now lives with me" be given his estate during her lifetime and then James Brown of Lyme as residuary legatee. Fashion Freeman, East Haddam, 1823, CPR, VIII, 535-36.

The James Brown who was born in East Haddam in 1806 was almost certainly a different individual, because it was highly unlikely that a fourteen-year-old boy would have co-signed a debt by note in 1820. Brown and Rose, *Black Roots*, 45.

10 *Benjamin Banning v. Prince Brown and James Brown*, NLCC, African Americans, November 1822, Box 6, folder 14; Petition of Samuel B. Mather, Ibid, November 1823, Box 6, folder 18; *Oliver Comstock v. James Brown*, Ibid, June 1833, Box 7, folder 7.

11 Brown and Rose, *Black Roots*, 143, 512. Brown and Freeman were the most likely surnames for the Browne slaves.

12 Brown and Rose, *Black Roots*, 567; *Connecticut Gazette*, June 4, 1800, [3]; *Norwich Packet*, July 15, 1800, [3]; *Jesse Brown v. Charles Lathrop*, NLCC, Files, February 1804, Box 263, folder 23, no. 95; *Jesse Brown v. Charles Lathrop*, NLSC, Files, September 1805, Box 69, folder 14, no. 39. The Rose who was Lathrop's servant appears to be too young to be the right person.

first name for people of color and these possibilities are highly unlikely.[13]

Cato, who was six in 1779, represents a similar problem. The nearest thing to a match is a runaway notice for a Negro man Cato, age 23, who left the service of Benjamin Buell of Hebron in the summer of 1795.[14] Another possibility is Cato Negro of Lyme who in 1823 was being cared for by the town. The town paid Joel Loomis for his support.[15]

Phillis, a 10-year-old girl, has likewise left no records of a conclusive nature. The likelihood exists that she received medical care from Dr. John R. Watrous of Colchester beginning in July 1783 when he bled and provided medications at a cost of one shilling. Her account also lists an April 1785 expense of one shilling for bleeding "Cesar." She paid her bill of six shillings and two pence by her labor in 1787.[16] Perhaps she was the Phillis cared for by Israel W. Wells of the same town in 1802.[17] Other records that may or may not be relevant are for a Phillis Negro who was provided care by East Haddam in 1813 and of a Phyllis [Negro], a State Pauper, from Norwich who received financial support in 1817.[18]

For adult male **Luke**, no clue exists. Luke was an extremely unusual name to be given to a person of color and nothing has been found that gives even a hint of what happened to him.[19]

Historical records, however, provide a good deal of solid data on Caesar, Old Fashion, Paddy, Pomp, and Prince Brown, three of whom were State Paupers.

Paddy Brown lived in Colchester.[20] "A native of Africa," he was one of several slaves that William Browne purchased and brought to New Salem in 1759 or 1760. An order of Judge of Probate Benjamin Huntington set him free after the confiscation of Browne's estate.[21] He was the only person with that first name living in southeastern

---

13 *Black Roots* has an extensive list of women named Rose. Brown and Rose, *Black Roots*, 565-68.

14 Ibid, 478.

15 Lyme Day Book, 1810-1827, September 8, 1823, CSL. Lyme records contain numerous references to Cato Huntley who was 28 in 1796 and a slave to Amos Huntley. A Cato Ransom lived in Colchester from 1803 until his death in 1838 at age 78. He was much too old to have been the Cato on the estate of William Browne. Brown and Rose, *Black Roots*, 192, 336.

16 Dr. John Watrous, Medical Account Book, 1781-1798, Vol. A, 2, CSL. Watrous made four visits to Phillis and one to Caesar.

17 Colchester Treasurer Records, 1791-1830, 1802, CTH.

18 RG 062, East Haddam Town Records, Box 7, folder 26; RG 019, Department of Social Services, State Board of Charities, Pauper Accounts, Vol. 2, 35, CSL.

19 Despite its biblical provenance, Luke was an uncommon first name even for whites. One other African American Luke has been found. In September 1747, the New London County Superior Court found Luke of Lyme not guilty of poisoning the daughter of his master. *Dom Rex v. Luke*, NLSC, Files, Box 19, folder 18, no. 27.

20 The authors of *Black Roots* reasonably but inaccurately conflated Pemberton Brown of Hebron with Paddy Brown of Colchester. Pemberton Brown died in Hebron on July 1, 1807 and Paddy Brown in Colchester on June 4, 1808. Brown and Rose, *Black Roots*, 47; RG 008, Office of the Comptroller, Journal C, 380, CSL.

21 As the Colchester memorial stated, "And when the State's Agent was selling the real estate of the said William it was asked if he intended to sell the Negroes, which he answered in the Negative." CA, Miscellaneous, Series 2, I, 93.

Connecticut at that time, so it is clear that the Paddy located in New London court records is the same man.[22] The November 1785 session was presented with a lawsuit in which "Paddy a Negro man late of said Colchester and now residing in Lyme" sued Joshua Rathbone, Jr. in a case of debt by book to recover £6-6.[23]

Seventeen years later on May 10, 1802 the selectmen of Colchester sent a memorial to the General Assembly stating that William Browne formerly owned a number of Negro slaves one of whom was Paddy. After the State seized his estate, all his property was sold except for the Negroes. They "were left and they took various ways & means for a living." Paddy, "a harmless Fellow and not able even to this day to speak English so as to be understood by a Stranger," remained on the same farm in Colchester on which his master had left him until the fall of 1801 and was adequately clothed and fed until that time.[24] He was about seventy-five years old. Since that time, however, he had become a charge of the town and the Colchester selectmen argued that since Connecticut had confiscated the estate on which he lived, that Paddy should be "maintained at the Cost of this State." The legislature agreed and Paddy became a State Pauper.[25] Between November 1801, when the town reimbursed Ralph Isham £3-17-2 for clothes, and 1808, the records contain numerous accounts for reimbursement of expenses for the care of Paddy. In addition to payments for Brown's general support, the town also appropriated funds for clothes, specifically, boots, a frock, a handkerchief, shirts, shoes, trousers, and tobacco.[26]

On five occasions between 1805 and 1808, the State Comptroller paid the town of Colchester to take care of Paddy Brown.[27] He died on June 4, 1808.[28] When the inventory of the Colchester portion of Browne's estate was taken in January 1781, the appraisers set his value at only one shilling.[29] This provides evidence for the supposition

---

[22] Brown and Rose, *Black Roots*, 47. Paddy Brown was the only man with that first name found in this essential work.

[23] *Paddy v. Joshua Rathbone Jr.*, NLCC, Files, November 1785, Box 195, folder 10, no docket. Judge Benjamin Huntington drafted the writ and, since it was filed in the no docket section, the suit was probably withdrawn. The possibility exists that either Joshua Rathbone, Sr. (d. 1807) or Joshua Rathbone, Jr. (d. 1810) cared for Paddy while he was able to earn his keep and they turned that responsibility over to the town once he became too feeble to work. Barbour Collection, Connecticut Vital Records, Colchester 1699-1750, 138.

[24] John Mumford testified on May 15, 1802 in support of the petition that "Paddy is now by reason of age and infirmity became incapable of procuring his living by labour." CA, Miscellaneous, Series 2, I, 94.

[25] Ibid, I, 93, 94. Connecticut assumed the responsibility to support all paupers who did not have a stated town of residence during the colonial era and continued to do so until 1820. The Comptroller was made auditor for all charges for state paupers in 1799. Edward Warren Capen, *The Historical Development of the Poor Law of Connecticut* (New York: 1905), 138-42.

[26] Colchester Town Records, 1797-1805, CTH; Colchester Town Records, 1805-1842, CTH. The persons paid to care for Paddy were Caesar Beckwith, Warren Fuller, Ralph Isham, Abner Kellogg, Gibbons Mather, Elias Newton, Jerusha Skinner, John Treadway, John Wills, plus Wright and Worthington. On January 29, 1806, the town paid former Browne slave Caesar Beckwith $18.08 to care for Paddy.

[27] RG 008, Comptroller, Journal C, 176, 229, 282, 338, 380. Journal C records payments to Pemberton Brown of Hebron on pages 191, 237, and 291.

[28] The Comptroller paid $63.01 to Colchester on November 22, 1808, "For supporting in sickness & funeral of Paddy Brown & Charles Linson State Paupers until their decease on 4 June 1808." Ibid, 380.

[29] The unknown Colchester farmer with whom Paddy lived between 1779 and 1801 appears to have provided most of his care.

that Paddy had physical and/or mental impairments and perhaps a jaw or throat condition that prevented him from speaking clearly.

The best documented Browne slave is **Pomp Henry**, aka Sambo Brown, thanks to the exhaustive research of Vicki S. Welch.[30] She wrote that Pomp was born around 1747 in Lyme to a Nehantic father and slave mother.[31] The first reference to him appears in a runaway notice posted by John Mumford in April 1770.

> Ran way from the Subscriber on the 9th of April Instant, a Negro Man, named Sambo about five Feet and a half high - Had on a lightish colour'd Kersey Jacket and Breeches striped Flannel under Vest, white Flannel Shirt, and dark grey Stockings, - Whoever will return said Negro to the Subscriber, in Lyme, shall have THREE DOLLARS Reward, and all necessary Charges paid by John Mumford.[32]

Sambo returned to Mumford and two years later ran away from Samuel Browne, Jr. of Stockbridge, Massachusetts.[33] The *Connecticut Courant* [Hartford] advertisement described the runaway as "a negro man named Pomp, about 25 years old, a thick set fellow, about 5 feet 6 inches high [who] Speaks quick broken English." In addition, he had lost the first joint of his right thumb and wore colorful clothing. Browne offered a $5.00 reward for his return.[34]

Pomp ran away again in October 1774 and was the subject of three different advertisements. The first, published in the *Newport Mercury*, provides more detail on

---

30 Welch, "Keys to the Shackles," *Connecticut History*, Vol. 40, no. 2 (Fall 2001), 228-36; Vicki S. Welch, *And They Were Related, Too* (n.p.: Xlibris Corporation, 2006), 49-57.

31 Her belief is that Pomp was a Native American of Nehantic ancestry. The Henrys of Rhode Island were Native American and his colorful attire was more typical of Indians than of Negroes. Welch, *And They Were Related*, 52; Welch, "Keys to the Shackles," 228-29, 234.

One can speculate that Pomp was originally a slave of Captain Nathan Jewett of Lyme whom William Browne and Jacob Bailey visited Captain Jewett on July 15, 1754. The inventory of his estate taken on March 10, 1761 listed five slaves, including a Negro Boy Pomp. Bartlett, *Frontier Missionary*, 25; Nathan Jewett, Lyme, 1761, NLPR, Vol. G, 591. Of course, Pomp was a common slave name and the first runaway notice gives his name as Sambo, but the possibility is interesting to contemplate.

32 Welch, "Keys to the Shackles," 230; Welch, *And They Were Related*, 50; *New London Gazette* (aka *Connecticut Gazette*), April 27, 1770, [4]. The runaway notices of 1770, 1772, and one of three for 1774, together with the 1776 theft notice can all be found in Welch, *And They Were Related*, 50-51.

33 Samuel Browne, Jr. was likely related to William Browne of Salem, Massachusetts, perhaps descended from Captain John Browne, a cousin of Colonel Samuel. Samuel Browne, son of John and Mary Browne of Salem, was born in March 1709 and published an intention to marry in 1733. He is the right age to be the father of Samuel, Jr. The legislature appointed Samuel, Jr. a justice of the peace for Berkshire County on February 10, 1774. *Vital Records of Salem, Massachusetts to the End of the Year 1849*, 6 volumes (Salem: The Essex Institute, 1916-25) I, 131; III, 155; Whitmore, *Massachusetts Civil List*, 132.

Unlike William Browne, Samuel, Jr. was a Patriot, as was his father. A Samuel supported a Stockbridge January 1773 memorial opposing the extension of the power of the Vice Admiralty Courts and freeing judges of the superior court from dependence on the Massachusetts legislature and, as a member of the legislature in March 1774, voted to impeach Loyalist Judge Peter Oliver for high crimes and misdemeanors. *Massachusetts Spy*, January 21, 1773, 195; *Boston Gazette*, March 7, 1774, [1]. Samuel Browne represented Stockbridge in the February 1775 session of the Provincial Congress. Force, *American Archives*, Vol. 1, 1328.

34 Welch, "Keys to the Shackles," 230; Welch, *And They Were* Related, 50. The advertisement was first published on September 29, 1772.

Pomp's third runaway attempt than the one found by Welch and published a month later in the *Connecticut Gazette*.

SIX DOLLARS REWARD

RAN away from the subscriber, last night, a Negro man, an indented servant for 6 years, named POMP, a well made fellow, of middling stature, lively and active, about twenty five years old, speaks quick, and something broken English, can talk some Dutch, has lost the upper joint of his left thumb, the nail turns down partly over the end of the same; carried away with him a home made mix-coloured blue and red coat, lined with blue shallow, trimmed with yellow metal buttons, cloth colored duroc jacket and breeches, two pair of leather-breeches, a new felt-laced with yellow tinsel; old ditto not laced, a white shirt, and striped ditto, linen trowsers, cloth coloured great coat, much worn, a pair of turn'd pumps, and double soled shoes, silver-plated shoe buckles, and sundry pair of stockings: — Whoever will take up said Negro, and bring him to his master, or secure him, and give notice thereof to his master, shall have the above reward, and all necessary charges, paid by the subscriber. All masters of vessels, and others, are forbid carrying off, or harbouring, said Negro at their peril.

SAMUEL BROWN, jun

Stockbridge, Oct. 9, 1774.[35]

Ten days later a second version of this runaway notice with some minor changes was published in Boston's *Massachusetts Gazette*. It gave the information that the breeches "were made at Philadelphia"[36] The *Connecticut Gazette* notice published the third notice on December 2, 1774.

Ran-away from the Subscriber, on the 12th day of Octo. last a Negro man Servant about 27 Years old, speaks fast and broken English, well-set, about 5 and Half Feet high, has had a Fillion on one Thumb and the Nail grows quite over the End of the Thumb; he was formerly own'd by Col Brown of Salem, and liv'd with Mr. John Mumford of Colchester, where he was call'd by the Name of SAMBO, but since by the Name of POMP; had on when he went away a yellow lac'd Hat, white Shirt, red and blue mist homemade Coat, and new buckskin Breeches. Whoever shall take up said Negro and secure him in any of his Majesty's Goals, and send me Word or bring him to me the Subscriber, shall have Six Dollars Reward, and all necessary Charges paid by me, November 18th 1774, Samuel Brown, jun.[37]

The Newport and Boston runway notices contain some significant information not found in New London's *Connecticut Gazette*. It refers to Pomp as "an indented Servant for Six Years." Since Pomp was a slave in 1781, the inexact phrase probably meant that he had been leased to Browne for a term of six years. Then there is the ques-

---

35 *Newport Mercury*, November 7, 1774, [1].

36 *Massachusetts Gazette*, November 17, 1774, [4].

37 Welch, "Keys to the Shackles," 230; Welch, *And They Were Related*, 51; *Connecticut Gazette*, December 2, 1774, [3].

tion, how did a New England slave learn to speak "a little Dutch?" Pomp's penchant for wearing and taking away colorful clothing is noted in all of the runaway notices. It was unusual, but not unknown, for a slave to run away more than once, but almost unprecedented to escape on three separate occasions. It was likewise unprecedented for a master to place advertisements in three newspapers in three different colonies and, moreover, the reward was a high one, two indicators of the great value Browne placed on the slave.

He was probably never recaptured for in 1775 and 1776 Pomp served briefly as a private soldier in Newport and South Kingstown, Rhode Island under Captain Billings and was paid for two months of service. A few months later he broke into the house of Samuel Dorrance of Voluntown and stole clothes and currency. In June 1776, Dorrance offered a $3.00 reward for the capture of the thief "one SAMBO, a Negro Fellow, formerly belonging to Col. *William Brown* of *Salem*; was last Year a Soldier at *Newport*; he is very black, something short, talks very broken. . . his Wool cut off the Top of his Head, a Felt Hat, cut very beauish."[38] In all advertisements, Sambo/Pomp is described as wearing extremely colorful clothes. When the State seized Browne's property, Pomp was one of the estate's slaves in the inventory for his Colchester lands in January 1781.[39]

These five runaway notices make clear that, despite being referred to by two different names, Pomp and Sambo were the same person. Four of the five advertisements emphasized that Pomp spoke "fast and broken English" and this seems unusual for a person born in New England. Perhaps he did not have a great deal of contact with whites as a youth and spoke a combination of Indian language and fractured English while growing up.[40] The author has found just one instance of another slave escaping from his master on three occasions and seven others in which they ran away twice.[41] Did Pomp return voluntarily after extended "joy rides" or did his propensity for wearing colorful garb lead to his recaptures? Interesting questions.

Pomp married Betsy Rodman who was of Narragansett or Nehantic blood around 1777 and thereafter his jaunts ended. Betsy was free, came from Rhode Island, and was the daughter of Abiather Rodman, a Native American. Pomp may have come in contact with the Rodmans while in military service in Rhode Island, yet it is also possible that he was related to the Henry family of Charlestown, Rhode Island and became acquainted with Betsy through that connection.[42] Although Pomp was a slave

---

[38] Welch, *And They Were Related*, 51.

[39] William Brown[e], 1779, NPR, no. 1760.

[40] Another possibility is that Pomp had a speech impediment.

[41] Nine newspapers from eastern Connecticut placed advertisements for runaway slaves between 1759 and 1805 and some 320 records for about 310 different individuals have been found. In addition to Sambo/Pomp, seven men and one woman escaped from their masters multiple times, Cloe of Groton, Derry of New London, Frank from Lyme, Jack from South Kingston, Rhode Island, Newport from Lebanon, Newport from Hartford, Sampson of Canterbury, and Sy from New London. Frank ran away from Joshua Powers three times between 1797 and 1804 when slavery was on its last legs in the state. All the others absconded twice. The newspapers examined were the [Norwich] *Connecticut Centinel, Connecticut Gazette,* [Stonington] *Journal of the Times,* [New London] *Bee, New London Summary,* [Norwich] *Courier, Norwich Packet,* [Norwich] *Weekly Register,* and *Windham Herald.* Except for one runaway notice in the *Summary,* all the above named were published in the *Connecticut Gazette.* Advertisements almost invariably appeared in just one newspaper and were printed for several weeks in a row

[42] Due to the fact that Pomp took the surname Henry, Welch believes that he took the name from his father

and living in Colchester at the time of the inventory of Browne's lands there in January 1781, his wife and children were all free. In August 1789, Pomp was mentioned in the diary of Moses Warren, Jr. when he sent his servant Lem for "Pomp Henry to fiddle for Thos. G. Wait & others at Dr. Calkins's" house in Lyme East Society, the first indication of the use of a surname.[43]

"Negro Pomp" is found in the 1790 Federal Census in Lyme as the head of a family of seven people.[44] The family consisted of Pomp, wife Betsy, and children Pompey, Sally, Hannah, Levi, and Abiather.[45] Landless, they lived near the Lyme-Colchester border, two houses away from John Mumford in Lyme, seven from Fashion Brown in Colchester, and ten from John Henry, on property formerly owned by William Browne.[46] Although called "Negro Pomp" in the 1790 census, all subsequent references to Pomp and members of his family use the surname Henry.[47] By 1798, Pomp, despite being only a little over sixty years old, could no longer provide for his family. The selectmen of Lyme petitioned the General Assembly in May stating the situation regarding Pomp Henry and his family.

> The petition of the subscribers, being the Selectmen of the town of Lyme, sheweth, that there are in said said town several negro slaves, the property of William Brown whose estates in said town . . . have been confiscated, sold, and converted to the use and benefit of the State, whereby the said slaves were left without support and homes, and sometimes are reduced to want and distress, so as to become chargeable to the said Town - more especially a family consisting of five in number, hath of late been confined by sickness for a great length of time, to the expence of the town twenty dollars, which hath been paid to David Johnson of Colchester for medical assistance . . . . Your Petitioners further state that the town of Lyme is not under any obligation to support said slaves, and therefore request that as the State is possessed of the said Browns property, they will support said Slaves when sickness

who may have been one of the Henry men of Charlestown identified by Ezra Stiles in 1761. Welch, *And They Were Related*, 52. Another possibility exists. One of the tenants of William Browne was John Henry of Colchester and it is possible that the surname came from that source. That renter had a black servant called John Henry.

[43] Welch, "Keys to the Shackles," 234; Moses Warren, Jr., Diary, 1789-90, 40, CHS. Moses Warren is the great-great-great grandfather of the author.

[44] Welch, "Keys to the Shackles, 234; 1790 Census, 101. The census classified, free Negroes as other free people.

[45] Pompey, the eldest, was born about 1778 in Colchester and became a seaman. Sally (b.c. 1780), Hannah (b.c. 1782), Levi (b.c. 1784), and Abiather (b.c. 1787) were born in Lyme. Welch, "Keys to the Shackles," 235-36.

[46] 1790 Census, 101. The strong likelihood exists that the Henry family lived on land managed by John Mumford for most of the rest of their lives. Welch, *And They Were Related*, 57.

[47] The 1800 census disclosed that Henry had five people in his household, including himself and that of 1820 showed that the number had risen to six. The Henry family contained one male under 14, one male under 26, one male over 45, one female under 14, one female 26-45, and one female over 45. The 1820 census also showed that son Abiather Henry had seven in his household, one male under 14, one male 26-45, four females under 14, and one female 26-45. AncestryHeritageQuest.com; Fourth Census of the United States, 1820. New London County, Vol. 3, Photostat, 1419, 1444, CSL. Pomp is not found in the 1810 census.

and infirmity render it necessary and repay to your petitioners said Twenty Dollars, as is duty bound.

The Assembly resolved that the "slaves viz Pomp Henry so called his wife Betsey, Sally, Hannah, Levi, & Abiather Children of the said Pomp be considered as the Paupers of this State" and ordered that $20 be paid to the town for medical services provided to the family.[48] A little over a year and a half later, Pomp was tried for theft in Colchester, although the records do not reveal the adjudication of the case.[49]

Lyme Day Books and State Comptroller Records contain extensive information to document the last years of Henry's life, consisting of records of payments to several individuals for the care of Pomp and his family. These records become most useful beginning in 1815 when the General Assembly again designated Henry as a State Pauper upon the request of the Lyme selectmen.[50] In a petition dated May 18, 1815, the Lyme selectmen repeated many of the arguments made seventeen years previously, that "Pomp Henry black man" had become poor, infirm, and unable to support himself and that the town had "already expended considerable sums" for his care. They again stated that "Pomp was a servant and slave for life of one William Brown . . . and that no provision was made nor is their [sic] any person known . . . that can be rendered liable for the said Pomp's support and maintenance." The selectmen requested reimbursement for all the town had previously spent and that Pomp henceforth be considered a State Pauper. The General Assembly granted the memorial.[51] The bulk of the accounts covered the period from May 1815 until his death on May 16, 1823. They consisted of payments to seven people in Lyme for clothes, medical care, shoes, supplies, and for his general care and support.[52]

In a cemetery on property on which the Mumfords once lived in Salem, stands a small stone with initials PH and a heart carved upon it. This is probably Pomp's grave and his wife Betsy who died in March 1826 is likely buried nearby.[53] About a quarter mile from the Mumford house on the right side of Darling Road as the driver is heading

---

[48] CA, Miscellaneous, Series 2, I, 68-69; Welch, "Keys to the Shackles," 232-33, 235-36; *State Records*, IX, 245-46.

[49] Colchester Town Records, 1797-1805, January 29, 1800, CTH. The town paid Samuel A. Peters four shillings for the complaint and warrant, John C. Bulkeley twelve shillings to arrest and hold Pomp, and John Isham, 3d thirteen shillings and a six pence for prosecution.

Son Abiather Henry also faced legal problems. In 1813, a Lyme grand juror accused him of stealing articles worth $1.00 from George Anson Miller and three years later Abiather charged Daniel Brown with passing a $3.00 counterfeit bill. Smith Family Papers, Lyme, 1723-1841, folders 24, 28, CHS.

[50] Lyme Day Book, 1810-1826, CSL; Lyme Town Records, LTH; Colchester Town Records; RG 008, Comptroller Journals and Waste Books; and RG 019. Pauper accounts contain sixty-two records concerning Pomp Henry and his family, mostly payments for their support.

[51] CA, Miscellaneous, Series 2, I, 88-89.

[52] RG 019, Pauper Accounts, Vol. 2, 97; Lyme Day Book, 1810-1827, CSL. The Lyme persons who received reimbursements for their assistance to Henry and his family consisted of Samuel Ingraham, David Johnson, Lemuel Lee, Dr. John Moore, Martha Rogers, Joshua R. Warren, and Wanton A. Weaver. The Day Book also contains twelve listings of payments to daughter Sally for keeping other people of color and six to son Abiather, most for care of his father.

[53] Welch, *And They Were Related*, 57.

towards Salem Valley Farms one can see the foundation of a small building when snow is on the ground, perhaps the house of Pomp Henry.

Old **Fashion Freeman**, aka Fashion Brown, Jack Brown, and Jack Fashion, lived in Colchester and East Haddam.[54] The 1790 Federal Census recorded that "Negro Fashion," who lived in New Salem Society near the Lyme line, headed a household of three people.[55] Six years later he purchased two small plots of land in the Millington section of East Haddam, the first containing two acres and the second seven rods with a house, for £34.[56] In 1800, Fashion, "a free Negro," purchased seven acres for $3.24 in Lyme North Society from George W. Jewett. This land bordered in part on the property of Prince Brown and Dan Lee.[57] In 1821, Dan Lee sold Fashion Freeman two and one quarter acres in Millington for $30.[58]

His will dated March 13, 1821 directed that "Silva a black Woman that now lives with me" be granted all his personal and real estate during her lifetime and then everything to James Brown of Lyme upon her death. He requested that Dan Lee administer his estate.[59] He signed with a mark. Fashion Freeman died in the first week of November 1823. Lee and Sylvia Maynard appeared before the judge of probate on November 8 to attest that he had signed his will in March 1821. It was probated on December 12, 1823. Fashion's extremely modest estate totaled just $133.92 divided among household goods worth $4.17, a cow $12, and three pieces of land, an "Old House and two Acres of Land" valued at $60, seven acres at $42, and "two acres & one quarter of Land" $15.75.[60] Additionally, the probate documents tell us that Dan Lee resigned as administrator in December due to infirmity and the probate court appointed Erastus Stark in his stead. The notice for persons having claims against the estate was placed on the Millington Society signpost, an addition to the inventory of August 1824 increased the value of the estate by $5.75, and charges against the estate from nine men amounted to $20.69.[61]

Both the inventory of the confiscated estate and statement by Governor Browne list Great Prince and Little Prince. Documentation exists for a Prince Brown

54 Brown and Rose, *Black Roots*, 139.

55 1790 Census, 101, CSL. Fashion, one of twenty-one African American heads of families in Colchester, lived ten houses away from Pomp Henry in Lyme. Ibid, 84-101. The federal censuses for East Haddam in 1800, 1810, and 1820 listed Fashion. He is called Jack Negro in 1800, as Fashion Brown in 1810, and as Jack Brown in 1820. In all three instances the household consisted of two persons. AncestryHeritageQuest. com. The 1820 Census recorded that the family of Jack Brown consisted of one "Males of forty-five and upwards" and one "Females of forty-five and upwards." Fourth Census, 1820, Middlesex County, Vol. 7, photostat, CSL.

56 Josiah J. Baker to Fashion Freeman, East Haddam Land Records, September 8, 1796, XII, 529.

57 George W. Jewett to Fashion, LLR, August 26, 1800, XXI, 435.

58 Dan Lee to Fashion Freeman, EHLR, April 27, 1821, XVIII, 780. James Brown sold this plot to Noah Chapman of East Haddam five years later. James Brown to Noah Chapman, Ibid, January 25, 1826, XIX, 59.

59 Nathan Stark, Dan Lee, and Sophia Maynard witnessed the will.

60 Appraisers Nathan Stark and Nathan Jewett.

61 Fashion Freeman, East Haddam, 1823, CPR, Vol. 8, 535-36; Fashion Freeman, East Haddam, 1823, CPR, no. 1261.

of Lyme, but we do not know which Prince became a landowner.[62] A Lyme Day Book, e.g. Treasurer's Records, contain payments for the care of a Prince Negro who was a town charge and died in March 1818. The strong likelihood exists, however, that this was Prince Griswold who died that year.[63] The records also list two Prince Freemans, one who spent most of his life in Colchester and the second in Lyme. Neither is a likely candidate for the second Prince.[64] A hint exists, however, to indicate that the Prince Brown who spent his life in Lyme may have been Great Prince because a letter about him written in January 1831 says the following, "he is verry old, probably seventy five or eighty" and "not able to labor."[65] Great Prince was valued at fifty per cent more than any other Browne slave and some sixty per cent more than Little Prince, a hint that he had higher mental and/or physical ability than any of the other slaves and an indicator that Prince Brown of Lyme may have been the older man.

Prince Brown of Lyme purchased a small plot in the North Society of Lyme from Harris Colt on August 31, 1790 for £9 lawful money.[66] "Negro Prince," living in the North Society, is found in the 1790 census as the head of family that consisted of five persons.[67] Brown is found in two subsequent censuses, as Prince in 1800 in a household of seven and as Prince Brown in 1820 in a family of six persons.[68] In 1792, Prince Brown, "a free Negro," bought another two pieces of land land totaling "fifteen acres

---

[62] The 1790 census lists a Negro Prince of Colchester with three in his family, but he was probably the man that *Black Roots* identifies as Prince Williams, former slave of Thomas Williams. 1790 Census, 94; Brown and Rose, *Black Roots*, 445.

[63] Lyme Day Book, 1810-1827, November 2, 1818, CSL; LLR, XV, 4. The town paid Ruel Beckwith for supplying a coffin.

[64] A Prince of Colchester was freed by Jacob Loomis, served in the French and Indian War, and married Hannah Burgin. He is probably the Prince Freeman who served in the Continental Army and purchased land in Colchester in 1791. The second lived in Lyme by 1798, purchased land in 1800, and died in 1826 in what is now Old Lyme. If this is the same Prince who married Jenny, he was most assuredly not the right Prince. Jenny died in 1832. Both are buried in Duck River Cemetery in Old Lyme, whereas the Prince who can be documented lived several miles north near the Lyme-East Haddam border. One of these men sold land in New Salem in 1795. Brown and Rose, *Black Roots*, 146; RG 008, Comptroller, Register for Army Notes, Vols. 222, 223, CSL; CLR, XIII, 225; XIV, 16-17; LLR, XXII, 30.

[65] Oliver Raymond to Isaac Spencer, January 15, 1831, CHS. The evidence is far from conclusive. A confiscation document states that Great Prince was twenty-six and Little Prince twenty-two, making is somewhat more likely that Prince Brown was the older man.

[66] Harris Colt to Prince Brown, LLR, August 31, 1790, XIX, 17. The deed of sale was first recorded in East Haddam by Isaac Spencer, Jr. and then in Lyme. The small piece of land bordered on the road from the house of Captain Abner Lee to that of James Gould and also on the land of Thaddeus Phelps. Gould, a tavern keeper, lived on what is now called the Old Salem Road in Lyme not far from the East Haddam line. Isaac Spencer, Jr. some six years earlier took over the care of Jimm, another of the former slaves of William Browne.

[67] 1790 Census, 104. The authors of *Black Roots* believe that Negro Prince was probably Prince Brown. Since a Prince Brown became a landowner in Lyme in 1790, this supposition is no doubt correct. The alternative is Prince Mather who was emancipated by Captain Joseph Mather in 1779. Tax records show that Mather paid taxes in 1782. He is listed, however, as living in the First Society and not the North Society, where Negro Prince lived. Brown and Rose, *Black Roots*, 47; LLR, XV, 4; RG 062, Lyme Town Records, 1781-1910, Lyme Tax Lists, Box 6, Vol. 1, 8, 60, 108, 148, CSL.

[68] The family consisted of one male under 14, two males under 26, one male over 45, one female under 14, and one female age 26-45. AncestryHeritageQuest.com; Fourth Census, 1820, Vol. 3, 1425, CSL.

with a small house" in the North Society from Joshua Jewett for £35.[69] Negro Prince married Phyllis Williams of Norwich in 1792 and they had two daughters, Sylvia and Nancy.[70] Selden Warner's ledger makes several references to Prince Negro between 1800 and 1811, but that man was almost certainly Prince Griswold who lived in the Hadlyme region of town.[71]

Lyme Land Records contain several more Prince deeds. Like many in the first generation of freed men, Brown encountered serious economic difficulties and sold plots of land in 1811 and 1826 and mortgaged portions of his property on four occasions in 1820 and 1823. In October 1811, Prince Brown sold John Sterling thirty rods for $12.[72] Almost nine years later in June 1820 he signed three mortgage deeds, the first to Allen W. Griffin of twelve acres and a house in Lyme "3d Society."[73] By a second transaction five days later, Brown mortgaged two pieces of land in the Third Society for $55.48 to merchants Mather & Griffing, the first of eight acres and the second his first purchase of land from Captain Harris Colt.[74] A third mortgage was also contracted in June 1820 was for $21.04 with surety of a "tract of Land situate in sd Lyme 3d Society.

Brown is also represented in New London County Court Records and, like the mortgages, they provide ample evidence of his financial difficulties. In June 1814, John Turner of Colchester sued Prince for $40.00 damages due to Brown's failure to pay a debt by note of January 19, 1813 for $35.21. The suit was withdrawn.[75] Eight years later Benjamin Banning of East Haddam filed suit against Prince Brown and James Brown for failure to pay off another debt by note for $61.03 dated September 16, 1822. To ensure that the defendants appeared at court, Constable Benjamin Brockway, Jr. attached a pair of oxen and a stack of English hay. The plaintiff withdrew the suit doubtless due to the fact that the defendants paid off the debt.[76] In November 1823, Samuel B. Mather and Nathan Griffing sued Brown for the "seisen and quiet and peaceable possession" of two pieces of land in Lyme Third Society that the defendant mortgaged to the plaintiffs in June 1820 by a $55.48 note of hand signed by Prince Brown, James

---

69 The first plot bordered on the lands of Captain [Harris] Colt and Josiah Jewett and the second on that of Silva "a free Negro of Norwich" and the aforementioned Jewett. Joshua Jewett to Prince Brown, LLR, October 13, 1792, LLR, XIX, 486.

70 Brown and Rose, *Black Roots*, 47. The two daughters are referenced in 1823 and 1826 deeds. LLR, XXVIII, 630; XXXI, 346.

71 This Prince purchased rye, flour, salt, potatoes, and salt fish from the Hadlyme shopkeeper and paid for these goods by mowing, breaking flax, cutting timber, shoveling dung, and catching fish. The nature of these transactions has the ring of Prince Griswold. Selden Warner, Ledger, Hadlyme, 1790-1809, 73, 114, CHS.

72 Prince Brown to John Sterling, LLR, October 15, 1811, XXV, 26.

73 Prince Brown to Allen W. Griffin, LLR, June 21, 1820, XXVIII, 531. Brown signed the mortgage deed with an X. According to the terms of the mortgage, Brown "signed" a "note of hand" for $43.24 and the date of repayment was not stated. The property was described in part as bounded by the highway from Lyme to Millington, the land of Calvin Selden, and the East Branch of the Eight Mile River. The East Branch of the Eight Mile River runs parallel to the Lyme section of Old Salem Road.

74 Prince Brown to Samuel B. Mather and Nathan Griffing, 2nd, LLR, June 26, 1820, XXVIII, 557. Like the previous mortgage, Prince provided the defendants with a note of hand payable with interest on demand.

75 *John Turner v. Prince Brown*, NLCC, Files, African Americans, June 1814, Box 5, folder 22, CSL.

76 *Benjamin Banning v. Prince Brown and James Brown*, Ibid, November 1822, Box 6, folder 14.

Brown, and Ichabod Brown. The court decided that the defendant was obliged to repay the sum borrowed together with interest for a total of $66.92 plus $10.42 costs by the beginning of April 1824.[77] The last transaction involving Prince Brown occurred in June 1826 when he sold one and one quarter acres to Oliver Comstock for $89.87, a piece of land that bordered on property owned by himself and daughters Sylvia and Nancy.[78]

Brown's economic circumstances continued to decline in his last years and his poverty prompted Selectman Oliver Raymond to write State Treasurer Isaac Spencer on January 15, 1831. "Theire is near me a man of colour the name of Prince or to take the name of his former Master Prince Brown" who was "poor and destitu[t]e of the comforts of life." He was old, probably between seventy-five and eighty, unable to work, and living with his wife. "I wish . . . you would direct some on[e] to furnis[h] him with as much as the State allows per week and lit [let] him remain where he is for he is much attached to his present home."[79] In January 1831, State Comptroller Elisha Phelps wrote to Raymond in response to his inquiry. With regard to Prince Brown, the "law provides, that whenever any person becomes destitute, & needing relief, his condition must be made known to the Selectmen" whose duty it was "to furnish the necessary supports, at the expence of the town." If, however, "such person is entitled to support by the State, measures will be taken to provide for such pauper."[80]

Illustration 9: Probate Notice for Prince Brown[81]

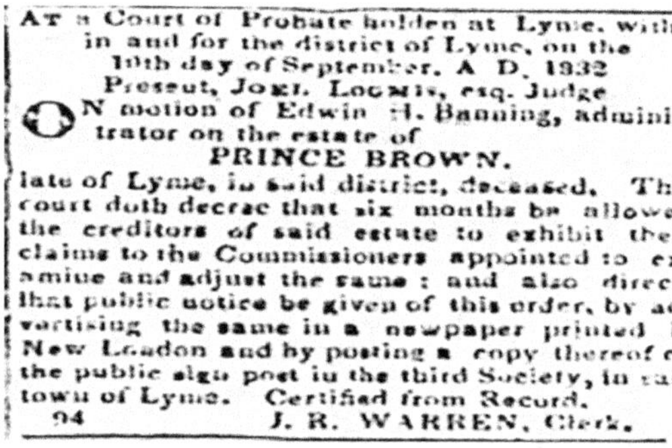

AT a Court of Probate holden at Lyme, within and for the district of Lyme, on the 10th day of September, A. D. 1832

Present, JOEL LOOMIS, esq. Judge

ON motion of Edwin H. Banning, administrator on the estate of

PRINCE BROWN,

late of Lyme, in said district, deceased. This court doth decree that six months be allowed the creditors of said estate to exhibit their claims to the Commissioners appointed to examine and adjust the same: and also directs that public notice be given of this order, by advertising the same in a newspaper printed in New London and by posting a copy thereof on the public sign post in the third Society, in said town of Lyme. Certified from Record.

94 J. R. WARREN, Clerk.

It appears as though the town wanted to turn over the burden of caring for Brown to the state, as was done in the cases of Caesar Beckwith and Pomp Henry, but he died in the spring of 1832 before any action was taken. After Prince's death, Lyme

77 *Samuel B. Mather and Nathan Griffing v. Prince Brown,* Ibid, November 1823, Box 6, folder 18. The first nine acre plot was called the "Schoolhouse lot" and adjoining landowners consisted of Dan Lee, Nathan Sisson, Lucretia Lee, and Jack Fashion. The second piece was described as the one that Brown purchased from Captain Harris Colt.

78 Prince Brown to Oliver Comstock, LLR, June 19, 1826. XXXI, 346.

79 Oliver Raymond to Isaac Spencer, January 15, 1831, CHS. No evidence exists in Lyme records that Brown ever received any support from the town. Raymond likely wrote the letter in anticipation of future needs. Lyme Land Records show that he lived within a quarter mile of the Raymond residence.

80 E[lish]a Phelps to Oliver Raymond, January 25, 1831, RG 062, LTR, Box 4, folder 21, CSL.

81 *Connecticut Gazette,* September 26, 1832, [3]. Joshua R. Warren is the author's great-great grandfather.

Probate Judge Joel Loomis appointed Edwin H. Banning administrator of Browne's estate and the inventory was taken on April 17. His property consisted of a house lot, thirteen acres of land, one cow, plus household goods, including two iron pots, table, spinning wheel, feather bed, bedding, and candlesticks. Its total value was $164.08.[82] In September, Lyme town clerk Joshua R. Warren published a probate notice concerning possible claims against his estate followed by a statement from the Court of Probate one and a half months later that Brown died insolvent.[83] When all the claims had been gathered, the Court determined that Brown's debts by note and book amounted to $179.11 and on October 20, 1834 administrator Edwin H. Banning sold "so much of the real estate of PRINCE BROWN . . . as will raise the sum of $179.11 cents with incident charges of sale."[84]

Prince's widow Phillis was living in Norwich in December 1838, the place of her birth, when time one of its selectmen wrote to the Lyme selectmen concerning her destitute status. "She is an old Colored Woman an inhabitant of Lyme [and] the Widow of the Late Prince Brown." Norwich intended to send her to the alms house unless Lyme provided for her.[85]

Although land and court records provide considerable information about the life and trials of Prince Brown, several questions about him remain. In the 1790 census, Negro Prince was the head of a family of five persons, 10 years later Prince had seven in his household, and the number in 1820 was six.[86] Who were these people? He married Phyllis Williams of Norwich in 1792 and is known to have had two daughters, Sylvia and Nancy. The three females may well have been represented in the 1800 and 1820 censuses. Other Brownes of color that lived in Lyme at this time were Ichabod, James, and Samuel P. Brown whose lineage is not known, but James Brown is listed as co-defendant in two lawsuits and Ichabod Brown in one, indicating the possibility that they were related to one another.[87] We cannot with any degree of certainty, however, know who the people in the Brown household were, although they were almost certainly other free persons of color.

Caesar Beckwith, aka Caesar Brown, was eleven years old when the estate of his master was taken over by the state.[88] On May 10, 1793, Judge Benjamin Huntington wrote that in 1784 when Caesar was about sixteen he was bound out to Jedidiah

---

[82] Prince Brown, Lyme, 1832, Old Lyme Probate Records, no. 92. The house and land was given an appraised value of $143.00 and the cow $17.00.

[83] Persons with claims against the estate were directed bring them to the house of Major John G. Jewett of Pleasant Valley in Lyme on the second Monday in March 1823 to appear before commissioners Zebulon Brockway, Jr. and Nathan Stark, 2d. *Connecticut Gazette*, September 26, 1832, [3]; November 7, 1832, [3]. Pleasant Valley is located less than a mile from where the author lives.

[84] Prince Brown, Lyme, 1832, Old Lyme Probate District, no. 92; *Connecticut Gazette*, October 8, 1834, [1].

[85] Charles Bliss to Sele[c]t Men Lyme, December 21, 1838, RG 062, LTR, Box 4, folder 21.

[86] It is possible that one of the five persons in the household in 1790 was Pru.

[87] Brown and Rose, *Black Roots*, 45, 47-48, 139.

[88] His first name is spelled inconsistently in documents - Cesar, Ceasar, Cezar, and Caesar. The most normal spelling is used in the text, although the original spelling is used in footnotes. The almost always reliable *Black Roots in Southeastern Connecticut* thought that Caesar Beckwith and Caesar Brown were two different men. Brown and Rose, *Black Roots*, 23, 43.

Beckwith of Lyme because "the Boy was lame and infirm" and since that time "his Infirmities have greatly increased." This statement accompanied a petition from the Lyme selectmen to the General Assembly concerning the situation of "Cesar Negro man formerly the Property of William Brown of Salem" who when a minor was apprenticed until he reached the age of twenty-six at which time his master returned him "to the Gov[erno]r & Company of this State." Caesar had lost the use of his limbs by reason of sickness and was "wholly incapable in any measure to support himself." The selectmen asserted that "the land belonging to said Brown before Confiscation was liable for the Support of said Negro," and since the State had taken over and benefited from the sale of the estate, he should be considered one of "this States poor."

The General Assembly agreed and designated Caesar "as One of the Poor of this State."[89] It paid the Town of Lyme £10-13 in August 1794 for the care of an unnamed pauper, almost certainly, Caesar Beckwith; another £12-18 in August 1795; £19-19 in May 1796 for the care of "a State Pauper;" £11 in November 1796; and two years later $20 for the "Support of [a] Negro Pauper."[90] Another source that documents "Charges of Paupers & Vagrants" noted that the State Comptroller paid the Town of Lyme £12-18 on August 31, 1795, £10-19 on July 28, 1796, $13.21 of August 21, 1797, and $20 on September 8, 1798.[91]

Beckwith appears in a number of records between 1800 and 1839. In 1800, he was a party in three court cases concerning the lease of a fifty-acre farm in the East Society near the Baptist meetinghouse.[92] The following year Ezra Maynard of Lyme sued Reynold Huntley and Caesar Beckwith in an action of trespass demanding $15. Justice of the Peace William Noyes found the defendants guilty and ordered them to pay $15 damages and $4.04 costs of suit. That same month a Lyme grand juror filed a complaint against Reynold Huntley and Beckwith for assaulting Phineas Huntley. Found guilty, the defendants were each ordered to pay a fine of $1.50 plus court costs of $5.30.[93] When Ezra Maynard of Chesterfield in Lyme petitioned "for an Act of insolvency" in April 1803, he listed the names of some thirty people to whom he owed money, including $9.00 to Beckwith.[94] One year later the town of Lyme sued Waterford in a debt

---

89 CA, Miscellaneous, Series 2, I, 71-72; *State Records*, VIII, 45-46.

90 RG 008, Office of the State Comptroller, Audited Vouchers, 1757-1819, Box 4, folders 5, 16, CSL; RG 008, Ledgers, 1788-1852, Ledgers 9-10, CSL. During the 1790s, State of Connecticut payments to towns for the care of paupers and transients did not identify for whom the funds were being expended. This changed at the beginning of the nineteenth century, when Comptroller reports specifically identified all State Paupers, the towns in which they lived, and the amount each received. Lists of State Paupers began to be found around 1800 and Caesar Beckwith's name is not among them. Between 1800 and 1809, Lyme paupers were "Benjamin White & Wife," Joseph Martin, and "Jacob Briggs & Wife." RG 008, State Comptroller, Ledgers, 1788-1852, Reports, Vol. 1, 1800-09, CSL.

91 RG 008, Comptroller, Journal B, 5, 19, 65, 110, 151.

92 *Caesar Beckwith v. James Huntley*, NLCC, Files, African Americans, June 1800, Box 1, folder 26; *James Huntley v. Reynold Huntley and Cesar Beckwith*, Ibid, June 1800, Box 1, folder 26; *Reynold Huntley v. James Huntley & Elkanah Huntley*, Ibid, June 1800, Box 1, folder 27. Court documents refer to Beckwith as "a free Negro."

93 RG 003, Justice Court Records of William Noyes, 1790-1806, January 3, 1801, January 29, 1801, Box 554, CSL. If Beckwith was involved in an assault, one wonders about the extent of his infirmities.

94 Petition of Ezra Maynard, April 24, 1803, CA, Insolvent Debtors, Series 2, 50; *State Records*, XI, 237-38.

by book for the care of paupers, one of the unpaid bills for $3.87 was due to "Casar Beckwith for House rent for Hannah Chandler, a Pauper of the Town of Waterford."[95] Beckwith found himself before the New London County Court again in June 1805 when William Moore, 4th of Waterford sued him in a debt by note for $73.00 signed on April 30, 1804 by which Caesar and Daniel Miller promised to repay the loan in one year together with lawful interest. The defendants defaulted and Moore recovered $77.93 for debt and interest plus $5.34 for court costs.[96]

Between approximately 1805 and 1807, Caesar lived in Colchester and the town paid him $18.08 in January 1806 for caring for State Pauper Paddy Brown.[97] In another court case, Moses Warren of Lyme sued Caesar Beckwith, "a Black man," in June 1809 for failure to pay a debt by note signed on March 16, 1805 for $15.45 plus interest. The defendant defaulted and Warren recovered judgment for $17.88 debt plus $4.43 costs of suit.[98] The Town of Lyme paid Beckwith $1.50 in January 1815 for taking "Bazil (Negro) to the Court at New London & paying [toll] Gate fees."[99] Beckwith found himself before the bar again in July 1817 when Sabin K. Smith and Joseph A. Smith of New London sued the free Negro in a debt by book for $51.08. Beckwith pleaded not guilty, saying that "he owes Nothing," but the court found him in book arrears for $30.13 plus costs of suit of $9.61.[100] No further information on Caesar is found until 1831, when the ledger of Peter Comstock of Lyme East Society showed that Beckwith owed him money for brandy, crackers, and "sundries."[101]

The most complete exposition of the life story of Caesar Beckwith came with a series of memorials sent to the General Assembly on his behalf between 1832 and 1837, the first by Lyme selectmen Sylvester Champion, Andrew Griswold, and Thomas W. Strickland on April 26, 1832. The selectmen stated that "Ceasar Brown (alias Ceasar Beckwith)" was born about 1768 and a slave to William Browne "in the family of Benjamin Beckwith then a tenant to said Brown" living in the Lyme portion of what became the town of Salem. Browne joined the enemies of the United States and his estate of around 9,000 acres of land, buildings, improvements, and slaves "became forfeit to this State." With regard to the slaves, "none of them [were] sold but were permitted

---

Beckwith's signature is found on the Maynard petition.

95 *Lyme v. Waterford*, NLCC, Files, African Americans, June 1803, Box 1, folder 33. The town of Lyme paid Beckwith $7.75 on January 3, 1803 for the care of an unidentified Negro, perhaps the same person referred in the court case. Lyme Day Book, 1796-1809, January 3, 1803, LTH.

96 *William Moore 4th v. Ceasar Beckwith and Daniel Miller*, NLCC, Files, African Americans, June 1805, Box 4, folder 40. He signed the note "Ceasar Beckwith."

97 Colchester Town Records, 1805-1842, January 29, 1806 CTH; Colchester Treasurer Records, 1791-1830, 68, CTH.

98 *Moses Warren v. Cesar Beckwith*, NLCC, Files, African Americans, June 1809, Box 5, folder 7. He signed the note, "Ceasar Beckwith."

99 Lyme Day Book, 1810-1827, January 30, 1815, CSL.

100 *Sabin K. Smith and Joseph A. Smith v. Caesar Beckwith*, New London Justice of the Peace Records, 1755-1903, July 22, 1817, Box 14, folder 8. Beckwith incurred the debt for foodstuffs like butter, crackers, flour, molasses, sugar, tea, "Cherry Rum," and "5 Gallons Cordial."

101 Peter Comstock Account Book, 1825-1838, 55, 58, CHS.

to remain in the families of the tenants of said Brown or to provide for themselves." Caesar remained in the household of "Benjamin Beckwith & Sons" and, while living with the family of Jedidiah Beckwith, "became a cripple in consequence of fever sores on his limbs" and "a Charge to the State." Infirm ever since, he had recently become "affected with a cough or disease of his lungs" and was consequently unable "to sustain himself." Since the state had benefitted from the sale of the estate to the amount of around $70,000, "your petitioners deem it right that the State should provide for the said Ceasars support" at the rate of $50.00 per year. The General Assembly continued the petition, e.g. postponed any action.[102]

On April 29, 1833, Beckwith sent a petition drafted by Joshua R. Warren asking the legislature examine the case presented on his behalf "last year." He stated that he was a member of the First Baptist Church of Lyme and argued that he deserved additional support because "the State having taken the property of his former master are in justice bound to support his declining life."[103] The legislature referred the petition to a select committee who reported that it believed "the facts stated to be true but there is provisions made by Law for the support of all State Paupers your Committee think it not expedient to make any grant at this time."[104] In 1836, another reference to Caesar appeared. He mortgaged the "house where I now live" on the highway in the East Society near the house of Elisha Way to Francis B. Loomis for $12.[105]

Beckwith sent another petition in 1837 asking for support and added some new information. The administrator of the confiscated estate freed all slaves "over twenty-one years of age," but since he was a minor he was bound as "an Apprentice to Jedidiah Beckwith" until he became twenty-one in 1789. Three years later in 1792 he became "sick with a fever which caused him to be crippled in one of his legs and one hand." He thereupon became a State Pauper, yet continued to "support himself by his industry, but by reason of Age and infirmity he is unable to labor much, and is poor and destitute." He added that he had lived about seventy years "amongst old Neighbors and feels much attached to them & the place of his nativity," and prayed to remain with them in his declining years. He asked for a small annual sum "from the State Treasury" for his care. The memorial was continued and later withdrawn.[106] More information on Beckwith appeared in 1838-39 when the Lyme treasurer paid W. H. H. Comstock, James L. Strickland, Job Tubbs, and Daniel Watrous for wood and food supplies furnished to the

---

102 "Petition of Sylvester Champion, Andrew Griswold and Thomas W. Strickland," RG 002, General Assembly Papers, 1821-1870, African Americans, Box 1, folder 8, CSL.

103 Beckwith joined the Baptist Church in the East Society on May 31, 1806. "After Solemn Prayer. the Door was opened to here [sic] Experiances. Then Came before the Ch[urc]h Brethren and Sisters Abel Smith and his Wife Polly Smith, Harris Beckwith, Cathy Manwaring, Daniel Huntley, Deliverance Smith, Fanny Ayer, [and] Cesar Beckwith. These all told their Experiances and offered them selves to Ch[urc]h." East Lyme, Baptist Community Church of Flanders (formerly Lyme First Baptist Church) Records, Volume 2, 31, 131.

104 "Petition of Ceasar Beckwith (alias Brown)," RG 002, Rejected Bills, 1808-1870, African Americans, Box 2, folder 5.

105 Ceasar Beckwith to Francis B. Loomis, April 25, 1836, LLR, XXXIV, 585. Since no other land record exists, the likelihood is that he was given the house by one of the persons who helped care for him, almost certainly a member of the Beckwith or Huntley families.

106 "Petition of Ceasar Beckwith," General Assembly Papers, African Americans, Box 1, folder 13.

elderly pauper.[107] The last reference to the former slave is found in a list of paupers on October 1, 1839 when a division of them was made between Lyme and newly constituted East Lyme. He probably died soon thereafter for no further record of him exists.[108]

The State classified Caesar Beckwith as a State Pauper in 1793, yet he never received the level of assistance accorded to Paddy Brown or Pomp Henry. He was just twenty-four years old when he became an official charge of the State. Nevertheless, despite physical impairments, he appears to have cared for himself, perhaps with the assistance of his neighbors, between around 1798 until the 1830s when the town began to provide for his support.

Three former slaves of William Browne - Paddy Brown, Pomp Henry, and Caesar Beckwith - became State Paupers which meant that it became responsible for their care. They were not, however, considered mentally incompetent persons over whom an overseer was appointed because such were generally only selected over those who owned real property. A process had to be followed before a conservator could be appointed to take charge of the affairs of any person deemed "labouring under a state of mental derangement," "now impotent & unable to provide for himself," "impotent & insane," "Lunatic," "non compos mentis," or "naturally wanting in understanding." Usually, a relative or acquaintance would contact the town selectmen who after investigation were fully "empowered to take such person . . . under their care." The selectmen then appointed a conservator over the person considered to be "wanting in understanding" and to take charge of his or her property.[109] The conservator used the assets of the person to pay for the care of the distracting individual.

This process was not followed for Beckwith, Brown, and Henry because they had few, if any, assets, thus responsibility for their support devolved upon the towns in which they dwelled and treasurer records show that the selectmen devoted a great deal of attention and considerable funds to caring for their own poor.[110] The selectmen could, however, petition the General Assembly to ask the state to take over the responsibility of caring for poor people who did not have permanent residence in the towns in which they then lived or were victims of special circumstances, like being slaves of a Tory, disabling injuries suffered during Revolutionary War service, or illnesses suffered by itinerants and sailors while in the state. The town of Lyme sounded out the State in 1831 in reference to Prince Brown, but he died before any further steps were taken.

Several questions remain unanswered about the former slaves of William Browne and, indeed, many in the first generation of freed people in Connecticut. For example, as already noted, little authoritative information has been found about seven of the twelve Browne slaves and we do not know if the Prince Brown who lived in Lyme was Great Prince or Little Prince. The 1790 Census lists Negro Fashion [Fashion Freeman], Negro Pomp [Pomp Henry], and Negro Prince [Prince Brown]. Fashion had three in his family, Pomp seven, and Prince five. Except, however, for those in Pomp

---

107 RG 062, LTR, Box 3, folders 2-4, 8-10. The seven town orders dated from January 1838 to March 1839.

108 Lyme Pauper Lists, LTH. No mention is made to Beckwith in early East Lyme town records.

109 *Public Statute Laws*, 382-83; Bruce P. Stark, "Connecticut Court System During the Time of Zephaniah Swift," *Connecticut Supreme Court History* IV (2009), 43-44.

110 In 1808, for example, Lyme provided full or partial support to forty-three people, only one of whom was a person of color, Hiram Still, the son of Pember W. Still. Lyme Day Book, 1796-1809, LTH.

Henry's household, we do not know who lived in the other two. Census records for the period between 1800 and 1820 provide additional data on Prince Brown, Fashion Freeman, and Pomp Henry, but Caesar Beckwith is not found, a clear indication that the census takers classified him as a dependent.

One final note. Two of six adult males, Prince Brown and Fashion Freeman, became land-owners.[111] They lived in close proximity to one another and near land owned by Sylvia Freeman of Norwich.[112] Considering the fact, however, that three of the Browne slaves were females and the remaining three males, Cato, Caesar, and Jimm, were minors, one of whom had physical impairments, the number, one third of males over 21, who acquired real property was probably typical for the times.[113]

---

[111] Probate records exist for them because they owned land.

[112] Ten of 14 Negro heads of families in 1790, including Prince Brown, lived in Lyme North Society, much closer to one another than to the rich and powerful in town. Stark, "Decoding the 1790 Federal Census," 330-31.

[113] The jury is out on Jimm, aka James Brown.

Chapter 10

The Last Browne Tenants

In addition to slaves, a number of tenants farmed the estate at the time of confiscation, a list of which is found in Governor Browne's Loyalist claim that provided data for 1774.[1] Nothing similar exists for any previous time period. As the table indicates, information provided consisted of the tenant's name, the length of the rental, the year of the contract, and the rental terms.

Table 5. Tenants in 1774 [2]

Tenant	Tenure		Rent		
			In money	Walls	L. Clearing
J. Henry	7 years March 1773		£100	80 rods	
J. Mumford	7 years	1774	£20 yearly first 4 years	30 rods 1st year	to clear 70 acres
			£30 yearly the last 3	20 rods after	
J. Ransom[3]	5 years	1774	£15 yearly	20 rods yearly	
Jos. Hastings	5 years	1770	£30 yearly	40 rods yearly	
Jos. Colt	6 years	1773	£15 Mar. 1778 £10 Mar. 1774		
Jos. Beckwith	5 years	1773	£20 yearly	20 rods yearly	
J. Minor	7 years	1773	£5 2/yearly		
S. Gilbert	10 years	1772			to clear 60 acres
B. Beckwith[4]	5 years	1772	£22 yearly	20 rods yearly	

---

[1] As recounted in Chapter 7, one of the most valuable farms, one that encompassed some 677 acres was untenanted at the time confiscation occurred.

[2] "The foregoing Lands were in the year 1774 farmed in the following manner viz." Browne Tenants, AmLC, AOP, AO 13/50, 142, NAUK. First names were abbreviated. It can be ascertained that B. represents Benjamin, W. William, J. stands primarily for John, although one J. is Joshua, Ja. for James, and Jona. for Jonathan, and Jos. represents both Joseph and Joshua. One S. is a Samuel and the second Stephen. Due to uncertainty about first names, the project to track down the tenants took longer than expected. After working on and off for some three months to positively identify them, the author finally tied down Joseph Hastings in June 2017.

[3] According to Mary E. Perkins, Joshua Ransom was a Browne tenant in 1760 and during the 1770s. Perkins, *Connecticut Farm*, 39-40, 52.

[4] Lease shared with Jedidiah Beckwith *State Records*, I, 311. There may well have been other leases in 1774 with two names on them.

Tenant	Tenure		Rent		
			In money	Walls	L. Clearing
Jona. Gilbert	5 years	1773	£27 yearly	20 rods yearly	
W. Carr	5 years	1769	£12 yearly		
S. Gardner	5 years	1770	£14-8 yearly		
Ja. Kelly	3 years	1770	£30 yearly		

The total for yearly rents amounted to around £215 per annum in the years just before the American Revolution, not a princely sum, but far from inconsequential.[5] The improvements required in most leases had equal importance. Seven specified that the renter constructs stone walls.[6] The lease of Jonathan Gilbert, for example, required that in addition to £27 annual rent, that he construct twenty rods (330 linear feet) of stone walls per year for five years. Two stipulated that land be cleared for future agricultural use, for John Mumford seventy acres and for Samuel Gilbert sixty acres. The extent of the tenanted farm can be inferred from the rental amount. The rent for the farm of John Minor, for example, was just £10 per year, while that for James Kelly was £30 yearly.[7] According to Ebenezer Backus, Jr. of Norwich in 1786, the Browne estate "was properly divided into Farms and Tenements, in some Parts with Stone Walls which Farms and Tenements were in the Occupation of Industrious and Thrifty Tenants."[8] A fourteenth farm leased to Samuel Hazard in 1767 was unrented in 1774.

The first person on the list, **John Henry**, lived in Colchester. Born in Rhode Island and raised in North Killingly, Connecticut, both he and his wife Hannah attended the Congregational Church there, owned the covenant on April 3, 1763, and had their son Francis baptized on the same day.[9] While living in that community, John and his brother Robert owned a not insignificant quantity of land, forty acres purchased in 1760 and sold in 1771, plus another 274 acres. In January 1772, John and Robert sold their Killingly farm for £660.[10]

---

[5] In his application for reimbursement from the British government, Governor Browne stated that rents yielded around £300 Lawful [money] p[e]r Annum with other Covenants on the part of Tenants." Perhaps the Massachusetts Tory counted the Hazard farm, unrented in 1774, or the value of walls and clearing of forests as part of the total. Memorial of William Browne, AmLC, AOP, AO 12/10, 227.

[6] The renters also had to pay all town and colony taxes.

[7] Without knowing the monetary value attached to building each rod of walls or clearing one acre of forest, one cannot know for certain the relative worth to the absentee of each lease, but the approximate scale of value from most to least monetary significance is as follows: 1) John Mumford, 2) Joseph Hastings, 3) Jonathan Gilbert, 4) James Kelly, 5) Benjamin Beckwith, 6) Joshua Beckwith, 7) Joshua Ransom, 8) John Henry, 9) Stephen Gardner, 10) William Carr, 11) Samuel Gilbert, 12) John Minor, and 13) Joseph Colt. Had the farm occupied by Samuel Hazzard been included, that property would have probably ranked in the top four in rental value.

[8] One can infer both from the Backus statement and knowledge of land quality that the fourteen farms did not take up the entire 9,600 acres of the confiscated estate. Affidavit, Ebenezer Backus, Jr. June 29, 1786, AOP, AO 13/50, 133-34.

[9] Putnam First Congregational Church Records (formerly North Killingly), Index, 93, CSL.

[10] William Henry Elbridge, *Henry Genealogy: The Descendants of Samuel Henry* (Boston: Press to T. R. Marvin, 1915), 131-34. Joseph Cutler and his wife Mary to John Henry, March 3, 1760, Killingly Land Records, VII, 26-27; John Henry and Robert Henry to Andrew Harris, December 5, 1771, Ibid, VIII, 249-50; John Henry and Robert Henry to William West, January 3, 1772, Ibid, IX, 139. The latter deed was also signed by

The chances are that they came to Colchester in March 1773 when John rented a Browne farm for seven years, living on property formerly occupied by John Mumford, Sr. That same year Henry acted as a representative for William Browne in a dispute over the boundary of the church lot donated to the society by Browne's grandfather.[11] The following year he was licensed as a tavern keeper by the Hartford County Court, a position he retained for as long as he lived in Colchester.[12] A strong Patriot, when Colonel Henry Champion of Colchester organized "a drove of Cattle" from Colchester to Roxbury, Massachusetts to provide food for General George Washington's army in December 1775, Henry furnished eight to ten head. Three years later Captain David Phelps of Simsbury and his unit of troops stopped for the night at John Henry's inn.[13] He was first elected to town office in December 1776 as surveyor of highways and took the "Oath of fidelity to the State of Connecticut" on December 1, 1777. During the Revolution, Henry served on Colchester's Committee of Inspection and Committee to Secure Provisions in 1780.[14]

An active member of the community, Henry's name appears several times in newspapers between 1776 and 1791. Three and one-half years after moving to town, he was designated as one of three commissioners on the insolvent estate of Thomas Gustin, late of Colchester, and one week later reported that a heifer had come on to his property that could be returned to its owner upon paying costs for its upkeep.[15] In June 1779, he advertised that he had taken up a stray sorrel mare and two years later for a second horse that had broken "into the Enclosure."[16] When the estate of William Browne was being sold at "PUBLIC VENDUE," in September 1781 and January 1783, the sales took place at "the Dwelling-House of Mr. John Henry, in Colchester."[17] He took up a stray horse, "a Natural Trotter," in March 1782.[18] In addition, he sold tickets for the Pier at Point Judith, Rhode Island lottery in 1791 and "the dwelling-house of Mr. John Henry, innholder" in Colchester served as the site for those bringing claims against the estate of Nehemiah Huntley for whom he was one of two commissioners.[19]

In January 1784, Major Theodore Woodbridge of Glastonbury and Dr. John R. Watrous petitioned the General Assembly to be granted the Harding Farm in Lyme, "nearly opposite the dwelling House where John Henry now lives," encompassing 288

Agnes Henry, John's second wife. Both grantees lived in Rhode Island.

11 CLR, IX, 69. The boundary agreement was signed by Jabez Jones, James Ransom, and Nathaniel Harris on behalf of Colchester with John Henry as attorney for William Browne.

12 HCC, PbyS: Travel, Box 541, April 1774, April 1778, April 1783 packets.

13 CA, Revolutionary War, Series 1, IV, 198; XII, 308. The fact that a man who had lived in Colchester for just two and one-half years could furnish so much livestock attests to the fact that he brought considerable personal property with him when he moved to the town or had the assets to purchase the same.

14 ColchesterBMD, Vol. 1, 246, 252, 254; Vol. 2, 343.

15 *Connecticut Gazette,* December 20, 1776, [1]; December 27, 1776, [1].

16 Ibid, June 17, 1779, [4]; July 6, 1781, [3].

17 Ibid, August 24, 1781, [3]; December 27, 1782, [4].

18 ColchesterBMD, Vol. 1, 258.

19 *Connecticut Gazette*, May 12, 1791, [1]; June 19, 1791, [4].

acres, "whereon Robert Henry now lives," in payment for their past military services.[20] The legislature granted the memorial.[21] Henry did not purchase any of the lots into which the confiscated estate was divided, although the house where he lived is mentioned in documentation for the sale of Lots 15, 16, and 23 in 1784 and 1786.[22] He lived in Colchester just over the Lyme border.[23] The 1785 Colchester tax list for New Salem states that Henry's assessment amounted to £18-14-3, the second highest in the parish. References to Henry occur in Lyme tax records for the years 1781-86 and indicate that a portion of the land he farmed was in that town. According to the "State Rate on Levy 1781," his property was worth £88 and he owed £1-2 in state taxes.[24]

The New London County Court called Henry twice in June 1783 as a witness in prosecutions instituted by Judge Benjamin Huntington.[25] In addition, Nathan Chapman of Colchester sued Henry in November 1784 for nonpayment of a £16 note dated July 18, 1776.[26] The town sold some of his personal property, perhaps livestock, at auction for failure to pay taxes on October 13, 1786.[27] A New Salem list of polls and ratable estates for 1787 lists both John and his brother Robert.[28] The New London County Court upon the recommendation of the civil authority of Colchester made Henry a tavern keeper in June 1785 and he continued to be reappointed through 1792.[29]

Colchester elected him surveyor of highways three more times in 1782, 1786 and 1789.[30] Another reference to Henry occurred in court records. Nathaniel Harris, Jonathan Rathbun, and others petitioned the New London County Court on May 16, 1787 on the need for a new road beginning near the Baptist Meetinghouse to connect

---

[20] Robert Henry is not found in Governor Browne's list of tenants despite living on Browne property. Perhaps he shared his brother's lease.

[21] CA, Revolutionary War, Series 3, II, 29, CSL; *State Records*, V, 56-67. Woodbridge and Watrous purchased the Harding Farm (Lot 23) on September 29, 1784 for £1,154 "in Securities for Service in the Continental Army" and Watrous on his own bought Lot 22 containing 148.75 acres on November. 30, 1786 for £402 in "Liquidated Securities." Perkins, *Connecticut Farm*, 218-19.

[22] Perkins, *Connecticut Farm*, 28, 52, 83, 212, 219.

[23] The household of his brother Robert consisted of nine persons and, if the 1790 federal census placed families in proximity to one another, seven households separated John Henry from that of John Mumford. 1790 Census, 101.

[24] Levy for 1785, Colchester Town Records, 1708-1884, Box 1, folder 3, CHS; RG 062, LTR, Box 6, Tax Lists, Vol. 1, 33. John's brother Robert's assessment was £67.

[25] *Benjamin Huntington v. Bliss Ransom and Alpheus Ransom*, NLCC, Files, June 1783, Box 179, folder 18, no. 343; *Benjamin Huntington v. Bliss Ransom*, Ibid, Box 179, folder 18, no. 344.

[26] *Nathan Chapman v. John Henry*, Ibid, November 1784, Box 190, folder 6, no docket.

[27] RG 062, LTR, Box 6, Tax Lists, Vol. 1, 33; Vol. 2, 274-75, 323; Vol. 3, 408-09, 421, 502, 530; Vol. 4, 602, 688, 753, CSL.

[28] Charles M. Taintor, *Extracts from the Records of Colchester, with some Transcripts from the Recordings of Michaell Taintor, of "Brainford"* (Hartford: Press of Case, Lockwood and Company, 1864), 155. Dr. John R. Watrous provided medical care to John Henry and his son Samuel between 1787 and 1790. Watrous, Medical Account Book A, 188, CSL.

[29] NLCC, PbyS: Travel, Box 95, folders 7-9. He was not chosen innkeeper in 1793.

[30] Colchester Town Meeting Records, 1780-1829, 10, 17, 33, CTH.

with the highway from Colchester to New London "by Henrys Tavern near a School house."[31] The 1790 Colchester census showed that his household consisted of three males over sixteen, four males under 16, six females, and two other free people, one of whom was also named John Henry.[32] He was one of fifty-three signers of a May 1792 memorial to the General Assembly asking for assistance in re-establishing New Salem Society because had been overrun by Baptists and other religious dissenters.[33] Henry departed the area in 1793 or 1794 and no further record of him is known.[34]

John Mumford (1740-1825), the Browne's last agent, lived on the farm in Lyme where he moved to shortly after coming to Connecticut.[35] He married Lucretia Christophers in 1770 and they became the parents of five girls. Elizabeth, the eldest, (1771-1795) married Nathaniel Shaw Woodbridge, later owner of much of the old Browne property in New Salem. Second daughter Mary (1774-1830) was followed by short-lived Lucretia in December 1775, Catherine (1777-1816), Sarah (b. 1780), and a second Lucretia in 1785. Mary married Elias Perkins of New London, Catherine became the wife of Dr. Isaac Thompson of New London, and Lucretia of Anthony Thacher of the same town.[36]

Mumford's father was an Anglican, as were at least two cousins from Groton, and he probably also supported the church identified so closely with the mother country.[37] Passive and quiet Loyalists, Mumford father and son remained undisturbed throughout the American Revolution.[38] He disappears from official records during most of the conflict and the first references to him appear in a 1781 medical bill for £2-15 paid in 1784 and his 1781 tax list of £205-5 on the state levy for that year.[39]

---

31 Petition of Nathaniel Harris, Jonathan Rathbun, and others, NLCC, PbyS: Travel, Box 95, folder 7.

32 1790 Census, 101; Rose and Brown, *Black Roots*, 181.

33 *State Records*, VII, 423-25. Three other men with the same surname signed the petition - Francis, Robert, and Samuel. Francis Henry, probably the son of John, was elected surveyor of highways in 1784 and 1787 and Samuel became a freeman in 1791. Colchester, Town Meetings, 1780-1828, 20, 30, CTH; ColchesterBMD, Vol. 2, 1751-1894, 351, CTH.

34 Henry is not found in the 1793 tax list and an advertisement for the 1795 sale of the "Harding Farm" noted that it was situated "one mile from the dwelling-house where Mr. John Henry formerly lived, and Mr. John Johnson, 3d, now lives." "A Rate Bill for State Rate," 1793, Colchester Town Records, 1709-1884, Box 1, folder 3, CHS; *Connecticut Gazette*, February 19, 1795, [4].

35 See Map 2, Lot 26 on page 144. Lot 26 is located in the lower left quadrant of the map.

36 Perkins, *Connecticut Farm*, 67, 139, 141, 143-44, 155.

37 Thomas Mumford III and Thomas Mumford IV (1728-99). Bruce E. Steiner, "Anglican Officeholding in Pre-Revolutionary Connecticut: The Parameters of New England Community," *WMQ*, XXI (July 1974), 373 376, 404. Episcopalian Bishop Samuel Seabury presided over the nuptials of John's daughter Polly with Elias Perkins of New London. *Connecticut Gazette*, February 13, 1805, [3].

38 He only took the oath of allegiance after the Revolutionary War ended. Oath of Allegiance, Lyme, Conn. 1777-1784, Lyme Public Hall Archives; Perkins, *Connecticut Farm*, 149, 151; Stark, *Lyme*, 97. The Connecticut General Assembly passed a law in May 1777 stipulating that "no freeman within this State shall be allowed to vote in the election of any of the officers of government" until he took the oath of allegiance in an open freemen's meeting. *State Records*, I, 226-27.

39 Samuel Mather Account Book, 1773 – 1796, 164, CHS; Dr. Daniel Caulkins Account Book, 1766-1788, Folio 106, CHS. The assessed value of his property was the highest in Chesterfield, the Lyme portion of New Salem. Additional medical visits by Dr. John R. Watrous took place between 1798 and 1806. Dr. John R.

Illustration 11: John Mumford, Jun., 1740 - 1825 [40]

In November 1781, Mumford sued Jacob Tillotson, collector of Chesterfield Society, for £150 in a case heard the following February. Mumford charged that the defendant had assaulted and falsely imprisoned him on November 5. Tillotson testified that the plaintiff owed the parish twelve shillings for taxes to support the gospel ministry. Tried by jury, the court found the defendant not guilty, ordered Mumford to pay court costs, whereupon Mumford appealed.[41] The Superior Court at its March 1783 session reversed the holding of the inferior court. The jury found Tillotson guilty and ordered him to pay Mumford £16 damages plus court costs.[42] A year later he advertised that "a small Boar PIG" had come onto his property, the return of which could be secured by the owner upon paying costs for its care.[43] Lyme chose John Mumford, Jr. to serve on the New London County Court jury in February 1784 for its next session and in 1783 and 1790 he had letters waiting for him at the New London Post Office.[44]

Watrous, Account Book C, 35, CHS; RG 062, LTR, Box 6, Tax Lists, Vol. 1, 33.

[40] Perkins, *Connecticut Farm,* p. 154. Image courtesy of The Connecticut Historical Society.

[41] *John Mumford, Jr. v. Jacob Tillotson,* NLCC, Files, February 1782, Box 172, folder 16, no. 65. With regard to the assault, Mumford asserted that the defendant with force and arms "Made a Violent and Forceable Assault upon the Body of the Plaintiff . . . and unlawfully Imprisoned" him "for the Space of Eight Hours . . . and Conveyed the Plaintiff . . . from Lyme to Norwich" and threatened to commit his to the "Common Gaol."

[42] *John Mumford v. Jacob Tillotson,* Early Records, CSC, March 1783, Vol. 23, 175.

[43] *Connecticut Gazette,* June 6, 1783, [4].

[44] NLCC, PbyS: Jurors, February 1784, Box 75, folder 4; *Connecticut Gazette,* October 3, 1783, [4]; July 7, 1790, [3].

In May 1784, the *Connecticut Gazette* published a runaway notice from Mumford in which he offered a ten dollar reward for the return of "a short thick negro man about 38 years of age named PONTO."[45]

The farm on which he lived encompassed 1,094 acres and was purchased by Thomas Shaw of New London of March 7, 1783 for £3,938.[46] Mumford remained on this property in New Salem for most of the rest of his life. According to the 1790 census, the family consisted of five males aged 16 and above, three males under 16, seven females, one free person of color, and three slaves, for a grand total of 19.[47] He became active in Lyme politics during the 1790s and early 1800s and held several public offices, including surveyor of highways in 1791, selectman in 1795-97 and 1803-04, and fence viewer in 1805-06. In addition, the Lyme Town Meeting appointed Mumford to a committee of eight men to consider the propriety of "building a Town House" in November 16, 1801.[48] In September 1791, he signed a petition to improve the highway from New London to Colchester.[49]

The 1800 census showed that the Mumford household in Lyme consisted of one free white male under 10, one free white male 16-25, one free white male 45+, three free females under 10, one from 10-15, two from 16-25, and one of age 45+, together with two other free persons. The total for the household was 12, only two of whom were over 25.[50] In 1808, Mumford was owed $250 by insolvent debtor Francis Hazard of New London.[51]

In old age, he and wife Lucretia moved to New London.[52] Lucretia Mumford died there on March 19, 1825 and John died four months later in his 86th year.[53]

---

45 *Connecticut Gazette*, May 7, 1784, [4]. Thirteen years later he advertised for a dairy woman and in February 1801 reported that indented apprentice Samuel Newbury had run way. Ibid, April 20, 1797, [4]; Perkins, *Chronicles of a Connecticut Farm*, 157.

46 According to Mary E. Perkins, Mumford would have liked to have purchased the farm, but felt that the seizure of the land by the State was so unjust that he did not bid on the land. At the request of Thomas Shaw, however, he continued to manage and live on the estate until 1819. Perkins, *Connecticut Farm*, 149, 166.

47 1790 Census, 101. The household probably included Mumford's father and disabled brother Caleb. Perkins, *Connecticut Farm*, 82-83. Lyme Tax Records show assessments for Mumford for the years 1784-88, RG 062, Lyme Town Records, Tax Lists, Box 6, Vol. 2, 324; Vol. 3, 476, 503, 521; Vol. 4, 688, CSL. Mumford's mother died at the end of March 1790 before the census was taken. *Connecticut Gazette*, April 3, 1790, [3].

48 RG 003, Justice Court Records of William Noyes, 12-13; Lyme Day Book, 1796-1809, May 2, 1796, April 3, 1797, LTH; Lyme Town Meeting Records, Vol. 3, 1801-1855, 2, 6, 17, LTH.

49 CA, Travel, Series 2, VII, 39.

50 1800 Census, AncestryHeritageQuest.com. Mumford is not found for 1810 and 1820 censuses in either Ancestry or the copies at the Connecticut State Library. One of the two other free persons was "his Negro Providence." Other Mumford servants of color included Tapheny Indian and Thankful Bump. Dr. John R. Watrous, Account Book C, 35, CHS; Brown and Rose, *Black Roots*, 54.

51 CA, Insolvent Debtors, Series 2, V, 140.

52 He moved to New London around 1820. In November of that year, he quitclaimed his right to land he held as guardian to Mary and Lucretia Woodbridge. John Mumford to Elijah Ransom, Salem Land Records, I, 415, Salem Town Hall.

53 "DIED, In this city, on the 19th inst., *Mrs. Lucretia Mumford*, consort of Mr. John Mumford, aged 75." The death notice for her husband stated simply, "DIED, In this city, John Mumford, Esq. aged 85." *Connecticut Gazette*, March 23, 1825, [3]; July 20, 1825, [3]. They passed away at the home of their daughter Lucretia

Mumford drafted his will on March 17, 1818 and left all his "estate of any description to my beloved daughter, Lucretia Thatcher, wife of Anthony Thatcher." He appears to have been in poor health as his signature was shaky. The inventory of his estate taken in August 1825 listed no real property and little personal property. Mumford had $2,500 in cash and $2,088 in New London Bank stock.[54]

A number of Ransoms lived in Colchester and held offices in the town, two of whom Amasa and James, purchased lots of the confiscated estate of William Browne.[55] The tenant J. Ransom was **Joshua Ransom** (1715-1806) who lived on a rented farm in 1760.[56] According to the 1762 Colchester Tax List, Ransom's property was assessed at £117-6.[57] Born in Colchester, he married Sarah Brown, a step-daughter of Pelatiah Bliss, and they became the parents of seven children, four sons and three daughters.[58] He lived for several years in New London and the court summoned Ransom and three others, including Lebbeus Harris, as witnesses in a lawsuit between Joseph Ely and Jonathan Harris in November 1759.[59]

He served five times in the minor office of surveyor of highways between 1740 and 1771.[60] Both Joshua, the renter, and son Joshua, Jr. served as militia officers, Joshua and three sons took the oath of fidelity in Colchester, but only youngest son Bliss still lived in Colchester in 1790.[61] Ransom was chosen ensign of the New Salem militia company in the 12th regiment in May 1769. He resigned nine years later due "to his Long Services, advanced age, and bodily Infirmity." In June 1776, his son Joshua, Jr.

Thatcher, buried in a cemetery in the city that later became a public park, and their stones removed to Cedar Grove Cemetery. John Mumford (1740-1825), *WikiTree, wikitree.com*

[54] John Mumford, New London, 1825, NLPR, no. 3783.

[55] William C. Ransom, *Historical Outline of the Ransom Family in America and Genealogical Record of the Colchester, Conn., Branch* (Ann Arbor, MI: The Richmond & Backus Company, 1913), 71-94. Amasa and James jointly purchased Lots 7 and 14 and James acquired Lot 15. The total acreage was 502.5.

[56] Although the first two tenants having the initial J. were John Henry and John Mumford, the third J. was Joshua Ransom, the same man who was a Browne tenant in 1760 and lived in Colchester at least as early as 1759. Twelve Ransoms took the Revolutionary War oath of fidelity in Colchester and two in Lyme, including James, Joshua, and Joshua, Jr. but no John. The 1790 census lists nine Ransoms in Colchester and four in Lyme, two different men with the first name James, but no John or Joshua. Perkins, *Connecticut Farm*, 40, 52; NLCC, PbyS: Summons for Evidence, November 29, 1759, Box 90, folder 5; ColchesterBMD, Vol. 2, 342-45; Lyme Oath of Allegiance; 1790 Census, 86, 94, 97, 98, 100, 101, 104, 107, 109.
    See Map 1, Lot C2 for the location of the house of Joshua Ransom.

[57] 1762 Colchester Tax List, CTR, folder 10, CHS.

[58] Ransom, *Ransom Family*, 76-77. Children: Alpheus (b. 1742), Joshua (b. 1744), Elizabeth (b. 1747), Anna (b. c. 1749), Sarah (b. 1750), Pelatiah (1752-1807), and Bliss.

[59] NLCC Files, *Joshua Ransom v. William Gardner*, June 1749, Box 86, folder 20, no. 30. The suit was a debt by note when both were then residents of New London. NLCC, PbyS: Summons for Evidence, November 29, 1759, Box 90, folder 5. When trial took place the following June, the court issued another summons to several people, including Joshua and Sarah Ransom. The lawsuit concerned a dispute over livestock worth £35. NLCC, Files, *Joseph Ely v. Jonathan Harris*, June 1760, Box 113, folder 16, no. 18.

[60] ColchesterBMD, Vol. 1, 152, 213, 216, 217, 232, CTH. Joshua, Jr. served as grand juror in 1775 and surveyor of highways in 1777. Ibid, 242, 248.

[61] Joshua, Jr. took the oath of fidelity to Connecticut on September 16, 1777 and his father followed January 19, 1778. ColchesterBMD, Vol. 2, 342-44; 1790 Census, 98.

received an ensign appointment and was promoted to lieutenant in October 1782.[62] A number of Ransoms owned land in Colchester, but neither Joshua nor Joshua, Jr. did. According to family tradition, Joshua, Sr. was a physician. His son Joshua, Jr. practiced medicine and removed to Otsego County, New York in the 1790s.[63] Joshua, Sr. left Colchester shortly after the Revolution and died in Barkhamsted on September 14, 1806 "aged 91 years."[64]

Jos. Hastings was **Joseph Hastings** (1710-1787) of Norwich. He rented a 500-acre farm from March 1773 to March 28, 1778 and continued to occupy it thereafter. After Connecticut took over the Browne estate, administrator Benjamin Huntington petitioned the New London County Court on May 21, 1781, stating that Hastings "refuseth to pay the rents . . . due on said Lease and holdeth said Lease." The court appointed referees and they determined that the tenant's debt to the estate came to £174-19-9, the equivalent of almost six years rent.[65] Hastings appears to have been a man of solid circumstances, so one wonders why did he lease such a large farm in a neighboring community? Perhaps he considered it to be a relatively inexpensive way to provide for his sons and whose labor was needed to build forty rods of walls per year.

Hastings married Zerviah Crocker in 1737 and they became the parents of eleven children between 1737 and 1759, two of whom died in infancy. He subscribed to a 1740 statement opposing the building of a new meetinghouse. The amount of his taxable property that same year was £70-4 at the approximate middle point of the 150 taxpayers in the West Society of Norwich.[66] Seven years later he was among forty-seven signers of a petition to organize a new parish by splitting the West Society. He served as officer of the troop of horse of the Third Militia Regiment in New London County, appointed cornet in May 1763, lieutenant in October 1768, and captain four years later.[67] The New London County Court summoned him in February 1768 to give evidence in the case of *Samuel Gager v. Jedediah Hide*.[68] He protested against a new highway in Norwich in 1770 and signed a memorial two years later to construct a road from Norwich West Society to the Lebanon meetinghouse.[69] Hastings died on December 12, 1787 and

---

62 CA, Militia, Series 2, II, 304; VI, 1375; X, 1901; XV, 2832, CSL; *Colony Records*, XI, 376; XIV, 339; *State Records*, IV, 298. Joshua, Sr's 1760 militia appointment was prompted by the resignation of Lieutenant James Ransom. Upon his resignation, he was succeeded by Samuel Tenant. CA, Revolutionary War, Series 1, 267d, 277g.

63 Ransom, *Ransom Family*, 77 A Joshua Ransom, probably Joshua, Jr. lived in East Haddam in 1790 in a household of 11 that contained 5 free white males under 16, 1 free white male over 16, and 5 free white females. A decade later he was living in Springfield, Otsego County, New York in a household of 9, including 1 white male over 45 and 1 white female over 45. ancestryheritagequest.com

64 *Connecticut Courant*, September 24, 1806, [3].

65 *Petition of Benjamin Huntington*, NLCC, Trials, Vol. 25, February 1783, no. 83; *Petition of Benjamin Huntington*, NLCC, Files, February 1783, Box 177, folder 2, no. 83. The phrase "holdeth said Lease" indicates that he was still in possession of the property.

66 *Vital Records of Norwich, 1659-1848*, Part I (Hartford: Society of Colonial Wars in the State of Connecticut, 1913), 181, 280; CA, Ecclesiastical Affairs, Series 1, VIII, 301, 314

67 CA, Ecclesiastical Affairs, Series 2, III, 153; *Colony Records*, XII, 143; XIII, 97; XIV, 11.

68 NLCC, PbyS: Summons for Evidence, February 6, 1768, Box 91, folder 5.

69 NLCC, PbyS: Travel, June 20, 1770, Box 94, folder 14; Ibid, December 5, 1772, Box 94 folder 17.

his inventory was taken on January 21, 1788. His six plots of land totaled 219 acres, including 100 acres in New Hampshire, and was valued at £530. The total for the estate amounted to £1,059.[70]

The tenant Jos. Colt was Deacon **Joseph Colt** (1727-1787) of Lyme.[71] The farm he leased must have been relatively small and unproductive because the six-year total rent amounted to just £25, a rate of just over £4 per year, and the smallest for any Browne tenant. Colt served twice as juror at the New London County Court in 1755 and 1761.[72] We see him in November 1761 when Richard Mather sued Colt in a note debt, but the suit was withdrawn.[73] Deacon Joseph was a middle-class Lyme farmer who became prominent in town affairs during and after the American Revolution. The town meeting appointed him to a committee to secure supplies for the families of soldiers in March 1777. The Connecticut Council of Safety selected him to appraise Brown's confiscated estate in January 1781 and he served as a selectman in 1784 and 1786. In April 1787, he was one of some 105 persons presenting a memorial to the General Assembly asking for the formation of a new township from the "North Part of Lyme," Hadlyme, part of Chesterfield, and a small portion of Colchester.[74] Deacon Joseph Colt served as one of two messengers from Lyme North Society at the ordination of the Reverend Richard Ely in Saybrook in January 1786.[75] He married Desire Pratt of Saybrook in 1756 and the couple became the parents of eight children. His tax list for 1781 amounted to £205, the highest in the North Society.[76] The North Lyme man served as administrator of the insolvent estate of William Banning of Lyme in early 1787.[77] Upon death, his estate was appraised at £1,263, the real estate portion was worth £783-5.[78] Despite his relative prominence, Colt rarely appeared before the New London County bar.

The tenant Jos. Beckwith in 1774 was **Joshua Beckwith** of Lyme.[79] He rented a farm as early as 1763 and was owed £59-10 by the confiscated estate of William

---

70 Joseph Hastings, Franklin, 1788, NPR, no. 5011. Only four children still survived. "DIED . . . Capt. JOSEPH HASTINGS, in the 77th year of his age." *Norwich Packet*, December 13, 1787, [3]. A notice for claims against his estate appeared in April 1788 by administrators Rozel and Dan Hastings. *Connecticut Gazette*, April 25, 1788, [4].

71 Edward P. Jones, *Descendants of John Coult who sailed from England and arrived in America September 4, 1633* (n.p.: 1933), 20-22.

72 NLCC, PbyS: Jurors, November 1755, Box 75 folder 2; January 1761, Box 75, folder 3.

73 NLCC, Files, *Richard Mather v. Joseph Coult,* November 1761, Box 119, folder 18, no docket.

74 CA, Revolutionary War, Series 1, XXVII, 18, 19; XXX, 89c; CA, Finance and Currency, Series 2, IX, 169, CSL; CA, Towns and Lands, Series 1, IX, 147; *State Records*, III, 288; V, 309.

75 New London Association, January 7, 1786, 160.

76 RG 062, LTR, Box 6, Tax Lists, Vol. 1, 20.

77 *Connecticut Gazette*, January 19, 1787, [4].

78 Barbour Collection of Vital Records, Lyme, 48; *Connecticut Gazette*, October 26, 1787, 3; Joseph Colt, Lyme, 1787, NLPR, no. 1370. Colt possessed eight plots of land, a house, an old barn, and a "Molatto Girl named Cloe Age 6 Years."

79 He never owned any property in town and no obvious reference to him has been found in the Beckwith genealogy. See Map 1 at the top center of Lot B1 for the location of his residence.

Browne in 1779.[80] He left a handful of traces in Connecticut records. When the movement to form Chesterfield Society from parts of New London North Society, Lyme East Society, and New Salem began, a 1768 petition giving proposed boundaries states in part "to John Mumford Junr House thence Easterly Taking in Joshua Beckwith to A Certain Swamp" and one of its signers was Jonathan Beckwith.[81]

Joshua Beckwith of Lyme placed an advertisement in the New London newspaper in 1770 for a runaway apprentice named Ezra White.[82] A muster roll for a "Company of Minute Men' in May 1776 includes Joshua Beckwith.[83] The Lyme "State Levy" for 1781 lists Joshua Beckwith of Chesterfield being taxed for an estate worth £109-5.[84] In a November 1781 sale of 193 acres and 128 rods to James and Amasa Ransom, Lot no. 7, for £1,414-19-1 part of the boundary was "a highway that goes by Joshua Beckwith toward N London."[85] Some 170 people from New London, Montville, and Colchester sent a memorial to the General Assembly in October 1791 asking that repairs be undertaken on the post road from New London, through Montville, to Colchester and Joshua was among the signees.[86] This is all that can be discovered for certain about the renter.

A Joshua Beckwith, almost certainly not the tenant, began to acquire small parcels of land in Colchester in 1793.[87] John Palmer of Colchester sold him 3 acres and 10 rods in the town for £9-3 in October 1793 and a year later Palmer sold another plot consisting of 16 acres and 14 rods that bordered in part on his previous purchase, both in Colchester First Society.[88] Joshua Beckwith of the First Society is found in seven other Colchester land transactions between 1805 and 1818.[89] What happened to the tenant after 1791, however, cannot be determined.

John Minor rented a small property in 1773 for £10 per year.[90] The New

---

80 He shared the 1763 tenancy with Jonathan Beckwith and perhaps the 1773 one also. The Browne estate owed Jonathan £32-11-5 in 1779. Perkins, *Connecticut Farm*, 45, 51, 202.

81 CA, Ecclesiastical Affairs, Series 1, XIII 142.

82 *Connecticut Gazette*, May 25, 1770, [3].

83 CA, Revolutionary War, Series 1, XI, 120. Other Minute Men in the company of Captain Eliphalet Holmes included Elisha and Martin Beckwith and the lieutenant was John Tenant who had formerly rented Browne land.

84 RG 062, LTR, Box 6, Tax Lists, 31.

85 CA, Revolutionary War, Series 1, XXXIV, 154.

86 CA, Travel, Highways, Ferries, etc. Series 2, VIII, 38.

87 The Joshua Beckwith, Jr. who died in 1826 was also a Colchester landowner, buying his first property in 1815. Joshua, Jr., too, however, was also not the tenant Joshua. CLR, XVII, 323; Joshua Beckwith, Colchester, 1826, CPR, no. 175. The probate documents generally refer to him as Joshua, Jr. No reference to any Joshua Beckwith is found in either Lyme or Colchester vital records.

88 John Palmer to Joshua Beckwith, October 1, 1793, CLR, XIII, 42; John Palmer to Joshua Beckwith, November 1, 1793, Ibid, 14, 338.

89 CLR, XV, 351; XVI, 144, 275: XVII, 111, 223, 369; XVIII, 81. The land described was in Colchester's First Society and in one Beckwith was called a resident of Lebanon.

90 Spelled both as Miner and Minor. The Minor genealogy lists a number of Johns, but none of them lived in Lyme at the right time. John Augustus Minor, *Thomas Minor Descendants 1608-1981* (Trevett, ME: 1981).

London County Court awarded John Minor of Lyme a license to tan leather in 1733.[91] Originally from New London, he purchased forty acres in Lyme East Society "near Hog Swamp" from Jonathan Daniels in August 1734 that he sold two days later for the same price to John and Hannah Jo[h]nson. Probably he acted as a straw purchaser.[92] Two years later in April 1736 came his first permanent acquisition, five acres for which he paid £10. In March 1737, he paid £120 for thirty acres of land and a house that bordered in part on his previous purchase. Between 1764 and 1766 he bought three more small plots of land that totaled thirteen acres and sold a salt meadow of one acre and forty rods in 1776.[93] Minor represents an example of a lower-class farmer with insufficient land to support his family who hoped to increase his income by renting land. Dr. Daniel Caulkins of the East Society provided medical care and billed him £6-4-2 in 1778-79 and attempted to collect £4-2-11 from his estate. In August 1778, he placed a notice in the *Norwich Packet* reporting the theft of a bay horse.[94]

After his 1781 death, his widow Deborah petitioned the General Assembly for permission to sell some of his land because "the Debts due from said Estate, together with allowances made to the Widow, with the Charges of Administration . . . surmounts the sum of the Inventory of the Personal Estate" of the deceased by £79-11-10. The legislature granted her request.[95] In three deeds, she sold six pieces of land to pay off debts owed by his estate. Other small pieces of land were distributed to the widow and sons Jeremiah and Samuel.[96]

Brothers **Jonathan** (c. 1730-1825) and **Samuel Gilbert** (1742-1813), tenants with two separate leases, were grandchildren of Captain Samuel Gilbert and sons of John Gilbert of Paugwonk.[97] Samuel Gilbert had a ten-year lease from 1772-82 and Jonathan a five-year lease from 1773-78. Neither took the oath of allegiance to Connecticut in either Colchester or Lyme.

Jonathan of Chesterfield in Lyme served in the French and Indian War, lived in Lyme East Society in 1767, was summoned to give evidence in a 1766 court case, reported in the local newspaper that he had taken up a stray in Chesterfield in 1773, and was one of a number of people during the 1780s who had property sold because of an inability to pay town and state taxes.[98] He paid rent to Benjamin Huntington in March

[91] NLCC: PbyS: Licenses, Box 81, folder 3, CSL.

[92] Jonathan Daniels to John Minor, LLR, August 1, 1734, V, 233; John Minor to John and Hannah Jonson, Ibid, August 3, 1734, V, 234.

[93] LLR, V, 552; VI, 124, 293, 294; XII, 25; XIV, 101.

[94] Caulkins Account Book, Folio 130, CHS; *Norwich Packet*, August 10, 1778, [4]. Caulkins received £1-4-6 from the estate. John Minor, Lyme, 1781, NLPR, no. 3644.

[95] "The Memorial of of Deborah Minor, CA, Estates of Deceased Persons, XIII, 223-25. According to the persons appointed to examine the claims, his personal estate amounted to £69-1 and the real estate £98-19.

[96] John Minor, Lyme, 1781, NLPR, no. 3644; LLR, XV, 379, 380; XVI, 50. Two plots were sold to Elisha Minor and one to Dr. Daniel Caulkins. The probate record does not contain an inventory of his estate. John had died by the time the 1781 tax list was gathered and his widow Deborah was rated at £13-5-6. RG 062, LTR, Box 6, Tax Lists, Vol. 1, 16.

[97] Brainard et al, *Gilbert Family*, 145-46, 148.

[98] CA, Ecclesiastical Affairs, Series1, XIII, 146, 147; NLCC, PbyS, Summons for Evidence, June 18 1766, Box 91, folder 2; *Connecticut Gazette*, May 14, 1773, [2]; December 22, 1786, [3].

1781 on the farm he leased from Browne and was classified as a non-resident proprietor of Lyme in December 1786.[99]

Married twice, he was the father of four children by his first wife Sarah Rogers and three with Mary Baker.[100] He briefly owned land in Lyme. Samuel Gilbert of Farmington, not the Browne tenant, sold Jonathan Gilbert a forty-five-acre tract on which Samuel Wickwire then lived for £165 in March 1770. Soon thereafter Gilbert deeded a portion of that land to the town of Lyme for a highway and in December 1772 sold that same forty-five acres to Jonathan Beckwith, Jr. and Samuel Beckwith, Jr. for £192.[101] He placed an advertisement in 1773 about "an old brown Mare" on his property in "Chesterfield Parish" and eight years later he noted that "a yearling brindle Bull" had entered his enclosure.[102] He was assessed for taxes in Lyme in 1781 and 1782.[103] Jonathan still lived in Lyme in January 1783 when the 207-acre farm he rented "in the N. E. corner of Lyme" was offered for sale by its new owner Samuel H. Parsons, but had moved to Fishers Island by 1785 when he sued Jonathan Latimer, clerk of Chesterfield Society, for payment of a £23-15 debt owed to him by its minister.[104] In 1790, he was living in Montville and was the head of a family containing nine people; three males under 16, one male over 16, three females, and two slaves and was a landowner there. He appears to have moved back and forth between Lyme and Montville and died in Montville. Both he and his wife are buried in Chesterfield.[105]

Samuel Gilbert of Chesterfield took part in military training on November 30, 1775 and was assessed for taxes in Lyme for 1781, 1782, and 1784.[106] He married Mary Dodge of Colchester and lived in the Millington section of East Haddam during the 1780s. His three youngest children were born there between 1783 and 1786 and two daughters were married in Millington in 1791 and 1793. The 1790 census for East Haddam notes that his household of 12 consisted of three free white males under 16, two over 16, and seven females. He removed to Luzerne County, Pennsylvania before 1796.[107]

---

99 CA, Revolutionary War, Series 1, XXXIII, 121.

100 Brainard et al, *Gilbert Family*, 145-46.

101 LLR, XII, 218, 418; XIII, 86. In one other transaction, Nathan and Clarina Eliot of Kent sold Jonathan their one-sixth share of twenty-two and three quarters acres in Lyme in August 1771. Jonathan's brother Samuel deeded whatever right he had to the property where Samuel Wickwire once lived and Samuel sold his right to the two Beckwiths in March 1773. LLR, XIII, 48; XV, 138.

102 *Connecticut Gazette*, May 14, 1773, [2]; December 28, 1781, [4].

103 Ibid, February 7, 1783, [3]; RG 062, LTR, Box 6, Tax Lists, Vol. 1, 32; Vol. 4, 753. He also received medical care from the region's doctor Daniel Caulkins in 1777. Caulkins Account Book, Folio 49.

104 *Jonathan Gilbert v. Jonathan Latimer*, NLCC, Files, June 1785, Box 192, folder 14, no. 221.

105 1790 Census, 128; *Connecticut Courant*, January 10, 1826, [3]; Brainard et al, *Gilbert Family*, 145-46.

106 CA, Revolutionary War, Series 1, II, 13; RG 062, LTR, Tax Lists, Box 6, 40, 323, 408-09, 753.

107 Brainard et al, *Gilbert Family*, 148-50; 1790 Census, AncestryHeritageQuest.com; CA, Susquehanna Settlers, Western Lands, Series 1, I, 186, CSL. Samuel was among a number of signers of a September 13, 1796 memorial to the General Assembly from Luzerne County, an area "under the claim of the State of Connecticut."

Benjamin and **Jedidiah Beckwith** of Lyme shared the five-year lease of a farm that ran from 1772 to 1777.[108] The family genealogy provides no useful information on the two tenants.[109] In May 1777, the General Assembly ordered that two executions against "William Brown, Esqr, of Salem, who is with the enemies of the United States" be rendered "null and void" because they had been levied against farms "improved by Benjamin and Jedidiah Beckwith of Lyme."[110] Two years later when Browne's estate was taken over by the State, his Lyme slaves were "in the Hands of John Mumford [and] Benjamin and Jedediah Beckwith living on said Lands."[111] Negro Caesar, a boy of eleven and another slave of William Browne were living with Benjamin and Jedidiah Beckwith at this time.[112] Both are found in the medical accounts of Dr. Daniel Caulkins.[113]

A Benjamin Beckwith of Lyme is found in New London County Court Records during the 1750s.[114] Benjamin of Chesterfield, the tenant, owed State and local taxes in 1781.[115] He died in Lyme in July 1785. The inventory of his estate amounted to just £37-12-11. One yoke of oxen comprised £14-15-0 of that total. His widow Hannah declined serving as administrator of his estate due to "Age and Infirmity" and that function was filled by Andrew and Martin Beckwith.[116] New London court records contain references to both a Benjamin and Benjamin, Jr. between 1759 and 1783. The tenant was likely Benjamin, Jr. in pre-Revolutionary War records and Benjamin without the appellation post-Revolution.[117]

---

108 How they were related to one another is uncertain. Lyme land records record both a Benjamin and Benjamin, Jr. and Jedidiah and Jedidiah, Jr., indicating the possibility that they could have been father and son, brothers, or cousins. In the eighteenth century, a Jr. did not always refer to a son of the person with the same first name, he could be a younger cousin or nephew. The 1832 memorial to the General Assembly referred to above regarding Caesar Beckwith, states that Caesar was born into the family of Benjamin Beckwith about 1768, remained in the household of "Benjamin Beckwith & Sons" for many years and was living in the family of Jedidiah Beckwith when he became partially paralyzed. The implication is that Jedidiah was the son of Benjamin, but since the petition was written many years after the events described, it is possible that the information was garbled. "Petition of Sylvester Champion, Andrew Griswold, and Thomas W. Strickland," RG 002, General Assembly Papers, African Americans, Box 1, folder 8.

109 Paul Beckwith, *The Beckwiths* (Albany, NY: Joel Munsel's Sons, Publishers, 1891), 81. The genealogy leaves a great deal to be desired. Jedidiah, Sr. was one of the creditors of Stephen Jerom of Lyme, an unsuccessful salt manufacturer. CA, Industry, Series 1, 190, 192, CSL.

110 *State Records*, I, 311; CA, Revolutionary War, Series 1, I, 311; VIII, 195.

111 CA, Revolutionary War, Series 1, XXIV, 462.

112 Petition of Sylvester Champion, Andrew Griswold and Thomas W. Strickland," RG 002, General Assembly Papers, African Americans, Box 1, folder 8.

113 Caulkins Account Book, Folios, 12, 37, 38, 125, CHS. The account book contains several different number sequences.

114 *Benjamin Beckwith v. Simon Armstrong*, NLCC, Trials, Vol. 22, February 1755, no. 61; *Benjamin Beckwith v. William Beckwith*, Ibid, February 1756, no. 135.

115 RG 062, LTR, Box 6, Tax Lists, Vol. 1, 31; Vol. 3, 274-75.

116 Benjamin Beckwith, Lyme, 1785, NLPR, no. 306.

117 Benjamin *Beckwith, Jr. v. Jonathan Smith*, NLCC, Trials, Vol. 24, June 1764, no. 35; *Benjamin Beckwith, Jr. v. Jonathan Smith*, NLCC, Files, November 1764, Box 135, folder 2, no docket; *Thomas Shaw v. Benjamin Beckwith*, NLCC, Files, February 1783, Box 178, folder 9, no docket.

Jedidiah Beckwith (1736-1801) lived in the East Society and Lyme land records show both a Jedidiah and Jedidiah, Jr.[118] Land records show that Jedidiah, Jr., perhaps the tenant, was a small farmer who often endured economic difficulties. Jedidiah
purchased two plots of land totaling eighteen acres from his mother Lucy in 1761 that
Jedidiah, Jr. sold to Stephen Gee nine years later.[119] Twice in 1769 the New London
County Court served executions on Beckwith for failure to pay small debts and costs
of £2-13-8 3/4 and £1-17-6 and the plaintiffs were compensated with small shares of a
sawmill for which Jedidiah was part owner situated on the land of Elisha Beckwith.[120] In
1768, he sold land in the East Society to Elisha Merrow and three years later conveyed
the house that he had purchased from Joshua Wade to Noah Miller, Jr.[121] Beckwith held
the position as Lyme lister for 1777 and 1779. The state tax levy for 1781 listed Jedidiah with taxable property worth £49 and he and Benjamin as joint tenants of property
rated at £27-10, probably that rented from William Browne. He signed a 1790 petition
regarding Connecticut River fishing rights and lived in a household of two people, one
of whom was female.[122] He died on March 12, 1801, age sixty-four, and is buried in the
Old Stone Cemetery in East Lyme.[123]

William Carr/Karr rented a Browne farm in Lyme between 1769 and 1774
and almost certainly for a number of years before that time, perhaps as early as the
1740s. He first appears in records as being from Lyme in 1743, when he sued Samuel
Mansfield, sheriff of New Haven County, for £30 damages. Once the details of the
lawsuit have been unpacked, a great deal was uncovered about this previously unknown
man. Court records show that Karr originally came from Boston, was "not long since a
transient person" living in Connecticut, and had recovered two judgments against James
Rood of Wallingford in 1/40.[124] Karr sued the sheriff because he had allowed Rood to
escape from jail. Mansfield claimed that Rood had not escaped, but had "enlisted in [an]
expedition ag[ain]st Spain."[125] Karr won his case before the New Haven County Court

---

118 Still another Jedidiah Beckwith, styled Jr., lived in the East Parish of Lyme. A mariner, he married Elisabeth Beebe in 1760, deserted her about eleven years later, removed to New York, and lived with another
woman that he called his wife. Elisabeth filed for divorce on December 8, 1775 on the grounds of desertion.
The court record contains three depositions by men who stated that Beckwith was living with another woman
and the New London County Superior Court granted her a divorce in March 1776. NLSC, PbyS: Divorces,
Box 10, folder 5, CSL.

119 Lucy Beckwith to Jedediah Beckwith, LLR, October 10, 1761, XII, 129; Jedediah Beckwith, Jr. to Stephen Gee, LLR, March 3, 1770, XII, 337.

120 Execution Absalom Beckwith against Jedediah Beckwith, April 12, 1769, LLR, XII, 132; Execution
Nathan Douglass against Jedediah Beckwith, LLR, May 3, 1769, XII, 127.

121 Jedediah Beckwith to Elisha Merrow, LLR, June 8, 1768, XI, 159; Jedediah Beckiwth to Noah Miller, Jr.
LLR, September 11, 1771, XI, 230.

122 CA, Revolutionary War, Series 1, VI, 104e; XIII, 388; CA, Industry, Series 2, III, 9, CSL; RG 062, LTR,
Lyme Tax Lists, 31; 1790 Census, 119.

123 "Inscriptions from Gravestones at East Lyme, Conn.," *NEHGR*, Vol. 79 (January 1925), 67.

124 Karr is called "A Transient Person" in both April 1740 trials. *William Karr v. John Rood*, April 1740 (2
cases), RG 003, New Haven County Court Records, Trials, Vol. 4, 41, CSL.

125 Nothing is known for certain about who William Carr was and where he came from until he sued Rood.
The strong possibility exists, however, that he was a runaway bound servant from the north of Ireland who

in 1742, Mansfield appealed to the superior court, Karr triumphed again, Mansfield petitioned the General Assembly to grant him a new trial, it did so, and the sheriff was found not guilty in the retrial before the New Haven County Superior Court.[126]

Karr signed a 1748 petition to the General Assembly complaining about the destitute condition of New Salem Parish after the dismission of the Reverend Joseph Lovett. He was probably renting a Browne farm at the time.[127] Our other knowledge of William Carr/Karr comes primarily from other court records. He is called a resident of Lyme in November 1752 when he was sued for debt.[128] In another case, Roland Rogers purchased a yoke of oxen from Carr and refused to pay because he claimed that he was a minor. The following July he recovered £37-1-8 from Rogers in a debt by note. The reverse of the writ contains notations for payments made by the defendant. He signed his name "William Carr" in acknowledgement of the receipt of the amount owed to him.[129] He is mentioned in a 1761 advertisement for the sale of a farm in Colchester and nine years later as having a letter at the New London post office.[130]

Karr married a daughter of William Dixon of Colchester and was living in Lyme in 1757.[131] Carr purchased twenty-one acres in Colchester in 1756 from Dixon and sold the land back eighteen months later.[132] In January 1767, he acquired forty acres of land from Jason Fargo located in New London North Society secured by a mortgage. In a February 1768 court case, Carr sued Fargo for the seisen and possession of the forty acres that he had purchased one year earlier. The defendant defaulted, Carr recovered the

---

escaped shortly after the ship carrying him reached Boston in November 1738.

John Pierce, Jr. of Portsmouth, New Hampshire contracted with merchant Robert Boyes of Londonderry, Ireland in November 1737 to provide him with Irish retainers. William Car (as the surname was spelled) was one of twenty-five servants who together with five others with the same surname escaped to freedom once they reached dry land. As such, he could well have been considered a transient person who had come from Boston. Ezra S. Stearns, "Contributions to the History of Londonderry, N. H.," *NEHGR*, 51 (October 1897), 467-70.

[126] RG 003, *William Karr v. Samuel Mansfield*, Early Records, CSC, August 1743, August 1744, February 1745, August 1745, Vol. 12, 191, 291-92, 348, 390-91; *William Karr v. Samuel Mansfield*, New Haven County Superior Court, Files, Box 309, CSL.

[127] Perkins, *Connecticut Farm*, 43, 51; CA, Ecclesiastical Affairs, Series 1, IX, 221.

[128] *David Gardiner v. William Karr*, NLCC, Trials, November 1752, Vol. 21, no. 109.

[129] *William Karr v. Roland Rogers*, NLCC, Trials, July 1753, Vol. 22, no. 16; Ibid, NLCC, Files, July 1753, Box 97, folder 3, no docket.

[130] The fifty-acre farm was in Colchester and interested parties were directed, "For further particulars, enquire of William Carr, near the premises." *New-London Summary*, April 3, 1761, [3]; *Connecticut Gazette*, January 5, 1770, [4]. In 1786, a William Carr, perhaps the same individual, owed taxes in Torrington. *Litchfield Monitor*, February 28, 1786, [3].

[131] For examples of Carr court appearances, see *David Gardiner v. William Carr*, NLCC, Trials, Vol. 21, November 1752, no. 109; *William Karr v. Roland Rogers*, Ibid, Vol. 22, July 1753, no. 16; *William Carr v. Jonathan Beckwith*, Ibid, Vol. 23, June 1762; *William Carr v. Jedidiah Chapel and William Chapel*, Ibid, Vol. 24, November 1766, no. 127; *William Carr v. Jason Fargo*, Ibid, Vol. 24, February 1768, no. 87; *William Carr v. Joseph Rogers*, Ibid, November 1770.

[132] William Dixon to William Karr, CLR, February 27, 1756, VI, 67; William Karr to William Dixon, Ibid, September 19, 1757, VII, 89.

land, five shillings damages, and court costs of £1-0-6.[133] But, unable to come up with the £20 purchase price, he quitclaimed the property back to Fargo in September 1769, yet later bought one half of Fargo's farm in the North Society for £90. The entire farm comprised ninety-six acres.[134]

In 1768 when efforts were being made to establish Chesterfield Society from parts of Lyme and New London, a copy of one of the key documents was left at the "usual Place of the abode of William Carr of Lyme who Is a Principle Inhabitant of New Salem Society."[135] One year later he sued Israel Jones of Colchester to collect a debt of £2-10.[136] In total, New London County Court dockets and trials show that he was involved in 13 cases, 10 as plaintiff and 3 as defendant between 1752 and 1770.[137] In addition, a William Carr, perhaps the tenant, served in the Continental Line during the Revolutionary War, the 6th Connecticut Regiment in 1780 and the 4th Regiment the following year.[138] That same year the Superior Court meeting in New London County heard a case involving James Karr of Lyme who sued Nathaniel Clark of Colchester in a plea of trover. The likelihood is that James was the son of William.[139]

The tenant S. Gardner was **Stephen Gardner** or Gardiner of the Gardiner family of the Narragansett region of Rhode Island. One of them, William Gardiner (1671-1738) of South Kingstown, owned and then sold 635 acres bordering on Great Pond, now Gardner Lake, in Colchester to Colonel Samuel Browne in 1724.[140] William's older brother Stephen (1668-1743) moved from South Kingstown to Norwich in 1730 and purchased land in New Salem at Great Pond, in the North Parish of New London, and the western part of Norwich.[141] He and his wife Amey Sherman became the parents of twelve children, the third of whom was Stephen (b. 1704) who moved to

133 *William Carr v. Jason Fargo*, NLCC, Trials, February 1768, Vol. 24, no. 87; *William Carr v. Jason Fargo*, NLCC, Files, February 1768, Box 146, folder 17, no. 87.

134 Jason Fargo to William Carr, NLLR, January 17, 1767, XVIII, 133; William Carr to Jason Fargo, Ibid, September 21, 1769; Jason Fargo to William Carr, Ibid, September 28, 1770, XIX, 323.

135 CA, Ecclesiastical Affairs, Series 1, XIII, 145.

136 RG 003, *William Karr v. Israel Jones*, January 23, 1769, John Watrous Court Records, [Colchester] 1767-1790, CSL.

137 The lawsuits spanned the time from November 1752 to November 1770 and, since Carr was plaintiff on most occasions, this shows that he was relatively prosperous.

138 CA, Revolutionary War, Series 1, XXX, 3j, 7f. Nothing has been found on Carr in census, probate, and vital records. The Carr who served in the Revolutionary War may have been a son of the tenant. Lyme tax records for Chesterfield in 1781 list a James Karr with an estate worth £74-10. RG 062, LTR, Box 6, Tax Lists, Vol. 1, 33.

139 *James Karr v. Nathaniel Harris*, Early Records, CSC, March 1780, Vol. 22, 199.

140 Caroline E. Robinson, *The Gardiners of Narragansett: Being a Genealogy of the Descendants of George Gardiner The Colonist 1638* (Providence: 1919), 10-11; Stark, "Myth and Reality," 161; Perkins, *Connecticut Farm*, 244. Gardiner's Rhode Island estate contained 1,620 acres at the time of his death. McBurney, "South Kingstown Planters," 85.

141 He bought and sold eleven parcels of land in Colchester between 1730 and 1739. CLR, III, 152, 163, 167, 303, 312; IV, 5, 29, 65; V, 17, 32, 262. By his will, Gardner divided his substantial estate among his six sons. Stephen and Peregrine shared ownership of one farm and the second Stephen was one of two executors of the estate. Stephen Gardner, Norwich, 1743, NLPR, no. 2168.

Connecticut with his father.[142] The younger Stephen Gardner lived on a Browne farm between 1744 and 1754 occupying a house near the center of the parish and serving as agent for the family.[143]

A third Stephen Gardner, called Stephen, Jr. in Colchester records, was likely the man who leased a farm from Browne for five years beginning in 1770.[144] In July 1757, Stephen, Jr. sued John Dixon of Colchester in a case of debt by bond for £80.[145] Stephen, Jr. was admitted a freeman of Colchester on April 8, 1765, was plaintiff in a New London County Court case in June 1767, was chosen surveyor of highways in December 1767, and his home in Colchester served in June 1767 as the site for persons wanting to present claims against the insolvent estate of David Dodge.[146] The Hartford County Court licensed him to keep a tavern in 1772, 1773, and 1774.[147] The one glimpse we have of Gardner during the American Revolution took place in February 1777, when a New London grand juror made a presentment against John Chapman for breach of the peace for "Striking and Beating Stephen Gardiner of Colchester.[148] By 1783, a court filing noted that Gardner, formerly of Colchester, was then living in New London.[149]

James Kelly who in 1770 took a three-year lease for a Browne farm in Colchester at the rate of £30 per year has left the fewest traces.[150] He never owned any land. He served in the Connecticut military in the waning days of the French and Indian War and took the "Oath of fidelity to the State of Connecticut and Freamans Oath" on September 16, 1777.[151]

---

142 Robinson, *The Gardiners*, 4, 11-12, 36; Hempstead, *Diary*, 224, 226-27

143 Perkins, *Connecticut Farm*, 50-51, Hempstead, *Diary*, 421, 436, 453, 497, 525, 540, 614. He held a number of town offices between 1742 and 1761, including surveyor of highways, lister, fence viewer, collector of excise, and agent on behalf of the town for 1757-58. ColchesterBMD, Vol 1, 194-95, 197, 199, 203-05, 207-09, 213, 217.

144 The Gardiner genealogy states that the third Stephen was born in 1735 and married Francis Congdon, while Colchester records say that he was born on March 7, 1725, the son of Stephen, and married Frances Brown in June 1760. Robinson, *The Gardiners*, 37; ColchesterBMD, Vol. 1, 86, 141.

145 The defendant defaulted and Gardner recovered damages and costs amounting to £24-17-8. *Stephen Gardiner v. John Dixon*, HCC, Records, July 1757, Vol. 16, 366.

146 ColchesterBMD, Vol. 1, 97, 226; NLCC, PbyS: Summons for Evidence, June 10, 1767, Box 91, folder 3: *Connecticut Gazette*, June 6, 1767, [4].

147 HCC, PbyS: Travel, Box 541, April 1772, April 1773, April 1774 packets.

148 *Governor & Co. v. John Chapman*, NLJP, Box 2, folder 21.

149 *Thomas Hambrough v. Stephen Gardiner,* June 1783, NLCC, Files, Box 181, folder 9, no docket.

150 He may have been connected to the Kelley family of Yarmouth, Massachusetts, but no direct evidence has been found for this supposition. Other sources point to the birth of a James Kelley, son of Edward and Alice Kelley of Medway, Massachusetts on August 8, 1732 and to the death of the wife of a James Kelly in Stratham, New Hampshire in April 1792. Eunice Kelley Randall, *Kelley Genealogy: David O'Killa the Immigrant of Old Yarmouth, Massachusetts with His Descendants and Allied Families* (n.p.: 1962); "Births in Medway, Mass., 1714-1744," *NEHGR*, 49 (October 1895), 446; "Deaths in Stratham, N. H.," Ibid, Vol. 73 (January 1919), 67. Other Kelleys lived in Norwich. See, for example, *Benjamin Kelley v. Samuel Thomson*, NLCC, Files, June 1761, Box 117, folder 20, no docket; *Daniel Kelley v. John Bliss*, Ibid, June 1767, Box 145, folder 2, no docket.

151 CA, Wars, Colonial, Series I, X, 39, 179; ColchesterBMD, Vol. 2, 342. He served in the 5th company of the 2nd Connecticut Regiment in 1762 and in Captain Joseph Wait's company in 1763.

Men became renters for different reasons.[152] Some like George Mumford of Fishers Island and John Mumford, Sr. owned slaves — George a large number — so it is difficult to argue that they lacked the resources to purchase land. John Henry and Samuel Hazard may also have fit this pattern. It could well have been a sound business decision to rent rather than to purchase. Why go into debt to buy a farm or struggle for years laboring to convert woodland into productive agricultural property? Why not take over a farm that already exists, pay an affordable rent, and reap the profits without a major capital outlay?[153] Others like Jedidiah Beckwith, Joseph Colt, Joseph Hastings, and John Minor owned real property but decided to supplement their agricultural holdings by renting additional land. Beckwith and Minor owned relatively little land and leased property in the hopes to become more prosperous. Still others like Joshua Beckwith and James Kelly were too poor to purchase even a small farm, thus renting was their best possibility for economic sustenance. Eight of the renters came from and lived in either Lyme or Colchester.[154] Four came from outside the region and one from a neighboring town.[155] Some tenants left relatively few historical traces, but through a thorough search of a variety of records, it was always possible to provide at least a faint outline of their lives.

New England in the colonial era was predominately a middle-class society in which yeoman farmers and their families made up the largest proportion of the population.[156] Renters were a much smaller segment of the population of New England than

---

152 The extent of tenancy (and absentee land ownership) could well have been much more significant than what has been discussed in most of the historical literature. The truth can only be determined, however, by a close examination of land records in scores of communities, a project far beyond the scope of the present study.

Given the lack of records on renters, the only way to gain a handle on this subject is to track down the holdings of absentees. Colonel Browne, for instance, owned some 29,540 acres of land in Colchester, Hebron, Lyme, New London, Stafford and Union in Connecticut and much more in other colonies. These properties encompassed thirty-two square miles and over one-twentieth of the area of the colony. Thomas Fitch and John Dolbeare controlled another 8.9 square miles of land.

153 One important advantage that Browne tenants had over ordinary Lyme and Colchester farmers was that their farms were consolidated into a single plot, while many landowners possessed land in several non-adjacent locations, the result of population growth and partible inheritance. As noted above in a footnote, Joseph Colt owned eight pieces of land.

154 Benjamin and Jedidiah Beckwith, Joshua Beckwith, Joseph Colt, Stephen Gardner, Jr., Jonathan Gilbert, Samuel Gilbert, John Minor, and Joshua Ransom. The Beckwiths who shared a lease are counted as one.

155 The "foreigners" were William Carr, John Henry, James Kelly, and John Mumford. Joseph Hastings came from Norwich, later Franklin, around ten miles from New Salem.

156 The classic formulation of this viewpoint is Robert E. Brown, *Middle-Class Democracy and Revolution in Massachusetts, 1691-1780* (New York: Harper & Row, 1955, 1969). For Connecticut, see Jackson Turner Main, *Society and Economy in Colonial Connecticut* (Princeton: Princeton University Press, 1985). Neither gave renters much coverage. Brown stated that just two per cent were tenants and Main wrote that young married couples with small farms often rented additional land to support their families and that about eight per cent owned no land. Brown, *Middle-Class Democracy*, 27, 33-34, 92; Main, *Society and Economy*, 28-29, 202.

One article that provides extensive coverage of tenancy, albeit for seventieth-century New England is Stephen Innes, "Land Tenancy and Social Order in Springfield, Massachusetts, 1652-1702," *WMQ*, XXXV, Third Series (January 1978), 33-56. The pattern of tenancy in this community looked much different than that practiced in New Salem. Around one third of all adult males for a period of some fifty years rented from William Pynchon and his son John, ranging from complete farms to one acre of meadow or a yoke of oxen for terms of up to twenty years. Innes, "Land Tenancy," 34, 43-44. No index term for renter or tenant exists in such classic formulations on the history of the New England town as Charles S. Grant, *Democracy in the Connecticut Frontier Town of Kent* (New York: Columbia University Press, 1961); Philip J. Greven, Jr., *Four*

in such colonies as New York, New Jersey, Pennsylvania, and Maryland.[157] What the story of the Brownes reveals is that at least part of this middle-class culture was made up of farmers who did not own their own land, but rented from rich absentees like the Brownes, Fitchs, and Dolbeares. They may have been relatively small in numbers, but if New Salem can be considered at all representative, renters often controlled more land than most farmers. Joseph Colt and John Mumford, Jr. were prominent enough to serve as selectmen, while others like Jedidiah Beckwith, Stephen Gardner, John Henry, and Joshua Ransom, helped to fill the many lesser town offices that were so necessary for communities to function. Good tenants, then, were just as valuable members of the communities in which they lived as landowning farmers.

Generations: Population, Land, and Family in Colonial Andover, Massachusetts (Ithaca: Cornell University Press, 1970); and Kenneth A. Lockridge, *The New England Town: The First Hundred Years* (New York: W. W. Norton & Company, Inc., 1970).

[157] For a good example of the importance of tenancy in the middle colonies, see Lucy Simler, "Tenancy in Colonial Pennsylvania: The Case of Chester County, *WMQ*, Third Series (October 1986), 542-69. In 1766, twenty-five percent of the householders were tenants. Ibid, 551.

Chapter 11

Memory and Traces of the Browne Estate

Colonel Samuel Browne purchased more than 9,600 acres in Lyme, Colchester, and New London between 1718 and 1729 and his grandson William lost the property during the American Revolution.

Relatively few traces of the presence of the Browne family remain in Connecticut. The most significant reminder is the name of the town Salem from the Massachusetts home of the Brownes. Although no one today remembers, Harris Brook and Harris Road honor James Harris, the man who sold Browne most of the land that comprised his estate.[1] The Mumford house still stands on White Birch Road in Salem and is owned by descendants of the last overseers. The back of the house can be seen from Route 82 and its front from Birch Road. Other town place names referring to the Browne era include Beckwith Hill, Carr Pond, and Ransom Brook. Beckwith Hill, at a height of 443 feet, is located in the southeast corner of town on the west side of Route 85. Carr Pond can be seen from Route 85 not far from Salem Four Corners, and Ransom Brook rises at the extreme southeast corner of town and flows north northwest across Darling Road and into the East Branch of the Eight Mile River.[2]

If someone wants to see the Browne lands, one of the easiest ways to do so is to drive along Route 82 east from the end of Route 156 in East Haddam until you reach the Salem bounds. All the property on both sides of the road running about 2.8 miles to Salem Four Corners and the intersection with Route 85 originally belonged to Colonel Samuel Browne. As you descend a hill and come to the East Branch of the Eight Mile River, you can look on both sides of the road and see agriculturally productive land. After about a half mile and on the right, the back of the Mumford House can be seen in the distance across a field. Shortly afterwards one comes to a farm for retired horses on the left and soon thereafter the driver sees Darling Road on the right with Salem Valley Farms, an ice cream bar, and the terminus of Route 11 that heads north to Colchester. If you stay on Route 82, you come to Salem Four Corners about half a mile beyond the entrance to Route 11. What used to be the intersection of Routes 82 and 85 marked by a light is now a traffic circle. Route 85 generally runs north from New London through Colchester and beyond. If you take a right at the traffic circle and follow Route 85 south

---

[1] A small shopping center at Salem Four Corners is called Harris Brook Commons.

[2] Hughes and Allen, *Connecticut Place Names*, 492-94.

towards New London, all property on both sides of the road belonged to Browne until the Salem-Montville bounds. Once into Montville, you drive through the hamlet of Chesterfield on the way to New London. On the way to Chesterfield, eight-tenths of a mile from Salem Four Corners on the left, you can see Carr Pond, named for tenant William Carr.[3]

If you take a right onto Darling Road from Route 82 near Salem Valley Farms and veer to the right at the stop sign onto White Birch Road, the dirt road entrance to the Mumford house is clearly visible. White Birch Road with fields on both sides merges into what is popularly known as the Old Salem Road. If one follows Old Salem Road southwest to the Salem-East Haddam line, you continue to travel along lands that once belonged to the Browne family.

The landscape of the southern part of Salem reveals its topography. Rambling its back roads shows just how minimal was the agricultural value of the lands. If one drives north on Gungy Road from Beaver Brook Road in Lyme, about a half mile on the left is the old Caples house, where a well-known family of color resided for over 100 years until the death of Joseph A. Caples in 1954. Gungy Road connects Beaver Brook Road in Lyme to Darling Road in Salem and was not paved until the 1950s. By driving slowly, particularly in winter months, you can still see remains of sections of the old road.[4] The power line used to end at the Caples house, but now extends another half mile to a house near a grouping of major power lines, called high tension lines, going south and north.[5] Like much of Connecticut, the region is traversed by decaying stone walls and occasional remains of cellars. The Salem line is about one mile beyond the Caples house and the terrain is rough, hilly, with ledges, and extremely rocky.

Once you cross into Salem, the scenery remains the same, although you gradually go downhill and near the intersection with Darling Road, the land becomes flatter and more arable. This section of Gungy Road contains a number of houses constructed since the road was paved. Turning right on Darling Road, within a quarter of a mile on the right stands the remains of a small dairy farm that formerly provided the milk for Salem Valley Farms. Not far beyond the dairy farm at 170 Darling Road stands the yellow house of Alfred Bingham, author of a family chronicle and the 1976 article that formed the basis for the slave plantation in Salem myth. At a stop sign at the intersection with White Birch Road, look left and you can see the Mumford house. The road goes on with old stone walls on both sides until you reach Salem Valley Farms near its end at Route 82. If you take a right at the stop sign onto Old New London Road, you travel through more mostly unproductive land that used to belong to the Browne family. The trip lasts 2.6 miles until you reach the Montville town line.

Despite the signs of Browne's presence — evident if one carefully looks for them — the small and unimportant town of Salem was best known (that is, until June 2001) as the home of Music Vale Seminary, an institution that lasted from 1835 to 1876. The Seminary was important enough to merit treatment in the Connecticut Tercentenary Series, was a significant feature in the sketch of Salem by Florence S. Marcy

---

[3] From map 2, it looks as though Carr Pond is located on lot 34.

[4] One Lyme portion of the old dirt road had a sharp curve popularly known as Cape Horn.

[5] The original white Caples house was enlarged in around 2013 and painted yellow.

Crofut, emphasized in the Connecticut volume of the Federal Writers Project American Guide Series, was the subject of three of the five entries for Salem in the standard Connecticut bibliography, and serves as the focal point for the Salem Historical Society.[6]

Unfortunately, the strongest memory people in twenty-first-century Connecticut now have of Salem, the Browne family, and New Salem parish of 250-300 years ago is a false one. It is the tale that the family brought a large contingent of slaves to Lyme and Colchester to conquer the wilderness so that the land could be productively farmed and the slave labor exploited for the benefit of white masters, a narrative put forth in 2001-02 in a number of published articles. The story of the origin and development of this incorrect narrative is a very important one and this study will conclude with an analysis of it.

No primary or secondary source published before 1934 gives any credence to the slave plantation story.[7] At that time, a pamphlet on an entirely different subject devoted two pages to Colonel Samuel Browne, noting that he acquired some 8,000 acres in what was then Colchester and Lyme. "Colonel Browne started to colonize this tract, and brought with him, to clear the land and work the fields over sixty families of slaves."[8] The next year, Ralph Foster Weld wrote that "when Colonel Samuel Browne settled the present town of Salem about 1720, he was said to have brought in more than sixty families to clear and work the land."[9] The words "was said" demonstrate that Weld was by no means certain of the veracity of the story. Within two years of the Weld statement, the Federal Writers Project in its Connecticut guide stated with much inaccuracy that Salem, "a hamlet, was originally purchased from the Indians by Colonel Samuel Browne of Salem, Mass., who settled here about 1700 with his household, including 60 families of slaves."[10]

The remaining piece of "evidence" came from an article published by Alfred M. Bingham in 1976 titled "Squatter Settlements of Freed Slaves in New England" in which he not only repeated the claims of Ralph Foster Weld, but also added new information from a family letter writing that when John Mumford moved to New Salem, he employed "a numerous gang of Blacks" to improve the land.[11] The tale remained quiescent until June 2001 when "Rewriting Slavery's History" burst upon the scene courtesy of *The Day* of New London. This highly publicized story based upon part of one sentence in Weld and a family letter written in 1900, quickly became dogma after "Rewriting Slavery's History" and *Complicity* in the *Hartford Courant* appeared.

---

6 Frances Hall Johnson, *Music Vale Seminary*, Tercentenary Pamphlet XXVII (New Haven: Yale University Press, 1934); Crofut, *Guide to Connecticut*, Vol. 2, 766-67; [Federal Writers Project, Conn.], American Guide Series, *Connecticut: A Guide to its Roads, Lore and People* (Boston: Houghton Mifflin Company, 1938), 396; Roger Parks, ed., *Connecticut: A Bibliography of Its History* (Hanover, NH and London: University Press of New England, 1986), 446-47. Music Vale Seminary has sometimes been inaccurately referred to as the first normal school for music in the United States.

7 This subject is also discussed in Stark, "Myth and Reality," 159-60, 170.

8 Johnson, *Music Vale Seminary*, 2-3. Johnson almost certainly got her information from Ralph Foster Weld.

9 Weld, *Slavery in Connecticut*, 6.

10 [Federal Writer's Project], *Connecticut*, 446.

11 Bingham, "Squatter Settlements," 75.

To get some historiographical background, no eighteenth-century primary or nineteenth-century secondary sources substantiates any aspect of a slave plantation in Salem story. Diarist Joshua Hempstead (1678-1758) of New London, a man who owned land in Colchester and knew several members of the Browne family, made no mention whatsoever to the existence of any slaves on his lands.[12] Jacob Bailey, who accompanied young William Browne and his sister Abigail on a trip to Connecticut in 1754, never remarked on any slaves on Browne property.

The inveterate scribbler Ezra Stiles (1727-1795), who like Hempstead commented on a tremendous variety of topics, made one brief mention of New Salem Society and one of William Browne. He noted in one work that "New Salem made about 1726, partly out of Lyme & part Colchester. Rev. Joseph Lovet ord[ained] 1729 or 1730, dism[issed] about 1745, no Pastor since; all become Bapt. &c but four." In his *Literary Diary* on February 6, 1775, he wrote that a new drama had been published in Boston. One of the characters, "Collateralis - a new made Judge" represented "Wm. Brown[e] Esq."[13]

Benjamin Trumbull (1735-1820), Connecticut's first historian, wrote *A Complete History of Connecticut* which covered the period from the colony's founding to the end of the French and Indian War. He corresponded with public officials and ministers from throughout the state asking for information on settlement, church societies, religious dissenters, and libraries. His Colchester correspondent noted the establishment of New Salem Society, but wrote nothing about either slavery or the Browne estate.[14]

John Warner Barber (1798-1885), engraver and book publisher, in *Connecticut Historical Collections*, first published in 1836, had short sections on Colchester, Lyme, and Salem, but wrote nothing about the Browne family or slavery in New Salem.[15]

Nineteenth-century historian Frances Manwaring Caulkins (1795-1865) wrote excellent studies of New London and Norwich and made several comments of note. In the New London book, she took information from Hempstead's diary concerning Samuel Browne, Jr.'s marriage to Katherine Winthrop and their journey to Fisher's Island in 1739.[16] In her history of Norwich, she wrote that "Capt. [sic] William Browne, a noted loyalist of Salem, Mass., connected with the Winthrop family of New London, was the proprietor of a large tract of land south of Colchester . . . and was

---

12 Hempstead served as business manager for the Winthrop family and made several references to Samuel Browne the younger and his wife Katherine Winthrop Browne between 1731 and 1743. In addition, the diary contains mentions Katherine and Epes Sargent three times in 1749 and 1755. Hempstead, *Diary*, 240, 244-45, 351-53, 356, 409. His diary made numerous references to New London area slaves.

13 Dexter, ed., *Itineraries of Ezra Stiles*, 311; Franklin Bowditch Dexter, ed., *The Literary Diary of Ezra Stiles, DD., LL.D* (New York: Charles Scribner's Sons, 1901), I, 515. The work may or may not have been *The Group*, a satirical play by Mercy Otis Warren concerning "toadies linked to Rapatio (Thomas Hutchinson)." Norton, *1774*, 300-01.

14 Benjamin Trumbull, D.D., *A Complete History of Connecticut: Civil and Ecclesiastical, From the Emigration of its First Planters, from England in the Year 1630, to the Year 1764; and to the Close of the Indian Wars* (New Haven: Maltby, Goldsmith and Co., 1818); Trumbull Manuscript Collections, Vol. I, 19, 20, 26, Beinecke Rare Book and Manuscript Library.

15 John Warner Barber, *Connecticut Historical Collection*, facsimile reprint (Storrs, CT: Bibliopole Press, 1999), 303-06, 328-34, 343.

16 Caulkins, *History of New London*, 408-09.

called by the owner New Salem." She added that a "portion of it under cultivation had been leased for a term of years, with nine slaves as laborers upon it." Caulkins also pointed out that when the State seized the land in 1779 "the slaves petitioned the legislature, through Benjamin Huntington, administrator on confiscated estates, for their liberty." The legislature failed to approve the memorial, "but the slaves had the benefit of the new laws regulating emancipation, and it is supposed that they were set free sooner or later." She accurately noted the existence of slaves, but made no mention of any plantation.[17] Discussing the construction of and history of the United States frigate *Confederacy* in Norwich under the supervision of Joshua Huntington, "who, as agent of the State, procured the materials and workmen." She noted that the vessel was "built chiefly of tory timber; the oak for her keel having been brought from the confiscated land of William Browne."[18]

Bernard C. Steiner wrote the first scholarly study of Connecticut slavery published in 1893. He emphasized the legal status of slaves, but also devoted one paragraph to William Browne, the 1779 petition for liberty by nine slaves on the Lyme portion of his estate.[19]

Guocun Yang's 1999 dissertation, the best single study of slavery in the colony/state, was primarily concerned with issues regarding slavery and freedom at the macro level and discussed such issues as the Connecticut slave codes, the slave trade, African American population, and crime and punishment. He made no mention of the Brownes.[20]

Historians who never read the 1900 letter that referenced events that took place almost one hundred and fifty years earlier, never saw the Weld booklet, and relied on other documentation had more accurate analyses of slavery on the Browne estate. Salem historian George N. Bates wrote an unpublished manuscript in 1935 that made no mention of any slaves on the property.[21] Lorenzo Johnston Greene, author of the classic *The Negro in Colonial New England*, stated in a footnote that Colonel William Browne "owned a large farm at Lyme" and that it contained nine slaves after Connecticut confiscated the estate.[22] Clifford K. Shipton, author of the most complete study of Browne, wrote that he owned a large amount of land in what is now the town of Salem "which he worked as a great estate with a few slaves."[23]

Joseph A. Caples (1873-1954), a man of color who lived on Gungy Road in Lyme and whose family had lived in the region since the 1780s, likewise did not

[17] Caulkins, *History of Norwich*, 330.

[18] Ibid, 404-05. She also reported that additional timber came from land in New London owned by a Boston Tory and the planks for the hull and deck came from the groves of other refugees.

[19] Steiner, *Slavery in Connecticut*, 27-28.

[20] Yang, "From Slavery to Emancipation."

[21] Bates, "History of Salem," 7-8, 46-51.

[22] Greene, *Negro in Colonial New England*, 107n. Greene's source was Bernard C. Steiner, "Slavery in Connecticut," 27. The number cited by Greene represents the number of those enslaved on the Lyme portion of the estate.

[23] *Sibley's Harvard Graduates*, XIII, 551.

mention the existence of a slave plantation within a couple of miles of his house.[24] In his memoirs, Caples wrote about about his ancestors, relatives, and others of African American and mixed blood from Lyme and the surrounding towns. He only wrote about the Browne estate in the context of wanting to believe that a son of Venture Smith called Cuff was his ancestor, Cuff Condol.[25] "There is a Mumford farm in Salem and as Venture was first sold to a man by that name, I assume there may have been a connection between the families and Cuff may have come in to the Gungy section via the Mumfords."[26]

The best-known Connecticut slaveholder until 2001 was Godfrey Malbone, a man who spent little time in the colony, and is now given scant mention in comparison to the Browne's "slave plantation" in Salem. His son of the same name lived a number of years in the Mortlake section of Pomfret.[27] As far as the history of New England slavery is concerned, he is a far more consequential figure than is Browne.

Born in Princess Ann County, Virginia, Malbone moved to Newport in the 1720s and became a wealthy merchant.[28] During the 1730s, Malbone inherited a large estate in Virginia, one that included some 50 slaves. He then had the resources to expand his activities and entered the African slave trade.[29] The bulk of his profits, however,

---

[24] Alfred Bingham, the author's family, and the author knew Joe Caples. He died more than twenty years before Bingham published his article. The likelihood is that Bingham did not know about the Gungy man's memoirs written in old age that had been donated to the Connecticut State Library by his nephew Jesse Caples.

[25] He based this supposition on the fact that one of the owners of Venture was Robinson Mumford, a cousin of the New Salem Mumfords. Joseph A. Caples, "Memoirs of the Caples Family," Volume 1, 50-58, CSL.

[26] Ibid, I, 52. Of personal interest from around 1949, was a note pasted into the Caples memoirs from "Life-long friends of Joseph and Martha Caples, two outstanding personalities in the Town of Lyme, beloved by all who know them." The lifelong friends were J. Warren Stark, Alione E. Stark, Ellen Stark Giaconia, Marion Stark, Hazel P. Stark, Reginald Stark, William G. Stark, Charlotte Stark Johnstone, and Jennie E. Stark. Hazel and Reginald Stark were my parents, the others were my grandparents J. Warren and Alione E. Stark, four aunts, and one uncle. The Caples lived about two and a half miles from the Starks. Joseph and Martha Caples, my grandparents, and two aunts listed here are buried in the same cemetery less than one hundred yards from where my wife and I live.

[27] Deutsch, "Elusive Guineamen," 229-30, 236-37, 245, 248, 252; Ellen D. Larned, *History of Windham County, Connecticut*, 2 vols. (Worcester, MA: Printed by Charles Hamilton, 1874, 1880), I, 353; II, 6-7; *Complicity*, 7; "Mortlake, Connecticut," *Wikipedia*, accessed September 12, 2016; "Malbone Castle and Estate," *Wikipedia*, accessed September 12, 2016. See also, Byrne, "The Wayward Squire of Kingswood Manor" and Preston, "Godfrey Malbone's Connecticut Investment."

[28] He owned a wharf on which he had a store and warehouse and the largest distillery in Newport. Bridenbaugh, *Cities in Revolt*, 38, 270.

[29] From 1736 to 1740, he sent three slavers to the Guinea coast, but all the vessels were eventually lost. He re-entered the trade during the 1760s and three of his daughters married slavers. Deutsch, "Elusive Guineamen," 229-30, 248, 252. In 1736, a Malbone slave ship on the Guinea coast "was over-set and intirely lost, having on board 8 Slaves and a Quantity of Gold Dust." Two years later another Malbone slaver "was totally consum'd by Lightning on the Coast of Guinea, with a great many Negroes on board." A Boston newspaper reported in May 1740 that "Just imported, directly from Guinea, a fine Parcel of Gold Coast Slaves, Men, Women, Boys, and Girls to be sold by Godfrey Malbone, Esq;," *New-York Weekly Journal*, March 21, 1734, [4]; June 19, 1738, [3]; *Boston Post-Boy*, May 26, 1740, [4]. In January 1744, the snow *Africa* and "seventeen fine Gold Coast Slaves" were sold at Malbone's wharf. *Boston Evening-Post*, January 23, 1744, [4]; Coughtry, *Notorious Triangle*, 45, 47, 58, 81.

were gained through the coastal and West Indian trade and privateering during King George's War.[30] He built a mansion in Newport that Dr. Alexander Hamilton described in 1744 as "the largest and most magnificent dwelling house I have seen in America."[31] A fire consumed it in 1766. He purchased some 3,000 acres in Pomfret on which he placed some 26 slaves in 1766, and bought another 1,900 acres in New London.[32] The wealthy merchant hosted "a grand Entertainment at his House" after the capture of Louisburg in 1745, suffered the loss of his tar house and wharf in 1752, and served as one of six directors of the "Newport Freemason's Hall Lottery."[33]

He appeared as plaintiff in thirty-two court cases and defendant in seven before the New London, Hartford, and Windham County Courts between 1731 and 1767, demonstrating the wide range of his economic activities. When he died in Newport in February 1768 "in an Advanced Age," the Providence newspaper noted that Malbone was "a very eminent Merchant of that Place."[34] His son Godfrey (1734-1786), attended Harvard and King's College, Oxford, and spent much of his adult life in Pomfret, although his loyalty to the British crown led to attempts, ultimately unsuccessful, to confiscate the estate.[35]

*****

No one intentionally spread the false story about a slave plantation in Salem, not Weld, not Bingham, not the two archeologists who worked on the site, and not the newspaper reporters. The myth resulted from a convergence of factors.

Ralph Foster Weld in his tercentenary pamphlet on Connecticut slavery pointed out that Connecticut masters seldom owned more than two slaves, although some more prosperous people had more, "but there was never in Connecticut a labor system analogous to that of the Narragansett planters in Rhode Island. When Colonel Samuel Browne settled the present town of Salem about 1720, he was said to have brought in

---

30 Malbone's sloop *Charming Betsy*, having been granted "Letters of Marque and Reprisals' by the governor of Rhode Island, sailed in September 1739 "against the Spaniards." In December 1739, the *Boston Evening-Post* reported that a privateer belonging to Malbone had seized two Spanish ships "and carry'd them to *Jamaica* to be condemn'd." *Boston Weekly News-Letter*, September 13, 1739, [2]; *Boston Evening-Post*, December 17, 1739.

31 Hamilton described the dwelling as "built intirely with hewn stone of a reddish colour; the sides of the windows and corner stones . . . being painted like white marble. It is three storys high, and the rooms are spacious and magnificent." In addition, the house was one of the first in the colonies to have a mahogany interior, the only one except for the Colony House to be made of brick as of mid-century, and the only true mansion in the colony. Bridenbaugh, ed., *Gentlemen's Progress*, 103, 151, n. 227; Bridenbaugh, *Cities in Revolt*, 17, 339.

32 *Newport Mercury*, June 9, 1766, [3]. According to one source, his vast Connecticut lands, "included large deposits of brown sandstone, which he quarried and imported to Newport for building material." Newport Historical Society, "History Bytes: Godfrey Malbone and Brownstone," March 29, 2012.

33 *The Pennsylvania Gazette*, July 18, 1745, [2]; *Boston Post-Boy*, September 25, 1752, [2]; *New-York Mercury*, July, 16, 1759, [2]; Bridenbaugh, *Cities in the Wilderness*, 326.

34 *Providence Gazette*, February 27, 1768, [2]. Another newspaper noted that the Newport man was "formerly a very considerable Merchant in that Place." *Boston-Gazette*, March 7, 1768, [3].

35 Larned, *Windham County*, II, 6-14, 133-34, 197, 257-58; Susan J. Griggs, *Early Homesteads of Pomfret and Hampton* (n.p.: Susan J. Griggs, 1950), 96-98, *Sibley's Harvard Graduates*, XI, 433-40. According to an obituary notice published in *The Gentlemen's Magazine* and quoted in his Harvard biographical sketch, "his farm contained 4,000 acres of land, well fenced and beautifully managed; on it were 50 negroes."

more than sixty families of slaves to clear and work the land." He added, however, that this was probably a unique case. If you look carefully at what Weld wrote about Browne, however, you will see the phrase "he was said to have brought in more than sixty families of slaves." In the bibliographical note at the end of the work, the author stated that he relied largely on two works, Bernard C. Steiner's *History of Slavery in Connecticut* and William C. Fowler's article "The Historical Status of the Negro in Connecticut." He also cited two additional works.[36] The author examined all the sources used by Weld and could not find any reference to Samuel Browne and sixty families of slaves.[37] What, then, was the source for the sixty families of slaves? A footnote in Steiner's book states that "Godfrey Malbone of Brooklyn owned 50 or 60 slaves." He cites an earlier work for this information. Is it possible that Weld mistakenly assigned this number to Browne?[38]

The second source for the slave plantation formulation comes from Alfred M. Bingham who wrote a 1976 article "Squatter Settlements of Freed Slaves in New England" published in *The Connecticut Historical Society Bulletin*. He had a lifelong interest in the history of his family and hometown of Salem.[39] The article begins:

> A grim aspect of black slavery in colonial New England is revealed by a study of a number of primitive stone structures in Southeastern Connecticut. I believe that they are the remains of settlements in which black slaves found temporary refuge after being turned loose to shift for themselves when their usefulness was ended.[40]

He discussed these stone structures, stone terraces, jumbles of rocks, dilapidated walls, crude enclosures, root cellars, and fieldstone markers in the rugged regions near his house in Salem and the Gungy section of Lyme and these observations represented the "proof" for the truth of the above statement. The article also included several illustrations, some from Salem and Lyme and others from Groton and Ledyard. With regard to slavery on the lands his Mumford ancestors farmed, he found two critical pieces of evidence. While examining a collection of family papers at Yale University, Bingham came upon a 1900 letter that his grandfather Alfred Mitchell received from a cousin that related the circumstances on how the Mumfords came to Salem. This is the

---

[36] Weld, *Slavery in Connecticut*, 6, 32.

[37] The other two were Greene, "Slave-holding New England," 492-533; William E. B. DuBois, *Suppression of the African Slave-Trade in the United States of America, 1638-1870*, Harvard Historical Studies, Vol. 1 (New York: Longmans, Green, and Co., 1896). Bingham also checked these four sources with the same lack of success.

[38] Steiner, "History of Slavery," 21; Fowler, "Historical Status of the Negro," 122.

[39] His father was Hiram Bingham III of Machu Picchu fame and his grandfather and great-grandfather were missionaries in Hawaii. Through his mother Alfrieda Mitchell, he was directly descended from the Mumfords of New Salem Society. Alfred M. Bingham, *The Tiffany Fortune, and Other Chronicles of a Connecticut Family* (Chestnut Hill, MA: Abeel & Leet Publishers, 1996). Pages 45-50 contain a discussion of his Mumford ancestors and the Browne family.

[40] Contrary to Bingham's belief, no evidence exists to support the theory that these foundations are the remains of slave settlements. They are, in fact, stone memories of families who lived in the Gungy region two or more centuries ago. At least one of these former homes belonged to the family of freed slave Cuff Condol, a man who never had any association with the Browne estate. On the Condol family, see Vicki S. Welch, *And They Were Related, Too*.

letter that is quoted in chapter seven, the critical passage being, "Mr. Mumford entered immediately upon his labor employing a numerous gang of Blacks whose graveyard was on a slope quite neighboring the [Mumford] house. . . . As I was informed in my youth, Mr. M. was kept in farm servants until the Revolution by Blacks from Rhode Island."[41] Bingham then quoted Ralph Foster Weld's assertion that Colonel Samuel Browne "was said to have brought in more than sixty families of slaves to clear and work the land."

Bingham used the evidence of his observations of abandoned stone structures, the remains of foundations, field stones in abandoned cemeteries, the statements in the letter to his grandfather, and the Weld booklet to reach the conclusion that these physical remains "were once places of refuge for outcasts, forced by neglect and abandonment . . . into a desperate struggle to survive as Stone Age men."[42] Bingham, however, never specifically claimed that the Browne absentee estate was a slave plantation, although such was strongly implied by the connection he drew between what Weld wrote and the 1900 letter. From the perspective of historians, however, the evidence for a slave plantation in Salem is remarkably sparse, an undocumented statement in a 1935 publication and a letter at Yale University written by an elderly man recalling events that took place 140 years previously.[43]

The story stayed out of the public eye for about a quarter century. In 1999, "[Gerald] Sawyer led a field school on an initial survey of the Salem site" after being alerted about the possibility of the existence of a slave cemetery in Salem by Colchester historian Abraham Abdul Haqq."[44] The likelihood is that Haqq and/or members of the Bingham family introduced Sawyer and Perry to the Bingham article and they drew the conclusion that the absentee estate was a slave plantation. The results were published in "Rewriting Slavery's History," "The Plantation Next Door" chapter of the *Hartford Courant's Complicity,* and related articles that further publicized the story.[45] The major difficulty with these articles is that the archeologists and reporters are not historians with a knowledge of the history of slavery and did not critically analyze the sources for the slave plantation formulation. It seemed to have never occurred to them to question the Weld statement that Browne "was said to have brought in more than sixty families of slaves to clear and work the land" or the Bingham belief that John Mumford "entered immediately upon his labor employing a numerous gang of Blacks" to work the land.[46] They and the reporters endorsed these questionable assertions and the tale of a slave plantation in rural Salem entered the mainstream.

The archeologists did so in part because they believe the hypothesis of Joanne Pope Melish in *Disowning Slavery: Gradual Emancipation and "Race" in New England, 1760-1860.* She argued that Northern whites embarked on a concerted effort to erase

---

41 The writer of the letter was seventy-eight-year-old Nathaniel Shaw Perkins and his source was Lucretia Mumford Thacher who was born in 1785.

42 Bingham, "Squatter Settlements," 65-80.

43 Stark, *Myth and Reality,* 161.

44 Hileman, "Rewriting Slavery's History."

45 Gerald F. Sawyer wrote a preliminary report on his archeological investigations in 2002.

46 Weld, *Slavery in Connecticut,* 6; Bingham, "Squatter Settlements," 75.

slavery from its collective memory after it had disappeared from the region.[47] The most detailed reference to Melish came in a 2002 *Norwich Bulletin* article in which Gerald Sawyer is quoted as saying that the history of "the enslavement of African Americans in Connecticut has really been hidden" and added that "it's an invisible history and we're working to uncover it." The author of the article added that "Sawyer subscribes to the theory of Joann [sic] Pope Melish wrote about when it comes to slavery in the north." She theorized "that when the north was getting to the point of abolishing slavery, they attempted to gain an edge on the south, not only economically, but morally, by first saying they didn't have slavery anymore and eventually saying they never had it."[48] Thus, peeling back the layers of hidden history uncovers a slave plantation in Salem, Connecticut.

The archeological and physical evidence is no more compelling. Those like Bingham, Caples, and the author who have walked the Gungy area woods near the border between Lyme and Salem and traveled on Gungy Road before the road was paved in the 1950s could readily see the old foundations of small buildings and stone walls.[49] They comprise the remains of small houses, outbuildings, spring houses, and root cellars from an area that was much more heavily settled in former times.

The archeologists paid special emphasis to cairns, e.g. mounds of stones and ancient burial grounds. As far as the cairns are concerned, Sawyer and Perry stated that they "are similar to the type used in traditional societies in Africa."[50] What they appear not to have known is that oval mounds of rocks are found in a number of eighteenth-century deeds, including several for property purchased by James Harris and sold to Colonel Browne. They include phrases like, a "black oak tree markt with Stones Layed about it" and "an ash Tree marked with stones about it." It is remotely possible that some of the cairns may mark the graves of Africans, but it is far more likely that they were boundary markers and piles of stones built by farmers after fields were cleared.[51]

Finally, the matter of field stones in long abandoned cemeteries must be considered. A graveyard exists on Bingham property in Salem that may well contain stones marking the graves of people of color, including Pomp Henry and his wife Betsy. Other cemeteries exist in the area, the best known one is located in Hartman Park off Gungy Road in Lyme.[52] Fieldstone graves can be found in numerous old cemeteries in the Lyme

---

[47] Joanne Pope Melish, *Disowning Slavery: Gradual Emancipation and "Race" in New England, 1760-1860* (Ithaca, NY: Cornell University Press, 1988), xlii-xliii, 3-6.

[48] Pencak, "A hidden history revealed." Additional references to the Melish theory are found in Hileman, "Rewriting Slavery's History," and Woodruff, Sawyer, and Perry, "How Archeology Exposes," 181, footnote 12.

[49] One can still see a foundation or two and stone walls in driving on Gungy Road. The most noticeable foundation located on the left as you are driving towards Salem may be the original home of the Condol family.

[50] Hileman, "Rewriting Slavery's History." On another occasion, Sawyer added, "'those cairns.' he says pointing towards mounds of rocks piled high in an oval shape, 'are more like burial markers found in Guinea, West Africa than anything in this country.' He speculates that the mounds might represent traditional African burials." Bingham, "Hallowed Ground," 30.

[51] Stark, "Myth and Reality," 170. The author has seen similar piles of rocks on family property in Gungy.

[52] Bingham, "Squatter Settlements," 75, 77-78; Welch, *And They Were Related,* 57.

region and elsewhere, many designated by a rough headstone, some containing illegible markings for names, and smaller foot stones. One cannot assume that all or most of these headstones mark the resting places of people of color because carved stones cost far more than many could afford.

*****

The strong likelihood is, however, that this story will never go away because the extensive newspaper coverage of the archeological dig in Salem has become embedded in popular consciousness.[53] Connecticut was, after all, just a bit player in the tragic history of slavery in the Americas, despite what was written in works like *Complicity.* Such needs to be recognized and understood, together with historical damage that can be done by false narratives.

Few understand that slavery was ubiquitous throughout the western world and that it endured until well into the nineteenth century. Nor is it well known that the Portuguese and Spanish introduced African slavery to southern Europe and the New World in the fifteenth and sixteenth centuries. Smallpox, the European disease that so decimated the Native American population of the Americas, arrived in the Caribbean with the Spanish in 1519.[54] What is needed, then, is a greater historical understanding of slavery in Connecticut as it actually existed and such knowledge can only be obtained by careful examination of primary sources. I hope that this work tells some of this important story and points the way for others to follow into the largely untapped archival records of Connecticut.

---

[53] One piece by a reputable historian and an online article written in 2015 appearing after the author's "The Myth and Reality in Salem, Connecticut" seemingly endorsed the Sawyer-Perry story. Forbes, "Grating the Nutmeg," 174; Barbara Wells Sarudy, "It's About Time: Searching centuries of History, Art, Nature, & Everyday Life for Unique Perspectives, Uncommon Grace, & Unexpected Insights," published November 19, 2015, accessed November 18, 2016.

Another piece containing falsehoods appeared in September 2019. The author stated inaccurately that New London County was the largest slaveholding region in New England just before the Revolution and that there "were more than 2,000 slaves in the county by 1774, including 60 slave families on a sprawling 4,000-acre southern-scale plantation in Salem." David Collins, "Ichabod Pease: A survivor of the dark days of New London Slavery," *The Day*, September 5, 2019.

[54] For information on the pernicious influence of Spain and the conquistadores on Indian society in Latin America and the bringing of Africans to the New World, see, for example, studies by the eminent historian Hugh Thomas, *Conquest: Montezuma, Cortez, and the Fall of Old Mexico* (New York: Simon & Schuster 1993) and *Rivers of Gold: The Rise of the Spanish Empire, From Columbus to Magellan* (New York: Random House, 2004).

Appendix A:

James Harris Before the Bar, 1699 - 1756

During the eighteenth century, individuals appeared much more commonly before the courts than they do in the twenty-first. Indeed, court dockets were so crowded with cases of debt that the historical caricature is that Connecticut Yankees were naturally contentious and that they enjoyed nothing more than suing each other.[1] This view does not represent reality. The overload of the colony courts was in large measure due to the adverse effects of the British Navigation Acts on commerce and the colony's lack of an adequate medium of exchange. Cash-poor artisans, farmers, merchants, and shopkeepers often had to resort to the courts to collect the debts due to them. The Connecticut economy thrived on debt and the relative leniency of creditors. The downside, however, was the clogging of the justice and county courts with a numbing quantity of debt cases. All one has to do is to examine eighteenth-century account books to see how normal it was for the purchasers of goods and services to be in arrears, sometimes for years, and payment, when tendered, was often in agricultural products, fowl, or labor.

The legal problems of James Harris were atypical because of the large quantity of court cases in which he was concerned, primarily as a defendant in cases of debt. Many other men and some women appeared before the bar on numerous occasions, although few in southeastern Connecticut as many times as Harris.

Some examples of persons who had contact with him confirm these realities.[2] Carpenter Daniel Galusha of Lyme and Colchester was plaintiff or defendant in fifty cases between 1720 and 1754.[3] Slaveowner and merchant Godfrey Malbone of Newport is represented in thirty-nine lawsuits before the Hartford, New London, and Windham County Courts, mostly as plaintiff in debts by bond. Businesswoman Mrs. Mercy Raymond of Block Island and New London is found some forty-two times from

---

[1] For excellent studies of debt in early Connecticut, see Richard L. Bushman, *From Puritan to Yankee: Character and the Social Order in Connecticut, 1690-1765* (Cambridge: Harvard University Press, 1967), 108-30, 297; John T. Farrell, ed., *The Superior Court Diary of William Samuel Johnson 1772-73* (Washington: The American Historical Association, 1942), xii-xxxviii; and Bruce H. Mann, *Neighbors and Strangers: Law and Community in Early Connecticut* (Chapel Hill: University of North Carolina Press, 1987), 11-46.

[2] The totals include suits that were withdrawn and those in which the two parties did not appear.

[3] Forty-nine lawsuits occurred between 1720 and 1745 with the final one in February 1754 when Galusha was living in Dover, Dutchess County, New York.

1712 to 1735 before the New London County Court, on eighteen occasions with her partner Major John Merrett and twenty-four as femme sole.[4] Tenant William Carr appeared as plaintiff or defendant thirteen times before the New London County Court and Browne's agent John Mumford, Sr. on eighteen occasions.[5] Finally, the author's disreputable great-great-great-great-grandfather Nathan Stark of Norwich, Colchester, and Lebanon appeared before the Hartford, New London, and Windham County Courts at least sixty-five times between 1749 and 1777,[6] the bulk before the New London County Court in which he was a defendant in debt cases.[7] The number of lawsuits involving Harris was abnormally high, but a small number of others, like merchants engaged in local and international trade are equally ubiquitous, but generally as plaintiffs. Harris ranked within the top one half of one percent of all those who appeared before the New London County bar.

The two tables that follow summarize the appearances of James Harris before the bar. The first provides an overview of all court cases in which he was either a plaintiff or defendant between 1699 and 1763 divided into four subject areas and the second focuses on debt suits for book, note, bill, and bond in which Harris was the defendant.[8]

Table 6. James Harris Before the Bar

	Plaintiff				Defendant				
Span/Dates	Debt	Bond	Land	Other	Debt	Bond	Land	Other	Total
1699-1710	1	—	—	2	7	—	—	6	16
1711-1720	1	2	—	2	15	18	4	1	43
1721-1730	10	5	1	3	14	19	—	4	56
1731-1740	19	—	1	5	69	16	3	6	119

---

[4] The last mention of her occurred in February 1740 when she served as a trial witness.

[5] The justice court records of John Watrous of Colchester contain information of a lawsuit in which William Karr of Lyme sued Israel Jones of Colchester. Watrous Court Records, January 3, 1769, Box 549.

[6] The justice of the peace records of John Watrous list six more cases involving Nathan Stark between the years 1769 and 1774.

[7] Statistics gathered through an exhaustive examination of county court dockets and volumes of trials/records supplemented by the extensive notes the author took while processing New London County Court Records. Trials for New London, however, do not contain all items of relevance. New London records for a number of years have a section called no docket and these materials are not found in the bound volumes. To cite two examples, the author found records for thirty-seven court cases in trials/dockets involving Godfrey Malbone, but when no docket materials are added, the total is 39. In addition, the number of lawsuits involving James Harris increased from 275 to 301. The New London County Court classified court cases as no docket when they were not adjudicated. They came under the categories of withdrawn, no appearance, and nonsuit. No docket files lasted from June 1744 to November 1768 and picked up again in November 1781.

[8] Totals include two cases brought to court after the death of James Harris.

Span/Dates	Plaintiff				Defendant				Total
	Debt	Bond	Land	Other	Debt	Bond	Land	Other	
1741-1750	4	2	1	2	36	11	2	—	58
1751-1763	—	1	—	—	8	—	—	—	9
Total	**35**	**10**	**3**	**14**	**149**	**64**	**9**	**17**	**301**[9]

Table 7. James Harris Defendant Debt Resolutions

Span/Dates	Conf/Guilty	NotGuilty	Withdrawn[10]	G/Appeal[11]	NotG/Appeal
1699-1710	2	—	5	—	—
1711-1720	24	—	6	2	1
1721-1730	28	—	3	2	—
1731-1740	61	1	21	1	1
1741-1750	26	1	19	1	—
1751-1763	2	—	6	—	—
Total	**143**	**2**	**60**	**6**	**2**

As can be seen from the first table, Harris was plaintiff in just 20 per cent of the occasions when he was called to appear before one of three county courts, 62 of 301 lawsuits. He was defendant in 213 cases for debts by book, bill, note, or bond. The courts found him guilty in 149 cases, while in another 60 instances, the suit was either withdrawn or both parties failed to appear when called. The court found Harris not guilty on only four occasions. Just 14 percent of all the suits, forty-two in all, involved

---

[9] Of a total of 301 lawsuits in which James Harris was a party, 269 came before the New London County Court, 21 in Hartford, and 11 in the Windham County Court. The totals do not include data on appeals to the superior court since such represent continuances of cases already decided.

[10] Includes nonsuit, no appearance, and unknown. The versos of writs of withdrawn cases usually contain either the word withdrawn or XX marks. The author has found additional documentation in just one instance when Harris and Daniel Shapley requested that Daniel Coit, clerk of the New London County Court, "to withdraw our Writt that are Each against [the] other." NLCC, PbyS: Travel, November 22, 1742, Box 88, folder 5.

[11] Abbreviations stand for Guilty and appealed to Superior Court and Not guilty and appealed to Superior Court.

matters unrelated to debt. Twelve concerned disputes over land, while sixteen more between March 1700 and June 1737 concerned the horse trade, both legal and illegal.

Moreover, these 301 cases do not exhaust the total for appearances before Connecticut county courts. For example, in New London County Court Records: Papers by Subject the series called Summons for Evidence contains thirty-eight more references to Harris. The court summoned him to appear as a witness on 24 occasions, he was a plaintiff or defendant in 10 other cases, and is named in four more. In addition, his name appears in the Travel series of Papers by Subject on four occasions.

These numbers demonstrate beyond a shadow of doubt that James Harris faced continuous financial difficulties and, thus, it can hardly be considered surprising that he died insolvent.

APPENDIX B:

Browne Family Before the Bar

The profile of appearances before the bar for members of the Browne family looks far different than those of James Harris. The prosperous Brownes were plaintiffs in fifty-six of the sixty court cases heard by the Hartford, New London, and Windham County Courts. The New London Court heard 35 of the 60 lawsuits, the Hartford Court 15, and Windham 10. In sum, the Brownes were plaintiffs in 11 debt lawsuits, 30 for bond, 14 involving land, and 1 for other or unknown reasons.

Table 8. Court Cases in Southeastern Connecticut[1]

	Plaintiff				Defendant				
Span/Dates	Debt	Bond	Land	Other	Debt	Bond	Land	Other	**Total**
1711-1720	—	1	—	—	—	—	—	—	1
1721-1730	—	7	—	—	—	—	—	—	7
1731-1740	2	6	4	—	1	—	—	—	13
1741-1750	6	2	—	—	—	—	—	—	8
1751-1760	1	4	—	—	—	—	—	—	5
1761-1770	1	4	4	—	—	—	—	—	9
1771-1780	—	—	—	—	1	—	—	1	2[2]
Total	10	24	8	—	2	—	—	1	45

[1] Family plaintiffs and defendants were Colonel Samuel Browne, William and Samuel Browne as executors, Samuel Browne, Katherine Browne, Epes Sargent and Katherine Sargent, and William Browne (1737-1802). The table includes ten lawsuits brought before the Hartford County Court relating to his New Salem lands.

[2] Information from 1777 petition to General Assembly. *State Records*, I, 311.

Table 9. Other Court Cases in Hartford and Windham Counties[3]

	Plaintiff				Defendant				
Span/Dates	Debt	Bond	Land	Other	Debt	Bond	Land	Other	**Total**
1711-1720	—	—	—	—					**0**
1721-1730	—	—	1	—					**1**
1731-1740	—	1	—	1					**2**
1741-1750	—	2	—	—					**2**
1751-1760	—	1	1	—	1				**3**
1761-1770	—	—	4	—					**4**
1771-1780	1	2	—	—					**3**
Total	**1**	**6**	**6**	**1**	**1**				**15**

William Browne (1709-1763) and son William Burnet Browne are represented in eight of the 15 lawsuits, while William Browne (1737-1802) by three in 1772 and 1773. The New Salem landowner sued Jacob Eliot of Lebanon twice and County Sheriff Eleazar Fitch of Windham, the future Loyalist, once.

---

[3] Family members consisted of William and Samuel Browne as executors, William Browne (1709-1763), Epes Sargent, William Burnet Brown, and William Browne (1737-1802).

Appendix C:

Browne Genealogical Charts

The Brownes of Salem, Massachusetts

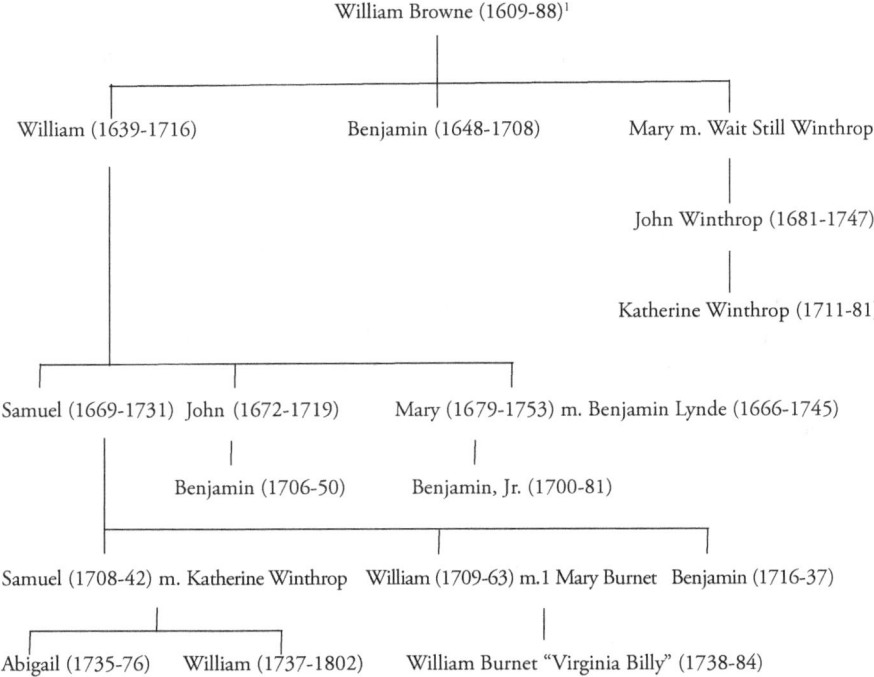

This condensed chart shows the relationships among the most prominent members of the family. Not included are those who are unessential to the narrative and children who died before reaching adulthood. For example, Samuel, Jr. and Katherine had three other children who died in infancy. His brother William married twice. His first wife Mary Burnet died in 1745 shortly after childbirth at the age of 22. William then married Mary French of New Brunswick, New Jersey and he fathered a total of nine children. The only one to marry and have heirs was William Burnet Browne. He wed Judith Walker Carter of Virginia and they had several female offspring.[1]

---

[1] "Descendants of William Browne," 160B; Lewis, "Record of Browne Family Portraits," 185-87.

Browne-Winthrop-Saltonstall[2]

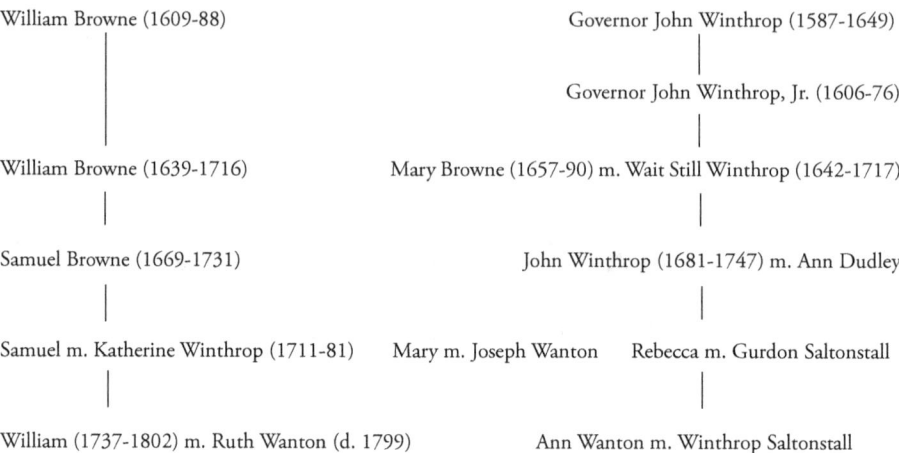

William Browne (1609-88)   Governor John Winthrop (1587-1649)

Governor John Winthrop, Jr. (1606-76)

William Browne (1639-1716)   Mary Browne (1657-90) m. Wait Still Winthrop (1642-1717)

Samuel Browne (1669-1731)   John Winthrop (1681-1747) m. Ann Dudley

Samuel m. Katherine Winthrop (1711-81)   Mary m. Joseph Wanton   Rebecca m. Gurdon Saltonstall

William (1737-1802) m. Ruth Wanton (d. 1799)   Ann Wanton m. Winthrop Saltonstall

Colonel Samuel Browne's aunt Mary married Wait Still Winthrop, son of John Winthrop, Jr., and Browne's eldest son Samuel (1708-1742) married his first cousin once removed Katherine Winthrop. One of Katherine's sisters married Joseph Wanton of Newport, the future governor of Rhode Island, and another sister married Gurdon Saltonstall of New London, son of the Connecticut governor of the same name. Governor William Browne married his first cousin Ruth Wanton and her sister Ann married first cousin Winthrop Saltonstall. The last absentee, therefore, was related to five New England governors - John Winthrop, John Winthrop, Jr., Joseph Dudley, Gurdon Saltonstall, and Joseph Wanton.

---

2 For information on the Wantons and Saltonstalls, see DuBosq and Jones, "Descendants of Gov. John Cranston," 252-53 and Richard M. Saltonstall, *Ancestry and Descendants of Sir Richard Saltonstall* (n.p.: Riverside Press, 1897).

Appendix D:

Browne Tenants

It is not known how many men leased land in New Salem from three generations of Brownes.[1] The only extant list of thirteen names comes from the Loyalist claim of Governor William Browne of tenants in 1774. Moreover, it was not uncommon for two or more men to share in a tenancy. As outlined in Appendix B, three generations of Brownes filed forty-two lawsuits in the New London and Hartford County Courts in cases of debt by bond, debt by note, and disputes over land against residents of Lyme and Colchester.[2] Several of the defendants rented farms from the absentees. The terms of contracts between the Salem, Massachusetts owner and the renters were secured by bonds that provided for monetary reimbursement if either side failed to fulfill the terms of the lease. An asterisk (*) is used to denote the thirteen leases listed by Governor Browne in his Loyalist claim. The evidence indicates that good tenants remained on the same lands for multiple leases, thus the foregoing list could well include around half of the total.[3]

Name (s)	Time Frame	Term	Acres	Town	Source(s)
Daniel Galusha & Samuel Gilbert	1718		300	Lyme	NLCC, NLSC
Ephraim Tiffany	1724-31	7		Lyme	Perkins, NLCC
Jonathan Culver & Aaron Stark	1724	7		Colchester	NLCC, NLSC
Samuel & James Grant	1720s			Lyme	Perkins

---

[1] As noted in chapter 2, absentee Thomas Fitch and New London's George Dolbeare also leased farms.

[2] A majority of bond debt cases brought before the New London County Court appear to be sureties for loans, as for example when William Browne sued David Dodge of Colchester in a debt by "bond or writing under his hand." On November 1, 1760, Dodge borrowed £30 from the Salem, Massachusetts man to be paid back with lawful interest when requested. *William Brown v. David Dodge*, HCC, Files,, November 1766, Box 183, packet 2.

[3] Information on tenants comes from several sources: Mary E. Perkins, Chronicles of a Connecticut Farm 1769-1905 (Perkins); New London County Court Records (NLCC); New London County Superior Court Records (NLSC); Connecticut Archives, Private Controversies, Series 2 (Private); William Browne, List of Tenants, AmLC, AOP, AO 13/50, 142 (AOP).

Name (s)	Time Frame	Term	Acres	Town	Source(s)
Jonathan Read & John Read[4]	1732-39	7	270	Lyme	NLCC, NLSC
Samuel Tubbs	1730s			Colchester	NLCC
Jacob Bacon, Jr.	1740s			Lyme	Perkins
Stephen Harding[5]	1744-62		288	Lyme	Perkins
Stephen Gardner, Sr.	1744-54			Colchester	Perkins
Nehemiah Royce & Daniel Gilbert	1748			Lyme	NLCC
Ebenezer Tiffany	1759-66	7	300	Lyme	Private
John Mumford, Sr.	1759-73			Col/Lyme	Perkins
Joshua Ransom	1760			Colchester	Perkins
Joshua & Jonathan Beckwith[6]	1763			Lyme	Perkins
Samuel, John, & Caleb Tenant[7]	1760s			Colchester	Private
Ebenezer Tiffany & Elisha Ely	1764		300	Lyme	NLCC, Perkins
Samuel Hazard[8]	1767-74	7	677	Colchester	Private, Perkins
*William Carr[9]	1740s-74	5		Lyme	AOP, Perkins
*Joseph Hastings	1770-75	5	500	Colchester	AOP, NLCC

---

[4] Read sublet the farm to Thomas Tozer in 1733 for the remainder of the seven-year term. *John Read v. Thomas Tozer*, NLSC, Files, September 1745, Box 18, folder 19, no. 14.

[5] Stephen Harding, originally from Warwick, Rhode Island, lived on what became known as the "Harden Farm" from 1744 to at least 1762. Perkins, *Connecticut Farm*, 52, 218; 1762 Tax List, folder 10, CTR, C. The Harding farm can be found on Map 1 at the northeast corner of Lot S

[6] The house of Jonathan Beckwith is found in Map 1. See the eastern part of Lot BI near the New London bounds.

[7] Samuel Tenant was appointed ensign of the New Salem militia company in April 1769. CA, Militia, Series 2, 1375.

[8] Samuel Hazard (1730-c.1788), son of Samuel of South Kingstown, RI, m. Catherine and their two oldest children were Samuel and George. It is likely that sons Samuel Hazard, Jr. and George Hazard lived on the farm and shared the lease. Samuel Hazard was admitted as a freeman in Colchester in 1769 and a "Samuel Hassard" took the oath of fidelity in September 1777. The person who took the oath of fidelity may have been Samuel, Jr. because a Samuel of Narragansett was expelled in 1779 for giving aid to the enemy, although he was allowed to remain on a promise of loyalty. ColchesterBMD, Vol. 1, 97, 154; Vol. 2, 342; Robinson, *Hazard Family*, 30, 69-70.

[9] As indicated in Chapter 10, the likelihood exists that Carr was a Browne tenant long before 1769, perhaps as early as the 1740s.

Name (s)	Time Frame	Term	Acres	Town	Source(s
*Stephen Gardner, Jr.	1770-75	5		Colchester	AOP
*James Kelly	1770-73	3		Colchester	AOP
*Samuel Gilbert	1772-82	10		Lyme	AOP
*Benjamin & Jedidiah Beckwith	1772-77	5		Lyme	AOP
*John Henry[10]	1773-80	7	[220][11]	Col/Lyme	AOP, Perkins
*Joseph Colt	1773-79	6		Lyme	AOP
*Joshua Beckwith[12]	1773-78	5		Lyme	AOP
*John Minor	1773-80	7		Lyme	AOP
*Jonathan Gilbert[13]	1773-78	5	207	Lyme	AOP
*John Mumford, Jr.[14]	1760-81	7	1,094	Lyme	AOP, Perkins
*Joshua Ransom[15]	1774-79	5	[245]	Colchester	AOP

Most farms had considerable size, much larger than that of the average Connecticut landowner, the known leases being for properties of at least 200 acres. In addition, each was a single plot and not, as with a number farmers by the mid-eighteenth century, made up of pieces of land that were not contiguous to one another. Moreover, the annual rents were relatively modest. To cite just one example, William Carr's farm of probably more than 200 acres in Lyme rented for just £12 per year.

According to the first advertisement for the sale of Browne's confiscated estate, the properties contained "eleven Dwelling Houses and as many barns."[16] On the assumption that this statement is correct, and one cannot be certain, three of the tenants rented agricultural, grazing, and woodlands. The most likely possibilities for tenants of lands without "Dwelling Houses" were Benjamin and Jedidiah Beckwith, Joseph Colt, and John Minor. All owned land in Lyme.

---

10 Lease may have been shared with his brother Robert.

11 Estimates for the size of the Henry and Ransom farms based upon a report from Probate Judge Benjamin Huntington of April 11, 1783. Report of Benjamin Huntington, AmLC, AOP, AO 13/50, 79.

12 Lease may have been shared with Jonathan Beckwith.

13 *Connecticut Gazette*, February 7, 1783, [3].

14 Since it is known from Governor Browne's Loyalist Claim that around 1760 Browne purchased a second lot of three to four slaves that "were sent to the farm on the Claim[an]t's Estate which the agent's son was in Possession," it is highly likely that Mumford's 1774 seven-year lease was the third of the same duration with the first beginning in 1760. Memorial of William Browne, AmLS, AOP, AO 12/10, 234

15 Lease may have been shared with Bliss Ransom.

16 *Connecticut Gazette*, August 24, 1781, [3].

Appendix E:

Tenant Contracts

No contract exists between any members of the Browne family and their numerous tenants, but lease terms can sometimes be inferred from court records.[1] The first of two examples dates from the November 1744 session of the New London County Court when Katherine Browne sued Jonathan Read and John Read for nonpayment of rent on a leased farm. The second came from after the American Revolution when Probate Judge Benjamin Huntington, administrator of the confiscated Browne estate, sued Joseph Hastings for not paying his rent. Both court cases provide details on the terms of leases. A significant proportion of the Browne debts by bond represented sureties for leases to farms.

1. *Katherine Brown v. Jonathan Read and John Read* [2]

To New London County Sheriff, his Deputy, or to Either of ye Constables of Norwich or Lyme Within Said County, Greeting.

In his Majesties Name you are hereby Required to Summon Jonathan Reed of sd Lyme and John Reed of sd Norwich, formerly John Reed June of Lyme, So that they appear before ye County Court to be holden at New London Within and for ye County of N: London on ye 2d day of June Instant, then & there to answer Unto Katharine Brown of Salem in ye County of Essex: She is Administrator of ye Last Will and Testiment of Small Brown Esqr Late of Said Salem Dec[ease]d in a Plea that ye Defend[en]tts Render

---

[1] The author found two contracts called lease indentures, one dated April 15, 1778 and the second March 25, 1782. By these indentures, Thomas Green of Newport rented a forty-acre farm in Lyme East Society to Elisha Smith. The first one-year lease stipulated that Smith pay Green £5 lawful money in produce at specified rates for each article of produce, for example, wheat at four shillings and a sixpence per bushel. The second lease for seven years required Smith to provide six cords of good "Merchantable Cord Wood" per annum delivered to the landing owned by George Griswold in Lyme. Smith Family Papers, folder 18, CHS.

[2] *Katherine Brown v. Jonathan Reed and John Reed*, NLCC, Files, November 1744, Box 78, folder 7, no.1. The Reads confessed judgement and the plaintiff recovered £73-13 damages and costs.

    Punctuation added to make eighteenth-century legalese somewhat more comprehensible. The punctuation could be a comma, period, or the making of a new paragraph. Legal language contains a number of long run -on sentences with numerous ands.

and pay to ye Plaintif ye Sum of Three Hundred Pounds Good and Currant Money of ye Coloney of Connecticutt Which to ye Plaintif the Defendants Justly owe.

Whereupon ye Plaintif Sayeth that ye defendants by there [sic] bond Under their hands & Seals by them Well Executed Dated ye 27th day of October AD: 1731 became bound and obligd to ye aforesd Small Brown in the afore mentioned Sum of Three hundred Pounds: to be Paid to ye Said Small Brown, his Certain attorney, Executors &c Which bond is Conditioned in ye following Words: Viz, The Condition of this obligation is Such that Whereas ye above bound John Reed Junr hath on ye day of Date of these Presents Taken Upon Lease of ye sd Small Brown one Certain Tract or farm of Land Lying Within ye Town Ship of Lyme aforesd With a mantion house and farm Standing theiron as by one Lease of Indenture bearing Even Date With these Presents Reference therein to being had May fully appear.

Now in Case ye sd John Reed Junr his Heirs Executors or administrators Shall Well and Truly fulfill Keep obey assume pay and Perform Every articul & Clause Contained in ye afforsd Indenture Which on his Part and behalf are Mentioned to be Performed & fulfiled according to ye True Intent & Meaning therof then ye above obligation Should Cease, but upon Defalt to Stand & Remain in full force. Now ye Plantif Sayeth that ye Defendants their bond aforsd Not in ye Least Regarding, have Never Performed ye Condition thereof Nor paid ye Same nor either of them and Still ye Some [sum] to pay or Condition to Perform Most unjustly do [   ], tho often there unto by ye Plantif Requested & Which is to ye Damage of Plantif as She Says three Hundred Pounds Law-full Money and therof She bring this Sute & Demands of ye defendants Said Sum With her Coast [cost], ye Plantif haveing Given Sufficient bond of Prosecution according to Law, hearof fail Not and due Return Make as ye Law Directs Dated in New London this 2d day of June AD 1744.

Clerk   Daniel Coit

This writ was followed by another court case heard by the New London Coun-ty Court in November 1744 and appealed to the Superior Court in 1745, one that contains much more detail on the lease. In this lawsuit, John Read sued Thomas Tozer to whom he sublet the property in 1733.

2. John Read v. Thomas Tozer[3]

To the Sheriff of the County of Hartford his Deputy or Constable of Colchester in sd. County, Greeting, or the Sheriff of the County of New London or his Deputy or the Constable of Say-brook in New London County.

In the Name of George the Second King &c you are Commanded to attach the goods or Estate of Thomas Tozer Late of Lyme in the County of New London now of Colches-

---

3 *John Read v. Thomas Tozer*, NLSC, Files, September 1745, Box 18, folder 19, no. 4. The New London Coun-ty Court found found Tozer guilty and ordered him to pay £102 damages and £9-8-3 costs. The defendant appealed to the Superior Court and the parties failed to appear.

ter aforeSaid to the vallue of Two Hundred pounds Bills of publick Creditt of the Old Tenor and for want thereof take the body of Said Tozer and him Safe keep so that you may have him before the County Court to be held at Norwich in New London County on the fourth Tuesday of November next to answer unto John Reed Late of Said Lyme more Late of Said Colchester now of Said Norwich.

In a plea of the Case whereupon the Plantiff Declars that in the year 1731 he took of Samuel Brown of Salam in the County of Essex and Province of the massachusets bay one farm of Land Lying and being in Sd Lyme Containing by Estimation 270 acres Sixty acres of which was then Cleared and fenced and fit for Either mowing or ploughing and Said farm is bounded north upon the Line Dividing between Said Lyme and Said Colchester west upon the Land Lately Least by Said brown to Samll Tubbs South by Land Lately Leased to Aaron Stark East upon the farm Lately sold by James Harriss to Said Samuel Brown of Said Salam. On which then Land Still is Standing a mantion house and barn which farm and Appurtinances the Said Brown Least by his Lease in writting for the Space of Seven years from the 25th of march 1732 to the Plantiff his heirs and Asigns for Rents and Servises to be paid and performed by the plan[ti]ff his heirs &c which Lease is Dated october 27th 1731 and the Plantiff by force thereof Entered into Said farm and Improved the Same the Space of one year from the Said 25th of march and then by his Lease perole he Least the Same to the Defend[an]t for the Remainding part of Said Seven years and the Defend[an]t Received the Same and Entered there into and Improved Said farm and Appurtenance the Remainder of Said Seven Years and took the Sole profit thereof to him Self and at the time the Defend[an]t Entering into Said Land he Did on him Self Assume and faithfully promise unto the Plantiff to pay him what the Improvement their of Should be worth yearly and Every year.

Now the Plantiff in fact Say that the use and Improvement was then well worth £25 old tenor bills of Publick pr year which the Defend[an]t hath never paid to the Plantiff nor made him any Satisfaction in any way whatever tho often Requested which is to the Plantiff Damage the Sum of £150 in publick bills of Creditt of the old Tennor and to Recover the Same with Just Cost the Plaintiff brings this Suit. Bond for Prosecution being given according to Law fail not but make return hereof with your doing thereon according to Law. Dated in Colchester this 9th Day of August anno Dom: 1744.

pr John Bulkley Assistant

3. *Benjamin Huntington Petition*[4]

To the Honourable County Court to be held at New London in and for the County of New London on the Second Tuesday of June next.

The Petition of Benjamin Huntington of Norwich in said County, Administrator of the Confiscated Estate of William Brown Esq. late of Salem in the Sate of the Massachusetts humbly sheweth that the said William Brown Exq. was for more than Ten Years next before the Year of our Lord 1773 the lawful Owner of a certain Tract

---

4 *Benjamin Huntington Petition*, NLCC, Files, February 1783, Box 177, folder 2, no. 83.

of Land in Lyme in the County of New London containing about Five Hundred Acres with a Dwelling House, Two Barns, and a Corn House thereon standing being the same Farm where Ebenezer Tiffany of said Lyme now dwells and the said Brown being the Owner of said Farm as aforesaid. At some time in or not long before the Month of March Anna Domini 1773 agreed with Capt. Joseph Hastings of said Norwich that the said Hastings should hire said Farm and Appurtenances thereof for a Term that should Expire on the 25th Day of March Anno Domini 1778 for his the said Hastings owns and improvement and that said Hastings should for this consideration of the use and improvement of said Farm dureing said Term pay to the said Brown the Sum of Thirty Pounds lawful Money per Annum for each Year of said Term and also make Forty Rods of good Stone Wall Five Feet High on said Farm where the same should be wanted for Fence in each Year dureing said Term and said Brown and Hastings haveing so agreed on the Rent of said Farm and completed their Leases thereof accordingly for the Term aforesaid.

The said Brown soon afterwards and before the first Day of June A.D. 1775 went into the Town of Boston in the State of Massachusetts and then and there joined with the Enemies of this and the rest of the United States of America and afterwards went with said Enemies from said Boston and still continues with and Screens himself under the Government and Protection of said Enemies carrying on Warr against this and the rest of the States aforesaid and the whole Estate of said Browne's Estate boath real and personal being in this State hath been by due course and judgment of law declared Forfeit and confiscated to this State and your Petitioner is lawfully and duely appointed and acting as Administrator thereon and the said Hastings by himself and such Persons as have improved said Farms under him by virtue of said Lease hath had the quiet and Peaceable possession, use, and Benefit of said Farm and Appurtenances dureing said Term but hath always neglected and refused and still refuseth to pay said Thirty Pounds lawful Money per Annum or to make said Stone Wall agreed as aforesaid or any part thereof for Four Years of said Term and the said Four Years Rent of said Farm is now due to the Estate of said Brown and the said Hastings hath in his power and conceals the said Lease and Evidence of said Contract or agreement and your Petitioner cannot obtain the same and your Petitioner hath by virtue of the Statute Law of this State in such Case made and provided a Right and it is his Duty as Administrator on said confiscated Estate to Institute this Suit in Equity for the Recovery of said Sums agreed for and due as aforesaid and the Interest thereof which is not less than One Hundred and Seventy Pounds lawful Money as also to recover the Damages sustained by the neglect of said Hastings to Build said Stone Wall which is not less than Thirty Pounds lawful Money more amounting in the whole for said Damages and rent due as aforesaid to the Sum of Two Hundred Pounds lawful Money to be recovered for the use of this State according to the direction of the Statute Law aforesaid .

Whereupon your Petitioner in his Capacity aforesaid prays your Honours as a Court of Equity to inquire into the truth of the Facts aforesaid by the Oath of said Hastings and such other Evidence as shall be adduced and Decree and order that said Hastings pay to your Petitioner in his Capacity aforesaid for the use of this State such Sums as shall be found due and Damage sustained as aforesaid together with just Cost as by said Statute Law your Honours are enabled to do and your Petitioner as in Duty Bound should ever Pray - Dated at Hartford the 21st Day of May Anno Domini 1781.

Benja. Huntington Adminis[trato]r

To the Sheriff of the County of New London or his Deputy either of the Constables of the Town of Norwich ins said County Greeting.

In the Name of the Governour and Company of the State of Connecticut, you are hereby commanded to summon Captain Joseph Hastings of said Norwich to appear before the County Court to be held at New London in and for said County on the second Tuesday of June next then and there to shew Reason if any he hath why the prayer of the foregoing Petition of Benjamin Huntington Administrator on the Estate Confiscated Estate of William Browne Esq therein named should not be granted and you are to leave a true and attested Copy of said Petition of this Citation with the said Hastings or at the Place of his usual abode in Norwich aforesaid at least Twelve Days before the sitting of said County Court. Hereof fail not but make due return of said Petition and Citation with your doings thereon as the Law directs. Dated at Hartford the 21st Day of May Anno Domini 1781.

Richard Law Assist[an]t

Norwich May 27th 1781. Then left a a true and attested Copy of this Petition and Citation in the House at the usual abode of the within named Defendant

Pros[per] Wetmore Sheriff

Fees for Copy &c 30/ L[awful] M[one]y.

Foregoing are true Copy from the Files of Court Examined

Wint[hrop] Saltonstall Clerk[5]

New London S[uperior] County Court June Term 1781

On the Petition of Benjamin Huntington of Norwich Administrator on the Confiscated Estate of William Browne late of Salem in the State of Massachusetts, setting fourth that said Brown was the Owner of a large Tract of Land in Lyme and that Jospeh Hastings of Norwich aforesaid hired of said Browne said Tract of Land pr Lease from March 1773 to 25 March 1778 for Considerations in said Lease expressed and that said Hastings has benign the improvement of said Farm said Term agreed that said Hastings refuses to pay the Rents &c. due on said Lease and holdeth said Lease.

And praying that said Hastings may be examined on Oath &c. and ordered to pay the Sum due together with Cost as Pr Petition dated 21st May 1781. This Court on Consideration of the prayer of said Petition appoint Messrs Guy Richards, Jacob Dewit,

---

5 Cousin of Loyalist William Browne.

Zabdiel Rogers and John McClaren Breed a Committee to examine into the Matters in said Petition contained and their Opinion thereon Report to this or the next Court.

Certified from the Records
Win[thro]p Saltonstall Clerk

Appendix F:

William Browne's Loyalist Claim

The Loyalist claim for William Browne offers a fascinating glimpse into both the processes by which claims were adjudicated and how the wealthy and influential often achieved success in their efforts to gain partial reimbursement for their losses.[1] Poorer Loyalists generally enjoyed no such success because they often lacked sufficient documentation to support their claims.[2] Readers will note the detail he and other claimants had to provide in order for their memorials to be favorably considered, ones that included biographical information, detailed lists of properties lost together with supporting evidence, and endorsements by acquaintances who could attest to the truth to what each claimant lost. In his property listing, Browne provided the cost both in New England currency and pounds sterling. The most important document in the series is the claim itself that consists of a narrative summary, an inventory of his losses, and a detailed explication of his losses.[3] Among the other noteworthy aspects of the documentation, is the fact that virtually all the property was acquired by Browne's grandfather Colonel Samuel Browne and most of it was entailed. In addition, it is clear from a careful reading of the texts that Browne appeared at the hearing, that he testified orally, and presented extensive documentation to buttress his case. The recorder/secretary did not quote verbatim, but provided the equivalent of minutes to the testimony, hence the short and choppy sentences.[4]

---

[1] For additional information on Loyalist claims, see E. Alfred Jones Jones, *The Loyalists of Massachusetts: Their Memorials, Petitions and Claims.*

[2] Monetary assistance was most likely to be given to those of high rank and importance in colonial society and those who had skills or information the British needed. Fingerhut, "Uses and Abuses," 246.

[3] In the transcriptions, the author has attempted to be faithful to the originals with regard to capitalization, punctuation, and spelling. The only liberties taken have been to supply periods and occasional capital letters at the beginnings of sentences.

[4] The first paragraph of the sworn statement of Governor Browne is recorded as: "Saith he is a native of Massachusetts, Representatives of two respectable Families by his Father and Mother's Side, the one Brown[e] the other Dudley, remarkable for their Attachment to the British Government, and of the most respectable Families in Massachusetts."

One can imagine, however, that the oral testimony by Governor Browne went something along these lines. "Good morning honorable commissioners and allow me on this occasion to offer you my most sincere

Although Browne was reimbursed for only a fraction of the amount he requested, the British government treated him well. After arriving in Great Britain, the government awarded him a pension of £200 per year and then gave him the appointment as governor of Bermuda at an annual salary of £750 Sterling per year.[5]

A. Peter Hunter to Governor William Browne, Halifax, May 17, 1786[6]

Office of Amer[ica]n Claims
Halifax 17 May 1786

Sir

I had the Honor of receiving your Letter of the 1st of March pr. Mr. Stockton which I immediately laid before the Commissioners & I am directed by them to inform you that they should be very sorry, if your Attendance here to Substantiate your Claim proved inconvenient to yourself, or Prejudicial to his Majesty's Service, but in no one Instance have they ever Dispensed with the Personal Attendance of a Claimant when his case being enquired into, more especially in one of such extent as yours.

The Commissioners remain in this Province till the Month of September next & should be glad that any Persons who have lodged Claims, should attend them here during that Period.

I have the Honor to be
Sir
Your most Ob[ient]t
Govr Browne   Humble Servant
        Bermuda   Peter Hunter
                                                    Sec[retar]y

B.1. The Memorial of William Browne[7]

To the Honorable the Commissioners appointed by Act of Parliament for enquiring into the Losses & Services of the American Loyalists.

---

gratitude for your kindness in giving me the opportunity to appear before you to discuss my losses as a result of the unfortunate late conflict. I was born in Massachusetts, like three previous generations of my family. I am descended from representatives of two of the most distinguished and respectable families in the province, one with the name of Browne and the other Dudley. One Dudley, my great-grandfather Joseph, was appointed governor of the commonwealth by the honored Queen Anne of beloved memory. All members of these families have been remarkable for their attachment to the British government, like many others in the most respectable families of Massachusetts."

5 A number of his acquaintances and colleagues also submitted claims, among them Jacob Bailey, Samuel Curwen, Daniel Leonard, former Chief Justice Peter Oliver, Timothy Ruggles, and Abijah Willard. Brown, *King's Friends*, 24, 32.

6 Peter Hunter to William Browne, May 17, 1786, AmLC, AOP, AO 12/139.

7 Memorial of William Browne, AmLC, AOP, AO 12/10, 217-44. A second set of printed page numbers go from 110-23.

The Memorial of William Browne late of Salem in the Province of Massachusetts Bay in New England.

Sheweth

That from the year 1762 to the year 1768 in which period a general uneasiness first manifested itself in the Colonies, your Memorialist was a Member of the House of Representatives of the Province aforesaid. That he uniformly supported with his voice, his vote and his influence, those measures which were then thought best Calculated to maintain the King's Authority, and in the year 1768 by his Submission to a Royal Requisition to rescind an Obnoxious Vote of a preceding Assembly, he lost his Seat, became an object of public Resentment, and in numerous Instances suffered in his Interest.

That he has been by several succeeding Governors appointed to places of Honor, Trust, or Profit, and when the disturbances began he commanded the first Regiment of Militia in the County of Essex, he was a Member of His Majesty's Council and one of the Justices of the Superior Court of Judicature with a yearly Salary of Two Hundred Pounds Sterling. That when the tumult happened at Cambridge in August 1774, he was attending his duty at the Superior Court at Boston, and was from that time obliged to reside there until the Town was Evacuated by the King's Troops in March 1776, that since he left his Home in August 1774 he has been entirely without assistance from his private Fortune and has solely depended for support upon the Bounty of Government. That he thankfully acknowledges the care and tenderness that has been shewn him, but in his Situation and Circumstances it has been unavoidable that he should incur Expences beyond what he had been enabled to defray. Your Memorialist further Sheweth that by an Act of the State of the Massachusetts Bay entitled "An Act to confiscate the Estates of certain Notorious Conspirators against the Government and Liberties of the Inhabitants of the late Province now State of Massachusetts Bay," made in 1779 your Memorialist was attainted by Name, and his Estate declared Forfeited to the use of the State. That by an Act of the State of Connecticut the Estate of your Memorialist laying within that Jurisdiction was Subjected to Forfeiture upon his Conviction of the Crime therein described and was accordingly Seized and Sold for the State. That by these several Acts of Legal Violence your Memorialist has lost a Fortune which he estimates to have been worth in 1774 at a moderate Computation Thirty three thousand two hundred and fifty six Pounds Sterling, and which he has endeavoured to describe in the Schedule hereto annexed, and will ascertain its Value by incontrovertible proofs if he should have an opportunity to be heard.

Your Memorialist therefore prays that his Case may be taken into your Consideration, that your Memorialist may be enabled under your Report to receive such Aid or relief as his Losses and Services may be found to deserve. And as in duty bound will pray.

(Signed) Will[ia]m Browne

B 2. An Inventory of the Estate of William Browne lat of Salem in the Province of the Massachusetts Bay

No. 1	9663 Acres of Land laying in Lyme, Colchester and New London in the Colony of Connecticut @ 40/	19,326
	11 Negroes upon the above Estate @ £30	300
	Rent in Arrear to March 25th 1776	500
	Due on a Judgement against J. Elliott	300
	Due on a Note of Hand by Fitch	100
2.	A Dwelling House in Salem occupied by himself	2000
	Furniture of the same, two Slaves &c	500
	Library of Books	150
3.	Dwelling House occupied by Cath. Sargent	750
4.	Dwelling House and Wharf	1000
5.	Warehouse and Land by T. Flagg	550
6.	4/9ths Dwelling House by H. Gardner	400
7.	37 Acres of Land in Salem called Stagepoint	1850
8.	Farm called Forrest River Farm by J. Vinning	1500
9.	2/3rds of 4000 Acres of Land in Charlton	2000
10.	Several Tracts of unimproved Land and other Real Estate in the province aforesaid	1000

Several Sums of Money due on Bonds, Notes of Hand, Accounts and for Rents		1000
		£ 33,256

(Signed) Will[ia]m Browne

Halifax 8th June 1786.

B.3. Evidence on the Claim of William Browne late of Salem.[8]

Claimant Sworn,

Saith he is a native of Massachusetts, Representatives of two respectable Families by his Father and Mother's Side, the one Brown, the other Dudley, remarkable for their Attachment to the British Government, and of the most respectable Families in Massachusetts·[9]

Was bred to the study of the Law, but turned his Attention to the Improve-

---

[8] Governor Browne was scrupulously accurate in the description of the offices he held and the extensive properties he owned and he provided detail about even the most minor of his assets, such as the "Rights for two Cows."

[9] Browne cited his Dudley ancestor because Joseph Dudley was Massachusetts royal governor from 1702 to 1715. *ANB*, s.v. Joseph Dudley.

ments of his Estate, was elected Representative for Salem in 1762.

Continued in the Assembly Seven years, in 1768 there was an Alarm about the Stamp Act [sic] which occasioned a Confederacy among the Colonies for Correspondence. The Assembly of Massachusetts Voted for Correspondence. Lord Hillsborough required the Vote to be rescinded.

Claimant voted for rescinding which lost him his Popularity. This lost him his Seat at the next Election.

In 1774 resided on his own Property at Salem. Colonel of Militia of Essex County and Judge of the Superior Court of Massachusetts.

Was one of the persons who addressed Governor Hutchinson. Never joined any Rebel Committee, or any Association.

Was appointed Judge of Superior Court by strong Recommendation of Governor Hutchinson.

Was one of the Mandamus Council. In August 1774 heard of the Danger in which Mandamus and continued at Boston till the Evacuation in March 1776. Went home to England in the Packet from thence. Bore Sir William Howe's Dispatches to Government, remained in England till February 1781, when he was appointed Governor of Bermuda.

Received his Salary as one of the Judges £200 pr Annum and Gratuities till he was appointed Governor. Salary was paid from the date of Commission [in] June 1774. Received in August 1775 by General Gage's Order £100 Sterling. In March 1776 received £200 in England of the Lord of the Treasury in common with the Mandamus Councillors.

On appointment to Bermuda applied to the Treasury and received £100, And £200 on the Expiration of Judge's Commission when his Appointment as Governor took place.

His present Salary £750 Sterling pr Annum in England. He went to Bermuda in December 1781, and has staid [sic] there ever since.

His Name is in the Act against notorious Conspirators.

Produces his appointment as Colonel of Militia by Governor Hutchinson in 1771.

Produces his Appointment of Judge of Superior Court of Massachusetts Bay by General Gage June 1774.

Produces Massachusetts Gazette 15th September 1774, containing resolve of a Committee that he should be requested to resign his Office as Mandamus Councillor, and his Answer that he would not from persuasion or threat do any thing derogatory to the Character of a Councillor of His Majesty's Province.[10]

Property No. 1.

Claimant was possessed of 9663 Acres in Lyme, Colchester, and New London in the County of New London Connecticut.

4000 Acres purchased by his Grandfather of J. Harris - 1718.

Produces Deed from James Harris to Colonel Samuel Browne of 4000 Acres in Lyme Township in Consideration of £1600 Currency of New England - £666 Sterling dated 1718. Produces Survey of said 4000 Acres.

Produces Deed from James Harris to Samuel Browne of 2865 Acres in Township of Lyme in Consideration of £2250 New England Currency dated 1723 - £803 Sterling.

Produces old Memorandum of a Deed from W. Gardner to Samuel Browne being in the hands of Samuel Huntington an Attorney at Norwich.

Produces Copy of said Deed, which appears a Deed from William Gardiner to Colonel Samuel Browne of 635 Acres in the Township of Colchester in Consideration of £1400 Connecticut Currency £500 Sterling dated in 1724.

Produces Copy of Deed from Aaron Stark to Colonel Samuel Browne of 45 Acres in Colchester in Consideration of £50 Currency dated 1725. £50 Currency equal to £15 Sterling.

Produces Copy of Deed from James Harris to Colonel Samuel Browne of 37 Acres in Colchester in Consideration of £50 dated 1726. £50 Currency equal to £15 Sterling.

Produces Deed from Daniel Davis to Colonel Browne of 80 Acres in Colchester in Consideration of £160 Currency dated 1727. £160 Currency equal to £51 Sterling.

Produces Deed from S Peck to Colonel Browne of 300 Acres in Lyme in Consideration of £700 dated 1728. £700 Currency equal to £225 Sterling.

Produces Deed from James Harris to Colonel Browne of 176 Acres in Colchester in Consideration of £316 dated 1728. £316 Currency equal to £102 Sterling.

Produces Deed from James Harris to Colonel Brown of 172 Acres in Colchester and New London in Consideration of £345 dated 1728. £345 Currency equal to £111 Sterling.

---

10 A copy of his response is located in Chapter 8 on page 135.

Produces Deed from Daniel Galus[h]a to Colonel Browne of 145 Acres in Lyme in Consideration of £350 Currency dated 1729. £350 Currency equal to £113 Sterling.

Produces Deed from S. Tubbs to Colonel Browne of 21 Acres in Colchester in Consideration of £42 dated 1729. £42 Currency equal to £13 Sterling.

Produces Deed from R. Stapples to Colonel Browne of 48 Acres in Colchester in Consideration of £110 dated 1729. £110 Currency equal to £35 Sterling.

Produces Deed from A. Gillet to Colonel Browne of 165 Acres in Consideration of £120 dated 1729. £120 Currency equal to £38 Sterling.

Produces Deed from James Harris to Colonel Browne of 200 Acres in Lyme in Consideration of £140 dated 1729. £140 Currency equal to £45 Sterling.

Produces Deed from James Harris to Colonel Browne of 626 Acres in Lyme in Consideration of £3450 dated 1729. £3450 equal to £1114 Sterling.

Produces Copy of Deed from James Harris to Colonel Browne of 26 Acres in Colchester in Consideration of £50 dated 1729. £50 Currency equal to £16 Sterling.

Produces Copy of Deed from A. Gillet to Colonel Browne of 128 Acres in Colchester in Consideration of £105 dated 1729. £105 Currency equal to £17 Sterling.

The whole contains 9663 Acres. Consideration amounts to £3883..13..8 Sterling.

Claimant's Grandfather continued in possession during his Life, died in 1731, then went to Claimant's Father by Will of his Grandfather.

Produces Copy of Grandfather's Will where by he devized all his Lands &c in Lyme, Colchester and New London to his Eldest Son Samuel Browne in Tail Male. Remainder in Tail Male to William like Remainder in Tail Male to Benjamin. Remainder in fee to his right Heirs.

William and Benjamin are dead without Heirs Male.[11] Claimant is the Eldest Son of Samuel Browne, but says the ultimate Remainder under his Grandfather's Will would go to the Children of all his Sons.

Claimant's Father was in possession [and] died in 1742 without a Will. Claimant is entitled as Heir in Tale Male. Claimant has been in possession ever since till the Troubles. There was no recovery suffered. This Estate has been Confiscated.

Produces Copy of Conviction February 1779 New London County and of

---

11 William married twice and had nine children, five of whom were sons. Four died young and only William Burnet "Virginia Billy" Browne married, but fathered only daughters. The third son Benjamin graduated from Harvard in 1735 and died shortly thereafter. *Sibley's Harvard Graduates*, VIII. 124; IX, 478-79.

Forfeiture of the Claimants Real and Personal Estate.

Produces Copy of Sale under hand of Benjamin Huntington who was appointed Administrator by the Court with Account of Sale of 5216 Acres for the Sum of £10,711 Lawful Money, and that there remained unsold 3600 Acres.[12]

Debts found due about £700 Continental Currency. Claimant admits a Debt of £900 Sterling with four years Interest due in 1774 and £480 Lawful with about a Year's Interest.

All this was under Lease. Tenants were to pay Money, were also to make Fences and other Improvements. Rent about £300 Lawful pr Annum with other Covenants on part of Tenants. Claimant produces Leases to prove as above. Values the Estate at 40/ Sterling pr Acre.

The Estate laid all together between Connecticut and Thames River and its Situation made it very valuable. Ten Miles from New London. Ten Miles from Norwich Market Towns and Seaports. One part was only 5 Miles from Connecticut River.[13]

Says he has laid out himself £7000 Sterling in Improvements. In Buildings, In repairs, In Clearing and Walls.[14]

Was laid out in different Farms.

Some of the best part was worth £3..12 Sterling per Acre. 1000 Acres of this were thus good.

Claimant says the best have been sold. The Administrator values what remains unsold at one Guinea pr Acre.

Claimant says he has generally known Farms in that Neighbourhood sell at more than 40/.

[Property] No. 2.

Was possessed of a House at Salem. This was his Grandfather's, bought at several Times, the whole of about two Acres.

Produces several Deeds of purchases of small pieces by his Grandfather, One by his Father, one by himself. Consideration about £240 Sterling.

---

12 The information in these two paragraphs must have come from Samuel Huntington.

13 The geographical location of the estate reads a lot better than the reality of the hills and poor roads from his lands to New London, Norwich, and Connecticut River.

14 This is about the only statement for which no evidence survives and on the face of it seems questionable. It is likely, however, that he counted clearing of fields and construction of walls as part of the £7,000 and the amount expended to purchase slaves. Physical improvements meant that the rent could be increased on the next lease.

His Grandfather built an House upon it and Wharf. Left it by Will to Claimant's Father in fee. His Father was in possession, and it came on his Death to Claimant and his Sister, they were the only Children.

Produces Deed from his Sister and her husband Joseph Blaney conveying to Claimant her Share in the premises and other Lands in Consideration of £800 dated 1762.

This Estate was afterwards divided and consisted in 1774 of House in which Claimant lived which he values at £2000 Sterling. 52 Feet by 37 a very handsome House in the Center of the Town.[15]

Values this House, Garden, Orchard and Offices at £2000 Sterling.

There was also another House on the Premises where Claimants Mother lived. Claimant built this in 1763, Cost £350 Sterling. Values this at £750 Sterling.

[Property] No. 3.

A House and Wharf on the above mentioned Grounds. This House was divided into two Tenements and one half Let at £12 Lawful pr Annum. Other half at ditto.

Wharf Let at £14 Sterling pr Annum. Values this at £1000 Sterling.

[Property] No. 4.

Land and Warehouse Let to S. Flagg. Claimant built the Store, cost £250 Sterling. Let at £20 Sterling pr Annum. Values it at £550 Sterling. It included a small piece of Land at £3 Sterling pr Acre.

Was also possessed of 4/9ths of a House in Salem and in another part of the Town. Claimant took this on a settlement of Accounts with the Executor of his Uncle and laid out about £145 Sterling in repairing it and Let it.[16] This had become dividable amongst the Family in these Shares. The whole House let at £20 Sterling pr annum. Values his Share at £400.

Produces Deed, shewing his Title to these 4/9ths. Was entitled to half a Cellar under the Town House built by his Grandfather and a Mr. Turner. Claimant entitled to one half. American Committee estimates it at £110 Sterling. Claimant values it at the same.

Was also possessed of 37 Acres at Stage point in Salem consisting of Eight parcels purchased at different times by Claimants Great Grandfather, his Grandfather,

---

[15] Elias Hasket Derby of Salem purchased the mansion and the other properties on the lot in December 1784. James Duncan Phillips, "Derby Wills and Land Titles, with Notes and Comments," *EIHC*, LXI (January 1930), 81-82.

[16] The uncle referred to was William Browne (1709-1763).

his Father and himself. Consideration £323 Sterling.

Produces the several purchase Deeds except one or two which had decayed. The Land lies opposite to the Town of Salem. Was in a State of great Improvement, divided into twelve Lots; Eleven Lots let at £53..15..6 per Annum Sterling, exclusive of Nine Acres worth £13..10 Ste[rlin]g. Values this Estate at £50 Sterling pr Acre.

Settled on Claimant by his Grandfather in the same way as the Lands in Lyme &c.

Was possessed of a Farm about four Miles from Salem called Forrest River Farm consisting of about 157 Acres with ten Rights, or Rights for 10 Cows, four Acres to a Right. Purchased at different times by his Grandfather, his Father and Claimant himself.

Consideration £397..4
23..5
£420..9 Sterling.

has not these Deeds.

This Estate is left in Tail Male to Benjamin Browne, then to Claimant's Father in Tail under his Grandfather's Will. Claimant now is entitled to it as Heir in Tail.

This was Let to one Vinning at £35 Sterling pr Annum, besides Rents, Tenant was to supply the Family with Butter Cheaper than the Market price 6d instead of 8d per Pound.[17]

Values this at £1500 Sterling.

Was possessed of 2/3 of 4000 Acres in Charlton. Produces Deed from W. Couper to Samuel Browne of 2000 Acres in Oxford in Consideration of £500 dated 1718. £500 equal to £208 Ster[lin]g.

Produces Deed of other 2000 Acres to his Grandfather in Consideration of £400 dated 1717. £400 equal to £166 Sterling.

Claimants Grandfather gives these Lands to Samuel Browne Father to Claimant in fee 2/3ds came to Claimant on his Father's Death. Values these at 15/. pr Acre.

Forrest Lands, no Improvements, brought in no Rent. The Lands are within 15 Miles of Worcester, the Shire Town which makes them Valuable.

Claimant also was possessed of 2/3 of 165 Acres in Fitchbury in Middlesex County purchased by Samuel Browne Claimant's Grandfather before the year 1731. Produces Survey taken in 1769, where by it appears that 165 Acres in Fitchbury are

---

17 He was ordered to leave this farm in April 1775. Oliver, ed., *Pynchon Diary*, 42fn.

Surveyed as the Property of William Browne.

Claimants Grandfather leaves these Lands to his Son Benjamin in fee, on Benjamin's death came to Claimant's Father and to his Uncle William. His Uncle William's Share was disposed of, and went to a Colonel Willard.[18]

The share of the Claimant's Father came by descent to Claimant and his Sister, part is sold. Claimant's present Share is 2/3 of 165 Acres. Forrest unimproved Lands. It appears by a Memorandum that Claimant asked £150 Lawful for these 165 Acres in 1774 £112 Sterling.

Claimant was entitled to 2/3 of 110 Acres in Ashby purchased by Claimants Grandfather before the year 1731. Left by him to Benjamin on his death descended to Claimants Father and Uncle William. This Uncle William's shares went to Colonel Willard. Father's Share came between him and his Sister.

Produces Survey in 1769 where by there appears a Lot of 110 Acres belonging to William Browne. This Survey was made for purpose of dividing the Estate.

Produces Receipt from Claimant of Tax for Lands in Ashby August 1773.

And produces Memorandum of an Agreement made by Colonel Willard who had authority to sell for Claimant, that one Laurence was to have these Lands at 18/ pr Acre. Forrest unimproved Lands. Was also entitled to 2/3 of 285 Acres in Fitchbury, the whole was purchased by Claimant's Grandfather, by him on his Death left to Benjamin, Came to Claimant's Father and Uncle William. Claimant's Father's Share came on his Death to Claimant and his Sister.

Produces Survey in 1768 where by 285 Acres are stated as belonging to Claimant. Claimant entitled to 2/3 of this.

Produces Quit Claim from persons who had purchased from the Representative of his Uncle William his Share. Should have expected three Dollars pr Acre.

Says that the Expences attending these Lands from payment of Taxes make them of high Value after the Taxes due for a Course of Years upon them, are discharged.

Claimant was entitled to a share of Lands in a large Grant in the province of Main[e]. This was originally of 600,000 Acres to Lacon Clarke. He did not perform Conditions, but his Representatives granted the whole (reserving 100,000 Acres to themselves) to ten Associates on Condition they performed. They granted to Twenty Associates reserving 100,000 Acres. These twenty Associates grant 300,000 Acres to Colonel Waldo on condition of his getting a renewal of the Patent and performing the Conditions.

---

[18] Probably Colonel Abijah Willard (1724-1789) from Lancaster, Massachusetts who was a Mandamus Councillor in 1774 and a Loyalist exile who died in New Brunswick. He claimed £6,314 for his losses and received £2,912. Jones, *Loyalists of Massachusetts*, 297-98; *Dictionary of Canadian Biography*, s.v. Abijah Willard.

Waldo got the Patent 40 years ago, and performed the Condition (as Claimant thinks). His Grandfather had one of the twenty Associates Share amounting to 5000 Acres. Half this came to Claimant's Father. Claimant now Claims 2/3 of 2,500.

Produces Receipt for Thirty Shillings of William Brown in full for Taxes on one half a Share in Lands belonging to the propriety called the Twenty Associates of Lincolnshire County.

Signed H. Appleton
Proprietor's Treas[ure]r

1768

Produces ditto Seventeen Shillings in 1768.

These Taxes were not annual but from time to time called for as the Expences were incurred in General about the Lands.

These Lands left to Claimant's Father and Uncle William. Claimants Father's Share came to 2/3 of it to Claimant.

Values the 2500 Acres at £150 Ster[lin]g.

Was entitled to several Lots in the Town of Hadley. Produces Account of the said Lots copied from Proprietor's Books. Where by appear 32 Lots in Claimant's Name containing different Quantities of Land. They are two Miles in length, but some of them very narrow, quite stripes. Knows not how to value them. Claimant's Share 2/3 of Moiety of 1060 Acres.

These Lands were left by Claimants Grandfather to Benjamin, came on his death to Claimant's Uncle and Father. Claimant is entitled to 2/3 of his Father's Share.

Claimant was entitled to a Moiety of a Proprietor's Right in Yarmouth No. 95. Produces Letter from Proprietor's Clerk. Values it at £33..15. Claims 2/3. N.B. The Lands are Sold & Claimant withdraws his Claim for them.[19]

Claimant cannot at present produce Evidence respecting his Lands in Springfield.

Claimant is in the Notorious Conspirators Act, under this Act the Estates of the Persons therein mentioned are forfeited. Claimant says this extends to forfeiture of Estates Tail.

Negroes.

Claimant was possessed of several Negroes on his Estate at Connecticut in No. 11.

When Claimant thought of improving his Farm in Connecticut he purchased three Negroes and one Woman whom he left on the Estate, afterwards purchased three

---

[19] N.B. placed to immediate left of the preceding paragraph.

or four which were sent to the Farm on Claimants Estate of which his Agent's Son was in possession.

These Negroes were on the Estate. The Administrator of the Estate would not sell them having doubt about the Legality of such Sale, but let them go away as they liked. They are all lost to Claimant.

The Administrator in his Account of Sales of Claimant's Estate mentions Eleven Negroes being on the Estate when Governor Browne left it, value £45 each.

Furniture at his Dwelling House at Salem [Massachusetts], proportioned to the goodness of the House. Saved his Plate and Linen.

This Loss appears to have been accidental. The Furniture was left in the House, and was removed on Account of Fires, by removal and pillaging most of it was lost or spoilt.[20]

The Library was under the same Circumstances.
Values Furniture £500
Library   150

£500 for Furniture includes two Slaves who have got their Liberty owing to the Confusion of the times.[21]

States Debts £1400.

Produces Certificate of Sale of Real and personal Estate of Claimant in the province of Massachusetts of a Sum equal (so far as had been sold) to £3024..11..6 Sterling.

Claims allowed by Commissioners on the Estate in Massachusetts £934 Lawful, Interest £40.

Claimant supposes about £700 Lawful fairly due.

Claimant says he was also in possession of some other Real Estate in Salem.

Two Rights or Rights for two Cows in great Pasture of Salem, purchased by his Grandfather. Values them at £9 Sterling each.

Had made use of one Right himself and let his Mother use the other.

Pew in first Meeting House belonged to his Grandfather, values it at £33..15..

---

[20] The diary of John Pynchon referenced the fact that his course was "broken [into] by the rabble." Oliver, ed., *Pynchon Diary*, 42fn.

[21] Two Massachusetts slaves, presumably household servants, and eleven Connecticut make a total of 13.

Pew in Saint Peters' Church. Value £9 Ster[lin]g.

Produces Deed from William Eppes to Claimant of a Pew in Saint Peters Church in Considerationof £12 Lawful.

Pew in a Meeting House. Produces Deed from Committee of Proprietors of North Meeting House to Claimant of half a Pew No. 16 in Consideration of £15..5 Lawful 1772. Values it at £12.

Produces Deed of another Pew No. 18 in Consideration of £28..10 Lawful 1772. £21 Sterling.

Ditto No. 19 1773. Consideration £24..10 Lawful.

*****

Doctor Jonathan Prince, Sworn,[22]

Remembers Governor Browne living at Salem, his Mansion House built by his Grandfather was a large House, three Stories, 17 Rooms, large handsome Rooms. Gardens, Offices, Stables compleat, thought best House and best Situation in the place.

It has been bought since the Confiscation by a Relative of Witness at about £2250 Sterling.[23] Thinks this a high price. Thinks would have fetched nearly the same Sum before the Troubles.

No. 2. Knew the House where Claimant's Mother lived. Remembers Claimants building it.

An handsome House with three Rooms on a Floor, this Floor, this has been sold since the Confiscation to Nathan Goodale who gave £750 Sterling. Values it in 1774 at near that Sum.[24]

No. 3. Remembers the House and the Wharf. There were several persons who held different parts of the Wharf. The Wharf run 200 Feet at least on the River. Should think this together must have been worth £1000.

No. 4 House where Flagg lived, remembers Claimant building the Store. Has been purchased by a Relation of Witness for £900 Lawful. Values it above £500 Sterling.

Knew the House where Gardiner lived, this belonged to the Family as Witness thinks undivided between Claimant and his Cousin.

---

[22] According to Salem vital records, a Jonathan Prince was born in that town on April 13, 1735, the son of Dr. Jonathan who died in November 1759. Vital Records of Salem, II, 198; VI, 162.

[23] The Commissioners awarded Browne just £500 sterling for this valuable property. Governor Willm. Brown late of Salem, AmLC, AOP, AO 12/61. The relative referred to was Elias Hasket Derby.

[24] Browne was awarded just £200 for this house. Ibid.

This House has been purchased since Confiscation at £900 Sterling. Thinks the whole House worth that Money.

On being asked how it could be worth so much, as Rent was so little. Says purchasers used to think themselves well off it they got 3 or 2 1/2 pr Cent for their Money.

Knew his Lands at Stage point. Remembers Claimant in possession, opposite to the Centre of the Town on the other Side of the River. Divided into different Lotts, thinks it consisted of about 40 Acres. One spot was particularly valuable. It was a place where Ships were hauled down, to repair.

Claimant has been told by a Tenant since the Confiscation that a small spot of half an Acre brought in £45 Sterling in one year from the Profits of Ships hauling on it.

That near the River was useful for drying Fish, the other Land was chiefly Grass, very convenient to the Town. A very valuable Tract. Thinks this would fairly have been worth from £50 to £60 Sterling pr Acre. That next the Water was richly worth £60 Sterling pr Acre.

Remembers him in possession of Vinning's Farm. Was Valuable. It was good Land well situated. Values the Farm at £10 Sterling pr Acre but speaks doubtfully.

As to Charlton Lands, Witness had himself Lands in a Town near Charlton which he sold at 30 Shillings Sterling pr Acre. They had small Improvements upon them. Such Lands were obliged to pay Taxes. Tho' unimproved, but it was not usual to Escheat them. Used to be Sold for Non Payment of Taxes.

His House at Salem was well furnished.

Remembers he had Rights in the Great Pasture of Salem. Thinks them worth £9 Sterling each.

Has heard he had large Property in Connecticut. It was reckoned very Valuable from being so near [New] London and Norwich.

Speaks highly in favor of his Character.

August 11th 1786.

****

As to Property in Massachusetts.

Produces Copy of Deed from Joseph Bowditch to Claimant of a piece of Land in South field in Salem in Consideration of £75 Lawful. 1764.

Produces Copy of Deed from Samuel Swazey to Colonel Samuel Brown for a parcel of Salt Marsh in Salem containing one Acre and an half, in consideration of £20 passable Money. 1728.

Produces Deed from Ebenezer Bowditch to Claimant of a lot in Salem containing 4 1/2 Acres in Consideration of £200 Lawful. 1760.

Produces Copy of Conveyance from Israel Hutchinson, Dummer, Jewett, three Commissioners of Forfeited Estates, of a parcel of Land in Salem, on part of which the Mansion House formerly of Claimant stands to Elias Heshel [sic] Derby in consideration of £6050 in Massachusetts Gov[ernmen]t Securities. They sell the same in fee, and Warrant the same in the name of the Commonwealth to the Purchaser in fee.

Produces Copy of Deed from William Hynd to Colonel Brown of 12 Acres in Marblehead in a place called the plain Farms in Consideration of £50 Current passable Money of New England.1728.

Produces Copy of Deed from John Marston to Colonel Samuel Browne of a parcel of Land in Stage Point in Salem containing about 3 Acres in Consideration of £54 Currency, dated 1718.

Produces Deed from William Saunders to Colonel Samuel Browne of 100 Acres with in the Township of Salem, in consideration of £400 Currency, dated 1711.

Produces Copy of Deed from James Darling to Colonel Samuel Browne of a House and Land in Salem in Consideration of £60 Currency, dated 1716.

Produces Copy of Deed from Joseph Flint to Colonel Samuel Browne of 3 or 4 Acres in Salem, in Consideration of £50 Currency dated 1722.

Produces Certificate to Claimants being possessed of a Pew in Meeting house at Salem and values it at £20 Sterling.
(Signed) James Jeffery - Clerk of the Proprietors of Meeting House - April 1, 1786.

Produces Certificate that Claimant was intitled to 2/3 of 18 1/2 Common Rights in great Pasture of Salem, which have been sold by Commissioners of Confiscated Estates.
(Signed) Jos. Clough — Clerk of Proprietors - April 1786.

Produces Certificate that Colonel Samuel Browne was one of original 20 Associates Grantees of Land in Penobscot 5000 Acres to each Share
(Signed) Silvanus Burn — Proprietors' Clerk   May 1786

Certificate that Claimant was owner of one half of the aforesaid Share in 1774.

Produces Certificate Signed John Downing & Peter Boyer, Committee for settling with Commissioners of Sale. That Commissioners of Sale sold in the County of Worcester Lands the Property of Claimant to the amount of £2480 Lawful, equal to £1860 Sterling. May 1786.

N.B. Claimant's Agent Joseph Blaney says in a Letter he is informed the Commissioners sold 1700 Acres for the Sum mentioned in the above Certificate.[25]

As to Property in Connecticut.

Produces affidavit of Eliazer [sic] Backus - that heard Claimant's Estate in Colchester, Lyme and New London, tho' not the exact Number of Acres, very valuable from its Situation. Good Farms and Buildings, well timbered, as valuable as any Land in the Province, divided into Farms. Values it at 15 Dollars pr Acre.

Montreal 11th. Feby. 1788.

John Fisher Esqr. Sworn,[26]

Is acquainted with Governor Wm. Browne, he was one of the Mandamus Council, did not know his Property in Connecticut, knew his House at Salem, a large good House near the Town House, one of the best Houses in Town.

Thinks £1000 Sterling a very considerable Valuation. Catherine Sargent's was a small House.

Knows not the Wharf and Warehouse. Knew he had a Farm at Stage Point, very Valuable.

*****

Joseph Chew Sworn,[27]

Knew the Governor's Estate in Connecticut. It was a large Tract of Land, a good many Tenants upon it. The Tract was between 9 & 10000 Acres 14 Miles from New London, ten from Norwich, 8 from Connecticut, good Lands, fine Ship Timber.

*****

17th February 1788.

Samuel Fitch Sworn,[28]

---

[25] Joseph Blaney was Browne's brother-in-law.

[26] It is not known who John Fisher, Esq. was. It is possible that he belonged to the Fisher family of Dedham and Wrentham, Massachusetts. Four Johns are possibilities but none were Tories. Philip A. Fisher, *The Fisher Genealogy: Record of the Descendants of Joshua, Anthony and Cornelius Fisher, of Dedham, Mass. 1636-1640* (Everett, MA: Massachusetts Publishing Company, 1898), 70, 73, 102, 108.

[27] Loyalist Joseph Chew (1720s-1798) lived in New London during the 1750s and 1760s, worked for Sir William Johnson on Indian Affairs, and moved to Canada after the Revolution. *Dictionary of Canadian Biography*, s. v. Joseph Chew.

[28] Loyalist Samuel Fitch (1724-1784) of Lebanon, Connecticut graduated from Yale College in 1742 and served as a junior officer in King George's War. He moved to Boston, served as *pro tempore* Advocate General for the Court of Admiralty, and departed with the British troops in March 1776. His brother Eleazar (1726-1796), Yale 1743, attained the rank of colonel of Connecticut troops during the French and Indian War,

Knew a good deal of Govr. Brown's Estate in Connecticut. It was a large Estate about 10,000 Acres, frequently passed by the Estate. The Situation makes the Land valuable. Lands sold by the Acre.

Values the Tract if there are Improvements such as he has heard, at £3 pr Acre.

C. Affidavit of Ebenezer Backus, Jr., June 29, 1786[29]

Province of Nova Scotia |
Halifax to wit |

Ebenezer Backus[30] of Norwich in the County of New London in the State of Connecticut Merchant being of the Age of thirty eight Years, deposeth and saith that he was born in Norwich aforesaid, served an Apprenticeship there to Messrs Trumbull, Fitch and Trumbull Merchants and hath been an Inhabitant of said Norwich during his past Life. That he well knows an Estate which formerly belonged to Colonel William Brown late of Salem in the Province of Massachusetts Bay which lies part in the Township of Colchester, Part in the Township of Lime and Part in the Town of New London all in the County of New London aforesaid, and in the Vicinity of said Norwich and New London two Trading Towns scituate on a navigable River. That this Deponent doth not know the exact Number of Acres of which said Estate consisted, but knows that is was an extensive Tract of Land of several Miles in Length and Breadth. That this Deponent well knew the situation and Condition of said Estate in the Year 1774; that there then were a great Number of valuable Farms, Dwelling Houses, Barns and other necessary Building thereon. That a considerable Part of said Estate was then covered with an excellent Growth of good Oak and other Timber fit for the Purpose of Shipbuilding, which from its Situation, being between two navigable Rivers and in no Part more than ten Miles distant from one or the other of them, was very valuable; That the Timber on said Estate, having been, while in the Possession of said Colonel Brown, particularly attended to and preserved, was of a Size and Quality superior to any other

---

formed a mercantile partnership with future governor Jonathan Trumbull and eldest son Joseph Trumbull, became sheriff of Windham County, and like his brother was loyal to the Crown. Dexter, *Yale Graduates*, I, 706-07, 735-37.

29 Affidavit of Ebenezer Backus, June 29, 1786, AOP, AO 13/50, 133-34 and written by him. AO 13/50 also contains copies of records from the Norwich Probate Court on the sale of Browne's lands, including the names of eleven slaves, a list of tenants in 1774, a list of money owed Browne by note and bond, and two lists of lands belonging to Browne's estate.
  This testimony is especially important because it was not made by a Loyalist exile who knew Browne. Backus, a Patriot, happened to be in Halifax at the time Browne's case was being heard and provided contemporary and knowledge based evidence about the value of his New Salem properties. He had no reason to inflate the value of the Connecticut lands. His statement provides confirmation that the former Massachusetts magistrate did not submit a fraudulent claim that magnified the extent of his losses. Fingerhut, "Uses and Abuses," 252-53.

30 Backus was born in Norwich in January 1743/4 and was a merchant in Norwich. He placed an advertisement as early as December 1772 for the sale of goods newly imported from London. *Vital Records of Norwich*, 254, 393; *Connecticut Gazette*, December 11, 1772, [1].

in that Part of the then Colony of Connecticut near the Sea Coast or navigable Waters, and for that Reason most of the Timber used in Constructing the Continental Frigate Confederacy which was built in the Year 1779 was procured from said Estate; That said Estate was properly divided into Farms and Tenements, in some Parts with Stone Walls which Farms and Tenements were in the Occupation of Industrious and Thrifty Tenants, was well watered and was estimated to be as good and as valuable a Tract of Land as any equal Quantity, lying in any Place within said State, it being to this Deponents Knowledge very productive, he having purchased in the Year 1781 and carried from of the same several hundred Tons of English Hay, the Produce of one Season as he supposed, which he transported to the State of Rhode Island for Use of the French Army then stationed there. This Deponent further saith that he verily believes that the said Estate taking the Whole of it together was in the said Year 1774 reasonably worth fifteen Dollars Per Acre at a moderate valuation, and he further saith that he hath Known it to have been estimated at a higher Rate particularly by one Thomas Shaw of New London aforesaid an opulent and principal Merchant there who declared that he should be glad to lay out the whole of his Property, so far as it would go, in the Purchase of said Estate at the Rate of five Pounds lawfull Money of said State at six shillings the Spanish Mill'd Dollar Per Acre, if he could obtain it at that Price.[31] That this Declaration was made by said Shaw in the Year 1783 when said Lands were of much less Value than in the Year 1774 and further this Deponent saith not.

Ebenr Backus Junr	Sworn at Halifax this | 29th day of June 1786 before | William Taylor Just P

D. Peter Hunter to Governor William Browne, July 20, 1786[32]

Office of Amer[ica]n Claims
Halifax 20th July 1786.

Sir.

I am directed by the Commissioners of American Claims to inform you that in deciding upon your Claim.

They have considered your Property in the Estate in Lime, Colchester, New London, at Stage Point & Forest River Farm only as a Life Interest, as these Estates appear to have been entailed & you have produced no Proof of the Entail being cut off.

The Commissioners further desire to inform you that they shall not report upon your Claim until they shall hear further from you, or satisfy them that those Entailed Estates are held to be forfeited and not recoverable by the Issue in Tail.

---

31 As can be seen in Table C, Shaw purchased lot 26 containing 1,094 acres on March 7, 1783 and after the date of the Backus deposition purchased Lots 4, 8, 34, 46, and 17 with another 1,287 acres. Thomas's father Nathaniel bought Lots 12 and 21 with a total of 217 acres in 1782.

32 Peter Hunter to Governor Brown, AmLC, AOP, AO 12/139.

I am Sir &,

His Excellency
Govr. Brown   Peter Hunter Secy.
Bermuda

E. Award to William Browne[33]

Governor Will. Brown late of Salem

Claim   £32,256

Determination 15th. July 1786.

Loyalty.   The Claimant is Loyalist & Rendered Services to Great Britain.

Losses

Real Estate	9663 Acres in Lime, Colchester & New London in Connect[icu]t Province. ~~Entailed the Comm[issione]rs give the Claimant for his Life Interest therein after deducting his Share of Incumbrances~~	£5000
	A House in Salem where Claimant lived	500
	A House where Claimants Mother lived	200
	A House & Wharf in Salem	170
	Ware House & Land in Do.	120
	4/9ths. of a House in Do.	70
	1/2 of a Cellar under theTown House in Do.	25
	37 Acres at Stage Point in Salem ~~the Estate being entailed the Comm[issione]rs give the Claimant~~	245
~~for his life Interest therein~~		

A Farm called Forrest River Farm ~~but being entail'd the Comm[issione]rs gives the Claimant for his Life Interest therein~~   335

6,665

Amount Brought forward[34]		£6665
2/3rds of 4000 Acres in Charlton	£333	
His Share in several Tracts of Land ~~unimproved~~	150	
	483	
		£7,148
Persl. Estate Negroes		210
Furniture & Library		200
For several Pews in Churches and meeting Houses		100

---

[33] Governor Willm. Brown late of Salem, AmLC, AOP, AO 12/61.

[34] From previous page.

at Salem

510

£7,658

Pr. Annum Income

Judge of the Superior Court of Mass[achuset]ts   200

Observation.

The Claimant was on of the Mandamus Councillors & his Name appears in the Notorious Conspirators Act. The Claimant has recovered 400£ for occasional Assistance from Government &c Pension of £200 pr. Annum till February 1781 when he was appointed Governor of Bermuda which he now enjoys with Salary of £750 pr. Annum.

Confiscation proved.

Resides at Bermuda.

Glossary

debt by bond -   a written promise to pay money or do some act by a specific time

debt by book -   the record of a sale in an accounting journal of a shopkeeper or merchant

debt by note -   a written promise by one party to pay money to another party

default -   failure of defendant to appear at the court date and, therefore, admitting guilt

execution -   the act of carrying out or putting a court order into effect

femme covert -   a married woman under the protection or cover of her husband

femme sole -   an unmarried woman

grantee -   purchaser of plot of land

grantor -   seller of parcel of land

no appearance -   both parties failing to appear at court date

nonsuit -   a plaintiff's voluntary dismissal of a case without a decision on its merits

tenant -   a householder who rents and occupies lands and/or buildings from another

withdrawn -   to take back or refrain from prosecuting, often by an agreement by parties in court filing before trial

Bibliography

The Connecticut Archives (CA), Connecticut General Assembly Records to 1820, are an invaluable resource for anyone studying the history of the state to 1820. The records are divided into twenty-eight subject categories, like Ecclesiastical Affairs, Militia, Revolutionary War, and Towns and Lands, fifteen of which have been used in this work. They are further subdivided into series. The Connecticut Archives are superbly indexed and every name mentioned in any volume is listed. Thus, it is possible after examining the indexes for each person of interest to find out out how many times James Harris is mentioned. The records were organized and bound between 1841 and 1843 and are readily available on microfilm at the Connecticut State Library in Hartford.[1]

Connecticut court records comprise an equally important primary source.[2] For this essay, two series of Hartford County Court Records (HCC), New London County Records (NLCC), Windham County Court Records (WCC), and Connecticut Superior Court Records (CSC) have special relevance. The first consists of bound volumes called Trials or Records that contain summaries of court cases usually a paragraph in length. For most purposes, the bound volumes are sufficient, but those needing more information must examine Files, the original documents filed with each court and stored in boxes. For debts by note, for example, the original writ or summons is invariably found and often the note is included in the documentation for the lawsuit. For bond debts, one can sometimes learn about the conditions of the bond. Sometimes the volume merely states that the suit was for damages and one must go to Files to find the specifics. As a rule, when a case was appealed and tried before the superior court, more information is found, as all documentation gathered for trial before the county court is included and often more data gathered for the new trial, like depositions and lawyers' arguments. In addition, several series of New London County Court: Papers by Subject also contain useful information, in particular those for Summons for Evidence and Travel.[3]

---

1 Sylvie J. Turner, "The Connecticut Archives," *Connecticut Historical Society Bulletin*, 33 (July 1968), 81-89. Special permission is required to examine the originals.

2 For an overview of the Connecticut court system during the eighteenth century, see, Stark, "Connecticut Court System," 21-82. For more detail on the organization and content of Files and Papers by Subject, see the following finding aids: Finding Aid to New London County, County Court, Files, 1691-1855, 70 pages; Finding Aid to New London County, County Court, Papers by Subject, 1685-1856, 21 pages; Finding Aid to New London County, Superior Court, Files, 1711-1800, 33 pages; Finding Aid to New London County, Superior Court, Papers by Subject, 1711-1900, 22 pages. Approximately half of each finding aid is devoted to description of the contents of the records and half to the box and folder list. All include illustrations of selected documents. In addition, each gives guidelines on how to use court records.

3 The records in Papers by Subject consist of materials that were removed from Files after the the court records

The author has made extensive use of court records.[4] They are, however, difficult to use because the sole indexing consists of dockets for each court session that list plaintiffs and defendants, not all of which are extant, and relatively few scholars have the fortitude for this endeavor.[5] Despite the fact that I spent a good part of my career at the Connecticut State Library processing, arranging, and describing New London Court Records, additional months were still devoted to ploughing through the bound volumes of Trials/Records in the search for relevant information.[6] The task is not for the meek, but the rewards for this labor are significant.[7]

Justice of the Peace records can also be of considerable assistance. Many are no longer extant because justices usually held court in their homes or taverns and the records documenting their work were considered personal papers. Hence, most have disappeared. In this endeavor, only a handful of relevant justice records have been used.

The third important primary source is land records. Original manuscript volumes can be examined in town halls, while microfilm copies are located at the Connecticut State Library. The author examined them both at the CSL and in town clerk offices. Land records are indexed by grantor and grantee. Typed master grantee and grantor indexes exist for each town. In addition, each volume of land records has its own handwritten index that may include references to transactions not recorded in master indexes. Land records for Colchester (CLR), Lyme (LLR), and New London (NLLR) have been extensively cited.

With regard to probate records, two forms exist, first, the record books kept by the judges for each district and, second, separate packets of probate files arranged by district and then by surname and first name containing loose copies of wills, inventories, etc. Copies for both exist on microfilm at the Connecticut State Library. The former are cited by probate district, volume, and page and the latter by town, date, probate district, and number. The State Library has a master card index that gives citations to the file packets, but no master index exists for the probate record books. Researchers must look at the handwritten indexes at the front of each volume to find the page(s) for

---

had been transferred to the Connecticut State Library. Although this practice violates archival principles, the results do make court records somewhat more user friendly, for most researchers who examine Files do not find it necessary to look for supplementary information in Papers by Subject. Stark, "Connecticut Court System," 42-47. Anyone who examines this set of records, however, will see that some items are misfiled. In the Summons for Evidence series, as an example, the researcher will also find depositions, costs, orders, and presentments among other papers.

[4] Records for the New London County Court from 1775 to June 1781 were destroyed when the British under Benedict Arnold raided New London on September 6, 1781 and Files for Hartford County contain a number of gaps and are in extremely poor physical condition.

[5] The dockets are generally arranged by name of the plaintiff usually either in numerical or alphabetical order.

[6] Trials or Records do not generally contain information on cases not brought to trial, like those in which there was no appearance or the parties withdrew the suit. Records of these lawsuits, some of which are important, can only be found by a thorough examination of Files.

[7] In many instances, if the person of interest has spent most his or her life in a single town or area, then the researcher can find most of the court data in the records of a single county court and whatever scattered justice of the peace records from the jurisdiction that are extant, but economic lives were not necessarily restricted to activities in one county. Such was especially true if the individual or individuals of interest lived in a town bordering on another county. Throughout much of the eighteenth-century Colchester was part of Hartford County, yet it bordered on New London and Windham Counties, thus necessitating a search of these records.

the individuals sought because sometimes the will, inventory of the estate, and other documentation are not adjacent to one another. The file packets are more user friendly. In theory, both the bound volumes and the file packets contain the same information, but this is not always the case.

Town records, in particular, accounts of the town treasurers provide detailed information on expenditures, for the poor, maintenance of highways, etc. Town meeting records and tax lists are also fruitful sources for examination. Unfortunately, town meetings records for Lyme are missing from the early 1730s to 1801, as are those for New London from around 1690 to 1740. The earliest town meeting records for Colchester can be found in Volume 1 of Colchester Record of Births, Marriages, Deaths (ColchesterBMD).

A good deal of scattered information of value can also be found in eighteenth-century newspapers, around twenty-five of which have been used in this study. The easiest way to access them is through the American Antiquarian Society's Early American Newspapers Project and searching by name, subject, or town. Early American Newspapers use Optical Character Recognition (OCR) to retrieve data and OCR will capture much useful information, but not all due to the limitations of the technology. To derive maximum value from this important resource, the researcher should search by colony and not specifically by newspaper and be aware of name variations, for example, William Browne, William Brown, W. Browne, etc. Early American Newspapers are generally good enough, but people need to understand that only a page-by-page examination of individual titles will retrieve all relevant information.

Finally, for those who wish to really get down into the weeds and have too much time on their hands, account books can provide bits and nits of important information. For this study, the medical account books of John R. Watrous of Colchester and Daniel Caulkins of the East Society in Lyme have proven to be particularly useful.

Some reference, then, to all but the most obscure white males can be found in at least one these resources and, in addition, to a significant proportion of females and people of color.

As one can see from below, the collections at the Connecticut State Library have been essential for this project, as, indeed, they are for virtually all studies of Connecticut history.

Manuscript Collections

American Loyalist Claims, Audit Office Papers, National Archives of the United Kingdom

Connecticut Archives, CSL
        Civil Officers, Series 1
        Ecclesiastical Affairs, Series 1
        Ecclesiastical Affairs, Series 2
        Estates of Deceased Persons
        Finance and Currency, Series 2
        Industry, Series 1
        Industry, Series 2
        Insolvent Debtors, Series 2

Militia, Series 1
Militia, Series 2
Miscellaneous, Series 1
Miscellaneous, Series 2
Private Controversies, Series 2
Revolutionary War, Series 1
Revolutionary War, Series 3
Susquehanna Settlers, Western Lands, Series 1
Towns and Lands, Series 1
Trade and Maritime Affairs, Series 1
Travel, Highways, Ferries, etc., Series 1
Travel, Highways, Ferries, etc., Series 2
Wars, Colonial, Series 1

Early General Records, Connecticut Colonial Records, CSL

Land Records, CSL and town halls
Colchester Land Records
East Haddam Land Records
Hebron Land Records
Killingly Land Records
Lyme Land Records
New London Land Records
Salem Land Records
Stafford Land Records
Union Land Records

Probate Records, CSL
Colchester Probate District
New London Probate District
Norwich Probate District
Old Lyme Probate District

Barbour Collection, Connecticut Vital Records, CSL
Colchester
Lyme
Norwich

Church Records, CSL
East Lyme, Baptist Community Church of Flanders (formerly Lyme First
Baptist Church) Records, Volumes 2-3, 1797-1859
Lyme Church Records, Vol. 1, 1787-1850
Montville Congregational Church Records, 1722-1827, Vol. 3
Putnam First Congregational Church Records (formerly North Killingly), Index

RG 002, General Assembly Records, CSL

General Assembly Papers, 1821-1870, African Americans (photocopies of
    originals)
Rejected Bills, 1808-1870, African Americans (photocopies of originals)

RG 003, Court Records, CSL
    Early Records, Connecticut Superior Court, 1713-1798
    Hartford County Court Records. Dockets and Records
    Hartford County Court Records. Files
    Hartford County Court Records. Papers by Subject
    Hartford County Court Records. Records
    John Watrous Court Records, [Colchester] 1767-1790
    Justice Court Records of William Noyes, [Lyme] 1790-1806
    New Haven County Court Records. Trials
    New Haven County Superior Court Records. Files
    New London County Court Records. Files
    New London County Court Records. Papers by Subject
    New London County Court Records. Trials
    New London County Court Records, African Americans (photocopies of
        originals)
    New London County Court Records, Native Americans (photocopies of
        originals)
    New London County Superior Court Records. Files
    New London County Superior Court Records. Papers by Subject
    New London Justice of the Peace Records, 1755-1903
    Windham County Court Records. Trials

RG 008, Office of the Comptroller, CSL
    Audited Vouchers, 1757-1819
    Journals B-C
    Ledgers, 1788-1852
    Reports, Vol. 1, 1800-09
    Register of Army Notes
    Waste Books 9-14

RG 019, Department of Social Services. State Board of Charities. Pauper Accounts, CSL

RG 062, Municipal Records, CSL
    East Haddam Town Records, 1762-1896
    Lyme Town Records, 1781-1910
    New London Town Records, 1674-1925

Bermuda Archives and Government Records Center
    Deeds and Plans of William Browne's Estate in the United States
    The Letters of William Browne, Esq. of Salem, Mass.
    Transcripts of Deeds and Plans of William Browne's Estate in the United
        States

Colonial North America at Harvard Library

Dreer Collection, Historical Society of Pennsylvania

Essex County Probate Records, Massachusetts State Archives

Gratz Collection, Historical Society of Pennsylvania

Massachusetts Historical Society Trumbull Papers, CSL

Manuscripts

1790 United States Census, Connecticut, microfilm, CSL.

American Revolution Collection, Box 10, Letters (Copies), CHS.

Caples, Joseph Albert. "Memoirs of the Caples Family," Volume 1, CSL.

Caulkins, Dr. Daniel, Account Book, 1766-1788, CHS.

Colchester Accounts of Expenses, 1779-1797, Colchester Town Hall.

Colchester Record of Births, Marriages, Deaths, 1713-1894, Volumes 1-2, Colchester Town Hall.

Colchester Town Records, 1708-1884, CHS.

Colchester Town Records, 1797-1805, Colchester Town Hall.

Colchester Town Records, 1805-1842, Colchester Town Hall.

Colchester Treasurer Records, 1791-1830, Colchester Town Hall.

Colchester Town Meeting Records, Vol. 1, 1780-1828, Colchester Town Hall.

Comstock, Peter, Account Book, 1825-1838, CHS.

Confederacy (Ship) Papers, Historical Society of Pennsylvania.

Fourth Census of the United States, 1820. Volumes 3, 7, Photostat, CSL.

Lyme Day Book, 1796-1809, Lyme Town Hall.

Lyme Day Book, 1810-1827, CSL.

Lyme Pauper Lists, Lyme Town Hall.

Lyme Town Meeting Records, Vol. 3, 1801-1855, Lyme Town Hall.

Mather, Samuel, Account Book 1773-1796, CHS.

Mitchell-Tiffany Family Papers, Manuscripts & Archives, Yale University Library.

New London Town Meeting Records, 1740-1789, New London City Hall.

New London Town Records, Freeman, 1730-1775, New London City Hall.

New London Town Records, Record of Ear Marks, 1691-1807, New London City Hall.

Raymond, Oliver to Isaac Spencer, January 15, 1831, CHS.

Smith Family Papers, 1723-1841, CHS.

Trumbull, Jonathan, Sr. Papers, CHS.

Trumbull Manuscript Collections, Vol. 1, Beinecke Rare Book and Manuscript Library.

Warner, Selden, Ledger, Hadlyme, 1790-1809, CHS.

Warren, Moses, Jr., Diary, 1789-90, CHS.

Watrous, Dr. John. Medical Account Book A, 1781-1798, CSL.

Watrous, Dr. John R. Account Books B-C, 1791-1818, CHS.

Will of Samuel Browne, Essex County Probate Records, MSA.

Newspapers

Boston Evening-Post

Boston Gazette

Boston News-Letter. Later the *Massachusetts Gazette.*

Boston Post-Boy.

[Boston] *Weekly Rehearsal.*

The City Gazette [Charleston, SC].

Connecticut Gazette [New London], originally the *New-London Gazette.*

The Day [New London].

Essex Gazette [Salem], later *Salem Gazette.*

Essex Journal.

Hartford Courant. Formerly called the *Connecticut Courant.*

Litchfield Monitor.

Massachusetts Gazette

Massachusetts Spy.

New-England Weekly Journal.

New-York Weekly Journal.

New London Summary.

Newport Mercury.

New York Evening Post.

New-York Gazette and Weekly Mercury.

Norwich Bulletin.

Norwich Packet.

The Pennsylvania Gazette.

Pennsylvania Journal.

Providence Gazette.

Weekly Rehearsal [Boston].

Printed Primary Sources

"Abstracts from Wills, Inventories, &c., on File in the Office of Clerk of Courts, Salem, Mass." *Historical Collections of the Essex Institute,* I (April 1859): 3-5.

Acts and Laws of his Majesty's English Colony of Connecticut in New-England in America. New-London: Timothy Green, 1750.

Adair, Douglas & John A. Schutz. *Peter Oliver's Origin & Progress of the American Revolution: A Tory View*. Stanford, CA: Stanford University Press, 1961.

"An Order to Warn Soldiers." *Historical Collections of the Essex Institute*, II (June 1860), 154-55.

Bartlet, William S. *The Frontier Missionary: A Memoir of the Life of the Rev. Jacob Bailey, A.M. . . .* Boston: Ide and Dutton, 1853.

"Births in Medway, Mass., 1714-1744." *New England Historical and Genealogical Register*, 49 (October 1895): 444-49.

Boyle, John. "Boyle's Journal of Occurrences in Boston, 1759-1778. *New England Historic and Genealogical Register*, 90 (October 1931).

Bridenbaugh, Carl, ed. *Gentleman's Progress: The Itinerarium of Dr. Alexander Hamilton 1744*. Pittsburgh: University of Pittsburgh Press, 1948.

"Browne Family Letters." *New England Historical and Genealogical Register*, 25 (October 1871): 352-55.

Burr, Jean Chandler, ed. *Lyme Records, 1667-1730: A Literal Transcription of the Minutes of the Town Meetings with Marginal Notations, to which hath been Appended Land Grants and Ear Marks*. Stonington: The Pequot Press, Inc., 1968.

Collections of the Massachusetts Historical Society, Series 1-7. Boston: Massachusetts Historical Society, 1792-1915.

Connecticut Headstone Inscriptions, Charles R. Hale Collection. Vol. 106. Connecticut State Library.

"Deaths in Stratham, N. H." *New England Historical and Genealogical Register*, 73 (October 1895): 62-77.

Dexter, Franklin Bowditch, ed. *Extracts from the Itineraries and Other Miscellanies of Ezra Stiles, D.D., LL.D. 1755-1794 with a Selection from his Correspondence*. New Haven: Yale University Press, 1916.

———. *The Literary Diary of Ezra Stiles, D.D., LL.D*. 3 Volumes. New York: Charles Scriber's Sons, 1901.

Donnan, Elizabeth. *Documents Illustrative of the History of the Slave Trade to America, Vol. III, New England and the Middle Colonies*. Washington, DC: Carnegie Institution of Washington, 1932.

Dow, George Francis, ed. *Records and Files of the Quarterly Courts of Essex County*. 9

volumes. Salem, MA: Essex Institute, 1911-75.

"Essex County Estates Administered in Suffolk County, Prior to 1701." *Essex Institute Historical Collections*, XLI (April 1905): 180-82.

"Essex County Notarial Records." *Essex Institute Historical Collections*, XLI (April 1905): 183-92; (October 1905): 381-98; XLII (April 1906): 153-68; XLIV (October 1908): 130-36.

Farrell, John T., ed. *The Superior Court Diary of William Samuel Johnson 1772-1773*. Washington: The American Historical Association, 1942.

Five Black Lives. Introduction by Arna Bontemps. Middletown: Wesleyan University Press, 1971.

From Wills, Inventories, &c., on File in the Office of Clerk of Courts, Salem, Mass." Historical Collections of the Essex Institute, April 1859, 3-12.

The General Laws For the People of Connecticut. Cambridge, MA: Printed by Samuel Green, 1673.

"Gleanings from the Records of the County of Essex." *Essex Institute Historical Collections*, XIII (April 1877): 135-42.

Governor and Company of Connecticut and Moheagan Indians, by their Guardians. Certified Copy of Book of Proceedings before Commissioners of Review, 1743. London: W. & J. Richardson, 1769.

Harvard College Records, Parts I and II, in *Publications of the Colonial Society of Massachusetts*, 15-16. Boston: The Society, 1925.

Heads of Families at the First Census of the United States Taken in the Year 1790. Washington: Government Printing Office, 1908.

Hempstead, Joshua. *The Diary of Joshua Hempstead, 1711-1758*. New London: The New London County Historical Society, Inc., 1901, 1999.

Hoadly, Charles J. et al. *The Public Records of the State of Connecticut*. 21 vols. Hartford: various publishers, 1894-2015.

Howes, Martha O. and Sidney Perley. *Town Records of Salem, Massachusetts*. 2 vols. Salem: The Essex Institute, 1868, 1913.

Jackman, Sydney W., ed. "Letters of William Browne, American Loyalist." *Essex Institute Historical Collections*, 96 (January 1960): 1-46.

"James Jeffry's Journal for the Year 1724." *Essex Institute Historical Collections*, XXXVI (October 1900): 325-30.

Jenks, John of Salem to Cotton Tufts of Weymouth, August 26, 1774. *Essex Institute Historical Collections*, XLVII (April 1911): 230-32.

Law, Jonathan. *The Law Papers: Correspondence and Documents During Jonathan Law's Governorship of the Colony of Connecticut, 1741-1750.* Volume I. Hartford: The Connecticut Historical Society, 1907.

"A List of Subscribers Towards the Bell of St. Peter's Church." *Essex Institute Historical Collections,* II (October 1860): 258-59.

Loring, George B., ed. "Some Account of Houses and Other Buildings in Salem, From a Manuscript of the Late Col. Benjamin Pickman." *Essex Institute Historical Collections*, VI (June 1864): 93-109.

Mather, Cotton. *Johannes in eremo: memoirs relating to the lives of the ever-memorable . . .* [Boston]: Michael Perry, 1695.

Mather, Cotton. *Virtue in it's verdure.: A Christian exhibited as a green olivetree, in the House of God; with a character of the virtuous Mrs. Abigail Brown: (the amiable and memorable consort of the Honourable Samuel Brown, Esq;) who expired Feb. 18. 1724,5.* Boston: Printed by B. Green, 1725.

Monday, Robert E., ed. *The Saltonstall Papers, 1607-1815.* 2 Volumes. Boston: Massachusetts Historical Society, 1972, 1974.

"Newspaper Items Relating to Essex County, Massachusetts." *Essex Institute Historical Collections*, LI (April 1915): 131-36; (October 1915): 282-89.

Nicolson, Colin, ed. *The Papers of Francis Bernard: Governor of Colonial Massachusetts, 1760-69.* 5 vols. Boston: The Colonial Society of Massachusetts, 2007-15.

Norwich, Vital Records of, 1659-1848. Part 1. Hartford: Society of Colonial Wars in the State of Connecticut. 1913.

Oath of Allegiance, Lyme, Conn., 1777-1784. Lyme Public Hall Archives.

Oliver, Andrew, ed. *The Journal of Samuel Curwen, Loyalist.* Cambridge: Harvard University Press, 1972.

Oliver, F. E., ed. *Diaries of Benjamin Lynde and Benjamin Lynde, Jr.* Boston: privately printed, 1880.

Oliver, Fitch Edward, ed. *The Diary of William Pynchon of Salem.* Boston: Houghton,

Mifflin and Company, 1890.

Perley, Sidney. "Evidence Relative to the Authenticity of the 'First Church' (So-Called in Salem." *Essex Institute Historical Collections*, XXXIX (July 1903): 229-93.

————, compiler. "Extracts from Salem School Committee Records." *Essex Institute Historical Collections*, XCI (January 1955); 24-72.

Pierce, Richard D., ed. *The Records of the First Church in Salem, Massachusetts, 1629-1716*. Salem, MA: Essex Institute, 1974.

The Public Statute Laws of the State of Connecticut. Hartford: Printed by Hudson and Goodwin, 1808.

Records of the Court of Assistants of the Colony of Massachusetts Bay, 1630-1692. 3 volumes. Boston: Published by the County of Suffolk, 1901-28.

Records of the Particular Court of Connecticut 1639-1663. Hartford: The Connecticut Historical Society, 1928.

"Representatives of the Town of Boston in the General Court before the American Revolution." *Collections of the Massachusetts Historical Society*, Second Series, X (1823): 23-29.

A RETURN of the Number of INHABITANTS in the State of CONNECTICUT, February 1, 1782; and also of the Indians and Negroes. Broadside, CSL.

"Salem Commoners Records, 1713-1739." *Essex Institute Historical Collections*, XXXVI (April 1900): 161-84; XXXVII (January 1901): 81-104.

"Sam'l Browne - Merchant in Salem - His Instructions to Capt. John Touzell - Voyage to the West Indies." *Historical Collections of Essex Institute*, I (May 1859): 66.

Sewell, Samuel. "Diary of Samuel Sewall." *Collections of the Massachusetts Historical Society*, Fifth Series, V-VII (1878-82).

Sewell, Samuel. "Letter-Book of Samuel Sewall." *Collections of the Massachusetts Historical Society*, Sixth Series, I-II (1886, 1888).

"Suffolk County Deeds. Volume I." *The Essex Antiquarian*, IX (July 1905): 97-104.

Taintor, Charles M. *Extracts from the Records of Colchester, with some Transcripts from the Recordings of Michaell Taintor, of "Brainford."* Hartford: Press of Case, Lockwood and Company, 1864.

Talcott, Joseph. *The Talcott Papers: Correspondence and Documents (Chiefly Official) during Joseph Walcott's Governorship of Connecticut, 1724-41*, 2 volumes. Hartford: The Connecticut Historical Society, 1892, 1894.

"To Coron'll Samuel Brown Esq." *Historical Collections of Essex Institute,* I (July 1859): 83-84.

Trumbull, J. Hammond and Charles J. Hoadly. *The Public Records of the Colony of Connecticut.* 15 volumes. Hartford: Brown & Parsons, 1850-1890.

Tyler, John W., ed. *The Correspondence of Thomas Hutchinson. Volume I: 1740-1766.* Boston: The Colonial Society of Massachusetts, 2014.

Vital Records of Salem, Massachusetts to the End of the Year 1849. 6 Vols. Salem, MA: The Essex Institute, 1916-25.

Ward, George Atkinson. *The Journal and Letters of Samuel Curwen, An American in England, From 1775 to 1783.* 4th edition, Boston: Little, Brown and Company, 1864.

"Will of Samuel Smith." *The Essex Antiquarian,* I (March 1897): 44-45.

Unpublished Secondary Sources

Avitable, Joseph. "The Atlantic World Economy and Colonial Connecticut." Unpublished Ph.D. Dissertation, University of Rochester, 2009.

Bates, George N. "History of Salem, Connecticut." Unpublished manuscript, 1935. Connecticut State Library.

Conroy, Douglas C. "A Disputatious People: New London's Wartime 'Illicit Trade' with the French West Indies (1755-1763)." Unpublished manuscript, 2017.

Grant-Costa, Paul. "The Last Indian War in Southern New England: The Mohegan Tribe of Indians v. The Governour and Company of Connecticut, 1703-1774." Unpublished Ph.D. Dissertation, Yale University, 2008.

Loucks, Rupert Charles. "'Let the oppressed go free': Reformation and Revolution in English Connecti-cut, 1764-1775." Unpublished Ph.D. Dissertation, University of Wisconsin - Madison, 1995.

Pierpiont Bacon Files. Town Historian's Notes, Colchester Town Hall.

Van Dusen, Albert Edward. "The Trade of Revolutionary Connecticut." Unpublished Ph.D. Dissertation, University of Pennsylvania, 1948.

Villiers, David Henry. "Loyalism in Connecticut, 1763-1783." Unpublished Ph.D. Dissertation, University of Connecticut, 1975.

Yang, Guocun. "From Slavery to Emancipation: The African Americans of Connecticut 1630s - 1820s." Unpublished Ph.D. Dissertation, University of Connecticut, 1999.

Published Secondary Sources

American National Biography, s.v. William Browne, Joseph Dudley, Joseph Wanton.

Anderson, Robert Charles, George F. Sanborn, Jr., and Melinde Lutz Sanborn. *The Great Migration: Immigrants to New England 1634-1635.* VII Volumes. Boston: New England Historical Genealogical Society, 1999-2011.

Anderson, Robert Charles. *The Great Migration Begins: Immigrants to New England, 1620-1633*, II. Boston: New England Historic Genealogical Society, 1995.

Archer, Richard. *Jim Crow North: The Struggle for Equal Rights in New England.* New York: Oxford University Press, 2017.

Bailyn, Bernard. *The New England Merchants in the Seventeenth Century.* New York: Harper Torchbooks, 1955, 1964).

————. *The Ordeal of Thomas Hutchinson.* Cambridge, MA: Harvard University Press, 1974.

Baker, Henry A. *History of Montville, Connecticut.* Hartford: Press of The Case, Lockwood & Brained Company, 1896.

Barber, John Warner. *Connecticut Historical Collection.* Storrs, CT: Bibliopole Press, 1999. Facsimile reprint.

Barnes, Eric W. "All the King's Horses . . . All the King's Men." *American Heritage* XI (October 1960): 56-59, 86-87.

Barrow, Thomas C. "The American Revolution as a Colonial War of Independence." *William and Mary Quarterly*, Third Series, XXV, no. 3 (July 1968): 452-64.

Beckwith, Paul. *The Beckwiths.* Albany, NY: Joel Munsel's Sons, Publishers, 1891.

Bentley, William. "A Description and History of Salem." *Collections of the Massachusetts Historical Society*, First Series, VI (1799): 212-88.

Bickford, Christopher P. "The Lost Connecticut Census of 1762 Found." *Connecticut Historical Society Bulletin*, 40 (April 1979): 33-43.

Bingham, Alfred M. "Squatter Settlements of Freed Slaves in New England." *Connecticut Historical Society Bulletin*, 41 (July 1976): 65-80.

————. *The Tiffany Fortune, and Other Chronicles of a Connecticut Family.* Chestnut Hill, MA: Abeel & Leet Publishers, 1996.

Bingham, Lucretia. "Hallowed Ground." *Smithsonian*, Vol. 32, no. 8 (November 2001): 30, 32.

Black's Law Dictionary. Seventh Edition. St. Paul, MN: West Group, 1999.

————. Tenth Edition. St. Paul, MN: Thompson Reuters, 2014.

Boucher, Ronald L. "The Colonial Militia As a Social Institution: Salem, Massachusetts, 1764, 1775." *Military Affairs*, Vol. 37, no. 4 (December 1973): 125-30.

Brainard, Homer Worthington, Harold Simeon Gilbert, and Clarence Almon Torrey. *The Gilbert Family: Descendants of Thomas Gilbert, 1582? - 1659.* New Haven: A. C. Gilbert, 1953.

Bridenbaugh, Carl. *Cities in Revolt: Urban Life in America 1743-1776.* New York: Oxford University Press, 1955, 1970.

————. *Cities in the Wilderness: The First Century of Urban Life in America.* New York: Oxford University Press, 1938, 1954.

Brown, Barbara W. and James M. Rose. *Black Roots in Southeastern Connecticut, 1650-1900.* New London: The New London County Historical Society, Inc., 2001. Reprint of 1980 edition.

Brown, Robert E. *Middle-Class Democracy and the Revolution in Massachusetts.* New York: Harper & Row, 1955, 1969.

Brown, Wallace. *The Good Americans: The Loyalists in the American Revolution.* New York: William Morrow and Company, Inc., 1969.

————. *The King's Friends: The Composition and Motives of the American Loyalist Claimants.* Providence: Brown University Press, 1965.

Browne, Benjamin F. "Youthful Recollections of Salem." *Essex Institute Historical Collections*, L (January 1914): 8-16.

Burkley, Kathryn Harris. *The Walter Harris Family of New London.* Privately published, 1991.

Bureau of the Census. *Heads of Families at the First Census of the United States Taken in the Year 1790: Connecticut.* Washington: Government Printing Office, 1908.

Burt, John H. "The Early Church Plate of Salem." *Essex Institute Historical Collections*, XLIII (April 1907): 97-114.

Bushman, Richard L. *From Puritan to Yankee: Character and Social Order in Connecticut.*

1690-1765. Cambridge: Harvard University Press, 1967.

Byrne, Leonard. "The Wayward Squire of Kingswood Manor." *The League Bulletin.* 30, no. 2 (May 1978): 26-31.

Calhoon, Robert McCluer. *The Loyalists in Revolutionary America 1760-1781.* New York: Harcourt Brace Jovanovich, Inc., 1973.

Capen, Edward Warren. *The Historical Development of the Poor Law of Connecticut.* New York: 1905.

Case, Jon B. "Northern slavery is well-documented." *The Day,* August 3, 2001.

Caulkins, Frances Manwaring. *History of New London, Connecticut From the First Survey of the Coast in 1612, to 1852.* New London: The Author, 1860.

————. *History of Norwich Connecticut: From Its Possession by the Indians, to the Year 1866.* Hartford: Published by the Author, 1866.

Chever, George F. "Some Remarks on the Commerce of Salem from 1626 to 1740." *Historical Collections of the Essex Institute,* I (July 1859): 78-119.

Clark-Pujara, Christy. *Dark Work: The Business of Slavery in Rhode Island.* New York: New York University Press, 2016.

"Col. William Browne House." *Essex Institute Historical Collections,* LXXII (1936): 283-86.

Collier, Christopher. "The hyperbolic ranting of deluded writers." *Hartford Courant,* December 1, 2002,

————. "Saybrook and Lyme: Secular Settlements in a Puritan Commonwealth," 9-28. In George J. Willauer, Jr., ed., *A Lyme Miscellany, 1776-1976* (Middletown: Wesleyan University Press, 1977.

Collins, David. "Ichabod Pease: A survivor of the dark days of New London slavery." *The Day,* September 5, 2019.

Connecticut Register and Manual, 2003. Hartford: Secretary of the State, 2003.

Contributions to the Ecclesiastical History of Connecticut. New Haven: William L. Kingsley, 1861.

Corriveau, Cindy Lee. *Images of America: Salem.* Charleston, SC: Arcadia Publishing, 2006.

Coughtry, Jay. *The Notorious Triangle: Rhode Island and the African Slave Trade, 1700-1807.* Philadelphia: Temple University Press, 1981.

"Courant Complicity In An Old Wrong." *Hartford Courant.* July 4, 9, 2000.

Cregeau, Damien and Dayne Rugh. "USS *Confederacy*: The Life and Service of Connecticut's Continental Frigate." *Connecticut History Review,* 58, no. 2 (Fall 2019): 36-48.

Crofut, Florence S. Marcy. *Guide to the History and Historic Sites of Connecticut.* 2 vols. New Haven: Yale University Press, 1937.

Crompton, Karin. "Archeologists explore Salem site." *The Day,* September 1, 2002.

Curtis, Ellwood Count. *Descendants of Edward Dolbeare, Sr. (c. 1644-1711).* Cedar Rapids, IA: Galactic Press, 2007.

Daniels, Bruce C. *The Connecticut Town: Growth and Development, 1635-1790.* Middletown: Wesleyan University Press, 1979.

————. *Dissent and Conformity on Narragansett Bay: The Colonial Rhode Island Town.* Middletown: Wesleyan University Press, 1983.

Davisson, William I. and Dennis J. Dugan. "Commerce in Seventeenth Century Essex County, Massachusetts." *Essex Institute Historical Collections,* CVII (April 1971): 113-42.

Deming, Judson Keith. *Genealogy of the Descendants of John Deming of Wethersfield, Connecticut.* Dubuque, Iowa: Press of Mathis-Mets Co., 1904.

Desrocher, Robert E., Jr.. "'Not Fade Away': The Narrative of Venture Smith, an African American in the Early Republic." *Journal of American History,* 84 (June 1997): 40-66.

Dexter, Franklin Bowditch, ed. *Biographical Sketches of the Graduates of Yale College.* 6 volumes. New York: Henry Holt and Company, 1885-1912.

Deutsch, Sarah. "The Elusive Guineamen: Newport Slavers, 1735-1774." *New England Quarterly,* 55, no. 2 (June 1982): 229-53.

di Bonaventura, Allegra. *For Adam's Sake: A Family Saga in Colonial New England.* New York: Liveright Publishing Corporation, 2013.

Dictionary of American Biography, s.v. William Browne.

Dictionary of Canadian Biography, s.v. Jacob Bailey, Joseph Chew, Abijah Willard.

"Dig Into History Yields Another View Of 'Free' North." *Hartford Courant,* June 11, 2001.

Donoghue, John. "'Out of the Land of Bondage': The English Revolution and the Atlantic Origins of Abolition." *American Historical Review*, 115 (October 2010): 943-74.

DuBois, William E. B. *Suppression of the African Slave-Trade in the United States of America, 1638-1870,* Harvard Historical Studies, Vol. 1. New York: Longmans, Green, and Co., 1896.

DuBosq, Charles Albert and William Jones. "Descendants of Gov. John Cranston of Rhode Island Addendum 1, Joseph Wanton Cranston and His Descendants." *New England Historical and Genealogical Register*, 80 (July 1926): 251-57.

Dunn, Richard S. *Puritans and Yankees: The Winthrop Dynasty of New England, 1630-1717*. Princeton, NJ: Princeton University Press, 1962.

Elbridge, William Henry. *Henry Genealogy: The Descendants of Samuel Henry.* Boston: Press to T. R. Marvin, 1915.

"Essex County Loyalists." *Essex Institute Historical Collections*, XLIII (1907): 289-316.

Farrow, Anne, Joel Lang, and Jennifer Frank. *Complicity: How the North Promoted, Prolonged, and Profited from Slavery.* New York: Ballantine Books, 2005.

[Federal Writers Project, Conn.]. American Guide Series. *Connecticut: A Guide to its Roads, Lore and People.* Boston: Houghton Mifflin Company, 1938.

Felt, Joseph B. *Annals of Salem.* Second edition. Volume II. Salem: W. & S. B. Ives, 1845.

Ferguson, Henry L. *Fishers Island, N. Y., 1614-1925.* New York: privately printed, 1925.

Fingerhut, Eugene R. "Uses and Abuses of the American Loyalists' Claims: A Critique of Quantitative Analyses." *William and Mary Quarterly*, 3rd Series, XXV, No. 2 (April 1968): 245-58.

Fisher, Philip A. *The Fisher Genealogy: Record of the Descendants of Joshua, Anthony and Cornelius Fisher, of Dedham, Mass. 1636-1640.* Everett, MA: Massachusetts Publishing Company, 1898.

Fiske, Jane Fletcher. *Gleanings from Newport Court Files, 1659-1783.* Boxford, MA: 1998.

Fitts, Robert K. *Inventing New England's Slave Paradise: Master/Slave Relations in Eighteenth-Century Narragansett Rhode Island.* New York: Garland Publishing, Inc., 1998.

Forbes, Robert P. "Grating the Nutmeg: Slavery and Racism in Connecticut from the Colonial Era to the Civil War." *Connecticut History*, Vol. 52, no. 2 (Fall 2013): 170-201.

Fowler, William Chauncey. "The Historical Status of the Negro in Connecticut." In, *Local Law in Massachusetts and Connecticut Historically Considered*. Albany: Joel Munsel, 1872: 111-48.

French, Elizabeth. "Genealogical Research in England." *New England Historical and Genealogical Register*, LXIII (1909): 356-63.

A Genealogical Register of the Descendants in the Male Line of Robert Day, of Hartford, Conn. 2nd edition. Hartford: J. & L. Metcalf, 1848, 1913.

Gerlach, Larry R. *Connecticut Congressman: Samuel Huntington, 1731-1796*. Hartford: American Revolution Bicentennial Commission of Connecticut, 1976.

Gidwitz, Tom. "Freeing Captive History." *Archeology*, Vol. 58, no. 2 (March/April 2005).

Gigantino, James J. II. *The Ragged Road to Abolition: Slavery and Freedom in New Jersey, 1775-1865*. Philadelphia: University of Pennsylvania Press, 2015.

Gildrie, Richard P. "'The Gallant Life': Theft on the Salem-Marblehead, Massachusetts, Waterfront in the 1680s." *Essex Institute Historical Colletions*, 122 (October 1986): 284-98.

Gipson, Lawrence Henry. *Connecticut Taxation, 1750-1775*. Tercentenary Pamphlet, X. New Haven: Yale University Press, 1933.

Goen, C. C. *Revivalism and Separatism in New England, 1740-1800*. (Middletown: Wesleyan University Press, 1962, 1987. Reprint of 1962 Yale University Press publication with a new introduction by the author.

Goodell, A. C. Jr. "The Centennial Anniversary of the Meeting of the Provincial Legislature in Salem, Oct. 5, 1774." *Essex Institute Historical Collections*, XIII (January 1877): 1-52.

Grant, Charles S. *Democracy in the Connecticut Frontier Town of Kent*. New York: Columbia University Press, 1961.

Greene, Lorenzo J. "Slave-Holding New England and Its Awakening." *Journal of Negro History*, 13 (October 1932): 492-533.

Greene, Lorenzo Johnston. *The Negro in Colonial New England*. New York: Atheneum, 1942, 1969.

Greven, Philip J., Jr. *Four Generations: Population, Land, and Family in Colonial Andover, Massachusetts*. Ithaca: Cornell University Press, 1970

Griggs, Susan J. *Early Homesteads of Pomfret and Hampton.* N.p.: Susan J. Griggs, 1950.

Griswold, Mac. *The Manor: Three Centuries at a Slave Plantation on Long Island.* New York: Farrar, Straus and Giroux, 2013.

Harris, Gale Ion. *Harrises of Connecticut: Scattered Descendants.* Salina, MI: McNaughton & Gunn, Inc., 2012.

———. "James and Sarah (Eliot?) Harris of Boston and New London." *New England Historical and Genealogical Register,* 154 (2000): 3-27.

———. "Thomas Harris, Merchant of New England." *National Genealogical Society Quarterly,* 80 (1992): 36-56.

———. "Thomas Harris, Sawmiller of Hartford, Connecticut." *National Genealogical Society Quarterly* 78 (1990): 182-203.

Hedges, James B. *The Browns of Providence Plantations: Colonial Years.* Cambridge: University Press, 1952.

Hileman, Maria. "Rewriting Slavery's History." *The Day* (New London), June 10, 2001.

Hines, Ezra D. "Browne Hill and Some History Connected with It." *Essex Institute Historical Collections,* XXXII (1896): 201-38.

Hinks, Peter P. Book Review Essay on Chandler B. Saint and George A. Krimsky, *Making Freedom: The Extraordinary Life of Venture Smith. Connecticut History,* 49, no. 1 (Spring 2010): 134-43.

———. "'Nought from nought leaves nought': Figuring Venture Smith," a review essay of James Brewer Stewart, ed., *Venture Smith and the Business of Slavery and Freedom. William and Mary Quarterly,* 3rd Series, 65 (July 2011), 490-99.

Holman, Winifred Lovering. "Early Dolbeares." *New England Historical and Genealogical Register,* 112 (1958): 170-84.

Holmes, Ellwood Count. *The Descendants of Edmund Dolbeare, Sr. (c. 1644-1711).* Cedar Falls, Iowa: Galactic Press, 2007.

Hughes, Arthur H. and Morse S. Allen. *Connecticut Place Names.* Hartford: The Connecticut Historical Society, 1976.

Ingersoll, Thomas N. *The Loyalist Problem in Revolutionary New England.* Cambridge, UK: Cambridge University Press, 2016.

Innes, Stephen. "Land Tenancy and Social Order in Springfield Massachusetts, 1652-

1702." *William and Mary Quarterly*, Third Series, XXXV (January 1978): 33-56.

"Inscriptions from Gravestones at East Lyme, Conn." *New England Historical and Genealogical Register*, 79 (January 1925): 66-80.

Jackman, S. W. "Salem and St. George's, William Browne, Loyalist." *Essex Institute Historical Collections,* 118 (July 1982): 172-85.

Jackman, Sydney W. "A Tory's Claim to the Wanton Estates." *Rhode Island History*, 19 (1960): 1-7, 50-61, 79-88.

————. "William Browne, Governor 1782-1788: A Study of his Early Life in his Native Massachusetts." *Bermuda Historical Quarterly*, XIII (Spring 1956): 17-24.

Jacobus, Donald Lines. *The Bulkeley Genealogy.* New Haven: The Tuttle, Morehouse & Taylor Company, 1933.

James, May Hall. *The Educational History of Old Lyme, Connecticut 1635-1935.* New Haven: Yale University Press, 1939.

James, Sydney V. *Colonial Rhode Island: A History.* New York: Charles Scribner's Sons, 1975.

Jarvis, Michael J. *In the Eye of All Trade: Bermuda, Bermudians, and the Maritime Atlantic World, 1680-1783.* Chapel Hill: University of North Carolina Press, 2010.

Jewett, Frederic Clarke. *History and Genealogy of the Jewetts in America.* Volume 1. New York: The Grafton Press, 1908.

Johnson, Frances Hall. *Music Vale Seminary.* Tercentenary Pamphlet XXVII. New Haven: Yale University Press, 1934.

Jones, E. Alfred. *The Loyalists of Massachusetts: Their Memorials, Petitions and Claims.* London: The Saint Catherine Press, 1930.

Jones, Edward P. *Descendants of John Coult who sailed from England and arrived in America September 4, 1633.* n.p.: 1933.

Jordan, Winthrop D. "The Influence of the West Indies on the Origins of New England Slavery." *William and Mary Quarterly*, Third Series, 18 (April 1961): 243-50.

Labaree, Benjamin W. *Colonial Massachusetts: A History.* Millwood, NY: KTO Press, 1979.

Lane, William C. "Early Silver Belonging to Harvard College," 165-76. *Publications of the Colonial Society of Massachusetts*, 24. Boston: The Society, 1923.

Lang, Joel et al. *Complicity: How Connecticut Chained Itself to Slavery, Northeast*, magazine of the *Hartford Courant*, September 29, 2002.

Larned, Ellen D. *History of Windham County, Connecticut.* 2 Volumes. Worcester, MA: Printed by Charles Hamilton, 1874, 1880.

Lawson, Henry M. *The History of Union.* New Haven: Press of Prince, Lewis & Atkins, Co., 1893.

Lewis, Gilbert Burnet. "Records of Browne Family Portraits." *Essex Institute Historical Collections*, LXXXVI (July 1950): 285-87.

Lewis, Theodore B. "Land Speculation and the Dudley Council of 1686." *William and Mary Quarterly*. 3rd Series, XXXI (April 1974): 255-72.

Lim, Susan. *Sola Scriptura and Sectarianism: The Rise of the Rogerenes in Colonial New London, 1664-1721*. Cheshire, CT: The Connecticut Press, 2019.

Litwack, Leon. *North of Slavery: The Negro in Free States, 1790-1850.* Chicago: University of Chicago Press, 1966.

Lockridge, Kenneth A. *The New England Town: The First Hundred Years.* New York: W. W. Norton & Company, Inc., 1970.

Lovejoy, David S. *The Glorious Revolution in America.* New York: Harper & Row, 1972.

McBurney, Christian. "The South Kingstown Planters: Country Gentry in Colonial Rhode Island. *Rhode Island History*, 45 (August 1986): 81-93.

McDermott, William P. *Stafford, Connecticut, 1719-1740: From Farm to Factory.* Tolland, CT: Kerosene Press, 2010.

McLoughlin, William G. *Isaac Backus and the American Pietist Tradition.* Boston: Little, Brown and Company, 1967.

———. *New England Dissent, 1630-1833: The Baptists and the Separation of Church and State.* 2 Volumes. Cambridge, MA: Harvard University Press, 1971.

McManus, Edgar J. *Black Bondage in the North.* Syracuse: Syracuse University Press, 1973

———. *History of Slavery in New York.* Syracuse: Syracuse University Press, 1966.

Main, Jackson Turner. "The Economic and Social Structure of Early Lyme," 29-47. In George J. Willauer, Jr., ed., *A Lyme Miscellany, 1776-1976.* Middletown: Wesleyan University Press, 1977.

————. *Society and Economy in Colonial Connecticut*. Princeton: Princeton University Press, 1985.

Manegold, C. S. *Ten Hills Farm: The Forgotten History of Slavery in the North*. Princeton, NJ: Princeton University Press, 2010.

Mann, Bruce H. *Neighbors and Strangers: Law and Community in Early Connecticut*. Chapel Hill: University of North Carolina Press, 1987.

Mayo, Lawrence Shaw. *The Winthrop Family in America*. Boston: The Massachusetts Historical Society, 1948.

Melish, Joanne Pope. *Disowning Slavery: Gradual Emancipation and "Race" in New England, 1780-1860*. Ithaca, NY: Cornell University Press, 1998.

Menchel, David. "Abolition without Deliverance: The Law of Connecticut Slavery 1784-1848. *Yale Law Journal*, Vol. 111, no. 1 (October 2001): 183-222.

Middlebrook, Louis F. *History of Maritime Connecticut During the American Revolution 1755-1783*. 2 Volumes. Salem, MA: The Essex Institute, 1925.

Miller, William Davis. "The Narragansett Planters." *Proceedings of the American Antiquarian Society*, 43 (1933): 49-115.

Minor, John Augustus. *Thomas Minor Descendants 1608-1981*. Trevett, ME: 1981.

Morgan, Mont. *The Soil Characteristics of Connecticut Land Types*. New Haven: Yale University Press, 1939.

Morgan, Nathaniel Morgan. *Harris Genealogy: A History of James Harris of New London, Conn. and his Descendants from 1640 to 1878*. Hartford: The Case, Lockwood & Brainard Co., 1878.

Morris, Richard J. "Social Change, Republican Rhetoric, and the American Revolution: The Case of Salem, Massachusetts." *Journal of Social History*, Vol. 31, no. 2 (Winter 1997): 419-33.

Mumford, James Gregory. *Mumford Memoirs: Being the Story of the New England Mumfords from the Year 1655 to the Present Time*. Boston: The Merrymount Press, 1900.

Nelson, William H. *The American Tory*. Boston: Beacon Press, 1961, 1964.

Newell, Margaret Ellen. *Brethren by Nature: New England Indians, Colonists, and the Origins of American Slavery*. Ithaca, NY: Cornell University Press, 2015.

Norton, Frederick Calvin. "Negro Slavery in Connecticut." *The Connecticut Magazine*,

5 (1899): 320-28. *Connecticu*

Norton, Mary Beth. *1774: The Long Year of Revolution*. New York: Alfred A. Knopf, 2020.

———. *The British-Americans: The Loyalist Exiles in England, 1774-1789*. Boston: Little Brown and Company, 1972.

Oberg, Michael Leroy. *Uncas: First of the Mohegans*. Ithaca, NY: Cornell University Press, 2003.

Oxford Dictionary of National Biography, s.v. William Browne.

Palmer, Gregory. *A Bibliography of Loyalist Source Material in the United States, Canada, and Great Britain*. Westport, CT and London: Heckler Publishing, 1982.

Parks, Roger, ed. *Connecticut: A Bibliography of Its History*. Hanover, NH and London: University Press of New England, 1986.

Pence, David. "A hidden history revealed." *Norwich Bulletin*, January 13, 2002.

Perkins, Mary E. *Chronicles of a Connecticut Farm, 1769-1905*. Boston: privately printed, 1905.

[Perley, Sidney]. "Descendants of William Browne of Salem." *Essex Antiquarian*, XIII (Oct. 1909): 59-62.

———. *The History of Salem, Massachusetts*. 3 vols. Salem, MA: Sidney Perley, 1924, 1926, 1928.

———. "Salem in 1700. No. 16." *Essex Antiquarian*, VIII (July1904): 113-18.

Phillips, Edward Hake. "Salem, Timothy Pickering, and the American Revolution." *Essex Institute Historical Collections*, 111 (January 1975): 65-78.

Phillips, James Duncan. "Derby Wills and Land Titles, with Notes and Comments" *Essex Institute Historical Collections*, LXI (January 1930): 65-96.

———. *Salem in the Eighteenth Century*. Boston: Houghton Mifflin Company, 1937.

———. *Salem in the Seventeenth Century*. Boston: Houghton Mifflin Company, 1933.

Preston, Howard W. "Godfrey Malbone's Connecticut Investment." *Rhode Island Historical Society Collections*, XVI, no. 4 (October 1923): 115-20.

Putnam, Even. "Militia Officers, Essex Co., Mass. 1761-1771." *Essex Institute Historical*

Collections, XXXIX (October 1892): 177-80.

Randall, Emma Kelley. *Kelley Genealogy: David O'Killa the Immigrant of Old Yarmouth, Massachusetts with His Descendants and Allied Families.* n.p.: 1962.

Ransom, William C. *Historical Outline of the Ransom Family in America and Genealogical Record of the Colchester, Conn., Branch.* Ann Arbor, MI: The Richmond & Backus Company, 1913.

Rantoul, Robert S. "A Historic Ball Room." *Essex Institute Historical Collections*, XXXI (August-December 1894): 69-87.

Raymond, Samuel Edward. *Raymond Genealogy.* Vol. 1. Seattle: 1969.

Raymond, Samuel. *Genealogies of the Raymond Families of New England, 1630-1 to 1886.* New York: Press of J. J. Little & Co., 1886.

Robinson, Caroline E. *The Gardiners of Narragansett: Being a Genealogy of the Descendants of George Gardiner the Colonist 1638.* Providence: 1919.

————. *The Hazard Family of Rhode Island*, 1635-1894. Boston: Printed for the Author, 1895.

Rogers, James Swift. *James Rogers of New London, CT, and his Descendants.* Boston: Published by the Compiler, 1902.

Saltonstall, Richard M. *Ancestry and Descendants of Sir Richard Saltonstall.* n.p.: Riverside Press, 1897.

Sargent, Emma Worcester and Charles Sprague Sargent. *Epes Sargent of Gloucester and His Descendants.* Boston: Houghton Mifflin Company, 1923.

Schaeffer, Patricia M. *A Useful Friend: A Companion to the Joshua Hempstead Diary, 1711-1758.* New London: The New London County Historical Society, 2008.

Schwartz, Sydney. "Yankee Slavery." *Archeology*, Vol. 54, no. 5 (September/October 2001).

Shorto, Russell. *Revolution Song: A Story of American Freedom.* New York: W. W. Norton & Company, 2018.

Sibley, John Langdon and Clifford K. Shipton. *Sibley's Harvard Graduates; Biographical Sketches of Those Who Attended Harvard College . . . with Biographical and Other Notes.* 17 Volumes. Cambridge and Boston: Charles William Sever and Massachusetts Historical Society, 1873-1975.

Silvester, Harriet. "St. Peter's Church in Salem before the Revolution." *Essex Institute*

Historical Collections LXXX (July 1944): 229-60; (October 1944): 334-67.

Simler, Lucy. "Tenancy in Colonial Pennsylvania: The Case of Chester County." *William and Mary Quarterly,* Third Series (October 1986): 542-69.

Slosberg, Steven. "Auctioning slaves our legacy, too?" *The Day,* February 20, 2005.

Stampp, Kenneth M. *The Peculiar Institution: Slavery in the Ante-Bellum South.* New York: Vintage Books, 1956.

Stark, Bruce P. "The Connecticut Court System During the Time of Zephaniah Swift." *Connecticut Supreme Court History,* IV (2009): 21-82.

————. "Decoding the 1790 Federal Census for New London County African Americans. *Connecticut History Review,* 54, no. 2 (Fall 2015): 289-306.

————. Finding Aid to New London County, County Court, Files, 1691-1855.

————. Finding Aid to New London County, County Court, Papers by Subject, 1685-1856.

————. Finding Aid to New London County, Superior Court, Files, 1711-1800.

————. Finding Aid to New London County, Superior Court, Papers by Subject, 1711-1900.

————. *Lyme, Connecticut: From Founding to Independence.* Lyme: [Lyme Bicentennial Commission], 1976.

————. "The Myth and Reality of Slavery in Salem, Connecticut." *Connecticut History,* 50, no. 2 (Fall 2011): 158-81.

————. "The New London Society and Connecticut Politics, 1732-1740." *Connecticut History,* no. 25 (January 1984): 1-21.

————. "Slavery in Connecticut: A Re-examination." *Connecticut Review,* 9 (November 1975): 75-81.

State of Connecticut Register and Manual. Hartford: Secretary of the State, 2003.

"A Stately Pleasure-House." *Essex Institute Historical Collections,* XXXI (August-December 1894): 205-12.

Stearns, Ezra S. "Contributions to the History of Londonderry, N. H." *New England Historical and Genealogical Register,* 51 (October 1897): 467-71.

———. "The Descendants of Dea. Zachary Fitch of Reading." *New England Historical and Genealogical Register*, 55 (July 1901): 288-94.

Steiner, Bernard C. "History of Slavery in Connecticut." *Johns Hopkins University Studies in Historical and Political Science*. Baltimore: The Johns Hopkins Press, 1893.

Steiner, Bruce E. "Anglican Officeholding in Pre-Revolutionary Connecticut: The Parameters of New England Community." *William and Mary Quarterly*, Third Series, XXXI (July 1974): 369-406.

———. "New England Anglicanism: A Genteel Faith?" *William and Mary Quarterly*, Third Series, XXVIII (January 1970): 122-35.

Stewart, James Brewer, ed. *Venture Smith and the Business of Slavery and Freedom*. Amherst, MA: University of Massachusetts Press, 2010.

Streeter, Gilbert L. "Salem before the Revolution." *Essex Institute Historical Collections*, XXXII (1896): 47-98.

Tapley, Harriet Silvester. "The Province Galley of Massachusetts Bay, 1694-1716 (Part 1). *Essex Institute Historical Collections*, LVIII (January 1922), 73-88.

Thomas, Hugh. *Conquest: Montezuma, Cortez, and the Fall of Old Mexico*. New York: Simon & Schuster, 1993.

———. *Rivers of Gold: The Rise of the Spanish Empire, From Columbus to Magellan*. New York: Random Rouse, 2004.

Tracy, Joseph. *The Great Awakening: A History of the Revival of Religion in the Time of Edwards and Whitefield*. Boston: Tappan and Dennet, 1842.

Trumbull, Benjamin, D.D. *A Complete History of Connecticut: Civil and Ecclesiastical, From the Emigration of its First Planters, From England in the Year 1630, to the Year 1764; and to the Close of the Indian Wars*. New Haven: Maltby, Goldsmith and Co., 1818.

Turner, Sylvie J. "The Connecticut Archives." *Connecticut Historical Society Bulletin*, 33 (July 1968): 81-89.

Twombly, Robert C. and Richard H. Moore. "Black Puritan: The Negro in Seventeenth-Century Massachusetts." *William and Mary Quarterly*, Third Series, XXIV (April 1967): 224-42.

Tyler, John W. *Connecticut Loyalists: An Analysis of Loyalist Land Confiscations in Greenwich, Stanford and Norwalk*. New Orleans: Polyanthus, Inc., 1977.

Vickers, Daniel. *Farmers & Fishermen: Two Centuries of Work in Essex County, Massachu-*

setts, 1630-1850. Chapel Hill: University of North Carolina Press, 1994.

Waller-Fry, George. *Adam and Katherine Rogers of New London, CT.* Storrs, CT: Spring Hill Press, 1977.

Ward, Christopher. *The War of the Revolution.* 2 Volumes. New York: The Macmillan Company, 1952.

Warshauer, Matthew. *Connecticut in the American Civil War: Slavery, Sacrifice, and Survival.* Middletown, CT: Wesleyan University Press, 2011.

Waters, John J., Jr.. *The Otis Family In Provincial and Revolutionary Massachusetts.* New York: W. W. Norton & Company, Inc., 1968, 1975.

Welch, Vicki S. *And They Were Related, Too.* n.p.: Xlibris Corporation, 2006.

———. "The Keys to the Shackles." *Connecticut History,* Vol. 40, no. 2 (Fall 2001): 225-46.

Weld, Ralph Foster. *Slavery in Connecticut.* Tercentenary Pamphlet, XXXVII. New Haven: Yale University Press, 1935.

White, David O. *Connecticut's Black Soldiers.* Chester, CT: Pequot Press, 1973.

Whitmore, William H. *The Massachusetts Civil List for the Colonial and Provincial Periods, 1630-1774.* Albany: J. Munsell, 1870.

Wick, William M. "The Statutory Law of Slavery and Race in the Thirteen Colonies of British America." *William and Mary Quarterly,* Third Series, XXXIV (April 1977): 258-80.

Winthrop, Robert C., Jr. *A Short Account of the Winthrop Family.* Cambridge, MA: John Wilson and Son, 1887.

Withington, Lothrop. "English Notes about Early Settlers in New England." *Essex Institute Historical Collections,* XLVII (January 1911): 63-65.

Wood, Peter H. "'I Did the Best I Could for My Day': The Study of Early Black History during the Second Reconstruction, 1960 to 1976." *William and Mary Quarterly,* Third Series, XXXV (April 1978): 185-225.

Woodruff, Janet, Gerald F. Sawyer, and Warren R. Perry. "How Archeology Exposes the Nature of African Captivity and Freedom in Eighteenth Century Connecticut." *Connecticut History,* 46, no. 2 (2007): 155-83.

Zilversmit, Arthur. *The First Emancipation: The Abolition of Slavery in the North.* Chicago: University of Chicago Press, 1967.

Zobel, Hiller B. *The Boston Massacre.* New York: W. W. Norton & Company, 1970.

Online Resources

"A Brief History of Fishers Island Since European Discovery." fishersisland.net

Colonial North America at Harvard University. colonialnorthamerica.library.harvard.edu

Federal Census 1790, 1800, 1810, 1820. AncestryHeritageQuest.com

Force, Peter. *American Archives, Fourth Series, Containing a Documentary History of the English Colonies in North America, from the King's Message to Parliament, of March 7, 1774, to the Declaration of Independence.* Washington: M. St. Clair and Peter Force, 1837. archives.org/details/AmericanArchives-Fourth

General Association of Connecticut . . . htpps://congregationallibrary.quartexcollections.com
        New London Association, 1708 - 1788
        Windham County Association, 1723 - 1814

"Henry Hamilton." *Wikipedia.* Accessed March 2, 2021.

John Mumford (1740-1825). *Wikitree.* Accessed September 11, 2021.

"Malbone Castle and Estate." *Wikipedia.* Accessed September 12, 2016.

"Mortlake, Connecticut." *Wikipedia.* Accessed September 12, 2016.

Newport Historical Society. "History Bytes: Godfrey Malone and Brownstone. Accessed March 29, 2017.

Sarudy, Barbara Wells. "It's About Time: Searching centuries of History, Art, Nature, & Everyday Life for Unique Perspectives, Uncommon Grace, & Unexpected Insights." Published November 19, 2015. Accessed November 18, 2016.

Smibert, John. britannica.com/biography/John-Smibert. Accessed March 7, 2022.

Smith, Venture. *A Narrative of the Life and Adventures of Venture, a Native of Africa.* New-London: C. Holt, 1798. docsouth.unc.edu/neh/venture/venture.html.

Sweet, John Wood. "Venture Smith, from Slavery to Freedom. connecticuthistory.org/venture-smith-from-slavery-to-freedom/

Wordell, David Hazard. "Historical Sketches, of Salem, Connecticut." www.salem.

ctgov/Pages/SalemCT_Clerk/HISTORICALSKETCHESOFSALEM. Accessed June 10, 2017.

Index

About the Author

Bruce P. Stark is a native of Lyme, Connecticut. An Army veteran, he served two years in occupied West Berlin in the 78th USASOU. He graduated from Brown University, earned M.A. and Ph.D. degrees from the University of Connecticut, and a library degree from Southern Connecticut State University. In a forty year career as an archivist and historian, he worked at a number of institutions, including SUNY Plattsburgh, Yale University Library, Beinecke Rare Book and Manuscript Library, University of Connecticut Library, and the Connecticut State Library. He has published extensively on Connecticut history and crafted a number of finding aids on judicial, legislative, and municipal records while at the State Library, his particular areas of expertise. He devoted special attention to materials concerning people of color. He retired in 2009.

www.ingramcontent.com/pod-product-compliance
Lightning Source LLC
Chambersburg PA
CBHW062322120626
46553CB00015B/184